CORPORATE PLANNING

EDITORS:
Robert J. Allio
Malcolm W. Pennington

CORPORATE PLANNING

Techniques and Applications

In cooperation with
the North American Society
for Corporate Planning

 A Division of
AMERICAN MANAGEMENT
ASSOCIATIONS

All selections are reprinted from *Planning Review*, with permission from the North American Society for Corporate Planning.

Library of Congress Cataloging in Publication Data

Main entry under title:

Corporate planning.

   "All selections are reprinted from Planning review."
   Bibliography: p.
   Includes index.
   1. Corporate planning--Addresses, essays, lectures.
I. Allio, Robert J. II. Pennington, Malcolm W.
HD30.28.C67   658.4'01   78-25803
ISBN 0-8144-5497-6

First Printing

Acknowledgments

The editors wish to express appreciation to Margaret M. McIntyre, Sheila McCormack, Brigitte Gauthier, and Mary Prendergast, all of whom gave support as editorial assistants during various critical stages of *Planning Review*'s evolution. We also wish to give particular thanks to Ben Russak, *Planning Review*'s first commercial publisher; Robert Randall, our continuing consultant; and John Goodwin, NASCP's president during *Planning Review*'s year of conception.

Contents

E. PROCESS SKILLS

Part VII. PERSONALITIES

Introduction

EVERYBODY PLANS. Most of our plans are short-range and informal. We plan our day—how to get to work, what we are going to do, whom we are going to see and when, where we will have lunch and with whom. Sometimes we formalize these plans by keeping a daily or weekly schedule.

Our longer-range plans are likely to be fuzzier and less formal, covering such matters as fixing the roof on our house, getting a new car next year, and putting the children through college, for which we may not have a specific time assigned. We seldom write these personal plans down.

In contrast, organizations have a different time orientation—or should have—as well as different needs. Successful organizations generally have formal plans that extend over a period that works for their type of activity. In the garment industry, this period usually covers the six-month period preceding the new fashion season. In the lumber products industry, the appropriate span may be the 50 years required to grow harvestable trees.

The planning function belongs to management, and plans should be prepared by the managers who will carry them out. But even the most effective manager can benefit from the expertise of a staff planner. Staff planners help managers get the information needed for effective planning, set up a structure and schedule for planning, shepherd the plans along, assist the managers at each stage, and help work out inconsistencies between different elements of the organization's planning efforts.

This book is intended as a guide for people whose job it is to plan—managers and staff planners. It covers the science of planning (see the section on modeling, Part VIB). But since planning is really an art, more attention is given to ways to master, or at least cope with, this arcane activity, as shown in the cases on business strategy in Part IV.

We hope to provide you with some guidance that can be applied to your own specific needs, problems, and opportunities. We do not set out any planning recipes or specific rules (although we do present some general rules in Pennington's What's Wrong with Planning). Every organization, large or small, business or public service, young or old, has its own history, its own way of doing things, its own people, its own needs. Thus a planning system that works for one company may not work for another. It may not even work for the same company after two or three years—experience changes and so do needs. This book will help you build your own system for your own organization.

We begin with a short section that states our own views on, and approach to, planning. This introductory section leads into a selection of articles from *Planning Review*, the journal of the North American Society for Corporate Planning, founded in 1966. Most major corporations in the United States and Canada, along with many government agencies, are represented in its membership. *Planning Review* strives to provide its readers with articles whose perspectives will help them do their planning jobs more effectively—whether as managers or as staff planners.

PLANNING—A PRIMER

Most contemporary organizations accept the planning process as an integral element of management. Figure 1 depicts management as a simple input–output system requiring *planning* as a precursor to the *execution* of any work done by the organization. The *control* element in the system measures the results, providing information for modification of existing plans or generation of new ones.

Figure 1. The management system.

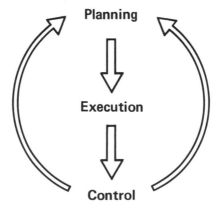

What is planning? The essence of most definitions is encompassed in the following statement: "Planning is the continuous and systematic process of making decisions that influence the future." The planner's lexicon contains few standard terms. A simple model, however, underlies all planning processes. The logic of this model is displayed in Figure 2.

Mission

The planning process begins with the mission of the organization. The mission, in the form of a charter or statement of business, indicates the

Figure 2. The planning process.

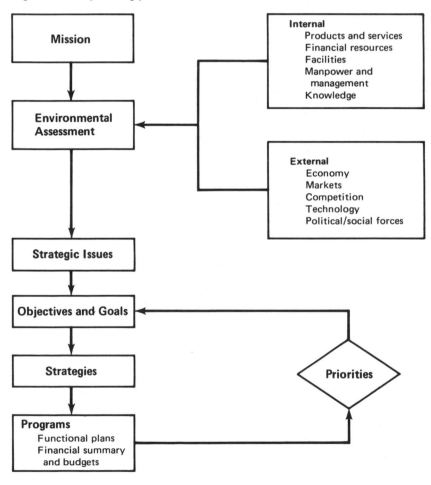

identity and fundamental purpose of the organization. Here are some examples of stated missions of several businesses:

Small appliance manufacturer: To develop, make, and sell specialized electric appliances to a consumer market that will pay for innovation and is large enough to offer a gratifying return, but which is not big enough to attract major competitors.

Large integrated paper company: To produce high-volume paper and paperboard products at minimum cost and to maintain a major share of these large-volume markets through production efficiencies and low prices.

City YMCA: To provide comfortable and inexpensive living accommodations for young men in our city and to provide at-cost educational and social programs to serve all adults in the area.

Food products company: To market a broad line of low-price food products throughout the Northeastern United States by offering our branded products as a house brand to independent groceries and small chains that do not offer their own brands. To keep investment at a minimum by contracting out all production.

Railroad: To provide profitable rail freight haulage on our existing track system in the Western United States. (It has been said that many railroads are in trouble as a result of limiting their mission to rail haulage, instead of something broader such as: Carriage of goods and people throughout the United States. With that mission, the railroad companies of the nineteenth century might now be the integrated transportation companies of the twentieth, offering a range of profitable transportation services including rail, truck, bus, air, barge, and pipeline.)

The mission, then, describes the organization's responsibility for supplying products, services, or systems to certain markets. It defines the boundary conditions within which an organization will do business. The markets, products, and services to be excluded from the company's business also may be identified in the stated mission.

Environmental Assessment

Stage two in the planning process is the environmental assessment, also known as situation analysis. This section of the plan describes the major environmental factors expected to present opportunities or problems over the planning period. The assessment can be conveniently divided into two major sections: the internal environment and the external environment. Some forecasting methods for making these assessments are discussed in the chapter by Chambers and Mullick, Forecasting for Planning.

Internal Environment

The internal environment comprises your firm's goods and services, as well as the factors of production. Most elements within the internal environment can be controlled by the organization. Important elements will include products and services, financial resources, facilities, manpower and management, and knowledge.

Products and services. The array of products and services produced for various markets should be carefully described. One helpful device is the product–market matrix, shown in Figure 3, which is often used in correlating sales to market sectors and for identifying the relative importance of specific products.

A product–market matrix can be used to develop new products as well. For example, several years ago an analysis was made of all the potential uses for business aircraft and the aircraft requirements that went with each use. These potentials and requirements were listed on one side of the matrix. On the other side of the matrix were listed all the aircraft either available at that time or in the proposal stage. The uses for which an existing aircraft already fit the required characteristics were eliminated. The few remaining uses constituted the market for entirely new aircraft. The Britten-Norman Islander was then designed to fit the required characteristics of an open use. It proved to be a successful aircraft. Figure 4 is an example of a product–market matrix used by a shipbuilding company.

Figure 3. Product–market matrix.

Markets ——→

	M$_1$	M$_2$	M$_3$	M$_4$
P$_1$				
P$_2$				
P$_3$				

Products

Figure 4. Product-market matrix for the shipbuilding industry.

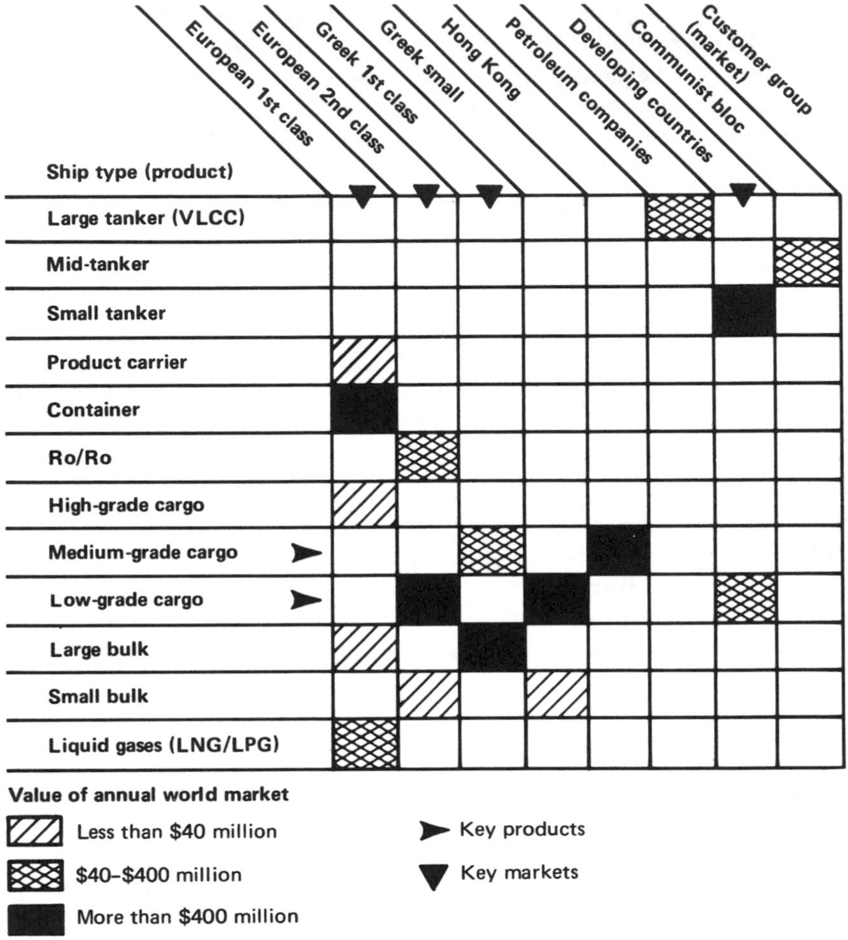
Customer group (market)
European 1st class
European 2nd class
Greek 1st class
Greek small
Hong Kong
Petroleum companies
Developing countries
Communist bloc
Ship type (product)
Large tanker (VLCC)
Mid-tanker
Small tanker
Product carrier
Container
Ro/Ro
High-grade cargo
Medium-grade cargo
Low-grade cargo
Large bulk
Small bulk
Liquid gases (LNG/LPG)
Value of annual world market
Less than $40 million
$40–$400 million
More than $400 million
Key products
Key markets

From *The McKinsey Quarterly.* Copyright ©1978, McKinsey & Company, Inc.

Product quality also must be assessed, along with the effectiveness of distribution, servicing, and marketing communications.

Financial resources. Money maintains your organization and provides for expansion. Is the balance sheet sound and are the financial ratios within prescribed limits? Will cash be available for dividends and debt service, or to finance working capital and new investments? Is the trend in earnings acceptable? For an unusual approach to financial analysis, see Christopher's chapter, Computing Who Deserves the Gold Stars.

Facilities. Your organization's manufacturing, distribution, and office facilities must be assessed. What changes would be required to accommodate growth or establish new regional or international branches? Does production equipment need to be replaced or augmented?

Manpower and management. The adequacy of your organization's productive and administrative workforce needs to be described. The quality of professional or managerial staff and the availability of key technical or administrative skills are particularly important. See Lee's chapter on Planning the Picking Order for the Company Totem Pole and Hawver's chapter, Management Potential—The Gap in Your Plan.

Knowledge. Proprietary information or patents give an organization a competitive advantage. Is the technology required for product or process design in hand? What is needed to develop it?

The complete analysis of the internal environment will yield a summary of your organization's strengths, competitive advantages, weaknesses, or its competitive handicaps.

External Environment

The external environment comprises those elements outside of your organization's control that affect industry and market demand and supply. Important elements may include:

Economy. Review the impact of the secular trend of the economy and the components of real and inflationary growth on your organization. Is a business cycle likely to affect demand or supply during this period? What constraints on supply or demand can you anticipate?

Markets. Consider the geography of markets and the concentration of customers in the major markets served. Is the market growing rapidly, or is it relatively static? What are the current prices and price trends? Is there a tendency for customers to reduce purchases as a result of backward or forward integration?

Competition. A good competitive analysis is a vital element of the planning process. The planner should identify present and potential competition, as well as the strategies of each important competitor. The possible introduction of new products or services by competitors requires careful scrutiny. The capacity of the industry to meet market needs and the impact of new capacity on the market must be reviewed.

Is your company the market leader? What is your competitive posture on price, performance, delivery, and service? Which way is the competitive equilibrium shifting? This part of the planning logic must clearly present market-share data both for the firm and for its principal competitors.

Technology. Assess the present state of technology that has relevance to the organization. What are the trends and potential new developments? (Will nuclear energy replace coal? Will solar energy replace both coal and nuclear energy?) See the Humphries article on technology assessment for pointers on how to go about making this type of assessment.

Political and social forces. The organization becomes more and more of an open system in which the influence of all stake holders must be considered. Thus, the forces operating derive not only from customers and suppliers, but from the consumer, the environmentalist, and the public at large. As a result you must assess the actual and potential impact of public groups, present and proposed government legislation, labor and union attitudes, and the like. The section on social responsibility, Part III, takes a look at these issues.

Changes in consumer values or new buying influences in the market may have a significant effect on demand for your firm's products. (See Part I, Futures.) National or world political issues or conflicts may have a severe impact on an organization, particularly one that depends heavily on an external supply of raw materials or energy. (See Part II, Resource Planning.)

Strategic Issues

Any comparison of the external environment with the internal environment inevitably reveals an area of tension or lack of congruence; that is, the requirements of the environment are not matched by the resources of your firm. This mismatch can be expressed as a set of opportunities and problems or of threats and challenges.

Vulnerability analysis represents a useful recent approach to identifying strategic issues. Developed by Stanford Research Institute, vulnerability analysis identifies the underpinnings of the organization as follows:

1. Needs and wants served by the business.
2. Resources and assets.
3. Stability of costs relative to competition.
4. Customer base.
5. Technologies.
6. Special abilities.
7. Strong corporate identity symbols.
8. Institutional barriers to competition.
9. Social values.
10. Sanctions, supports, and incentives.
11. Integrity of products and the organization.
12. Availability of complementary products or services.

Potential threats and challenges are enumerated and assigned both a probability of occurrence and significance of impact. Priorities for response can then be inferred from a display of the results, as shown in Figure 5.

The most important of your organization's opportunities and problems represent strategic issues. Although an organization may be faced with a multitude of opportunities and problems, the number of important strategic issues will rarely exceed eight to ten. Here are some examples of strategic issues:

- Competitor A has introduced a new product line that offers better performance and lower cost.
- The supply of high-purity raw materials could be interrupted by political unrest in the source country.
- Scientists in the corporate research center have developed an ef-

Figure 5. Vulnerability analysis — A threat assessment.

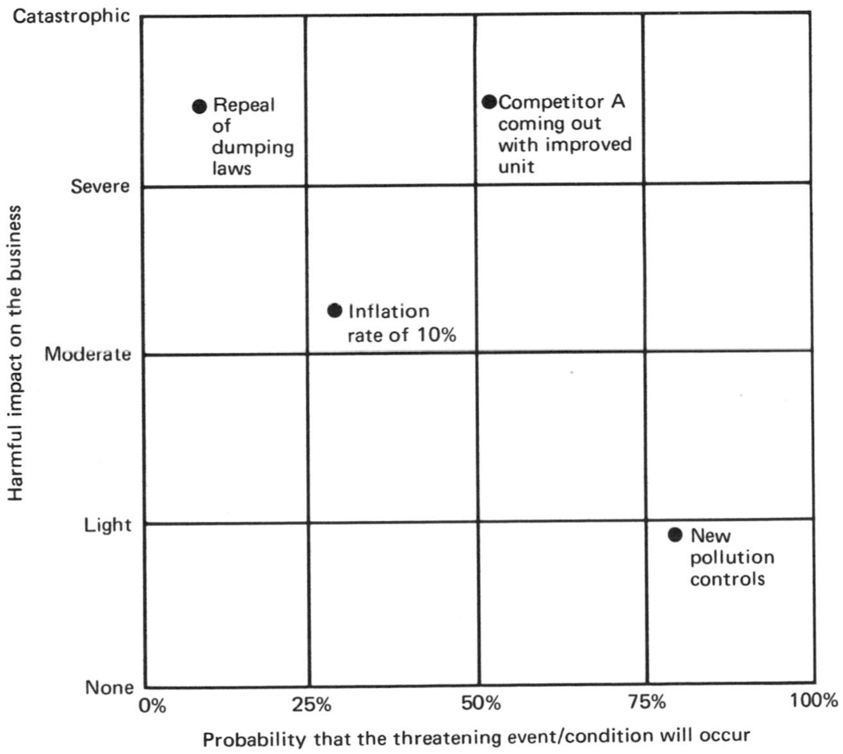

ficient new process that will significantly reduce the firm's manufacturing costs.

- The capacity of the firm's productive facilities is anticipated to be exceeded by demand in two years.
- Market share and profitability of the firm are declining.
- Potential new government regulations could create a legislated market for the firm's protection systems.
- Rapid decline of population in our urban service area as people move to the suburbs is changing both the numbers and the types of people served (for a nonprofit organization).

Often strategic issues will be confined to a single function of the firm, such as marketing or manufacturing. Some planners, in fact, prefer to identify a strategic issue for each of the firm's key result areas. More often, however, strategic issues will affect several functions and therefore require a response from the entire organization.

Objectives and Goals

Objectives and goals always describe where the organization is going, although the semantics may vary from organization to organization. We nevertheless find in any firm a hierarchy of objectives and goals, ranging from the abstract to the concrete and specific. We prefer to define objectives as the broad, general, and enduring statements of purpose, as significant end conditions or configurations the company wishes to reach, in contrast to goals, which are more specific. Here are two examples:

Increase earnings per share   (*objective*)
Increase earnings per share to $4 by 1980   (*goal*)

The goal, then, represents a measurable result to be achieved at a specific time. Goals generally are constrained—increase in market share may be limited in the short term by corporate requirements to maintain earnings; growth may be limited by the availability of cash.

Often a firm will begin the planning process by stating its objectives and goals. In the logic of all planning models, however, objectives and goals always represent responses to strategic issues. If other objectives appear important, they must derive from the feeling that other opportunities and problems exist.

Choosing your organization's goals isn't easy. Goals lay the groundwork for the organization's strategies. They must strike a balance between what the organization would like to do and what it is capable of doing, given its resources and the realities of the environment. To be useful in planning, goals must be:

Significant. Goals must have a real impact on the success of your organization's mission.

Reasonable. If the people in your organization don't believe the goals can be attained, they will not even try. For example, a goal of a 20 percent annual increase in sales for the next five years is obviously unreasonable for a company in a mature industry that has been growing at a rate of 5 percent over the past five years.

Challenging. Goals must be set high enough so that your people have to work hard to achieve them. Easy goals do not bring out the best in an organization, and they tend to give people the feeling that planning is unimportant. Even if past sales growth has averaged 5 percent, an 8 percent goal may reasonably be attainable with careful planning, and would certainly be challenging.

Specific and measurable. If your stated goal is: "To be a major factor in the small computer industry," how will you know whether you have succeeded? A more useful goal for planning might be something such as: "To achieve a 17 percent penetration of the minicomputer market in the United States by the end of 1983." At the end of 1983 you could count the number of minicomputers sold in the United States as against how many you sold, and know whether you reached your 17 percent goal.

Time-related. Getting 17 percent of the market is a fine goal, but it may not be of much significance to your firm if it is going to take you 30 years to do it. That 1983 target date is important.

Consistent with other goals. Expansion into a new market may require large investments that would make it impossible to reach a goal of increased profits at the same time.

Evaluated in terms of performance. Each month, quarter, or year—depending on the goal—you should evaluate progress made toward each goal. If you are not on your planned line to the target, you may have to change your plans in order to reach the goal, or perhaps change the goal to reflect the realities of the situation. If you are fortunate, that modification may be an increase in the performance numbers or an earlier target date.

Strategies

Strategy describes how your organization intends to achieve its objectives. This is a critical step in planning, for selection of strategies will also dictate how resources are to be allocated. Although simple to define, formulation of good strategies presents the greatest challenge to the planner. Strategy formulation also offers the greatest opportunity for creativity.

Strategy for a product or service in a given market requires that the number of variables be specified. Strategies can generally be located, therefore, in an n-dimensional strategy space, as illustrated in Figure 6a. Note that there are three variables in this diagram: y is the vertical axis, x is the horizontal axis, and z intersects the two coordinates to form the three-dimensional strategy space. If only two variables are important (for example, cost and quality), your strategy as against that of a competitor may be relatively easy to specify (see Figure 6b).

The firm that has a relatively simple product–market relationship can describe its operation in terms of its base business. The base business is the sale of existing products or services to existing markets, the matrix for which is shown in Figure 7. Several strategic options are available. If the firm wishes to improve the level of performance, it may elect one of the strategies shown in Figure 8a: extending the product line or expanding the market it serves. Needless to say, the company may improve performance by choosing to adopt the converse strategies of eliminating marginal products or markets.

The next set of alternatives will involve augmentation (Figure 8b). Augmentation may come through the sale of existing products to new markets. These new markets may represent new geographic regions or countries or alternatively, new groups of customers. Augmentation may also involve the sale of new products to existing markets. A firm selling high-voltage cable to electric utilities may wish to consider selling other

Figure 6. Strategies for a product or service. (a) n-Dimensional strategy space. (b) Strategies for book publishing.

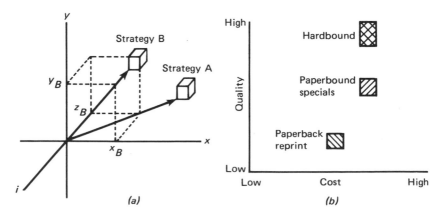

Figure 7. Product-market matrix for the base business.

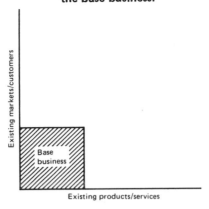

Figure 8. Product-market matrix strategies: (*a*) Expansion. (*b*) Augmentation. (*c*) Diversification.

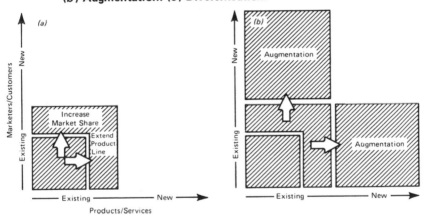

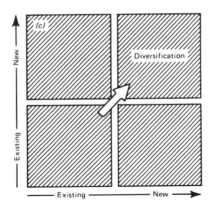

transmission hardware or engineering services. A firm selling razors may augment its products with a line of men's or women's cosmetics.

The final strategic option for a firm that has a well-defined base business may be to diversify (Figure 8c). Diversification is the sale of a new product or service to new markets. This strategy offers the greatest degree of freedom, but it also entails the highest risk. (See Part V on acquisitions.)

These strategic options arise because the firm perceives that its performance will fall short of its potential. This shortfall can be demonstrated by gap analysis (see Figure 9). The potential may be defined by a variety of methods ranging from simulation (to determine maximum growth possible if all the firm's cash flow were reinvested) to a simple statement of corporate aspirations (for example: Grow at 15 percent per year).

The performance projection is rarely a simple extension of historic performance. It is the purpose of the planning process, in fact, to demonstrate that the future will not replicate the past. A useful concept is

Figure 9. Gap analysis.

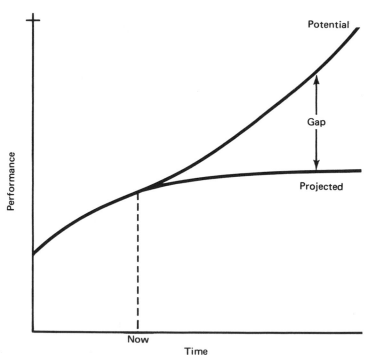

the strategy center, based on the hypothesis that businesses, like products, experience an evolution of their own. The evolutionary stages of development are illustrated in Figure 10. In the initial embryonic stage, earnings are low (or negative), and the business has heavy cash requirements. As a more stable growth period begins, earnings improve, and the business may finance its own growth. Ultimately, the business will mature, at which point growth will cease and cash flow will be positive. Finally, the aging business will enter a period of decline. The natural evolutionary process can, of course, be altered by strategic

Figure 10. The strategy center approach.

Category	Characteristics			
Market	High Growth/ Low Share	High Growth/ High Share	Low Growth/ High Share	Low Growth/ Low Share
Financial	Cash hungry Low reported earnings Good P/E High debt level	Self-financing, cash hungry Good to low reported earnings High P/E Low-moderate debt level	Cash rich High earnings Fair P/E No debt- High debt	Fair cash flow Low earnings Low P/E Low debt capacity
Title	Embryonic	Growth	Mature	Aging
Volume growth rate				
Managerial style	Entrepreneur	Sophisticated manager	Critical administrator	Opportunistic

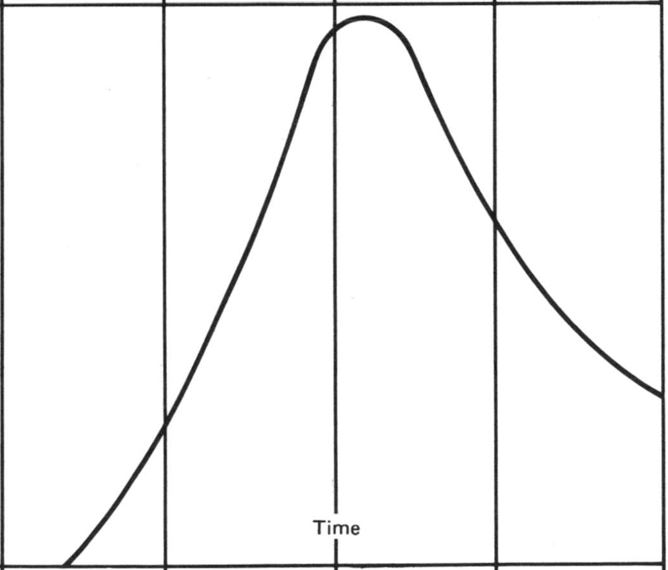

Source: Arthur D. Little, Inc.

intervention in the form of new products or markets—or the actions of competitors.

The planning process should identify the stage in the life cycle to which a business has evolved. Financial characteristics of the business clearly depend on evolutionary stage. Other characteristics, such as management style and organizational structure, also will correlate closely with the degree of evolution. (See Part IV on business strategy.)

Strategy appropriate for a growth business, say, will often depend on

Figure 11. Decreasing cost with production experience.

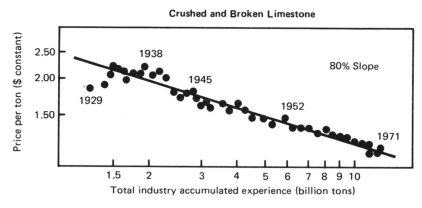

Source: U.S. Bureau of Mines.

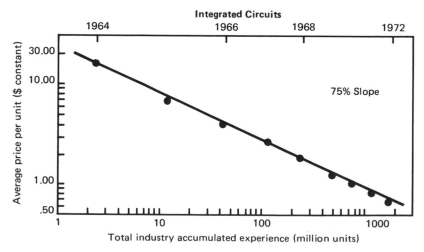

Source: Published data of Electronics Industry Association.

what other kinds of business are carried out by the firm. In such cases, the various portfolio analysis methods are invaluable strategic planning tools. These methods for assessing the strategic posture of a portfolio of businesses rely on characterizing businesses in terms of competitive position (for which market share is often a good proxy) and industry condition (for which industry growth rate is a good proxy). The important variables, usually expressed in matrix form, can be used to describe a given business strategy. Three well-known management consulting firms came up with three different approaches.

The earliest version of the matrix is the 2 × 2 portfolio developed by The Boston Consulting Group, known as the BCG matrix. The analysis begins with the empirical observation that cost decreases 20 to 30 percent in real terms each time accumulated experience doubles. This can be graphed on a logarithmic scale. A glance at Figure 11 shows that the lowest cost obviously derives from maximum production experience—or largest market share. The other variable to be considered is the maturity or growth rate of the industry. Businesses then can be positioned as shown in Figure 12:

> *Stars* (high market share, high growth potential). The strategy for
> stars is to maintain or increase market dominance.

Figure 12. The BCG matrix: The portfolio management concept.

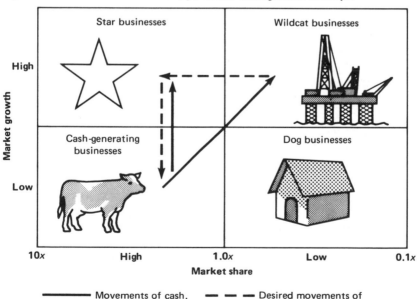

Cash cows (high market share, low growth potential). Profit is high because of market position, but little investment is required to finance the slow growth.

Wildcats (low market share, high growth). These businesses have potential to become stars, but may deteriorate into dogs if strategy is ineffective. They require high investment in order to reach star status.

Dogs (low market share, low growth). Dogs have little future and should usually be terminated or divested.

However, some who consider the BCG matrix too simplistic a model prefer to use the 3 × 3 McKinsey/GE matrix shown in Figure 13. Here we find competitive position replacing the market-share parameter of the 2 × 2 matrix, and industry attractiveness replacing market growth.

Even greater disaggregation is possible in the 5 × 4 matrix prepared by Arthur D. Little, Inc. In the ADL matrix the variables become market position and industry maturity, as depicted in Figure 14.

The implicit hypothesis in all portfolio approaches to strategy is that a firm seeks to create a balanced portfolio, having assets distributed in the several desirable sectors of the matrix. Satisfying this hypothesis assures the enterprise of continuity. Thus, embryonic businesses become growth businesses, which evolve into mature businesses. If competitive position is strong, the earnings and cash flow from the mature business will finance the embryonic growth portions of the portfolio.

Perhaps some of the most significant recent strategy guidelines are emerging recently from the PIMS project of the Strategic Planning Institute. PIMS, an acronym for *P*rofit *I*mpact of *M*arketing *S*trategy, takes a totally empirical approach. Data are collected on possible determinants of profit from a variety of businesses and are then compared by regression analysis. Results from more than 1,000 businesses over many years have suggested a number of important correlations. For example, analysis to date shows that 80 percent of a firm's profitability is the result of the complex interaction of nine strategic variables:

1. *Investment intensity.* Increases in fixed capital or working capital tend to reduce profitability and cash flow.
2. *Productivity.* Increases in value added per employee improve profitability.
3. *Market position.* Increases in relative or absolute market share have a positive impact on profitability and cash flow.
4. *Market growth.* Participation in growth markets will increase absolute profit, but requires additional investment.

Figure 13. The McKinsey/GE business assessment array.

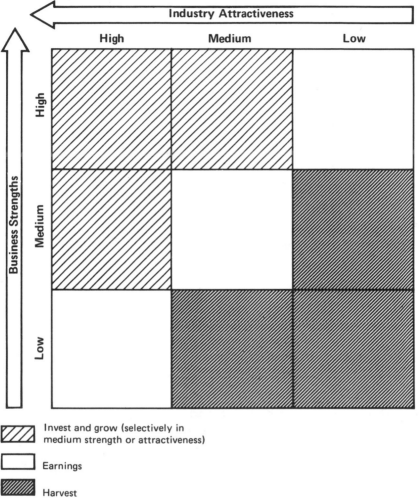

5. *Quality of products or services.* High product quality has a favorable impact on financial performance.
6. *Innovation.* Innovative activity, such as research and development and engineering, usually will have benefits only if the firm has a strong market position.
7. *Vertical integration.* If the market is stable and mature, vertical integration improves performance. If the market is changing rapidly, however, vertical integration is undesirable.

Figure 14. ADL's business profile.

Competitive Position	Stage of Maturity			
	Embryonic	Growing	Maturing	Aging
Dominant				
Strong				
Favorable				
Tenable				
Weak				

8. *Cost push.* The firm's response to increased costs will depend on its ability to accommodate them internally or to raise prices.
9. *Current strategic effort.* Change in any of the first eight factors may have effects that are negative at first. For example, getting additional market share is costly.

The major findings of PIMS, in most instances, do nothing more than confirm conventional wisdom. The empirical validation and quantification of these variables, however, represents a major advance in strategic planning. Especially significant is the finding that differences in industry, product, or company history have virtually no effect on the laws of the marketplace.

Programs and Supporting Plans

The natural sequel to formulation of strategies is the preparation of programs required to carry out the strategies, and the allocation of resources to these programs. Although strategic issues will cut across organizational boundaries, often a set of functional plans and programs will be desirable for marketing, manufacturing, research and development, engineering, capital investment, human resources, and the like. Nonprofit organizations may give special attention to community relations, funding, volunteer activities, or other aspects of their operation.

Financial Summary and Budgets

The final portion of plan development yields a set of financial statements for the period of your plan. Conventional profit-and-loss statements, balance sheets, and flow of funds statements will be presented, accompanied by appropriate commentary. The first year of the financial plan is usually devoted to the budget. Disaggregation into more detail (for example, month by month) may follow.

Recent advances in computer software make possible alternative displays of financial information. See Figure 15 for an example. These sophisticated advances provide manipulation by regression analysis. Important anomalies or trends in performance may be discerned and questioned. More sophisticated models, being developed in many firms, permit the simulation of many possible changes in external or internal variables. These are discussed in the modeling section, Part VII.

Priorities

The challenge in this part of your plan is to allocate resources to those activities or programs that have highest priority. An initial set of programs usually requires more resources than are available, and a series of iterations may be necessary. It may be necessary to revise objectives and goals and their supporting strategies. One important benefit of the planning process is, of course, that priorities have to be made explicit in a valid plan. For example, certain expenditures may have been required because of earlier decisions, particularly in the public sector. These decisions perpetuate the old system. Zero-base budgeting methods offer a new approach whereby all the resources of the firm are reallocated in terms of the new, forward-thinking plan. Zero-base budgeting, however, is so arduous a process that few large organizations have managed to use it successfully.

GENERALITIES

The preparation of a *plan* is considered by most to be only a secondary result of the *process*. Indeed, slavish devotion to forms and procedures will yield only a massive volume ignored by management at all levels. The process should be continuous, dynamic, and iterative, for the plan is a view of this process at a particular instant of time. As such, the planning document may have no more than symbolic value. The

Figure 15. Financial information ($000).

RUN 12/01/77 CURRENT YEAR 1977 XYZ DIVISION COMPOSITE PLAN

Account	Historical (1970–1976)					1977	Planned (1978–1982)				
	1970	1973	1974	1975	1976	1977	1978	1979	1980	1981	1982
Shipments	34,761	32,653	33,137	41,424	42,164	38,606	45,540	51,684	57,270	62,588	67,540
Cost of shipments	24,174	23,266	23,078	29,136	30,753	27,870	32,370	35,857	39,726	43,149	46,623
Value added	20,430	19,510	19,610	24,100	25,050	23,079	27,400	30,891	33,760	37,153	39,670
R&D expense	467	502	532	630	743	733	782	843	900	926	982
G&A expense	5,250	5,971	5,740	6,475	7,350	7,840	7,917	8,540	9,380	10,500	10,745
Supporting expense	7,500	8,530	8,200	9,250	10,500	11,200	11,310	12,200	13,400	15,000	15,350
Operating income	6,054	4,114	5,095	6,739	5,539	1,383	6,173	8,316	9,559	10,875	11,825
Operating cash flow	389	292	-1,739	-220	-1,094	808	3,039	3,084	4,855	6,384	5,336
Operating investment	29,790	34,901	38,847	44,031	48,684	49,279	51,139	54,605	57,816	60,153	63,261
Average accounts receivable	4,146	4,091	4,146	5,653	6,820	6,574	7,014	7,667	8,155	8,700	9,230
Average inventory	9,399	11,536	12,063	12,891	14,853	15,240	15,587	16,701	17,748	18,694	20,040
Plant and equipment	14,995	17,848	20,978	23,631	24,953	25,642	26,597	28,131	29,628	30,397	31,354
Capital expenditures	3,798	2,460	3,993	1,338	1,381	1,521	1,450	2,041	1,200	490	1,695
Production workers	1,165	1,148	893	1,184	1,190	984	1,019	1,078	1,128	1,174	1,194
Nonproduction employees	459	484	427	464	500	479	501	521	548	591	578

process has forced careful consideration on the part of the organization of its environment, resources, goals and objectives, strategies, and programs. The thought and effort that have gone into this process should have broadened the viewpoint of managers and helped them to coordinate their decisions. This is the real value of planning. (See Part VI on the planning process.)

The role of the planner is to facilitate preparation of the plan by operating management. But the responsibilities of the long-range planning executive tend to be rather broad in nature:

Basic Function

- Directs the corporate long-range planning and development program to ensure best use of its resources, in accordance with objectives for growth and profitability.
- Defines corporate goals and objectives and prepares plans for achievement.
- Plans and develops programs to ensure rates of growth and profitability.
- Prepares studies to assess corporate functioning and advises regarding its results.

Responsibilities

- Assists the president and other officers in developing corporate objectives and plans for their achievement (rate of return, rate of increase in sales and product line objectives), and develops and conducts continuing reviews.
- Exercises overall direction of preparation of programs for execution of corporate plans.
- Conducts ongoing assessment of corporate performance, as compared with corporate plans. Considers present and planned capacity of the company in financial terms, workforce, organizational facilities, and technology.
- Reviews proposals for major capital expenditures to ensure their conformity with corporate plans. Advises on their economic justification.
- Undertakes special studies requested by the president and other officers, usually involving growth planning of the company, and of new or improved products or processes.
- Keeps informed of, and coordinates, overall corporate plans, as well as other planning studies being conducted within the company. Encourages initiation of such studies when needed.

- Seeks out, investigates, and assesses outside opportunities for the company (licenses, patents, joint ventures, possible mergers).
- Assists other departments and divisions of the company in their planning activities.

This is because the planner's job is to facilitate, provoke, challenge, and encourage. (See particularly Jerstad's chapter, An Administrator's Manual of Planning.) It is a delicate and precarious role, at best (as witness the frequent turnover in the planning profession) and, justifiably, planners cannot commit themselves to the process with courage and integrity unless they consider themselves expendable. Helpful ways to get around this sticky area are found in the process skills contributions in the section on the planning process, Part VI.

Does planning really pay off? Several *ex post facto* studies present evidence that the financial performance of firms that plan most certainly exceeds that of firms that do not plan. But many of the benefits of planning are less tangible than financial performance, such as:

Better understanding of the business
Visibility for strategic issues
Explicit strategies and improved resource allocation
Improved internal communication

Having a plan establishes a strategy for existing resources, justifies new resources, and makes it easier to contend with change. That is, it sets forth alternatives if fewer resources prove available.

A good plan is based on reliable information and presents credible strategies. Results may track the plan if operating management has been involved in the planning process and is commited to its implementation. Nevertheless, the future is uncertain. As a result, many organizations require analyses showing the sensitivity of performance to variations in key assumptions. A few firms have also experimented successfully with contingency plans. These present a set of alternatives to be invoked when major perturbations are experienced.

Plans are usually prepared on an annual cycle. In a dynamic environment, frequent changes in strategy or resource allocation may be necessary, whereas plans in mature industries don't need to be revised as often. Here is a typical planning schedule:

Month	Event
January	Corporate statement of expectations
March	Organizational response, agreement on objectives

June	Preliminary plans submitted for corporate review
September	Final plan submitted
November	Approval of plans, resource allocation
December	Preparation of budget for first year of plan

WHERE TO GET MORE HELP

The bibliography will give additional sources of information. The various member organizations of the International Affiliation of Planning Societies are also excellent sources of guidance.

Part I
FUTURES

ARNOLD MITCHELL

Changing Life Ways and Corporate Planning

THE DRIVING FORCE in our society is no longer technology, economic growth, production, income, invention, and the like. Instead the driving force seems to lie in the inner realm of people's values. This contribution examines the effect of changing values on corporate planning.

To bring order to this confused and many-faceted field, I will discuss values in terms of what I call "ways of life," and I will begin by describing six ways of life characterizing America today. I will then sketch three national profiles of these life ways that might reasonably come to pass, and will indicate some of the changes in consumer values, needs, and beliefs that would accompany these possible scenarios and their changing life-way profiles. Finally, I will discuss some market implications of the changes I foresee.

SIX LIFE WAYS

The term "life way" differs from the common expression "lifestyle" by focusing on the inner drives of an individual. A person's way of life is defined by inner motivating, guiding, and meaning-giving values and feelings. "Lifestyle" describes how the inner drives are exhibited. For example, a life way revolving around the inner drive to achieve fame could be expressed by a number of different lifestyles, such as a devotion to athletics, to politics, or to academic pursuits.

I have identified six types representing six life ways: Makers, Preservers, Takers, Changers, Seekers, and Escapers (see Table 1).

Makers are the people who make things happen. Their distinguishing characteristic is visible achievement. Makers tend to strive for accomplishment, recognition, and prosperity. They are leaders in business, the professions, and politics.

Preservers are at home chiefly with the familiar, the tried and true. Proud of tradition, Preservers act as an anchor on change. They make up

Table 1. Summary of characteristics of the six life ways.

Life Way	Hallmark	Goals	Examples
Maker	Visible achievement	Accomplishment Recognition Prosperity	Liberal executives and professionals Salesmen Promoters
Preserver	Reverence for tradition	Preserving the status quo National security Salvation	Conservative executives and professionals Authoritative parents Fundamentalists
Taker	"Me first" attitude	Family security Pleasure Friendship	Disinterested bureaucrats Go-along union members Tenure-oriented employees Some welfare recipients
Changer	Out-of-phaseness	Changing the system Excitement Recognition	Consumer advocates Radicals Social critics Some cultists Liberationists
Seeker	Inner search	Serenity Wisdom Accomplishment	Some religious leaders Some businessmen Some artists Some innovative scientists
Escaper	Flight from reality	Happiness Freedom Pleasure	Drug addicts Alcoholics Walter Mitty types Total mystics Extreme dropouts

much of the "silent majority." They are also Makers who are winding down, the conservatives of some of the richest suburbs in the nation, and the staunch advocates of status quo middle America.

Takers coast. Creating as few waves as possible, they take what they can from the system. Takers inhabit the byways of business life; they are drawn to bureaucracies and tenured posts. With little interest in global and national issues, Takers find their rewards in family life, friends, and conventional pleasures.

Changers always have answers, are constantly trying to alter things to conform to their views. They are the critics, protesters, radicals, and complainers—and make up a significant percentage of the doers.

Seekers are the people whose life way drives them to search for a firmer grasp, a deeper understanding, or a richer experience. They have the courage to take seriously the unproved; they dare to live by rules not evident to others. Often unrecognized by their contemporaries, Seekers are sometimes noted in history as the great spirits and seminal thinkers of their times.

Escapers are the lotus-eaters. Their chief drive is to escape the pressures and demands of every day. Escape takes many forms, from dropping out to addiction to fantasy to withdrawal. It affects every age group and social class. These are the ones who cannot, or will not, cope.

A handful of life ways cannot describe all the variations within a large and diverse population. Nonetheless, most people can be identified with one of these patterns. Sometimes people change from one life way to another. Also, a person can practice two life ways at once. For example, a man may be a Maker at work and an Escaper in his home life.

DISTRIBUTION OF LIFE WAYS

How are these life ways distributed in the adult population of the United States, and how can they be used to describe a society?

About one-third of the population appear to be Preservers. Makers and Takers are equally numerous, at slightly over 20 percent. The remaining 25 percent is divided among Changers, Escapers, and Seekers.

On this basis, three-quarters of the population (the total of Preservers, Makers, and Takers) generally accept the way things are. One-fourth (Changers, Escapers, and perhaps Seekers) basically want change.

This provides us with a way of allocating the life ways in terms of social norms. The vertical line in the center of Figure 1a represents the cultural norm of the full spectrum of society. Since Makers and Preservers constitute the heart of the status quo, they are placed on either side of the center line. The Maker tries to nudge the norm in the direction of evolutional development; Makers want some, but not radical, change. The Preserver presses in the opposite direction; he would like a return to yesterday's ways. On either side of these middle groups are life ways further removed from the cultural heartland: Changers and Seekers on the develop/reform side and Takers and Escapers on the avoid/rigidify side. The curve in the figure approximates the life-ways distribution. This kind of spectrum has to be relative to current definitions of norms.

The most important point about the distribution curve is the general correspondence between the numbers in the life ways and cultural norms. The center groups of Makers and Preservers constitute more than half the population, the next two groups contain about 30 percent, and the two outermost groups about 15 percent.

Overlap between life ways and cultural norms is not to be taken for granted. For example, in a classical primitive society there is an enormous concentration in the traditional mode. Hence the huge hump in the Preserver portion of Figure 1b.

Figure 1(a). Present life-way profile.

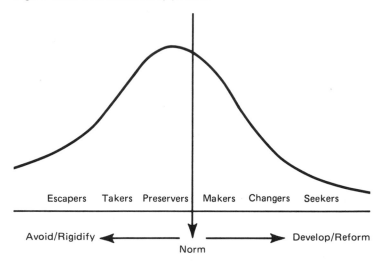

Figure 1 (b). Life-way profiles for a primitive society, a society in transition, and a defeated society.

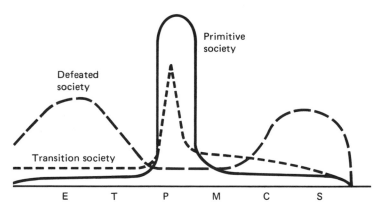

In an agrarian society undergoing a transition to industrialization, power is in the hands of Makers and Changers, but the largest share of the population remains in the Preserver mode. This explains the curious distribution of the dotted line in Figure 1b.

A nation defeated in war or undergoing severe depression would display the pattern of the dashed line: humps on the Escaper-Taker end and on the Changer-Seeker pole, but a low plateau in the Preserver-Maker portion.

The overall message is that stable societies show life ways clustered around their cultural norms. Unstable societies show the opposite pattern. Measured this way, our nation is on the stable side, but less so than in the past, when the curve was more concentrated around the center.

ALTERNATIVE FUTURES

There are three classes of plausible futures: regressive, conventional, and transformational. Let us look at some possible futures for our nation and consider how each of these might come about.

Regressive Futures

A regressive future would be marked by fear, authoritarian government, social regulation, and rigid economic controls. It represents human and economic regression. Undesirable as it sounds, how might we be catapulted into it? In terms of our life ways, how might a violent swing be generated toward the Escaper-Taker-Preserver side?

Many say such a swing is taking place now and that it is fully justified. They argue that the urban and campus riots of the late 1960s showed that permissiveness does not work. On the political level they point to assassinations. On the human level they point to rises in crime, pornography, and drugs. On the economic level there is a staggering GNP, inflation, unemployment, and dissident workers.

Table 2 shows some traditional views that command wide support. Of particular importance is the last item, which comes from a survey of students. Eighty-six percent of the students questioned thought society needed some legally based authority to prevent chaos. There is a striking amount of conservatism among segments of the population generally considered to be on the liberal side.

Table 2. Support for traditional views.

Statement	Percentage Agreeing
The Golden Rule is very important	93
Nothing is more important than family love and respect	90
Drugs are associated with moral corruption and decay	90
Love is very important	87
Friendship is very important	87
Children should respect their parents	87
Society needs some legally based authority to prevent chaos	86

I interpret these survey results as a reaction to excesses of wildness and violence. Since they appear to be directed toward preserving traditional values, they can be important stabilizing influences, even though they may be more reactive than leading.

If these restraining reactions *fail* to emerge promptly and decisively, it is possible that this country could move into a "slough of despond." The question is whether we are there now. This would be a period of confusion, improvidence, and economic recession born of chaotic moral, political, social, and economic actions. Unless restrained from the start, the trends might gather uncontrollable momentum. Dog-eat-dogism would predominate. Our system of checks and balances would be destroyed. Under such circumstances, we could be swept into a "collapse" future in which society as we know it would be obliterated. More plausible is the prospect of a wave of extreme authoritarianism following the "slough of despond." Such an antidemocratic surge could lead us to a "1984" type of future or to an ironly regimented "authoritarian recession." The best we could hope for in these circumstances would be a just-barely-making-it "industrial stalemate."

The national life-way profiles accompanying these events would oscillate wildly. Today's balanced pattern would fall apart as the nation entered the "slough of despond." Many would seek refuge in Escapism or a vicious brand of Takerism (Figure 2a). Many Preservers and Makers would resort to Changerism in attempts to get the nation back on its feet. A highly divided, leaderless profile would result.

Conventional Futures

What about conventional futures—those based on incremental or evolutionary change? Herman Kahn calls them "surprise-free" futures. They represent the status quo extended indefinitely. Tomorrow will be like today, only bigger, richer, better.

In a stable, growth-oriented society the presumption that tomorrow will be a somewhat shinier version of today is eminently sensible. If, in addition, most of the population is generally satisfied with the way things are, there is good reason to anticipate a smoothly unrolling future.

Table 3 shows happiness or life-satisfaction ratings of Americans during the past 15 years. The percent being "very satisfied" with life has ranged from 35 to 22. There is no discernible trend in the data. Considering the other extreme, as many as 17 percent and as few as 8 percent said they were "not too satisfied" with life. Again there is no apparent trend.

Satisfaction indexes in other realms are also positive. For example, 81

Figure 2. Profile of futures. (a) Regressive; (b) conventional; (c) midterm transformational; (d) transformational.

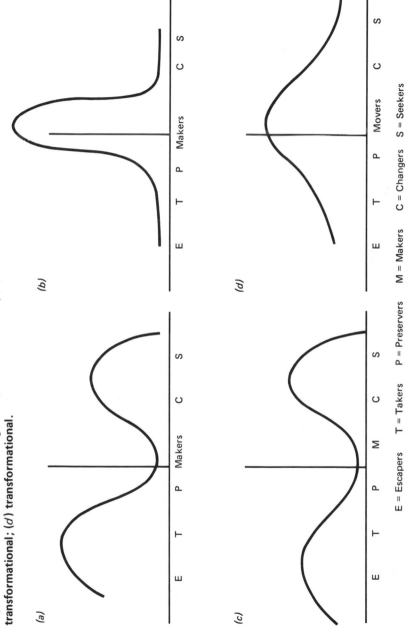

(a)

(b)

(c)

(d)

E = Escapers   T = Takers   P = Preservers   M = Makers   C = Changers   S = Seekers

Table 3. Satisfaction with life (percent).

Year of Survey	Very Satisfied	Pretty Satisfied	Not too Satisfied
1958	35	54	11
1962	24	59	17
1965	24	65	11
1968	24	66	10
1970	22	65	13
1971	34	57	8
1972	22	66	12

percent said they were satisfied with the work they did; 73 percent were satisfied with their housing; 62 percent were satisfied with their incomes. There are almost no differences between men and women, but blacks show up as only about half as satisfied as whites.

A final item is that Americans consider their lives better today than they were five years ago, and they expect the rate of improvement to increase during the next five years. This expectation of improvement applied to men and women of all age groups, all educational levels, all incomes, all occupations, all regions, all places of residence, all races, all religions, and all political persuasions. The two highest expectation ratings for the 1972–1977 period came from groups said to be most dissatisfied with America: the age group 18–29 and blacks as a whole.

It appears that most people not only expect but *want* tomorrow to be like today. This is a powerful combination.

If this expectation is realized, by 1990 we will arrive at something that might be called a "superstate," an enormously rich, productive, efficient, aggressive mass economy that has successfully used technology to overcome the hosts of shortages and negative industrial side effects that plague us today. Among those who believe that levels of economic growth of 5–6 percent per year are not only desirable but sustainable for 100 years ahead is Hermann Kahn. He is engaged in a massive study to demonstrate the feasibility of having the whole world get rich before it retires. If this happens, our life-ways profile will be shifted slightly to the right of today's pattern (Figure 2*b*).

The superstate has been defined as successful in overcoming the problems of industrialization and limits to growth. If it can do that, it might also be able to expand rapidly enough to reduce or eliminate poverty, inflation, unemployment, and other economic and social problems. The issue of unimpeded economic growth is central because if economic growth rates must be severely curtailed, important values and patterns of life ways will have to be changed. This brings me to plausible futures springing from the third, or transformational, route.

Transformational Futures

I should like to sketch a three-part scenario for the coming 15–20 years that takes into account many of the trends, pressures, and dislocations we are experiencing today and those that are looming ahead.

First, it is believed that Preserverism will continue to be the dominant life way in the immediate future. The conservative posture that developed in the early 1970s is still with us (Figure 1). The mood America reflects in the opinion polls is not one of a people about to throw away what they have for the "new values." But reservations and uncertainties do seem to be mounting.

Second, it seems plausible that adherence to the basic pattern of the status quo will sooner or later prove inadequate to cope with the combination of "external" problems such as resource depletion, pollution, economic uncertainty, and violence and "internal" problems such as rising expectations, alienation, moral indignation, and more explicit visions of what might be. Despite general prosperity, the gap between what people will accept as satisfactory and what actually happens might widen rather than narrow.

Increasing national tension may mark the late 1970s. A bimodal life way could develop, pitting the forces of change against the forces of the status quo. A profile such as that in Figure 2c could result.

Such a profile means that the nation has been robbed of the energy and creative leadership of its Makers and the stabilizing influence of its Preservers. The result would probably be a rise in societal anger, disillusionment, chaos, violence, and economic disruption. Such a development would destroy all prospects for a smoothly unfolding, "surprise-free" future.

Third, if the nation is lucky and/or wise enough to avoid the trajectory into an authoritarian state, the crisis I have described may trigger a swift metamorphosis in values. Some transformation in goals and priorities seems essential if we are to achieve the kind of postindustrialism many people claim they want.

If national values are to change so fundamentally as to accept a future marked by low economic growth, a new kind of Maker will have to emerge from this period of split national priorities. This will be the Mover, who will combine qualities from several of the basic six life ways. He will have many of the achievement drives of the Maker; he will share the Preserver's value of tradition; he will need some of the zeal of the Changer if he is to lead the way to postindustrialism. Finally, as a private citizen, the Mover will adopt the contemplative sensitivity of the Seeker, which is necessary for building a person-centered society.

With the emergence of Movers—an event which seems possible during the 1980s—the national life-way profile will undergo another major shift (Figure 2d). The pattern shown here has every chance of offering stability in a rapidly changing world. The key element is the shift from Maker to Mover in the leadership role. It is strong in the building mode of Movers and sufficiently interested in preserving the past not to fall apart from excesses of experimentalism. Such a society should have the economic resources to carry its Escapers and Takers with little trouble. And it should be able to hear its Changers and Seekers without being threatened by them. The profile is notable for the diversity it permits and encourages. Many people could be happy in this kind of a society. It should work if the Movers have sufficient influence and charisma to achieve the consensus that every democracy requires to be successful.

MARKET IMPLICATIONS

What do these possible changes mean for the marketer? What insights do these observations provide into what we might profitably do today and tomorrow?

The most fundamental point is this: These futures exist today in the sense that the patterns of values represented by regressive, conventional, and transformational worlds characterize many of today's consumers.

The typical consumer of the regressive future is today's security-oriented buyer, concerned primarily with price, conformity, and utility. The consumer of the conventional future is today's prosperous, possession-conscious, status-prone, pleasure-loving customer. And the consumer of the transformational future is today's frugal, person-centered, experience-seeking, inward-looking, ecologically aware buyer.

From this viewpoint, the futures analysis proves helpful to the marketer in several ways. In fact, the patterns of values associated with these three types of futures can serve as the basis for market segmentation.

If the marketer looks at the customers he is trying to please in terms of these three different clusters, he can ask and answer a series of questions pertinent to today's market. For example, he can ask what values would be dominant in each of the clusters. Table 4 shows a matrix opposing ten values important in marketing with the three types of customers. The marketer can rank each of the values in each of the buyer

Table 4. Consumer-value matrix.

	Regressive Future	Conventional Future	Transformational Future
Values			
Individualism			
Experimentalism			
Societal concern			
Person-centeredness			
Direct experience			
Sense of security			
Escape			
Conformity			
Naturalism			
Materialism			
Marketing Approaches			
Advertising themes			
Media			
Own/rent/lease			
Warranty			
Credit			
Distribution			
Product Characteristics			
Price			
Performance			
Durability			
Design			
Variety			

segments. Working with this matrix produces a rich sense of critical differences in customers.

Based on this, the marketer can analyze different marketing approaches. It is clear that each of the consumer types would respond differently to advertising themes and other marketing techniques.

Similarly, he can systematically probe which product characteristics would be most important and appealing to each of the three market segments. This sort of analysis can be applied to numerous other aspects of today's marketplace.

If you agree that the next five years will be decisive in determining the direction of our future, it becomes crucial to plan now for the market trends of the late 1970s and beyond. Figure 3a–c shows possible major market trends in the three futures.

In these three figures the vertical axis at the left shows the share of goods and services purchased; the horizontal axis represents time. The

Figure 3. Value segmentation.

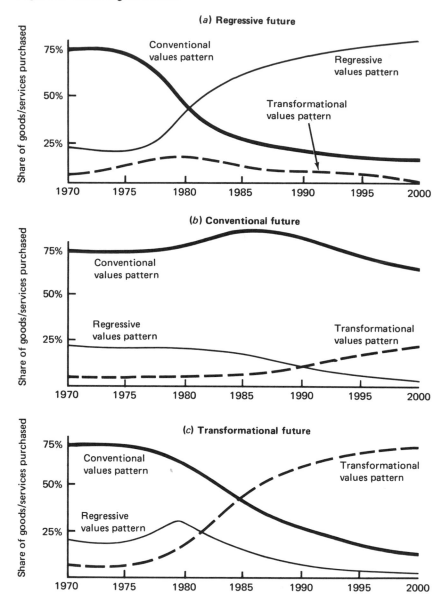

(a) **Regressive future**

(b) **Conventional future**

(c) **Transformational future**

thick solid line shows an estimate of the share of goods and services purchased by consumers who are dominated by the conventional values pattern. The thin solid line shows the share bought by consumers who possess regressive or group-oriented values. The dashed line depicts the share of purchases made by the frugal, transformational group. As shown on the figures, I have imputed 75 percent of consumer sales to the conventional pattern in 1970, 20 percent to the so-called regressive group, and 5 percent to the transformational pattern.

Figure 3a suggests trends in these three value segments if the United States veers off into a depressed and depression-ridden regressive type of future. In effect, market shares of conventional and regressive consumers switch over time, while those of the transformational consumer fade away almost completely. These would be grim times for income-elastic markets or products bought for status or visibility reasons. They would be better times for safe, groupy, big-name warranted, bargain, and security-inspiring products.

Figure 3b shows the bouncy, prosperous conventional future. Consumption continues to be dominated by materialistic buyers, and the contribution of the security-oriented fraction declines. I show a slow rise to perhaps 20 percent in the share of goods accounted for by transformational consumers. In general, markets in this future would be classic Americana. Also suggested is the prospect of a considerable antithesis-of-prosperity market within the main flow, composed of consumers who have "outgrown" old modes of market expression.

Figure 3c shows trends under conditions of an emerging transformational society.

What would you do if you became convinced that this kind of future actually was developing? It would be like no other society in history, so you would have to improvise. Here are some of the things I would do:

• I would collect all the data I could to support my thesis because I would surely encounter violent opposition from others in my company. I would try to publish my findings so I could claim to be an expert.

• I would locate harbinger samples of my emerging types of consumers and would conduct a series of in-depth interviews with them, with the aim of defining them statistically, demographically, psychologically, as consumers, as parents, and in every other way possible.

• Then I would draw up the longest list I could of the products and services these consumers would want, what they would pay, where they would buy, and similar matters.

• I would hedge my bets by figuring out "common denominator" markets among the three types of futures. I would emphasize these partly to convince my superiors and colleagues I still knew what I was doing.

• I would ferret out branch points leading to the different kinds of futures and would monitor these points closely for early warnings of market changes. I would devise rough contingency plans for the most critical forks in the future.

• When I was ready—when I thought I could handle the sarcasm and disbelief of my audience—I would ask my top management for a day to lay out my insights and what they mean for company planning. I would approach this meeting with extreme seriousness.

• If I could, I would get my management to participate in an involving exercise to get into the future themselves and to reach their own conclusions about tomorrow's consumers. These exercises are available and they do work.

• I would do one final thing: I would invest in a fatted calf and a full moon.

WILLIS W. HARMAN

Business and Society
in Transformation

ALTHOUGH most of us have to be concerned primarily with the welfare
of our own organizations, we recognize that these organizations prosper
only as the society as a whole prospers. Society presently faces a set of
complex problems, and neither the bureaucratic process of executive
decision making nor the adversary process of political decision making
seems well adapted to their resolution. What appears to be required is a
process for developing new perceptions of the situation, the facts, and
the action possibilities.

Several years ago the Kettering Foundation asked Stanford Research
Institute to help with a reassessment of contemporary societal problems
so that the Foundation could work toward their resolution. From our efforts emerged two views of our present situation which lead to very different kinds of policies. We call one a "conventional" view; this holds
that the problems of the 1970s are not essentially different from problems society has faced in the past, except that a number seem to have
developed at once. Thus by committing familiar problem-solving resources, we can assume that the problems will be adequately dealt with,
as past challenges have been. A second "transformational" view perceives that we have come to the end of an era, and a thorough systemic
change will be required to solve the problems.

As time has passed, the second view has become more plausible. In it
contemporary crises—energy and food shortages, inflation, recession—
appear as highly interrelated "transition pains" that will remain baffling
and unresolvable until they are viewed as part of the partial breakdown
of a system that has to precede a restructuring. In it seemingly diverse
forces and events, from changing cultural values and recent scientific
findings to the growing intolerability of tradeoffs in the energy-environ-
ment-economy arena, fit into a pattern that seems to make overall sense.

There can be little question that substantial changes in technology and patterns of living will have to take place within the next quarter century . . . if the sorts of events projected by the so-called "prophets of doom" are not to become a reality. The preoccupying question has become whether existing economic, social, and political institutions provide the means to bring these changes about in an evolutionary and benign manner. . . .

Business will be, is already, faced with doubts that private enterprise can . . . respond to the changed circumstances of the new economic era. . . . There is frank doubt in many quarters that private enterprise can take into account the social costs of its activities without being so heavily regulated as to defy the meaning of "private." There is frank doubt that what a great many people perceive as the "real needs" of society can be served at a profit sufficient to attract private enterprise and private capital. . . .

As long as people perceive that the interests of the profit-making enterprise differ substantially from their own, if people come increasingly to believe that private enterprise, because it must make a profit to survive, cannot produce the things that society most wants, the role of private enterprise can only decline, and its image and influence diminish.

From a draft report of the Council on Trends and Perspectives, U.S. Chamber of Commerce, September 1974.

OUR PREMISE: WORLD IN CRISIS

We start with the premise that the free enterprise system and the industrialization mode on which its success is based appear to be in trouble. There is enough evidence of this to warrant serious examination of this "crisis of crises."

The case for crisis is not, however, proved. In fact, it cannot be proved until after it is too late to do anything about it. Thus Herman Kahn, for instance, presents an impressive case for a "post-industrial perspective" in which, within the next century, "the more desperate and seemingly eternal problems of human poverty will have largely been solved or greatly alleviated," "most misery will derive from the anxieties and ambiguities of wealth and luxury, not from physical suffering due to scarcities," and "the post-industrial economy should be close to a humanistic utopia by most historical standards"—if we just don't falter or lose our nerve now. Kahn denies that "spaceship earth" limitations, increasing pollution, resource depletion, food and energy shortages, technological excesses, "limits to growth," rich-poor gaps, and supposed deterioration of "quality of life" constitute insurmountable problems, when approached with "technological progress . . . the systematic internalization of relevant external costs . . . the normal use of the price and other market mechanisms . . . and some degree of public regulation and international cooperation." As Kahn states, "New technology and capital investment are necessary . . . to help protect and improve the environment, to keep resource costs down, and to provide an economic surplus for problems and crises. . . . If we are reasonably prudent and flexible we will not have to contend with any really serious shortages in the medium run and the long run looks even better." In other words, there is no systemic crisis, just a crisis of will.[1]

In sharp contrast to this is the view that there *is* a systemic crisis and a need for systemic transformation if the fundamental humane values underlying the democratic free enterprise system are to be preserved. There is also a crisis of *perception* as well as will, of seeing and understanding the need so that the transformation can be as nondisruptive and nondestructive as possible.

Other views are being presented. Some of the pessimists, such as Robert Heilbroner, see the need for a systemic transformation and don't think we will make it.[2] Some of the "humanistic optimists" (in contrast to the "technological optimists" like Kahn) see the need for a transformation and perceive it as happening smoothly without serious disruption; Charles Reich[3] and George Leonard,[4] for example, espouse this view.

Thus with full recognition that other interpretations of our time are supportable, we propose to examine the implications of the transformational view. At the least, it deserves to be one of the alternative future contexts against which major action options are tested.

INDICATIONS THAT THE INDUSTRIALIZED WORLD IS IN TROUBLE

Consider these trends:

Public faith and trust in business are low, and this is partly because the business corporation does not know how to respond to the new demands that are being made. In the past it was enough to claim that the corporation's mission was to seek to make a profit in a competitive marketplace by the most efficient allocation of the firm's resources of capital, manpower, technology, management skill, and other corporate capacities. Today that sounds a little like asserting that the mission of an elected official is to get reelection votes, or that of a government agency is to balance its budget. True, but not enough.

There are indications of lasting changes in basic values and beliefs. These are mainly of three types:

• Observable cultural changes, such as survey and poll data; cultural indicators such as organizations joined or books read; "consciousness-expanding" activities such as yoga, meditation, biofeedback; evidence of changing values and attitudes toward a "new naturalism"; and growing interest in the spiritual, mystical, transcendental, suprarational, and esoteric.

• Awareness of the need for a new social paradigm, that is, of the inadequacy of the growth-and-consumption ethic of business-dominated affluent society for political guidance and for commanding the deepest loyalties of the citizenry.

• Developments within science supportive of a more transcendental image of humanity. Most significant here is the new legitimation of (and new research tools for) systematic exploration of subjective experience, varied states of consciousness, religious beliefs and mystical experiences, meditative insight, psychic phenomena, and occult mysteries.

Industrialized society faces new dilemmas of a sort that it does not know how to resolve. These include:

The growth dilemma. The environmental and social costs of continued exponential growth in energy and materials usage, and economic growth in the forms we have known, appear to be unacceptably high. But the costs of stopping that growth also appear to be unacceptably high. In the

---

From the study of the past it is evident that, throughout the ages, individuals and communities have repeatedly come upon the creative factors and forces at work in the human psyche. Great philosophies and great religions have time and again come into being as an outcome of such discoveries; and for a time stirred men to the depths. But as often as the discoveries have been made they have again been lost.

In this present age there is the possibility of making the discoveries in a new way: not as an outcome of some special revelation of extraordinary insight on the part of one man or a small body of men, but in the form of direct personal experience of a considerable number of intelligent men and women directing their awareness upon the inner world. For the first time in history, the scientific spirit of inquiry, the free search for truth, is being turned upon the other side of consciousness.

In place of *a priori* dogma there is a growing body of empirically established experience; experience which can be progressively funded, as our experience of the outer world has been funded, and its meaning learnt. Because of this, there is good prospect that the discoveries can this time be held: and so become, now and henceforward, no longer the lost secret but the living heritage of man.

P. W. Martin, *Experiment in Depth* (New York: Pantheon, 1965).

latter case the costs take the form of economic decline and unemployment, and further alienation of those with low incomes whose "slice of the economic pie" stops expanding.

The control dilemma. It is a truism that practically all contemporary societal problems are the result of past technological successes. Thus society is beginning to demand "technology assessment" to reduce future negative social and environmental impacts of new technologies. In short, we are talking here about intervening in the early stages of technological research and development to control what technologies are developed and applied. On the one hand, such interference in the free enterprise system seems imperative; on the other hand, it clearly puts in jeopardy certain basic characteristics of the private market system as it has been known in the past.

The distribution dilemma. The gap between the rich and the poor widens inexorably. Stability of the planetary order cannot be achieved when some millions are starving and other millions are compulsively consuming and wasting, yet there is no suitable mechanism (or even philosophy) within the industrial system for redistribution. The problem cannot be solved by making the poor nations more productive along the lines of industrial development, because the planet could not support its population if all peoples of the world consumed and polluted at the present U.S. level. On the other hand, it certainly seems unlikely that the advanced nations will voluntarily reduce their material standard of living to redistribute some of the wealth to the rest of the world.

The work-roles dilemma. This may be the most serious of all, because we have so effectively concealed from ourselves its frightening dimensions. Industrial society is increasingly unable to supply an adequate number of meaningful social roles.

Legitimated social roles in an industrialized society tend to be having a job, being married to someone who has a job, and being a student preparing for a job. But the number of jobs provided by the system is only with great strain and artificiality brought close to the number of contributive roles needed. The ability of new technology to create more jobs is limited by "new scarcity" considerations.

If unemployment were only an economic problem, it could be handled with some sort of income-maintenance program. But unemployment is more fundamentally a psychocultural problem. An increasing number of citizens are defined out of the mainstream, labeled as having little or nothing to offer in what are to be the primary activities of society, and come to accept for themselves the damning self-image of being superfluous. In a modern society, where productiveness comes from position in a productive organism, the individual outside the organization is unproductive and ineffective; unemployment and underemployment endanger effective citizenship and self-respect.

WHY THE PRESENT SITUATION IS DIFFERENT

These four dilemmas appear to be unresolvable without systemic change. They represent tradeoffs that grow steadily more intolerable, or situations that steadily worsen.

The first three dilemmas relate closely to what might be described as a "new scarcity." Where scarcity of food, clothing materials, shelter, game, and farmland has existed in the past, it has successfully been considered remediable by the extension of geographic frontiers and the improvement of technology. The "new scarcity" is of a different sort. It arises from our simultaneously approaching the finite planetary limits of:

Fossil fuels and strategic minerals
Natural freshwater
Food-producing land
Habitable surface area
Waste-absorptive capacity of the natural environment
Resilience of the planet's life-supporting ecosystems

These limits must be considered together, because they are interdependent; none has rigid limits. Materials can be substituted for one another; low-grade ores, for example, can be exploited if sufficient "clean energy" is available. Energy sources can be exchanged. Materials recycling can be accomplished, but that too takes energy. The amount of food-producing land can be effectively expanded, and the land's productivity increased, through expenditure of petroleum products including tractor fuel, fertilizer, and pesticides; and the resulting pollution can be cleaned up by the expenditure of still more energy. And so on.

The fourth dilemma, the inherent shortage of work roles, has provoked anxiety for the past half century, but it has been partly kept out of sight with wars and preparations for war. It was forecast as a key problem of the future in Donald Michael's book, *Cybernation: The Silent Conquest.*[5] For a time it seemed that this might have been a fallacious "cry of wolf," and technology really would generate more jobs than it displaced. But the "new scarcity" changed that. As Margaret Mead has succinctly put it, "It is being said that we do not need now, and may not need later, to exploit the marginal labor of the very young, the very old, the very uneducated, and the very stupid."[6] To say nothing of the very specially trained—in aerospace and automobiles, for instance.

This dilemma interacts particularly with the growth dilemma. The

We may be facing a decade or more of disasters, as our old institutions and nation-state structures are forced to deal with the new global crises. Our ability to handle these crises depends upon leadership and commitment and organizational structure and our ability to make necessary changes fast enough. But it probably also depends in a crucial way on how rapidly we all begin to accept and practice certain concepts about our relation to each other and to the world, concepts that are essential for global cooperation and survival. . . .

We are passing through a philosophical and religious transformation in this generation, a transformation consistent with our new scientific knowledge as well as with our new awareness of inner human meaning and outer global responsibility. It is a transformation that is even more remarkable and more necessary than the astonishing technological transformations and social transformations of our time. It is only on some new philosophical and religious foundation of this kind that any viable society for our children and grandchildren can be built.

John Rader Platt, "World Transformation: Changes in Belief Systems," *The Futurist,* June 1974, pp. 124–125.

primary barrier to doing otherwise reasonable things with regard to energy resource conservation and environmental protection is the fear that these actions might cost jobs. The overall consequence is vacillation or paralysis.

WHY PROFOUND CHANGE IS NECESSARY AND INEVITABLE

There is a still more basic dilemma that underlies the four mentioned above. It is that these problems are deeply rooted in the basic industrial era paradigm—the whole pattern of perceiving and believing and valuing and acting associated with that era's view of reality. They are probably not resolvable within that paradigm.

The basic paradigm that has dominated the industrial era (including emphasis on individualism and free enterprise, material progress, social responsibility as mainly the concern of the government, and few restraints on capital accumulation), and that involves striving toward such goals as efficiency, productivity, continued growth of production and consumption, and continued growth of technological and manipulative power, has resulted in processes and states (for example, extreme division of labor and specialization, cybernation, stimulated consumption, planned obsolescence and waste, exploitation of common resources), which end up counteracting human ends (for example, enriching work

> The new frontier of our age does not lie in outer space but in the human soul. All the bewildering events of this era are mere portents. They give warning that the torch of individual consciousness can no longer shed sufficient light and meaning on the vast expanse of man's material domains. New resources must be opened in the human soul, if man is not to lose himself in the conquest of outer space or turn his heart to stone while building a civilization of robots.
>
> We are living in a stage of history as much in need of inner exploits as the fifteenth century was of geographic exploration. But the oceans and mountains which must be crossed on this quest are not visible to physical senses and cannot be found on maps and globes. To find them we must restore the sight within, the sight which began to wane millenniums ago. There is no alternative, for "where there is no vision, the people perish."
>
> Franz Winkler, *Man: The Bridge Between Two Worlds* (New York: Harper & Row, 1960), p. 53.

roles, resource conservation, environmental enhancement, equitable sharing of the earth's resources). The result is a growing and massive challenge to the legitimacy of the present industrial system.

The implication of this is that, on the one hand, fundamental systemic change will be required and, on the other hand, there is no very orderly way in which this can be accomplished. Because different parts of the social system respond with different speeds, direct actions cannot accumulate sufficient political force by the time they are needed. Hence, during the next few years no programs for combating stagflation, energy shortages, food shortages, and so forth, can be expected to be very successful.

To clarify this point, consider two principles that are implicit in our industrial era society, but that no longer match reality. These are:

The principle of industrializing production of goods and services. Organizing and subdividing work into more and more elemental (and more meaningless) increments, and replacing human labors by energy-driven machines. The goals of industrialization include efficiency, labor productivity, and material growth (and consumption).

The principle of insatiable consumer demand. The assumption that whatever the great industrial machine can produce, consumers can (and should) be taught to want.

The principle of industrialization implies that human beings seek to escape from work, and that energy will remain cheap and plentiful. But both worker behavior and psychological research provide ample evidence that persons seek meaningful activities and meaningful relationships to their society. Individuals thrive not on mindless pleasure, but on challenge. Access to a satisfactory social role is a fundamental political right. And with regard to energy and most raw materials, never again will they be cheap and plentiful. Thus the principle of replacing humans by energy-driven machines no longer makes the sense it once did.

More and more the industrialized system has to condition consumers to want what it produces, against growing opposition from these consumers. Some sort of movement toward a "frugal society" seems inescapable ("frugal" connoting careful use, not necessarily austerity), yet the economic consequences of such a change are grave indeed.

In the long term the outputs of the economy must be thought of, not as goods and services alone, but as goods and services plus satisfaction of social roles. The industrial age "central project" of material progress must be replaced by a new "central project" capable of enlisting the energies and inspiring the commitments of society's members. This will no doubt emphasize quality of life and spiritual as well as continued technological development.

THE BASIC CHARACTERISTICS OF SYSTEMIC TRANSFORMATION

The essential characteristics of a "workable" post-transformation society are:

• It must build on the past if it is to be reached through a nondisruptive transition. This means that most existing institutions (for example, multinational corporations, the Congress, the stock market, the advertising industry, the military establishment) will probably retain more or less the same external forms, although their operative goals may be significantly different from past goals.

• Although in some sense it must be in equilibrium, to adapt to the limits imposed by the "new scarcity," it must also be open to myriad innovations, must be flexible and adaptable, and must celebrate diversity. Its vitality will probably come in part from its having strong public, private, and voluntary sectors.

• It must eliminate structured social and environmental irresponsibility. That is, the overall incentive system (economic benefits, community approval, encultured mores) must foster ecologically wholesome behavior, in the broadest sense.

• It must be a "learning and planning society," with all assured the right to be full and valued participants.

• It must be guided by an "ecological ethic," emphasizing the total community of all life in nature, and by a "self-realization ethic," placing the highest value on development of selfhood and declaring that an appropriate function of all social institutions is creation of an environment that will foster such development. (These two ethics are complementary, not inconsistent.)

• Large private-sector institutions will be recognized as quasi-public and responsible to the public affected by their actions.

• The society must have discovered an inspiring "central project."

The transition period will inevitably involve some degree of social disruption, system breakdown, and economic decline. The extent of this can be lessened by more thorough understanding of the nature and necessity of the transformation.

REFERENCES

1. From unpublished seminar materials issued by the Hudson Institute.
2. Robert Heilbroner, *An Inquiry into the Human Prospect* (New York: W. W. Norton, 1974).
3. Charles Reich, *The Greening of America* (New York: Random House, 1970).
4. George Leonard, *The Transformation* (San Francisco: Delacorte, 1972).
5. Donald Michael, *Cybernation: The Silent Conquest* (Santa Barbara, Calif.: Center for the Study of Democratic Institutions, 1962).
6. From a lecture.

GRAHAM T. T. MOLITOR

The Hatching
of Public Opinion

THE NEED FOR ANTICIPATING PUBLIC POLICY CHANGE

In today's fast-paced world merely muddling through—benevolent neglect, as some have described it—is too erratic, too costly, and too dangerous a course for arriving at sound public policy decisions. Reliance on little-understood forces—the "silent hand"—posited on innumerable unstructured events which somehow tote up to effective action, is increasingly outmoded. The management of massive, modern, complex, and qualitative technologies requires much more time and attention. Careful anticipation and explication of our problems is needed, more than ever before.

Through a better understanding of public policy issue genesis and development, wiser alternatives can be selected. That much is obvious. Change thus can be accommodated with minimal disruption. Public policy anticipation affords an opportunity to minimize the sometimes protracted and always costly defense of the indefensible. It means more effective and more efficient public policy determination.

PUBLIC POLICY PREDICTION MODEL

Over the past years I have developed a wide variety of techniques for forecasting not only the emergence of public policy confrontations, but also dates for probable implementation of public policy by law. Some 100 techniques for describing public policy "issue environments" have been developed. This article describes a few of these basic concepts.

The basic approach is worldwide, focusing on advanced industrialized nations with relatively high levels of affluence, urbanization, and literacy. It concentrates on the period of industrialization, starting from the mid-1800s. Based on an examination of thousands of issues with wide currency during this period in such countries, it appears possible to predict the emergence and probable implementation dates: first, of almost any new public policy (law); second, for any country; and, finally, at any point in history.

Anticipating the course of specific public policy developments ten years ahead is possible with very high accuracy. More general predictions can be made as far as 60 to 70 years ahead. However, such long-range predictions are less accurate.

Predictions are possible simply because public policy determinations do not occur as a bolt out of the blue. New public policy is not made overnight. Instead, new laws emerge in an evolutionary process. The actual appearance of the new law is preceded by long shadows, long trains of activity. Certain structural forces gather powerful inertia over time and give rise to what I term "issue environments." Some forces giving rise to public policy issue confrontations may span 100 years or even longer. Combinations of these structural undercurrents come together as an issue progresses. This convergence of several big forces raises such a dissonance that public attention and demand for action results. Political response usually follows quickly.

Most issues in this country require some ten years, as a general rule, to wend the course from initial appearance to final implementation. I have noted no recent federal issue which involved less than six to ten years to progress from initial discussion to enactment. A ten-year period, often a tortuous course of adversary confrontation, provides a protracted period of time for discussion and debate before a new public policy change is forged into law.

SIX INDICATORS OF CHANGE

Six key indicators can be used for tracking and measuring the evolution of public policy change. The process of change invariably starts with aberrant and unique events which, when aggregated, reveal meaningful patterns. Scientific/technical/professional authorities observe and analyze such phenomena. Shortly thereafter the observations of leading authorities begin appearing in leading literature. The written data base permits widespread dissemination of the ideas, and gives rise to various kinds of organizations which institutionalize the cause and provide a sustained base for advocating change. Politicians, who reflect the popular will, pick up such trends, and leading domestic and international jurisdictions implement them. The intensity of each of these indicators tends to follow an S-curve pattern. At the outset the intensity takes off slowly, then follows a steep slope, and then tapers off.

Each sequence of events plotted in Figures 1–6 leads or lags the others. When overlaid, plots of the six forces tend to converge. This confluence can be described as a critical takeoff point for intensified action on a public policy issue. When all six indicators concurrently advance at steep rates of increase, the momentum for public policy action is so great as to be well-nigh irreversible.

Leading Events

Figure 1 depicts how isolated events, often viewed at first as aberrant, bizarre, or unique, eventually converge. The aggregation of the events reveals patterns or trends. The first heralding of an idea may be an emotional response to limited data and inadequate supporting rationale. Early distortions are reduced, however, as new phenomena become understood.

Deployed in a time series, isolated events build up to a "data wall" describing an abuse or excess so unconscionable that remedial action is virtually assured.

> *Key tracking point:* "Data walls" amass to "critical mass," "takeoff" points, at which time (depending on "cost benefits") a virtually irreversible course for change is reached.

Leading Authorities/Advocates

Figure 2 describes how random phenomena or isolated events are discussed and interpreted by authorities and advocates. Although various authorities usually get involved with the issues, most politicians tend to take up causes rather late. The average elected official reflects the views of his constituency, so this general conclusion is not surprising. Statesmen and ideological leaders enter the process much earlier, of course. One commentator has suggested that politicians take up causes when 20 to 40 percent of the people have begun to think that an idea is right. Gaining so sizable a body of public support requires substantial time.

Figure 2 pertains to intellectual elites who analyze and articulate social problems and issues. Likewise the victimized, even though less capable of articulating their plight, emote their feelings and often become powerful propaganda symbols for change.

> *Key tracking point:* Usually fewer than 12 innate innovators can be pinpointed on any issue. By monitoring these early vanguards whose ideas are ultimately diffused widely, early indications of change can be forecasted.

Figure 1. Leading events.

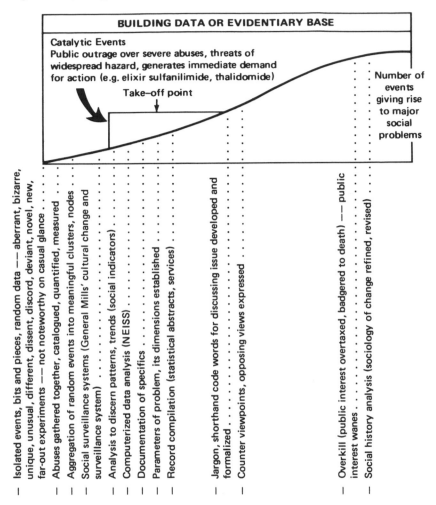

Leading Literature

After informal and oral commentaries, authorities begin to write about their ideas. Figure 3 displays the categories of literature which then emerge. Often there is as much as a one- to six-year lag between the time when an expert first talked about an idea until his views are finally published in a serious journal. Catalogued here are the various kinds of journals in a continuum indicating approximate lead-lag relationships between some classes of literature.

Figure 2. Leading authorities/advocates.

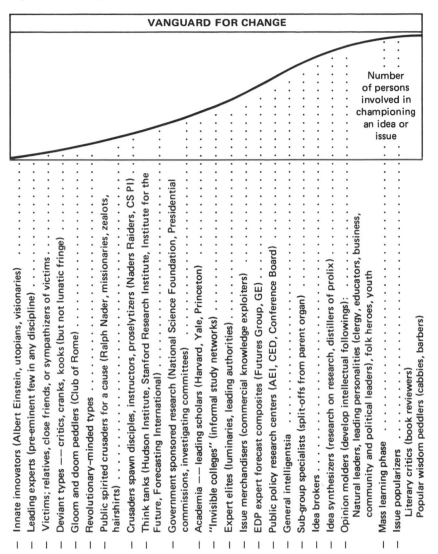

Written records progress from modest beginnings to the more prolix, which serve to explicate parameters and refine thinking, then to mass literature for public consumption.

Key tracking point: Various classes of literature emerge at different times—lead-lag times of up to 100 years can

Figure 3. Leading literature

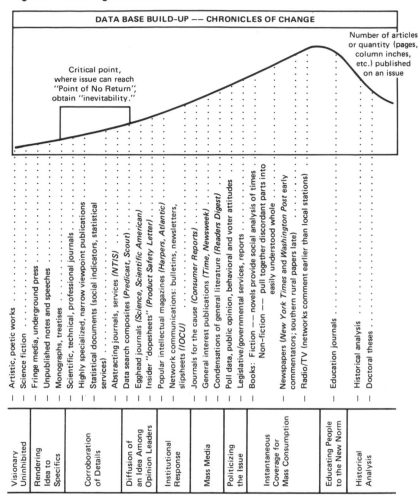

be involved. Therefore, "early warnings" about emerging problems can be obtained from a careful literature search.

Leading Organizations

As the issues emerge, various institutions organize, as shown in Figure 4. As these groups become established and better known, a lightning-rod effect attracts adherents and sympathizers from near and far. Organizations usually form locally, although they may spread toward in-

Figure 4. Leading organizations.

ORGANIZATIONAL SUPPORT FOR A CAUSE						

Number of organizations, persons, resources committed to the cause.

INFORMAL PHASE		FORMALIZATION OF UNDERTAKING				
Individuals	Informal Groups	Formal Local Organizations	State Organ.	Regional Organ.	National Organ.	International Linkages
		Associations, Leagues, Federations, International Networks				
Victims of a Problem	Crusaders	Building Together of Like-Minded				
UNORGANIZED		ORGANIZED				
Random, ad hoc		Institutionalizing the Cause				
Amateur, Part–Time Advocates		Professional, Full–Time Champions				
Issues Are Simple		Complexity Grows				
Issues Emotionalized, Naively Conceived		Serious–Minded, Rational Efforts Undertaken				
Unrefined Delineation of Issues		Highly Functionalized, Extremely Specialized Sub-Groups Emerge				
Amateur advocates generate publicity, attract interest to cause, build up a following — "lightning rod" effect		Amateurs burned out, except for few "diehards"				

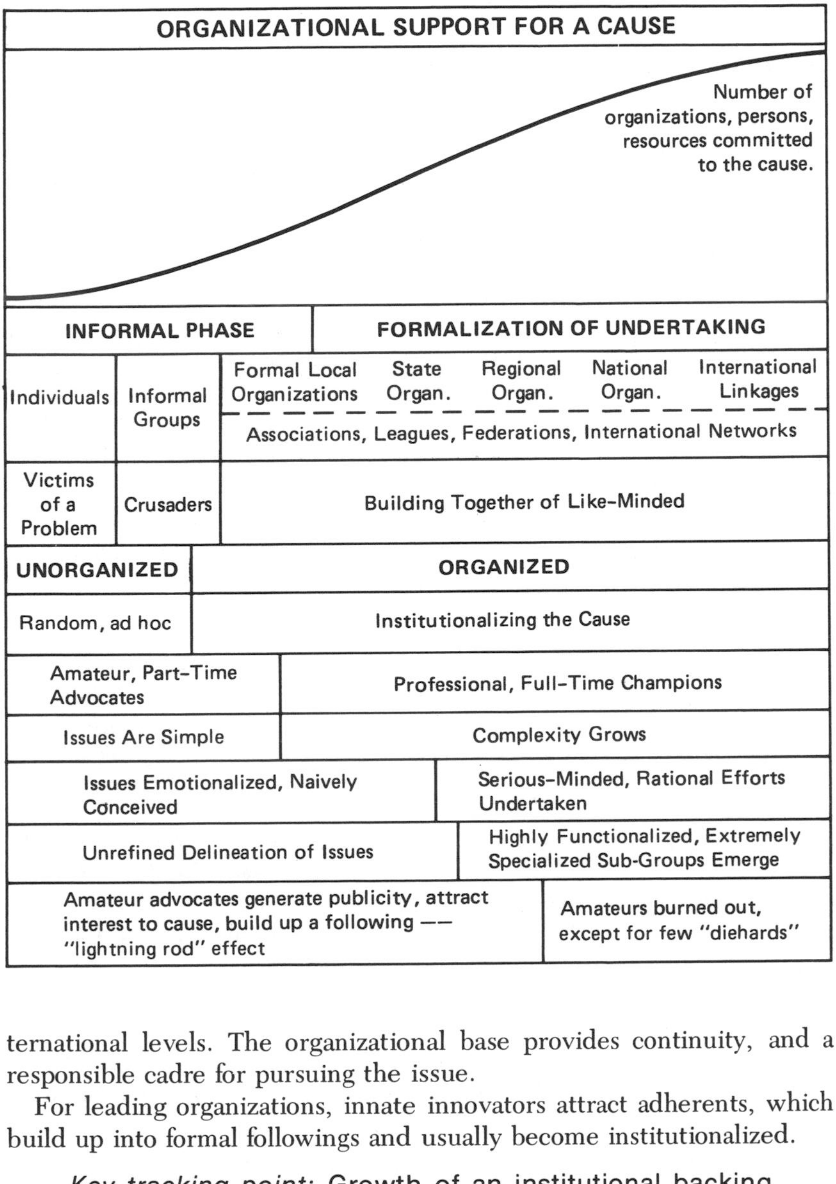

ternational levels. The organizational base provides continuity, and a responsible cadre for pursuing the issue.

For leading organizations, innate innovators attract adherents, which build up into formal followings and usually become institutionalized.

Key tracking point: Growth of an institutional backing for a cause—whether measured by number of organizations, persons involved, or resources committed—follows exponential increases which tend to force serious consideration of the issue by public policy-makers.

Leading Political Jurisdictions

During the course of these processes, certain political jurisdictions, which I term "precursor jurisdictions," begin to implement new policies (consult Figure 5). Once a new law is implemented by a number of leading jurisdictions—either internationally or domestically (at state and local levels)—other jurisdictions follow suit, provided, of course, that the policy proves workable. After actual implementation the idea, now enshrined as public policy, ceases to be merely theoretical and abstract. It has become a practical and realistic working solution. The process of other jurisdictions following the lead of early adopters results in "diffusion patterns." For a number of reasons during different periods of history particular countries or groups of nations have been "early adopters." Sweden is now such a leader, and has been an early implementer for at least 20 to 30 years. Such "bellwether" jurisdictions provide an early indication of probable action for other advanced countries.

Thus, early innovators and experimenters show the way to others. After the idea is proved, other jurisdictions emulate, follow suit.

> *Key tracking point:* Some four to six countries (and often simultaneously their internal local jurisdictions) invariably are the first to innovate by implementing new public policy ideas. These leading jurisdictions vary with different times in history and for different issues.

Recently I spent several weeks in Scandinavia, primarily in Sweden, interviewing some 100 private authorities and public officials to develop an in-depth understanding of impending consumer policy developments. In case after case—in fact, with respect to nearly every major consumer issue enacted in recent years—Sweden implemented the consumer policy provision some 2 to 10 years ahead of the United States. Some 2,000 consumer issues either implemented in some jurisdiction or at a serious stage of discussion, but not yet implemented by the U.S. federal government, have been identified. A substantial portion of these issues are likely to be implemented in the United States within the next 2 to 20 years.

To sum up, these six forces following S-curve patterns converge to create a dissonance within the system that demands public policy response. As events flow along over time, authorities/advocates pick up on them; next, the number of published articles builds up to provide a permanent written analysis and wider dissemination; at about this stage, a

Figure 5. Leading political jurisdictions.

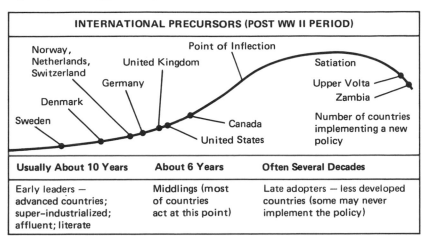

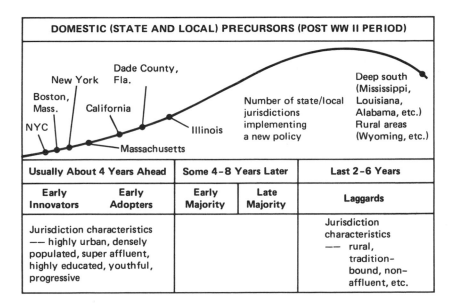

number of organizations begin to emerge around an issue; and, bringing the cycle to a close, political jurisdictions finally are pressured to respond. The typical convergence is shown in Figure 6.

None of these plotted data is subjective. All data plots are based on

Figure 6. Typical convergence of evolutionary waves of change.

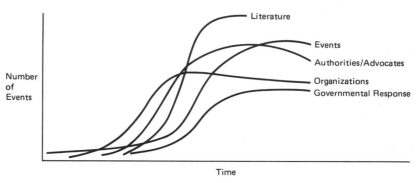

objective measurable data. Nothing other than hard evidence is relied upon. As these trends move along, the rates increase at a very rapid or exponential rate; at such "takeoff points" the pace of change itself creates pressures for action. Overlaying these six time-series plots reveals the point where data tracks coalesce. At this stage the issue begins to receive intense and special attention. From this point onward, forward momentum on the issue is very strong. One can begin now to make specific predictions. Application of this six-step model to several hundred historical issues shows it to be an accurate technique for anticipating public policy developments.

JEANNE BINSTOCK

Dr. Spock's Babies Take Charge

A SHIFT in values has been occurring among young adults in the United States with important implications for business planning, for it is altering and will continue to alter buying behavior. The "new morality," as Daniel Yankelovich calls it, seems to be symptomized in the sexual revolution; the anti-Vietnam War movement; antibusiness attitudes, including increased consumer sensitivity, environmental protectionism, and an antiprofit orientation; and an antigovernment mood.[1] In fact, the new values run deeper than even these movements suggest. They reflect an entirely new way of looking at the world that is going to spread and be expressed and acted upon with increasing energy and severity.

There was a time when executives did not have to be (or hire) social trend analysts in order to develop and market their companies' products profitably. But it is less true every day, particularly as concerns with long-range planning become more prominent. Using social trend analysis in marketing decisions means that the executive has been educated to understand the causes of change, to take advantage of its symbolic symptoms, and to provide what is wanted by others and profitable for the business. In short, analyzing social trends is adaptive behavior.

WHO ACCEPTS THE NEW MORALITY?

The new morality is an age phenomenon, started and still led by the generation born during and after World War II. At the moment its first wave is coming to adulthood (1976–1980) and making consumer choices. The post-Vietnam War generation has not yet come to adulthood and will not constitute a separate market until 1985 or 1990. Most of the impulses of change to the new morality in the under-35s (down to about 22) began in the "better" colleges and universities, spread from there to the East and West coasts, then to Northern industrial states, and moved into the Midwest and Sunbelt only in the last several years. In the most extreme expressions of the new morality, typical of many college-educated under-35s living in major coastal cities and coming from the upper-middle class (their fathers being educated executives and professionals), there is an actual effort to substitute one set of values for another. But for most of the post-World War II generation, it is simply additive. New values are grafted onto old. The actual life differences between the subscribers to the new morality and those who subscribe to what we might call traditional morality become apparent and understandable when adult under-35s anywhere in the United States are compared with over-55s; the dissimilarities in their life experiences turn out to be great. Particularly noteworthy is the enormous contrast in educational achievement of each of these two generations (Figure 1).

The more educated the over-35s, the more likely they are to share with the adult under-35s some of the values of the new morality. Also, since it is a value system that supports all forms of equality, it tends to recruit more than its fair share of adherents among over-35 women, particularly well-educated ones, and among blacks. It tends to recruit less than its fair share of adherents of over-35 men and whites, particularly if they are either very near the top of the heap or very near the bottom. And, as noted, it is also a regional phenomenon.

In sum, the new morality is most subscribed to by the following groups, in descending order of commitment:

College-educated adult under-35s on the East and West coasts
College-educated adult under-35s in the industrial and North-Central states
College-educated adult under-35s elsewhere
Noncollege adults under 35
Professionally educated over-35s
Women in general
Blacks in general

It is least subscribed to by the following groups, in descending order of rejection.

The superrich (who are rarely interested in change)
Over-55s
High-school–educated (or less) manual workers over 35
Rural communities in general

Of today's buying population of about 163 million (those 16 years of age or over), fully 73 million are the post-World War II generation, reared in an environment dramatically different in many ways from that of generations before. In addition to growing up at saturation levels of

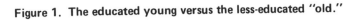

Figure 1. The educated young versus the less-educated "old."

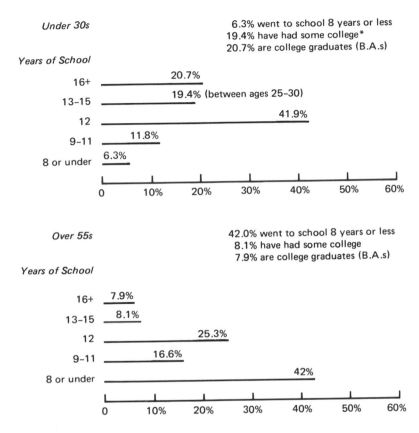

Source: Current Population Reports series P-20, No. 274; also reported in *Statistical Abstracts of the United States 1975,* Bureau of the Census, Table No. 192.
* These figures are accurate for women between the ages of 25 and 30; however, there have been increasing college enrollments for those under 25.

education, penicillin, mass contraception, and television—all or most of which simply did not exist for prewar generations—they are without personal knowledge of either the Great Depression or World War II.

Not all of these 73 million have fully embraced the new morality. It is, in fact, a phenomenon impossible to quantify, but its continued diffusion seems certain. Its youthful adherents may retrench a bit when they join the Establishment with its traditional morality, but they do not retrench much. As the under-35s become under-40s and each younger generation comes of adult-consumer age, the new morality will come to represent the world view of a substantial part, if not a majority, of the buying population.

WHAT IS THE NEW MORALITY?

The new morality[2] is not so much a new philosophy as it is the addition of a few crucial new values grafted onto basic traditional values. If we divide our everyday lives into their major sets of activities, we find that we all subscribe to several sets of goals:

Life goals (Where am I going?)
Personal goals (What must I do?)
Work goals (Why must I work?)
Social goals (How is happiness achieved?)

In each of these four areas, the new morality encompasses a major traditional value, shared alike by pre-World War II and post-World War II generations, and an added value, shared only among the post-World War II generation.

This concern with inner development, which we can summarize in the phrase "personal growth," is the new value that exists in the postwar generation, alongside social status mobility, the traditional value. Unlike previous generations, money is now the adult under-35s' secondary rather than primary concern—even in the midst of a recession (Table 1).

Table 1. Life goals.

Traditional Morality	New Morality
A. Social status	A. Social status
B. Money	B. Money
	plus
	C. New experiences, learning, creativity

The post-World War II generation, led by the college-educated, have added two new values: the rejection of boredom and the acceptance of social and economic responsibilities of a very broad sort. Unlike their elders, they do not think stability and security, on the one hand, and stimulation and excitement, on the other, are mutually contradictory. They want them both, in their personal lives and in their work lives. The desire to make an extended social contribution has two components: it is a reflection of their own preferences and of their guilts. People who believe it is important to grow and be enriched by experience and information assume that this is what others want as well.

Surprisingly, the under-35s are also considerably more guilt-ridden than prewar generations, not so much about sex as about social aggression and human brotherhood. The traditional Protestant and Catholic religious values stress guilt for acts perpetrated in a personal context. The new religious values produce guilt, not for what one did, but for what *one did not do*. In an effort to achieve relief from these feelings of guilt, the adult under-35s feel obliged to maintain responsibilities beyond family, community, and country, to unknown outsiders (Table 2).

Table 2. Personal goals.

Traditional Morality	*New Morality*
Economic	
A. Financial and personal security and stability (even at the price of boredom)	A. Financial and personal security and stability (but *not* at the price of boredom) plus, therefore
	B. Stimulation and excitement
Social	
A. Responsibility for making an economic contribution to family, community, and country	A. Responsibility for making an economic contribution to family, community, and country
	plus
	B. Social contribution to others: outside family, outside community, outside country

In their specific work goals, the same new preoccupations are evident: personal growth, counteracting boredom and seeking stimulation (even at the price of incomplete security and stability), and relieving guilt—about hurting other people or not helping them (Table 3).

In the areas of interpersonal relations, which include family, leisure activities with friends, and, not incidentally, work relationships at the office, there have been three substantial values added by the post-World War II generation. Peers are now as important as, if not more important than, authority; sex is now good (rather than bad) and subject to fewer

Table 3. Work goals.

Traditional Morality	*New Morality*
A. Making more money	A. Making more money
B. Increased power and authority	B. Increased power and authority
	plus
	C. Helping people
	D. Increased emotional gratification at work

feelings of guilt; women are regarded as somehow more worthy in the total sense than in the traditional morality.

The adult under-35s are against repressions and against formal power relationships; they are for increased self-consciousness and introspection and for getting rid of guilt rather than stockpiling it. With the increased importance of good communication has come an increased emphasis on equality and openness of approach. Thus, in work areas as well as interpersonal areas, the adult under-35s have developed new communications styles: open and sensual expression, reciprocity in information and feeling flow, a cooperative rather than a tough approach, and a greater and in many ways more detached interest in women's opinions and feelings (Tables 4 and 5).

Table 4. Social goals.

Traditional Morality	New Morality
Family Relationships	
A. Loyalty and support of spouse	A. Loyalty and support of spouse
	plus
	B. Good psychological communication
	C. Good mutual sex
Nonfamily Relationships	
A. Respect for authority	A. Respect for authority
	plus
	B. Respect for peers

Table 5. Personal style.

Traditional Morality	New Morality
A. Control of feeling and competitive behavior is how a man acts	A. Control of feeling and competitive behavior is how a man acts
B. Display of feeling and deferential behavior is how a woman acts	B. Display of feeling and deferential behavior is how a woman acts
	plus
	C. Each sex can develop the personal characteristics associated with the opposite sex

It is important also to note, for its business implications, that where once time equaled money, time is now connected more directly with emotional satisfaction. What is demanded is not only the end of boredom (the wasting of time), but more creative use of time (increased level of stimulation per unit of time).

WHY DID THE NEW MORALITY START?

The first wave of the new morality, the generation born between 1940 and 1955, was created by affluence; the rise of "mind" occupations; superb medical care; television; exclusively maternal child-rearing, highly psychological in orientation; higher education; and mass effective contraception and control of venereal disease through penicillin—in that order. The preoccupation with new experiences, creativity, and learning grew out of postwar prosperity.

The period after the war was marked by a dramatic increase in urban living, white-collar (middle-class) employment, and, more importantly, dramatic increases in the standard of living and in the variety of available and inexpensive consumer goods—from telephones, refrigerators, and cars to washing machines, vacuum cleaners, and mixers. By the mid-fifties, most Americans (a clear majority) owned every one of these items. By 1960, ownership of these items had reached almost saturation level.

Most American households had television. In 1955, the average household television set was turned on about five hours per day; by 1973, it had increased to six and a half hours per day.[3] The number of hours of television watching per day seems to be as high among people of high education and income as low.

The first adult wave of the new morality comprises those children born mostly between 1945 and 1955 in urban centers and of white-collar parents, brought up in material comfort, the omnipresent safety of wonder drugs, and the expectations of doing mind work rather than manual work—a generation of Americans as unfamiliar with physical pain and the possibility of death through disease as they are with material discomfort or economic scarcity.

In the optimism of the postwar environment, parents expected continued upward mobility as well as higher educational achievement and possibly professional or managerial work for their children. This, in fact, was an appropriate anticipation. Figure 2 indicates a dramatic rise in "information" occupations in about 1945, which is continuing even as agricultural and industrial occupations decline. The figure uses low estimates for information workers.

Urban middle-class children born between 1945 and 1955 were strongly influenced by the heavily psychological child-rearing of their mothers. Families were small, thanks to contraception, mothers were still at home, and labor-saving appliances and products allowed them to concentrate on the feelings, motives, and educational development of their children with an exclusiveness that must be considered new. They

Figure 2. Four-sector aggregation of the U.S. workforce, 1860–1980.

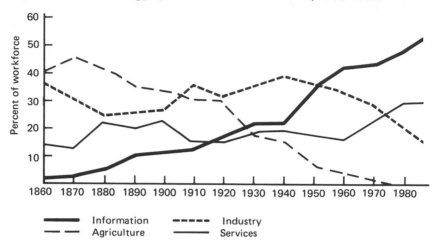

were even free from the traditionally most important chore of mothers since the beginning of time, nursing sick children and prevention of childhood death. This new intimacy of urban mothers and their children, particularly with their sons, is a cause of such features of the new morality as feminine identification, rejection of power relationships, and preference for an open, informal style of communication. Affluence and educational expectations were the cause of their being so learning-, experience-, and creativity-oriented.[4]

This intimacy also contributed substantially to higher levels of guilt, centered on aggressive behavior and feelings (particularly if expressed to Mom), maternal demands for cooperation, and worry about sins of neglect. Mothers were not only free to be preoccupied with their children's psychology but it is *they* who are the Spock generation: firm, natural believers in punishment by withdrawal of love or by guilt, not by authority or corporal punishment. This blossoming of guilt, encouraged by mothers who could not or would not use force, was further stimulated by television.

The emotional impact of television-watching on small children is underrated. Adults know the events on TV are not real life; children do not. Adults are skillful at avoiding painful identification with helpless or tragic people, seen so often in the course of news reporting; children are not.

TV singlehandedly produced the global perspective of American young adults. Because of TV, they were better informed than previous generations of children and more sympathetic to concerns outside themselves. Whatever the political leanings of their parents, these children, relatively powerless themselves, silently identified with all the helpless people being portrayed, their feelings transformed into vague guilt when normal defense mechanisms appropriate to adulthood began to emerge. TV produced commitment of feeling rather than withdrawal. Comparatively speaking, they had seen and heard and felt more joy and grief for people outside the neighborhood or the family than any generation anywhere in the world that had ever gone before.

The experience of the world through TV as much as their mothers' tender and omnipresent solicitations produced a generation obsessed with guilt by neglect, guilt about fancied and real aggression, and redemption by helping others.

When these children emerged from the protection of family life in the sixties, they found two new commonly shared experiences, which again separated them from their parents and previous generations—at least on massiveness of scale. One was the college experience of peers with whom they could exchange information and feelings in a leisurely environment virtually free from authority and interference. It solidified and dramatized opinions originally held only tentatively.[5] At the same time, there was the sudden availability of easily implemented, sure-to-work contraception—the Pill—and the final demise of syphilis and gonorrhea as dangerous and permanently mentally disabling diseases.

So, raised in comfort, reared to be seduced, watching the joy, grief, and horror of the whole world on TV, attended and overcontrolled by a mother who wanted them to be like herself, encouraged by peers, the first wave of the post-World War II generation in the first flush of adulthood invented the new morality.

WHY IS THE NEW MORALITY IMPORTANT FOR BUSINESS PLANNING?

We are now talking about a market of about 73 million. Few of this total generation (including the post-Vietnam generation) of 35- to 16-year-olds came from homes without telephones, washing machines, cars, freezers, and color TV. Of those now adult, about 20 percent have had some college and 20.7 percent have four-year bachelor's degrees. Television, further urbanization, the movement to the South and Southwest of industry, are homogenizing the experience among all members of these postwar generations, narrowing regional differences.

As the under-35s become under-40s and then under-45s by 1985, and continue to be copied or joined by the younger and the less educated, the new morality will determine the buying habits and advertising preferences of the majority of the buying population. The slowdown in its diffusion since the late sixties, apparent to us all, is just that, a slowdown. The new morality will continue to develop: more slowly if the economy does not recover, more rapidly if it does. Its causes are too profound to stop and its consequences are already expressed.

Some variation of the new morality is here to stay, having been produced by history. Moreover, it can be expected to further encroach on the priorities of traditional morality. The under-35s are very shortly going to be the major consumers of all consumer products and services, not just some. The business executives' choice is either to understand them or lose the market to those who, for one reason or another, do understand them.

The more businessmen stand still as a new value system develops around them, the wider the gap, the lower their penetration of the market becomes, and the less able they are to provide satisfaction in return for any one dollar spent in an effort to do so. To sell them, one must know what they are thinking and feeling. Otherwise, product development, packaging, promotion, advertising, and sales begin to function at increasing levels of inefficiency until the business is no longer profitable.

In the long run, when managers begin to perceive value shifts as a real problem, start taking the trouble to investigate these changes in relation to their own product or service, and modify their goals in order to increase their markets and penetrate them more efficiently, they will have to explore more fully the whys of the trends that appear to be obvious. If the whys of change are understood, managers have the internal gyroscope that permits them to make continued accommodations to the environment.

REFERENCES

1. See Daniel Yankelovich, *The New Morality: A Profile of American Youth in the Seventies* (New York: McGraw-Hill, 1964).

2. For exploratory reading, I suggest Philip Slater, *The Pursuit of Loneliness* (Boston: Beacon Press, 1970); Charles Reich, *The Greening of America* (New York: Random House, 1970); and Robert Flack, *Youth and Social Change* (Chicago: Markham Press, 1971).

3. *Social Indicators 1973*, Office of Management and Budget, Statistical Policy Division (Social and Economic Statistics Administration, U.S. Department of Commerce), p. 221.

4. Jeanne Binstock, "Motherhood: An Occupation in Decline," *The Futurist*, June 1972.

5. See Flack, *Youth and Social Change*.

Part II
RESOURCE PLANNING

HAZEL HENDERSON

The Entropy State

MANY MODELS exist of the unfolding shape of advanced industrial societies. Proposed here is yet another: that of the "entropy society."

Daniel Bell gave us the notion of a "post-industrial society" transcending via technology the ideologies of left and right, and one in which most of the labor force would be employed in service and knowledge-based industries. John Kenneth Galbraith sees a "new industrial state" of dentente between business and government: a "technostructure" with power falling to cadres of bureaucrats, technicians, and managers, and with only the vestiges of a market economy.

Gunnar Myrdal describes in *Beyond the Welfare State* the future evolving from the mixed market and planned economies of which Sweden is typical. And Roger Garaudy foresees in *Crisis in Communism: Turning Point in Socialism* the shape of advancing bureaucratized communism in the USSR, as well as the more decentralized worker-managed models of communism such as that now developing in Yugoslavia. And while Karl Marx's prediction of the decline of capitalism did not count on the labor force becoming bourgeois, as it has in today's highly industrialized societies, the crystal-ball-gazing of capitalism's school of market-oriented economics has proved equally cloudy.

Another model of the unfolding pattern of industrial societies might well be that of the "entropy state." Simply put, the entropy state is a society at the stage when complexity and interdependence have reached the point where the transaction costs that are generated equal or exceed the society's productive capabilities. In a manner analogous to the phenomenon that occurs in physical systems, the society slowly winds down of its own weight and complexity, with all its forces and counterforces checked and balanced in a state of equilibrium.

We seem unwilling to come to terms with the fact that each increase in the order of magnitude of technological mastery and managerial control requires and inevitably leads to a concomitant order of magnitude of government coordination and control. Thus we see the irony of those corporate technological innovators who decry the government bureaucracies that all technological innovations call forth. Worse, as the industrial system grows more complex, specialized, and differentiated, it becomes increasingly difficult to model the labyrinth of variables in such a web of social and physical systems. Any system that cannot be modeled cannot be managed. Indeed, systems analyst Jay Forrester has noted that such complex systems tend to behave counter-intuitively and are stubbornly resistant to human manipulation.

Because advanced industrial societies develop such unmanageable complexity, they naturally generate a bewildering increase in unanticipated social costs: in human maladjustment, community disruption, and environmental depletion. All these effects of uncoordinated, unplanned activities and suboptimization are called by economists, in almost a Freudian slip, "externalities." The cost of cleaning up the mess and caring for the human casualties of unplanned technology—the dropouts, the unskilled, the addicts, or those who just cannot cope with the maze of urban life or deal with Big Brother bureaucracies—mounts ever higher. The proportion of GNP that must be spent in mediating conflicts, controlling crime, protecting consumers and the environment, providing increasingly comprehensive bureaucratic coordination, and generally trying to maintain "social homeostasis" begins to grow exponentially. New levels of expenditure to maintain this social homeostasis are augured daily, as in the recent calls for new legislation to provide government compensation for crime victims and for new agencies to counsel and assist those who succumb to chronic debt.

Another emerging facet of complex societies is the newly perceived vulnerability of their massive, centralized technologies and institutions, whether manifested in the loss of corporate flexibility, urban decline, power blackouts, skyjacking, or the many frightening scenarios of sabotage and violence now occurring daily.

Meanwhile expectations are continually inflated by business and government leaders, and it becomes more difficult to satisfy demands of private mass consumption while trying to meet demands for more and better public consumption, whether for housing, mass transit, health, education, welfare benefits, parks and beaches, or merely to keep the water potable and the air breathable. The enormous burdens of military expenditures add to this allocation problem in most industrial countries. But even without such huge arms commitments, the ever-inflating bubble of expectations is cause for concern. The recent elections in Denmark are a case in point. Paradoxically, a taxpayer's revolt unseated a liberal government in irritation over the costs of a highly popular social welfare program—an apparent inability of voters to understand the inevitable trade-offs between high levels of public goods and services and private consumption.

The symptoms of the entropy state are also visible in Japan. Notwithstanding military expenditures held to less than 2 percent of the GNP, the ruling Liberal Democratic Party is strained by labor unrest, soaring wage settlements, growing social dissatisfaction as inflation reaches annual levels of 16 percent, and the rising public investment costs of pollution control, sewage treatment, housing, and social security benefits. Britain too is exhibiting signs of industrialism's next stage, the entropy state. Social conflict increases as the resource base shrinks, and more equitable sharing has become the inevitable demand. Rampant inflation, soaring public investment costs and social welfare services, and the ineluctable bureaucratization follow a pattern that grows more familiar each day. There seems now to be a dawning realization on the part of the stoic British that belt-tightening is a way of life and that achievement of even a modicum of satisfaction will now require nothing less than a new frame of mind and lowered expectations.

Inflation is now so ubiquitous in advanced industrial economies that it has become one of their structural features, rather than a temporary affliction. It can no longer be described by economists as a trade-off for unemployment, since in many countries, including our own, we have both. Traditional Keynesian remedies of pumping up the whole economy in order to ameliorate areas of structural unemployment and mask the true conflict over the distribution of wealth are now beginning to be felt as too costly in that they raise rates of inflation and deplete resources. Economist Irving Friedman suggests in *Inflation: A World Wide Disaster* that vastly inflated expectations for both public and private consumption are now a key factor.

Another explanation for inflation comes from thermodynamicists, who insist that economists don't yet understand the drastic multiplier effects of developing energy and resource scarcities. Simply stated, such energy researchers as the brothers Eugene and Howard Odum say that economists and Federal Energy Office officials have not yet grasped the crucial difference between *gross* energy and *net* energy. Gross energy is typified by all those theoretical barrels of oil locked in such less accessible forms as shale and tar sands. But it will take millions of barrels of oil to crush the rocks, heat and retort the shale and sands, not to mention the refining and transporting, as well as the millions of gallons of scarce water that would have to be diverted from farm use in the process. What is left over at the end of all this investment of energy and resources is net energy, only a fraction of the quantity theoretically available (gross energy). Indeed the Odums claim that so far the nation's entire nuclear power enterprise has only yielded a few percentage points of net energy, because the process is so heavily subsidized with coal and oil—for uranium extraction and enrichment and scores of other energy and capital-intensive steps that precede the final output of electricity from a nuclear plant. Inflation, in this explanation, is driven by the increasing amount of money and energy a society must keep diverting to the job of extracting and refining lower and lower grade energy and materials. Therefore, there are fewer real goods and services produced and prices soar, as the multiplier effect of additional energy-intensive processing of these resources into finished goods is felt.

But the energy situation has merely revealed and lent impetus to what may be the unfolding "end game" of industrial societies. First there will be the frantic efforts to invest more and more capital in energy exploitation and resource extraction, despite the already visibly diminishing marginal returns to much of our capital-intensive production. Consider, for example, the case of agriculture where, according to agricultural researchers David Pimental, Michael Perlman, and others, by a key measure—how much energy is used for a given output of calories—our U.S.-type highly mechanized, fossil-fuel subsidized farming is now the most inefficient in the world. In other overautomated processes as dissimilar as fishing and operating mass transit systems, the marginal returns to capital investment are falling: fish catches are now destructively overefficient, while on such transit systems as San Francisco's BART, workers are displaced by costly and erratic automated train controls.

The current stage of hurling massive quantities of capital at the increasingly fruitless endeavor of trying to produce greater supplies of energy and resources, will, in time, be played out. The learning experience will be horrendously costly because it will foreclose many other more realistic options. Capital, amassed from our previously bountiful sources of energy and materials, now represents our society's last diminishing store of low entropy (i.e., concentrated potential for useful work). As evolutionist Gregory Bateson illustrates, capital is our precious stock of stored flexibility for performing an orderly social transition to adapt to new conditions, just as a chrysalis uses its stored energy to turn itself into a butterfly. Instead we see a tragic situation developing, as oil companies, electric utilities, and basic manufacturing industries all attempt to borrow larger and larger quantities of capital to squeeze new supplies from degenerating and depleted deposits of fossil fuels, materials, and minerals.

Banks, in turn, oblige their corporate borrowers, if necessary, by borrowing expensive funds themselves and issuing their own debt instruments, thus adding to the mirage. Sometimes the wasteful, disastrous capital-spending plans of corporations and utilities can be halted only by massive pressures from consumers and environmentalists. By fighting rate increases and higher prices and by forcing companies to more fully internalize social and environmental costs, such groups may deflect company plans by "upping the ante" and making their own capital spending and borrowing plans less viable. We can see this occurring now in many energy companies and electric utilities.

As the emerging capital shortage becomes more acute and interest rates and inflation continue to soar, we may find that debt service will become the biggest item in corporate and municipal budgets. It will then become more evident that inflation is the manifestation of a massive, futile economic wheel-spinning, where money flows faster and faster, economic activity becomes more feverish, people work harder, and the GNP appears to be climbing reassuringly. The only problem will be that fewer and fewer products, goods, and services will result from this hyperactivity, and money will simply become less and less related to real value. At some point we will recognize that investing capital to call forth diminishing supplies is a tragic misdirected effort. At that point, presumably, interest rates will fall, in spite of the increasing scarcity and value of capital, since most of the precious remaining supply will be needed to maintain existing plants, equipment, housing stocks, public buildings, and amenities, and will not be available for whatever high-yield uses may still remain. At this point, we will have drifted to a "soft landing" in the steady-state economy, while symptomatic inflation will have masked our declining condition.

The entropy state may be the future of advanced industrial societies unless as yet unimagined advances in computer science enable us to manage and control the complexity of these societies, and unless we improve our ability to devise accurate social indicators. Even then, the attempt to control such impenetrable systems will inevitably mean greater government control, further loss of freedom and individuality, and will lead us closer to the computerized state of which George Orwell warned in his book 1984. Another path may lie in deliberately trying to reduce the interdependencies by simplifying some of the overly developed systems that have now reached such obvious diseconomies of scale. We might take, not the Luddite's axe, but the surgeon's scalpel, and with a delicacy borne of desperation, begin to isolate and sever some of the interdependencies in our social and technical systems, so that the variables might once more be reduced to a manageable number.

Some systems seem to work best on a very large scale. For example, the telephone system must be widely standardized and is, by definition, composed of interlocking elements. But other systems and institutions can be more efficiently operated on a smaller scale. Perhaps cities and many corporations fit into this category. Some have even suggested that if we convert individual homes and apartment buildings to solar, wind, and methane power generation, then the only reason that homeowners would need to be connected to central power stations would be to sell power back to utilities for resale to their own industrial customers! Certainly we are now seeing the trade-offs in building larger and costlier central power plants with longer, more expensive, energy-wasting transmission lines. But to expect existing utilities and energy corporations to develop such radically different systems would be as naive as it would have been to give the buggy whip makers the responsibility of developing the automobile.

Similarly, we might change the mix of human and machine energy that our production methods currently employ. Many of our farm families were driven off their land because of the now energy-wasteful automation and the large-scale investments that corporate farming requires. A return to smaller farms might yield benefits in human satisfaction and would save enormously on energy and transportation. This capital-to-labor equation has changed for hundreds of other production processes in our society, as the cheap energy trip comes to an end. We can communicate instead of commuting, fill in the wasted spaces in the suburban sprawl, use our existing buildings more efficiently and renovate old ones. Then we can bicycle more; perhaps one day walk the shortened distances more safely; grow our own vegetable gardens; and spend more time in family and community activities. As the Ford Foundation energy study shows, such changes in our life styles could stretch all our resources. The entropy state might be held at bay for many generations by such new values and symbols of success.

In the last analysis, Bell's "post-industrial society," the technostructure of Galbraith's "new industrial state," the various models of socialism, communism, and welfare capitalism mentioned earlier are all too heavily dependent on increasing economic growth and technological mastery. Even service economies are wholly dependent on their primary agricultural, manufacturing, and resource bases. The Bucky Fulfilling dreams of technologically based abundance of the sixties now seem adolescent and remote. Perhaps the crumbling faith in the gods of technology will be restored and justified, and premonitions such as this, of the entropy state, can be happily banished from our minds. But at least running scared may buy us some time and retain some of our precious store of flexibility, so that we may yet transform ourselves into a new culture in harmony with the earth.

BIBLIOGRAPHY

Bateson, Gregory. *Steps to an Ecology of Mind* (New York: Ballantine, 1973).

Friedman, Irving S. *Inflation: A World Wide Disaster* (Boston: Houghton Mifflin, 1973).

Garaudy, Roger. *Crisis in Communism: Turning Point in Socialism* (New York: Grove Press, 1972).

Myrdal, Gunnar. *Beyond the Welfare State* (New Haven: Yale University Press, 1960).

Odum, Eugene. *Georgia Conservancy Magazine,* Fourth Quarter, 1973.

Odum, Howard. "AMBIO," *Journal of the Royal Swedish Academy of Sciences,* Vol. 2, No. 6.

Pimental, David. *Science* November 2, 1973.

K. VALASKAKIS, J. G. SMITH, P. S. SINDELL, AND I. MARTIN

The Conserver Society

IN NOVEMBER 1974, GAMMA, an interuniversity futures studies group at the Université de Montréal and McGill, on the basis of an unsolicited proposal received a contract from the Canadian Department of Supply and Services, acting on behalf of fourteen federal government departments and agencies, "to provide a perspective on the implications for Canada and for Federal Government policies and programs of a future period of controlled, socially oriented growth generally described as the 'Conserver Society.'"

The work was carried out in two stages. The objective of the first stage was to define alternative conserver societies for Canada in a world setting. That of the second stage was to explore the desirability of this option for Canada. The results were submitted to the government in 1976 in a synthesis volume as *The Selective Conserver Society*, and in three technical volumes: *The Physical and Technological Constraints* (Vol. 2); *The Institutional Dimension* (Vol. 3); and *Values and the Conserver Society* (Vol. 4).

In this contribution we comment on one of our scenarios: conservationist growth. This, we feel, is of particular and immediate relevance for corporate, labor, and government planners. To place this one option into perspective, we note several of the other options which were developed in our work.

Conservation might be defined as those processes through which the useful lives of resources are prolonged. To accomplish this, resources may be used less, or less intensively, or not at all, or used and, where appropriate, recycled. A resource, it should be noted, is anything that can provide satisfaction. It may be concrete, abstract, raw, or transformed. Useful life refers to the time during which a resource is capable of providing satisfaction. Resources, of course, do not die. But a consumed ice cream changes its state and cannot continue to produce the initial satisfaction associated with it.

If conservation is thought of merely as nonuse, it is tempting to suppose that the only perfect conserver would be a corpse. But, in fact, a live consumer may also be very much a conserver. Nor is there any necessary implication that for a conserver society to exist, all its members must be conservers. It is theoretically possible for some segment of the population to conserve by preserving, for another to recycle, and for yet another not to conserve at all. To argue that a conserver society can exist only if every single member becomes a conserver is to commit the fallacy of division, which mistakenly assumes that what is true for the whole is necessarily true for the parts.

In a conserver society, high priority is placed upon: reducing waste in production and consumption, respecting ecological balance, developing a longer-term orientation in decision making such that attempts are made to measure the consequences of acts before these are undertaken.

THE CASE FOR A CONSERVER SOCIETY

If one likens the recent experiences of the industrialized West to a wild party, fueled by a wine cellar of cheap energy and raw materials, it is possible to adopt any of the following positions:

Position 1. The conserver society must be recommended on the grounds of ecological necessity. The argument runs as follows: "The party is unfortunately over. We are dangerously low on resources and high in environmental disruption. Therefore we must conserve. If we don't, there are ways in which Nature can force us to change our minds. These have been already identified by Parson Malthus."

Position 2. The conserver society is not recommended since there is no necessity for it. "The party is not over. There are many good resources left if we take the trouble of looking deep enough in our wine cellar. Therefore, instead of panicking and changing our lifestyles, let us instead step up exploration and technological change and maintain our high rates of consumption."

Postion 3. The conserver society is not recommended. What is recommended is a more equitable high-growth consumer society. "The party was nice for those invited. However, most members of the human species have never even heard about it. Our task is to invite these have-nots from both within Canada and abroad. What we need is a high-growth, high-consumerist, but equitable society where everybody has the opportunity to go to the party if he or she so wishes."

Position 4. The conserver society is recommended on the grounds of pure desirability, independent of necessity. "It was an awful party anyway. What disgusting waste. It was a breeder of alienation, competition, greed, and envy. Whether or not we have abundant resources in the future is immaterial. There is a nicer party across the street, where people are behaving responsibly."

Position 5. We must at this stage take an agnostic position. Let us prove or disprove the ecological need for conservation. Then let us examine the attractiveness or unattractiveness of the alternatives. If there is a case to be made for the conserver society, let us make it, rather than assume that problem away. "Any change involves a cost and this is particularly true for value change. For good or for ill, the Canadian public believes (in 1976) in a consumer ethic. If we are to challenge this belief, let us do so for good reasons. Therefore let us study carefully the situation with as neutral an initial position as possible and then assess the options."

In our work we adopted position 5, and attempted to develop detailed physical, technological, social, and institutional indicators of future input, output, and subjective constraints to continued undirected industrial expansion.

CONSTRAINTS: FOOD SUPPLY

Our future food supply is illustrative of more than 100 different types and levels of physical or institutional constraints which we looked at.

Although Canadian agriculture has recently enjoyed a period of large surpluses, this era may be coming to an end. The Achilles heel of modern agriculture seems to be its increasing dependence on nonrenewable inputs, in particular, petroleum. An inventory of inputs going into agricultural production would include:

- *Free inputs, such as sun and rain.* These are fully renewable and are not likely to be in scarce supply except for exceptional periods.
- *Human energy inputs, mainly labor.* These, however, are being replaced by machinery.
- *Inputs from the soil itself.* With crop rotation, other things being equal, there should be no long-term problem of soil exhaustion. Other things, unfortunately, are not always equal.
- *Direct and indirect energy inputs.* In this last category we have to count the high contribution of petroleum.

Agriculture is essentially an intricate energy conversion process where original energy resources are translated into a form eventually usable by human beings. Here the concept of net energy is particularly important. Other things being equal, the longer and more involved the agricultural process (the more industrialized agriculture becomes) the lower the net energy figure, if all energy inputs are taken into account. Table 1 illustrates this proposition.

Table 1. Net energy and protein of different foods (U.S. data, 1974).

Food	Ratio of Primary Energy to Food Energy Produced	Primary Energy (Kcal Required) for Protein (g) Produced
Fish		
Distant	15	25
Coastal	1	3
Meat		
Feedlot	12	100
Grassfed	4	—
Range	0.5	—
Eggs	5	22
Dairy	2	20
Flour and cereals	0.3	5

SOURCE: B. Warkentin, "Agriculture, Food & Renewable Resources," GAMMA, *Physical and Technological Constraints*, Vol 2.

In general, every additional link in the food transformation chain leads to energy losses. Thus eating steak is less energy-efficient than eating vegetable proteins, and so on.

If we consider that Canada presently feeds not only itself but much of the rest of the world, population growth must necessarily raise serious problems. The greater our population, the more intense the depletion threat becomes. Even if food shortages are avoided, the extraction cost (including fertilizers and eventually that of artificial food) will likely go up because of the high energy content in the food chain. This, combined with an ominous threat of world climatic change, with specifically negative consequences for Canada in terms of lowering of temperatures over the next 30 years, adds up to a strong case for conservation. Were this not enough, much of the best growing land in Canada has already been surrendered to urban sprawl. It is unlikely that this trend will be easily reversed in the shorter term.

In the light of the above, until a less energy-intensive agricultural technology is developed and/or the price mechanism makes it personally unprofitable for individuals to throw away the 2 to 3 lbs per person per day of leftover food as they do now, the need to reduce waste in both production and consumption—to conserve—will remain high.

CONSUMER AND CONSERVER SOCIETIES

GAMMA looked at two control scenarios, a business-as-usual one, close to the status quo, and an anticonserver, or squander, society.

Three conserver society scenarios were constructed, each of which differed from the others in its anticipated conservationist effect. As seen in Table 2:

CS_1 is a growth-with-conservation scenario and stresses maximum efficiency. Conserver growth is described by the phrase "doing more with less."

CS_2 is a high-stable-state option. Industrial growth is arrested and so also is the constant creation of new artificial needs. However, existing needs, whether innate or acquired, are catered to. The growth of industry is constrained, but at a high level. There is material affluence, but new creative energies are diverted to less material pursuits. CS_2 is described by the phrase "doing the same with less."

CS_3, the maximum conserver scenario, demands radical value change. There is a rollback of artificial needs and a program of deindustrialization and deurbanization. There is a return to a nonindustrial mode of production. Activity is diverted to spiritual endeavors. Akin to some of the principles of Eastern philosophy, this "Buddhist" scenario counsels doing "less with less."

Our proposed CS_1 scenario has as its underlying theme the elimination, or at least substantial reduction, of waste throughout the production–consumption continuity. This does not imply any reduction in overall industrial and economic growth, although it could mean a redistribution of effort and certainly implies a move toward less wasteful industrial practices. Strategies to accomplish this include RICH and sharing by renting.

REFORM OF INEFFICIENT CONSUMPTION HABITS (RICH)

The basic idea behind RICH is that marginal reforms in individual behavior can add up to a substantial conservationist effect. It is a question of weeding out the inefficient, unproductive, and unnecessary consumption practices that we have adopted during the era of cheap energy and underpriced raw materials. Such practices are extravagant without contributing much to our comfort or convenience.

Because there are millions of consumers in Canada, behavior changes that cost little to the individual will collectively save large amounts of energy and raw materials and free these resources for alternative use. Thus, RICH lies at the heart of the philosophy of CS_1—doing more with less. The exact conservationist effect of any particular measure will have to be specifically computed. However, it will be illustrative to mention a few examples of RICH.

Table 2. A comparison of the consumer and conserver societies.

	The Selective Conserver Society			Consumer Alternatives	
	CS$_1$ Efficiency Scenario	CS$_2$ High Stable State	CS$_3$ "Buddhist" Society	CS$_0$ Status Quo	CS$_{-1}$ Squander Society
Thematic description	Doing more with less	Doing the same with less	Doing less with less	Doing more with more	Doing less with more
Goal	Seek maximization of felicity by minimizing waste, living in harmony with nature, and keeping options open for the future			Seeking maximization of felicity without the constraints of conservation	
General objective	Efficiency	Industrial stability	Nonindustrial stability	Growth	Growth
Specific objectives	Reduce waste without changing values	Freeze demand at optimum level	Reduce demand	Mixed laissez-faire	Increase demand
Principal strategies	Rental schemes, RICH, tech. change, full cost-pricing public regulation	Demarketing, even-handed advertising, education	Education, demonstration of attractiveness of option	Mixed laissez-faire	Consumer sovereignty
Possible impact on inflation	Uncertain	Uncertain, probably antiinflationary	Probably antiinflationary	Inflationary	Very inflationary
Possible impact on unemployment	Reduces unproductive employment, increases productive	Uncertain	Create employment	High unemployment	Very low unemployment
Population policy	Zero growth, excluding immigration, unless otherwise shown	Zero growth, excluding immigration, unless otherwise shown	Zero growth, excluding immigration, unless otherwise shown	No definitive policy	No definitive policy
Implications concerning growth in forward throughput	Controlled growth in forward throughput matched by growth in reverse throughput	Zero growth in forward throughput	Reduction of existing forward throughput	High growth in forward throughput with very little recycling	Higher growth in forward throughput and no recycling
Possible impact on income distribution	Tendency toward egalitarian distribution	Very egalitarian	Egalitarian	Perpetuates income inequalities	Increases income inequalities
Possible impact on balance of payments	Uncertain	Probably improves B/P	Probably improves B/P	Worsens B/P	Worsens B/P
Impact on lifestyles	Behavior changes but not values	Some change in values and lifestyles	Radical change in values and lifestyles	Existing lifestyle	More wasteful practices

Packaging

We overpackage not only our own consumer goods but, in a totally unnecessary fashion, even pet foods. It is shocking to find in the supermarket elaborately packaged cans of dog food which supposedly cater to the owner's sensibilities. From a conservationist point of view, such a practice is absurd. If consumers were to refuse to subsidize such waste, the packaging industry would alter its policies. A significant proportion of the dollars we pay for commodities is used, not to enhance the objective quality of the products we buy, but to embellish their external appearance.

It is interesting to compare North American practices at the supermarket with European. The European shopper goes to the store with a durable shopping bag that is reused again and again. The North American comes home from a shopping spree with a plethora of paper bags, no-deposit, no-refill cans, and miscellaneous other packaging items that are then difficult to dispose of. Should we retain this wasteful way of doing things?

Home Use of Energy

A number of changes in consumer behavior within the household, some obvious, others less so, could reduce energy consumption. Among the obvious ones are maintenance of household temperature at 68°–70° F, rather than at 75°–80° F. The standard world practice of turning off lights in unused rooms could be profitably adopted in North America.

Another obvious conservationist measure for households is better insulation. Improving the thermal insulation of the home is an easy way to save energy and money. In Colorado, U.S. homeowners with good credit ratings can pay for home insulation in 30 months at 9.5 percent interest. The cost is about $150–$300 and the energy saving an average 15 percent. The program is funded by a federal grant used primarily to buy materials. An essentially similar program has just been proposed by the government of Canada.

Garbage Disposal

CS_1 stresses use and recycling of products to eliminate unwanted effluents from the biosphere. One of the unfortunate characteristics of modern Western megalopolises is their enormous garbage production. Garbage production can be reduced at source through more effective packaging. It could be made easier to recycle. In this connection, the segregation of garbage could contribute a great deal. The separation of organic from inorganic garbage and the further separation of inorganic garbage into simpler constitutents could facilitate the creation of reverse channels of distribution, recycling the used good back to its original raw state.

Driving Habits

Much of our energy is used in transportation, particularly car use. At the CS_1 level, the car as a method of transportation—or as an expression of machismo, extension of personality, or whatever—is not challenged. In CS_1 we accept the car culture, but, obviously, we would all benefit from more efficient cars.

SHARING BY RENTING

The rental scheme as a strategy for conservation is based on two simple ideas:

First, we own many things that we can use in a given time period. Because we own these things, we remove them from the public domain and prevent others from using them. If a satisfactory method of sharing what we have could be devised, more people would enjoy the luxuries of life without the need to produce ever more quantities of redundant commodities. Renting, which really means possessing only when using, is one possible method of achieving this greater efficiency. Hence a rental society would reduce energy used in production by making consumption more efficient.

Second, if a producer retains ownership of a good which he has produced, he has a strong interest in making that product more durable. More generally, if goods are produced for renting exclusively, whether or not the initial producer retains ownership, they must be built to last. Therefore, a rental scheme can be conservationist by reducing the need for new production.

THE DISADVANTAGES OF RENTING

Renting is not without disadvantages, and any careful study of its feasibility must consider both sides of the picture. Among the possible drawbacks is the question of the lease period. Renting over too-long periods is equivalent to ownership, since the commodity would, in fact, be removed from public use without necessarily being fully enjoyed by the lessee. It is possible to lease a car and leave it idle in the garage, in which case there is no conservationist effect.

Second, there is the double-edged sword of load equalization. On the one hand, utilization of idle resources is efficient and to be recommended. On the other, if, through rental schemes, all cars presently in circulation were to be on the road at the same time, there would be a nightmare of traffic jams, pollution, and energy use. One answer is that there may already be too many cars in circulation and that a better utilization of fewer cars would solve that problem. A more general answer lies in management of time. If we all have lunch at the same time, go off on weekends every Friday evening, return from work at 5 P.M., and so forth, there can be little renting because there are peak loads. To equalize the load and avoid peaks and troughs, time will have to be managed differently.

The third drawback of a pure rental scheme is inconvenience. Members of a tennis club who have to sandwich in their tennis between 4:45 and 5:30 on Wednesday have experienced the inconvenience of renting, rather than owning. It is much more convenient to have your own private tennis court. The question is, does the removal of the inconvenience justify the tremendous waste? Or can there be, instead, a way of minimizing the inconvenience by more careful load equalization?

The fourth drawback is the psychological value attached to ownership, which is lost in renting. To rent a Rolls-Royce is not the same as owning one. There is also the question of true or alleged health hazards associated with renting. The idea of sharing clothes is repugnant to many, and if people were to be asked to rent bed sheets rather than own them, they would probably react in horror. Yet this is exactly what we do when we stay in hotel rooms. In some cases the objection is legitimate; in others, a mere cultural whim.

To sum up the conservationist effect of renting: load equalization and building in durability reduce the need for new production and therefore the pollution and resource depletion associated with it, as well as reducing effluents associated with consumption.

CONSERVER TECHNOLOGY

Our present mode of production (or any mode of production for that matter) depends on a given technology. To alter our production methods usually implies changing our technology first. For this reason, conservation at the CS_1 level, far from requiring a stagnant technology, actually demands a dynamic, rapidly improving one. There can be no question of freezing technology levels; rather, new technologies must be developed that will allow us to do "more with less."

Technological improvements may perhaps be the single most important strategy for conservation within the logic of CS_1. The subject is so broad that it cannot be covered in detail here. However, in general terms, the main objectives of such a technology would be:

- Substitution of renewable and inexhaustible energy resources for nonrenewable ones.
- Development of ways of producing food with minimum energy loss.
- Development of solutions to the twin problems of pollution and recycling. Pollution refers to the unintended by-products and intended output. Reduction of pollution at source is by far the best solution. This can be done by developing low-pollution industrial processes, using clean, renewable energy, if possible. If pollution cannot be reduced at source, it must be neutralized ex post facto, mainly by recycling.
- Reduction in use of nonrenewable metals. An allied objective is the discovery of means to reduce the extraction cost of these metals when they have to be used.
- Increase in durability and quality of products. This may involve use of better-grade materials, superior assembly techniques, and quality workmanship.
- Development of new methods of population control.
- Reduction of health hazards and the maintenance of a high quality of life.

The expected conservationist effect of CS_1 is substantial. The actual quantities of energy and materials conserved cannot be accurately assessed at this time, but estimates for much less comprehensive high-efficiency scenarios vary from approximately 11 percent to 22 percent. Savings of this order may seem unsatisfactory to some but be welcomed by others. Some people will conserve even fully renewable resources, and this conduct may be considered praiseworthy or unnecessary, depending on one's view. Others will conserve only what they have to conserve. In the latter category probably lies, for good or for ill, the mainstream of the Canadian public.

Arriving at CS_1, then, may not be possible and will not be easy. One route is government fiat. It is often argued that because it is not constrained by the profit motive as the market is, the state can take a longer term view in planning and executing its activities than is possible for the individual or the corporation. In part this may be true and, when so, it is the great strength of the state. In this context, it is useful to recall that not only do future generations not vote, but politicians generally do not think much further ahead than the next election. Civil servants, of course, may think in much longer time horizons; so, too, in fact, do cor-

porate planners. But neither civil servants nor corporate planners occupy line positions. They are staff people. Their influence can be
brought to bear on decisions, but they do not, or should not, *make*
decisions, at least in a democracy.

The second avenue through which to reform growth so that it is less
pollution-intensive or resource-profligate is, of course, through a political and ethical revolution that substitutes altruism for selfishness as the
prime mover of human affairs. This is certainly the most attractive of all
alternatives. With education, dedication, and a great deal of luck, perhaps future generations will be more successful in accomplishing this
than we or our forebears have been. In the meantime, the CS_1 scenario
outlined in this contribution, if adopted, could provide future generations with the time necessary to learn, and to plan for, the restraints
implied in the CS_2 and CS_3 scenarios.

KENNETH R. FARRELL

Food and Agriculture in the Next Quarter Century

IN 1972 the world food situation made an about-face, turning from surpluses and low prices to relative scarcity and high prices. Those of a
Malthusian persuasion judged that we had entered a period of chronic
food scarcity in which demand, spurred by population growth and rising
affluence, had begun to outrun the productive capacity of the world's
farmers. Other, more sanguine, observers pointed out that man had
thus far avoided the Malthusian specter and would somehow have the
ingenuity, foresight, or luck to continue to "muddle through," except-
ing, of course, the occasional national or regional famine.

Both views are overdrawn. World food production can keep a half-
step ahead of population growth in the next quarter century, but only if
purposeful agricultural development plans are implemented in the near
future and if food production and distribution are viewed in a global,
rather than a nationalistic, context.

THE RECENT PAST IN PERSPECTIVE

During the 1960s and early 1970s total food production in both the
developed and developing countries rose about 3 percent per year. But
rapid population growth in the developing countries cut per capita food
production to about 0.4 percent per year, compared with 1.5 percent in
the developing countries. Low grain prices and concessionary terms facilitated grain imports by the developing countries and helped to improve diets, but may also have tempted governments there to delay
needed agricultural development efforts. Low grain prices also greatly
stimulated the production and consumption of livestock products in
many countries.

In the developed grain-exporting countries, the agricultural policy
during the late 1960s and early 1970s was designed to reduce surplus

stocks. By 1972 U.S. government policy had contributed to the retirement of nearly 60 million acres from crop production.

These trends set the stage for 1972, when bad weather in many parts of the world caused an unprecedented drop in world grain production. Large grain imports by the Soviet Union in 1972–1973 and increased grain imports by the developing countries combined with growing demand in the developed countries created by rapid income growth, rapid inflation, and monetary realignments to generate a tremendous surge in import demand. World grain stocks were pulled down to alarming levels. World grain output since then has been sufficient to avert large-scale shortages, but stocks remain very low.

High prices and spot shortages of food in recent years were the signs of a world food market seriously out of adjustment. Events had masked the fact that between 1967 and 1974 the world needed more food than was being produced and that, to meet these needs grain stockpiles were being drawn down. The trends were going in the wrong direction: demand was being stimulated and supply restrained. The year 1972 brought the unmasking, and producers could not adjust immediately. That producers are now expanding output does not, however, mean that the "world food problem" has been solved.

The basic imbalances in world food production and consumption remain uncorrected. Correction of these imbalances will require reevaluation of agricultural, food, and trade policies in many parts of the world.

RESOURCES FOR FUTURE FOOD PRODUCTION

What are the sources from which increased food production might be derived in the next quarter century? How limited are the traditional factors of land, labor, capital, and management likely to be in various parts of the world, particularly in the developing nations? Can resources used in agricultural production continue to be made more productive by infusion of new technology? What types of new technology might increase productivity?

Land

The U.N. Food and Agriculture Organization (FAO) estimates that about 1.4 billion hectares (3.4 billion acres) presently are being cultivated to grow food crops or to feed livestock. This is less than one-half of the 3.2 billion hectares (7.8 billion acres) that could be used (Table 1).

Although the world as a whole is clearly not running out of land, the potential new land is not equally distributed throughout the world's climatic zones. More than half the potentially arable land lies in the

Table 1. World agricultural land resources (million hectares).

Region	Total Land Area [a]	Potentially Arable Lands [b]	Cultivated Land [c]	Unused Potential [d]
Africa	2,987	732	209	523
Asia	2,739	633	482	151
Australia and New Zealand	795	146	46	100
North America	1,834	466	235	231
Europe	480	177	144	33
South America	2,070	680	126	554
U.S.S.R.	2,240	354	232	122
World	13,145	3,188	1,474	1,714

SOURCES: U.N. Food and Agriculture Organization, *1973 Production Yearbook,* Vol. 27 (Rome, 1974); Report of the President's Science Advisory Committee, "The World Food Problem," Vol. II (Washington, D.C., May 1967).

[a] Excludes areas under inland bodies of water (for example, rivers and lakes).
[b] Includes soils considered acceptable for production of food crops adapted to the environment.
[c] Includes arable lands (land under temporary crops, meadows, fallow, idle, and crops for market or garden) and land under permanent crops (which occupy the land for long periods, such as beverage crops, fruits, nuts, rubber, shrubs, and vines).
[d] Column 2 minus column 3.

tropics, and many people live in areas where the possibilities for expanding cultivated area are limited.

But land becomes relatively less of a limiting factor to agricultural production as people learn about and can afford other means of increasing output. The problem facing many of the developing countries is not simply limited land, but that their land produces so little. Land will continue to be especially critical in food production in the developing countries so long as they rely only on traditional agricultural practices and institutions which often constrain the farmer's productive capacity.

Other Inputs

As indicated, there remains a very large area of land in the world which could be transformed into cropland. To do so, however, would require large capital investment both directly and in terms of the marketing and social infrastructures which would need to accompany such development. Some of the potentially cultivable land would require very careful management and relatively large amounts of capital to develop and maintain.

We expect most of the future growth in food production to come from technologically induced higher yields. Most of the recent increases in grain yields in the developing countries have been brought about by the adoption of high-yielding varieties of grain—especially wheat and rice—and an associated package of inputs.

Fertilizer

The use of fertilizer is a key factor in increasing yields. But it must be combined with improved seed varieties, pesticides, and improved cultural practices if it is to have much impact on yields. We believe that the recent high prices for fertilizers primarily reflect short-term problems of adjusting supply to demand. Fertilizer production capacity had been overexpanded in the mid-1960s, driving prices down and discouraging new investment. When the events of 1972 led farmers to attempt a rapid expansion of crop production, fertilizer production capacity was strained and prices rose sharply.

In the longer run, raw material costs seem likely to be much less important determinants of fertilizer production than technology and production costs. Only 2–3 percent of current consumption of natural gas in the United States is used in fertilizer production, while Middle East oil countries each year flare enough natural gas equivalent to produce four times the world's present nitrogen fertilizer production. In addition, the technology already exists for converting coal—the most ample fossil fuel—to methane for producing nitrogen fertilizers.

Known reserves of phosphate rock are adequate for many years, but are concentrated in a few localities. Until the last two or three years the supplies of these two materials were so ample that their resulting low prices discouraged exploration for new sources.

Irrigation

Irrigation as an input for increasing production has become increasingly important. About 50 percent of the world's crop production depends on water control, primarily irrigation, drainage, and flood control. Irrigation is especially important in the developing countries, particularly those with arid or monsoon climates.

Present utilization of irrigated potential for the world is only about 40 percent, and is projected to reach 60 percent by the year 2000.[1] Developing this potential will require large capital investment. Such costs may be reduced with the development of new technologies, and new water resources may be discovered. Improved technological and institutional facilities for precise water management may well match in importance the need for greater investment and new technologies.

Farm Organization

The pattern of agricultural development throughout the world is quite diverse, reflecting both varying rates of economic progress and the distribution of resources, especially land and labor. At one extreme is that followed by the United States of a strong trend toward larger units, replacement of labor with machinery, a rapid increase in use of purchased inputs, and specialization in production with large increases in output per man-hour and per acre.

At the opposite extreme is the very successful development pattern of Japan. Instead of the consolidation of farms into large units, here tiny farms are remaining tiny, with small, two-wheel tractors replacing draft animals, and a good deal of part-time farming. Very high yields are being attained with emphasis on fertilization, crop protection, and high-response varieties, but also a good deal of labor input.

Two important points emerge: (1) Research results here and abroad show no compelling reason for farm firms to grow in size to achieve economies of scale; and (2) the technology most appopriate will vary among countries depending on several factors, including availability and relative costs of production factors, and, of course, the nature of the production activity itself.

New Technology

No discussion of the next quarter century would be complete without some speculation on new technology which might become available. The following are cited as examples of technology which might come on stream, economic conditions warranting[2]:

- Upgrading of the protein content of the cereal grains and other crops, for example, hi-lysine corn.
- Hybridization of additional crops, including wide crosses like triticale (rye and wheat cross).
- Development of soil-management techniques which would permit the use for agriculture of the fragile soils of the tropical rainforest.
- Biological rather than chemical control of harmful insects and diseases.
- Control of the tsetse fly, the vector for sleeping sickness in Africa, thereby opening for agricultural use vast areas of that continent which are now idle.
- Successful long-range weather prediction and possibly weather modification.
- Use of satellites for worldwide crop reporting.
- Extension of the principle of nitrogen fixation to new groups of plants in addition to legumes, thus cutting down the need for commercial fertilizer.
- Desalination of seawater, permitting human habitation and agricultural production in lands now unused.
- Conquest of the fuel problem, probably by the use of nuclear energy.

- Greater environmental control for both plants and animals, providing more economical production and high, more standardized quality.
- Advances in food technology, particularly the modification of plant protein to provide meat analogues to the many millions who cannot afford palatable and nutritious meat, milk, and eggs.
- Use of microbial action on various feedstocks (such as organic wastes or fossil fuels) for direct production of feed and food.
- Better systems of distribution to minimize the twin problems of overeating and poverty-related malnutrition.
- Improved understanding of relationships, so that the computers will give us more sense and less nonsense.

THE DETERMINANTS OF DEMAND

Resources are physically available to insure world food production, but how will demand affect the economic pressure on these resources?

Population growth, of course, provides the greatest stimulus, but income growth, the level and distribution of income, and consumer preferences can have a critical effect. It is a sobering thought that about 85 percent of the current annual population increase is occurring in the developing countries, and that reductions in growth rates in the past seem to have been caused not so much by the development of birth-prevention technology, but by improved well-being that changes both the economic and social incentives for having children.

As consumer incomes increase, a smaller proportion is spent for food. In most low-income countries half or more of income is spent for food, whereas the proportion drops to less than one-fifth in the highest-income countries. As real per capita income increases, cereals usually make up a lower proportion of the food budget. Income elasticities for livestock products (and therefore the indirect consumption of coarse grains) are relatively high.

We expect developing countries to continue to be heavily dependent on grains for food, while the developed countries will continue to consume less grain directly but will convert more grain to meat, milk, and eggs.

Now let us try to bring into perspective potential food supply and demand prospects. In our report *The World Food Situation and Prospects to 1985*,[3] we examined possible outcomes under several alternative sets of assumptions (Table 2). Our projections focus on grain (wheat, coarse grains, and milled rice), since this is the single most important component of the world's food supply.

Table 2. Alternative USDA projections to 1985 of cereal demand, production, and trade (million metric tons).

Item	Base	Low Demand	Moderate Demand	High Demand	High Demand and Increased Developing Country Productivity
World					
Demand	1,062.6	1,501.8	1,548.5	1,618.7	1,643.9
Production	1,081.8	1,503.6	1,550.4	1,620.6	1,645.7
Balance [a]	19.2	1.9	1.9	1.9	1.9
Developing countries [b]					
Demand	466.6	678.6	691.2	726.2	743.5
Production	443.1	626.2	632.4	648.7	721.0
Balance	−23.5	−52.4	−58.8	−77.5	−22.5
Developed countries [c]					
Demand	596.0	823.2	857.3	892.5	900.4
Production	638.7	877.4	918.0	971.9	924.7
Balance	42.7	54.2	60.7	79.4	24.3

SOURCE: U.S. Department of Agriculture, Economic Research Service, Foreign Agricultural Economic Report No. 98, "The World Food Situation and Prospects to 1985" (Washington, D.C., December 1974), p. 35.
[a] Imbalances between demand and production in base are due to stock buildup, timing of shipments, and missing data on a number of small importers. Projected equilibrium does not allow for building or reducing stocks.
[b] Includes the People's Republic of China.
[c] Includes the USSR and Eastern Europe.

We assumed world population growth to 1985 at the rate of 2.4 percent in the developing countries (including China) and 0.9 percent in the developed countries (including the USSR and Eastern Europe). Productivity was assumed to increase in line with historical trends modified by recent gains.

Under these alternatives the developing countries would experience net deficits in cereals. Output would fail to keep pace with the demand generated by both rising incomes and rapid population growth. But the developed countries, especially the United States, would have the productive capacity to meet those deficits as well as their own growing domestic requirements.

The net import deficit in the developing countries could vary between 52 and 78 million tons, depending on how much varying rates of economic growth affect demand.

Attempts to extend our projections to the year 2000 raise an important question: Can the developing countries maintain a modest increase in per capita food consumption which is based on a growing dependence on grain imports from the developed countries? Not likely. At current grain export prices (weighted by trade), it would cost nearly $12 billion annually even by 1985 to finance the high alternative deficit mentioned in our projections.

The alternatives facing the developing countries are (1) to meet such import deficits with large-scale food aid programs by the developed countries, and (2) to reduce the deficits by major efforts on the part of the developing nations themselves to increase food production.

Our fourth alternative projection suggests that the grain deficit of developing countries in 1985 could be reduced to a million tons less than the 24-million-ton base-period deficit if serious efforts are made to increase productivity there. Such efforts would have to be maintained or accelerated in future years.

Solving the world food problem in this manner would be costly, and probably could not be achieved by the developing countries alone. Still, the cost would be much less than financing the closure of the gap each year with increasing grain imports.

SOME POLICY ISSUES

It is apparent that the developing nations will need to provide assistance—capital, managerial, technological—if the food deficit is to be lowered by increased output in the developing nations. But the developing nations must first commit themselves to goals of increased output as well as goals of limiting population growth.

The most important policy questions for the long run are those concerned with the promotion of agricultural production in the developing countries. The stimulation of agricultural investment; the development, adaptation, and dissemination of new farm technologies; and the provision of adequate economic incentives to farmers should be high on the list of policy aims.

Many of the developing countries have policies that seriously limit the incentives to their own farmers to produce more food. Agricultural and food exports are sometimes taxed, or internal prices manipulated, in such a way that prices received by farmers are held down seriously. Monetary and trade policies often seriously discriminate against production by their own agricultural sectors.

In a number of developing countries governments follow policies that underpay their farmers, in part because they want to hold down the price of food for social or political purposes. While these policy goals are understandable with respect to consumers and to wageworkers in industry, their impact on the food production capacity and trade pattern of the developing countries needs to be evaluated carefully.

CONCLUSIONS AND IMPLICATIONS

Several conclusions may be drawn from the foregoing discussion.

• The developing countries of the world as a whole face growing food import deficits in the next quarter century.

• The reduction of potential food import deficits in these nations must come through some combination of major increases in the rate of growth in food production within the developing countries and reduced rates of population growth. A failure to adopt such a strategy implies increased dependency on food aid from developed countries or reduced levels of per capita consumption.

• There is, in fact, a large potential for increased food production in both the developing and developed nations during the next quarter century. To exploit these potentials requires, first and foremost, a commitment from the developing nations to step up agricultural productivity, including reassessment of food, agricultural, and economic policies to provide greater incentives to investment and production.

• Even with the commitment of the developing countries to increased agricultural productivity and output, massive assistance from the developed nations will be required.

• Technical assistance and training, the transfer and adaptation of technology, and the development of new technology designed for the particular conditions of developing nations are areas in which the private sector in developed countries can make substantial contributions to expanding food production.

REFERENCES

1. Based on Alan Strout, "World Agricultural Potential: Evidence from the Recent Past," March 1975, unpublished FAO data presented in a draft of the paper.
2. From Don Paarlberg, "Agriculture 2000 Years from Now," a paper presented to the Bicentennial Symposium at the Museum of History and Technology, April 23, 1975, Washington, D.C. Dr. Paarlberg is Director of Economics, U.S. Department of Agricultural Economics.
3. U.S. Department of Agriculture, Economic Research Service, Washington, D.C., December 1974.

JAMES R. COLLIER

The Thinking Man's Inventory of Natural Resources

TO THE WORLD at large, the problems of energy supply and demand
have tended to obscure the need to focus attention on what is happening
in the nonfuel minerals area. But to those of us in the business, the
problems are no less compelling and largely similar. Nonfuel minerals
demand for the year 2000 is estimated to constitute approximately two-
thirds of total minerals demand in the United States. The U.S. Geological Survey estimates that by the year 2000 U.S. dependence on imports
will be complete for 12 commodities and more than 75 percent for 19
others.

To reduce the supply/demand problem to a manageable size, I have
omitted those minerals that are available almost everywhere in unlimited supply (such as sand, gravel, and limestone; the gases extracted
from the air; and those minerals routinely extracted from seawater). I
have also omitted the precious metals because of their "exotic" nature
and the somewhat artificial nature of resulting demand, as well as those
minerals used principally as fertilizer ingredients (potassium, phos-
phorus, and sulfur) because of the complexity of the population and
world food problems involving them. The 12 minerals that remain,
listed in Table 1, represent almost 50 percent of the U.S. demand for
nonfuel minerals. The United States is largely dependent on foreign
sources for seven of these 12 minerals. Half the minerals on this list
relate to the manufacture of steel, and the use of aluminum and titanium
as substitutes for steel is increasing.

To understand the problems fully, we have to recognize the terminology developed by V. E. McKelvey for describing mineral reserves and
resources, depicted in Figure 1. In general terms, reserves are known
sources that can profitably be extracted with present technology at existing price levels. Resources include reserves, marginal or subeconomic
known deposits, and hypothetical and speculative unknown sources.
These definitions are further refined by (1) the degree of certainty

Table 1. Selected nonfuel minerals demand in 1968.

Mineral	1968 Demand (millions)	
	World	U.S.
Copper	$ 7,739	$1,300
Iron	6,591	1,294
Aluminum	5,247	1,983 [a]
Zinc	1,460	380 [a]
Titanium	1,265	414
Lead	931	242 [a]
Nickel	878	300 [a]
Tin	819	196 [b]
Manganese	457	64 [b]
Molybdenum	224	90
Tungsten	197	43
Chromium	105	24 [b]
Total	$25,913	$6,330

SOURCE: U.S. Bureau of Mines, *Mineral Facts and Problems*, Bulletin No. 650 (Washington, D.C.: Government Printing Office, 1970).
[a] Most from foreign sources.
[b] Almost all from foreign sources.

Figure 1. Mineral resources classification.

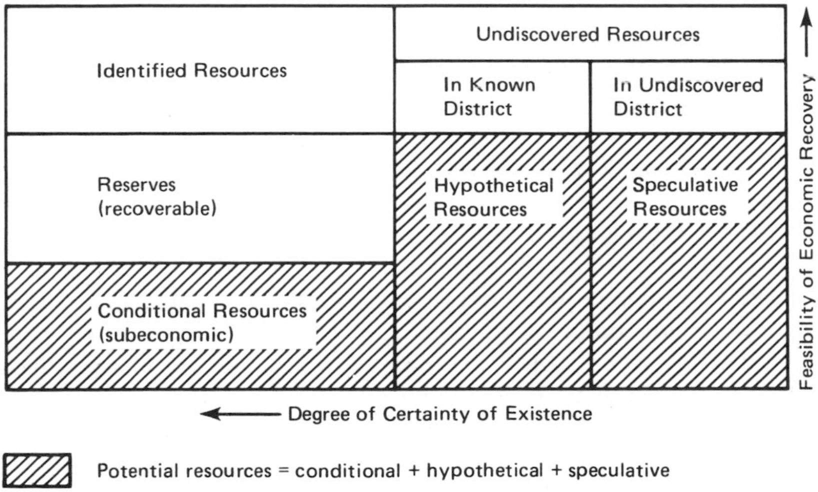

Identified Resources	Undiscovered Resources		
	In Known District	In Undiscovered District	Feasibility of Economic Recovery →
Reserves (recoverable)	Hypothetical Resources	Speculative Resources	
Conditional Resources (subeconomic)			

← Degree of Certainty of Existence

Potential resources = conditional + hypothetical + speculative

Source: V.E. McKelvey.

of the existence of the source, and (2) the relative feasibility of economic recovery. It is possible to add a third dimension to this chart to allow for materials substitution or interchangeability. Hypothetical resources may be inferred from the probabilities of known ore-bearing districts and speculative resources from our knowledge of broad geologic terrain or unconventional sources only recently recognized as having potential. So when we talk about supply, we are usually considering only the tip of the iceberg, as shown by the white area in the figure.

It is the task of planners to assess the total environment, present and future, to make critical assumptions, and to predict their implications. Unfortunately, there are no easy answers, no neat tables of projections, and there never have been. However, I will outline the factors affecting quantification and will discuss adequacy of resources for the future.

There are four principal influences to be considered in the evaluation of supply/demand: geochemistry, economics, politics, and demand itself. Geochemistry deals with the known existence of minerals as elements dispersed in the earth's crust. Of the nine elements that represent 98 percent of the earth's crust, only three—aluminum, iron, and titanium—are on my list of 12 selected minerals. The existence of minerals uniformly dispersed throughout the earth's crust is not necessarily of value to us since they may not have the crucial performance characteristics desired or we may not yet have learned how to extract them economically from every chemical combination in which they occur. Except for lead, the minerals most in demand occur in higher concentrations in the oceanic crust than in the continental crust.

Whether or not minerals are classified as resources depends, therefore, not only on their crustal abundance, but on their relative concentration, mineralogy, and location—hence their ease of identification. Some, such as sand, gravel, and limestone, occur extensively and quite close to the surface and are therefore easily quantified. Others, such as iron ore, potash, and phosphates, occur as concentrated sedimentary layers sufficiently close to the surface to make quantification reasonably easy. More difficult are those few, such as chromium, copper, lead, and zinc, which may occur as placements in igneous rocks in sufficient concentration to be mineable. Other minerals, such as sodium, potassium, and magnesium, occur as solutions in seawater and are readily quantified. Finally, some, such as manganese-copper nodules, phosphorites, and aragonite, occur as sea-bed deposits which have only recently been explored. As a result, our knowledge of potential resources from the point of view of the certainty of their existence can be highly variable from one mineral to another.

From the start we have added to our reserves from several sources.

The most obvious are new discoveries in previously unexplored or inadequately explored areas. Five of the major pre-Cambrian areas of the world, which contain the world's oldest rocks and are therefore likely to be rich in minerals, are still, to a large extent, unexplored. These areas are Siberia, Northern Canada, Western Australia, Eastern South America, and South Central Africa. But the most common sources are lower-grade ores and mineral values in old tailings which once were subeconomic. We have known of their existence but have not been able to afford them.

Unconventional sources increasingly present opportunities for expansion of our mineral reserves. Examples already mentioned are sea-bed deposits, the most publicized being manganese-copper nodules. However, now that we have learned what the *Glomar Explorer* was really used for, we may not be as close to that prospect as we previously had thought. Though not as exciting, the aragonite deposits, or calcium carbonate sands, now being successfully mined in the Bahamas represent a concrete example. This venture has added up to 100 billion tons of calcium carbonate to our known mineral reserves. In addition, aragonite is now being delivered to a titanium dioxide plant where it is used to neutralize waste sulfuric acid and, in the process, to produce more than 200,000 tons per year of high-quality synthetic gypsum, a new source.

From an economic point of view, increasing demand, followed by increasing prices, has the most direct impact on the cutoff grade for economic recovery. Improved technology is nearly as important in increasing reserves. For example:

• Advances in mining equipment have significantly reduced extractive costs and, in the process, increased the mineral values of lower-grade ores.

• Marconaflo, Inc., has developed a unique recovery system which will allow old lead/zinc tailings in Morocco to be reclaimed and reprocessed now that the price of zinc has increased above that existing at the time of their initial disposal.

• Iron ore pelletization and similar beneficiation increase the percentages of mineral values recovered from a given ton of ore and thereby reduce transportation costs and subsequent smelting or refining costs.

• Advances in transportation reduced the cost per ton of ore carried in dry bulk cargo carriers from the Marcona mines in Peru to Japan from $17.00 pre-Suez to $7.50 in 1975. Technology has made possible reductions in overland transportation as well.

• A high-capacity, long-distance belt conveyor system delivers run-of-mine ore from the Marcona mine in Peru over 15 kilometers and across a 510-meter-high escarpment to the beneficiation plant near the port. Power generated by dynamic braking of the conveyor going down the escarpment is used to drive the conveyor system with an additional 585 kilowatts of surplus power left over. Transportation costs from mine to plant have been reduced from 90¢ to 6.5¢ per ton.

• In New Zealand, Marcona is dredging iron sand, with metal values as low as 17 percent, concentrating it to 56 percent, pumping it as a slurry aboard large bulk carriers 2 miles offshore, and discharging it by clam shells at the destination.

Petroleum price increases suggest another significant factor in the economic consideration of supply: artificial restraints. Although the practical effect of such restraints is economic, an effect which can quickly change a potential resource to a true reserve, their genesis is largely political. Hence political considerations must loom large in any assessment of minerals supply. These arbitrary restraints may be imposed by the user country as well as by the supplier nation.

While the specific forms of government and their potential stability and attitudes toward private investment may themselves appear hostile, we must appreciate that host countries do have valid objectives. There is a great need to establish their sovereignty over internal affairs, obtain equitable prices and stable earnings in real terms with some protection from exaggerated short-term fluctuations, and finally, to offset declining trade balances. While a country's need for technical and investment assistance may be a favorable factor, the host country can increasingly select among sources of such assistance and pick one more nearly conforming to its own vision of what is best for the country.

A key issue is how widely dispersed, internationally, is the resource in question. The larger the number of producing countries, the more difficult it is to develop the community of interest essential to the imposition of such restraints. For example, the economics of aragonite, a low-value commodity found almost everywhere, simply cannot be changed arbitrarily by the Bahamian government as can that for bauxite by the Jamaican government.

For other reasons, a country may begin to place such a high value on environmental conditions that it raises the cost of extracting a mineral resource to the point at which it no longer fits our definition of a reserve. This could turn out to be the case for certain resources in the United States, such as western coal. Environmental considerations may increase reserves by reducing demand. Pressures to remove lead from gasoline and from paints, for example, have a significant impact on lead demand. Similarly, environmentalists are succeeding in having legislation passed which bans nonreuseable beverage containers. As a result, demand for primary aluminum most certainly will be reduced.

From the point of view of the user country, there also are political factors which affect resource economics and hence available supplies. The most obvious is national security, an issue used for some time in the United States to justify maintenance of government stockpiles of so-called strategic materials. Another is the monetary impact of rising imports. A study by the U.S. government estimated that by the year 2000 the United States would have to pay $44 billion per year for its nonfuel minerals imports. Such an outflow of money, when added to payments for energy, could easily lead to artificial restraints which would have the effect of raising prices in the United States and thereby increasing domestic reserves for many minerals.

The final consideration in the quantification of minerals supplies is demand itself. While increasing demand tends to deplete known reserves in the short run, it may have an opposing long-term influence. As known reserves begin to be used up, the price of the mineral goes up. If the commodity is genuinely scarce, this price increase forces substitution, or the stimulation of technology which reduces consumption. If the commodity is not truly scarce, the price increase results in increased exploration with new discoveries, the use of known subeconomic resources, or the exploitation of unconventional sources, all of which increase or expand supplies.

It is often possible to reduce demand through the use of scrap in lieu of ore. Table 2 shows the percentage of total consumption for four of our key minerals represented by recycled materials in 1974. Over the past two decades, recycling of aluminum has been on the increase, copper has averaged 40–45 percent, lead had declined slightly until 1970, after which it has increased dramatically from 35 to 52 percent, and zinc, one of our scarcer widely used metals, has declined from 30 to 15 percent.

Table 2. Selected use of recycled materials in 1974.

Material	Short Tons	Percentage of Total Use of Recycled Material
Aluminum	1,251,000	20
Copper	1,700,000	44
Lead	815,000	52
Zinc	224,000	15

SOURCE: *The New York Times,* April 11, 1975, p. 45.

Historically, possibilities for recycling have varied significantly among minerals.

When we use bauxite to make aluminum for beverage containers, we do not consume it. It can be recycled for subsequent reuse. Similarly, uneconomic tailings from one economic era may become valuable reserves during a subsequent era. On the other hand, when we burn certain resources and disperse them in the atmosphere, or dump a waste acid in the ocean, we do indeed lose them so that they cannot be reused. Recently, we have begun to change our views concerning such dispersal and consumption. I have already mentioned the creation of gypsum from waste sulfuric acid and abundant calcium carbonate. Other examples are sulfur removal from crude oil in lieu of its dispersal in the atmosphere and removal of sulfur from copper smelter gases and its conversion to sulfuric acid. This new availability of sulfuric acid near the sources of copper ore has begun to change the economics and use of oxide copper ores previously neglected.

The United States' first major evaluation of materials supply and demand prospects after World War II was made by the Paley Commission. The Commission's reserve estimates for lead were 7.1 million tons in 1952, of which only one million tons were proved. The Commission stated that "the poor discovery record of the past decades provides little basis for optimism. . . ." Yet by 1970 reserves of lead in Missouri alone were 30 million tons. I do not cite this example as a predictor but as an indicator of our predictive inadequacies. Table 3 shows changing reserve estimates resulting in the "expanding bucket" viewpoint of materials supply. For each mineral listed, not only have reserves provided for consumption during the period shown, but they have been greater at the end of the period than earlier.

Table 3. Increases in known reserves worldwide.

Material	1956	1960	1970
Chromium (million short tons)	200.0	—	775.0
Copper (million short tons)	100.0	170.0	307.9
Lead (million short tons)	40.5	48.8	95.0
Mercury (million flasks)	0.6	2.0	3.2
Platinum (million Troy ounces)	25.0	25.0	424.0
Tin (million long tons)[a]	5.0	5.0	6.5
Zinc (million short tons)[a]	70+	67.0	90.0

SOURCE: U.S. Bureau of Mines, *Mineral Facts and Problems,* Bulletin No. 650 (Washington, D.C.: Government Printing Office, 1970).
[a] Free world only.

This performance is understandable. Our views are most directly affected by what we can see in the short term with reasonable clarity. The nature of the minerals business has been to experience alternating periods of significant over- and undersupply. The problem is that there has been too little discrimination between over- and undersupply of extractive and processing capacity, determined by investment practices, as opposed to minerals in the ground. Because these anomalies from supply/demand balance cannot be corrected rapidly, we have perceived apparent shortages as inherent shortages.

At present, there are two differing points of view concerning the future adequacy of minerals supplies, characterized as anti-Malthusian and neo-Malthusian. The anti-Malthusians point to the "expanding bucket" concept as evidence that we really don't need to worry. The work done for the Club of Rome best characterizes the neo-Malthusian view that if current growth rates continue, the man-earth system will collapse in less than 100 years, on the basis of the most optimistic assumptions about reserves. William Vogely of the U.S. Department of Treasury said that "by 2000 A.D. world production of primary minerals will be declining and will be well below that now foreseen; mining from deposits, as we know it, will have disappeared in the United States; the minerals industry will be an industry concerned with the technologies of use of materials and the recycling of total minerals stocks."[1] Mr. Vogely based his view on a reasonably supportable assessment of the future influences which each of us will have to learn to deal with in our planning roles.

But the consensus is that, at least through the year 2000, the world will have adequate nonfuel mineral resources, perhaps with minor exceptions, to support continued predictable world economic growth. Table 4 summarizes the views of a panel of 15 international economists published in *Iron Age*. The greatest uncertainties surround lead, zinc,

Table 4. Estimated world demand and reserves for metals.

Material (million short tons)	Cumulative Demand, 1970–2000	Reserves
Bauxite	990	4,746
Chromium	102	1,863
Iron	19,800	96,700
Lead	181	144
Nickel	27	46
Zinc	283	131
Copper	573	370
Tin	10	5
Tungsten	2	1

SOURCE: *Iron Age*, January 6, 1975, p. 70a.

tin, and tungsten. Even these uncertainties with regard to tin are disputed by Mr. Harold Allen, Executive Director of the International Tin Council, who said, "All we know is that we have 31 years' reserves and very strong geological evidence that we shall find more."[2]

A more comprehensive estimate of nonfuel minerals resource adequacy to the year 2000 was made by the U.S. Geological Survey in 1970. This study indicates that, on a world basis, there appears to be no problem of resource adequacy. At the First World Symposium on Energy and Raw Materials, Mr. Wolfgang Sames, Director, Ministry of Economic Affairs, West Germany, concluded that there no doubt were theoretical absolute limits in the distant future, but that this was not a problem for the current generation. He said that the information available was sufficiently reliable for one to be sure that, in physical terms, resources were adequate to take the world beyond the year 2000. Dr. James Boyd, Executive Director, National Commission on Materials Policy, suggests that there are so many unknown factors about the supply–demand interrelationships that there is no reason to take too seriously anyone's forecast of what will happen to any specific commodity over a long period of time.

If all this is true, if we generally do have adequate resources for reasonably projected demands to the year 2000, but our predictive skills as applied to specific commodities are very limited, what should we as planners be thinking about? First and foremost is the necessity to recognize that we are concerned primarily not with adequacy of supply but with access to supplies. Access will be determined by the availability of investment capital, the political considerations of environment, supplier country stability, and supplier and user country monetary needs. Such thinking is increasingly leading to consideration of greater use of commodity agreements which address themselves not only to supply and demand but also to optimum stocks. One recent study in the United States indicated that inventory purchasing practices were a major factor in the current recession. The study showed that a change by one month in the purchasing lead time for aluminum alone has a $1.4 billion impact on the economy. The study also concluded that most inventory shifts were not mistakes but purposeful attempts to protect against possible shortages and price increases. The result is false prosperity followed by recession. It is one purpose of commodity agreements to eliminate uncertainty which leads to these unsettling actions.

The other major factor to be watched with regard to supply is the cost of energy. I believe that the relative cost of energy will come down significantly, although not to previous levels. I do not believe that arbitrary political restraints will be successful in preventing such a decline.

From the point of view of demand, product design, material substitution, and recycling seem to hold the greatest opportunities for amelioration of short-term problems, but only if responsible individuals give these matters greater attention than they have in the past. In the long term, conservation seems to be equally promising. The overall picture will most certainly respond to what we set as overriding priorities in the political arena, both domestically and internationally.

As a closing comment, I would like to quote François-Xavier Ortoli, recent President of the Commission of the European Economic Communities: "The important thing is to have an intimation, beyond the immediate moment, of new forms to which reason gives a certain face, but whose features are modified by dreams."[3]

REFERENCES

1. *Proceedings of the Council of Economics of the AIME Annual Meeting,* New York, March 1–4, 1971, p. 21.

2. Summary of *Proceedings of the First World Symposium on Energy and Raw Materials,* Paris, June 6–8, 1974 (New York: The Committee for Economic Development), p. 22.

3. Summary of *Proceedings of the First World Symposium on Energy and Raw Materials,* Paris, June 6–8, 1974 (New York: The Committee for Economic Development), p. 116.

Part III
SOCIAL RESPONSIBILITY

JOHN THACKRAY

Audits Aim
Social Strategy

THE BLACK RIOTS of the mid-1960s profoundly changed the atmosphere in the modern corporation—regardless of how little those protests may seem to have done for civil rights. After the fires of Watts, Detroit, and Newark were extinguished, large corporations reacted to the cries of frustration. But initially, there was much inflated rhetoric about how corporations, like knights in shining armor, could slay the dragons of racial hatred, unemployment, and slum housing. There were inevitable disappointments, and many false turnings. The problems of our urban society proved far more intractable than activists within corporations imagined. Nearly all corporations which sponsored projects of "social responsibility" found that their achievements—when there were any—fell far short of targets.

Prior to Watts, most corporations had tended to accept the world as it is, and society at face value—the face and faces seen from the executive suite. Corporations neglected the opportunity to improve society except as taxpayers and as the chief providers of employment and economic growth. Their attitude was passive. Society was for politicians, social scientists, or revolutionaries to fret about. To be sure, the corporation did *some* interacting with the fabric of society. It gave to charity, for example: typically the United Fund or the Chairman's favorite cause.

Today some corporations have decided to take a more direct and novel approach to social problems and to analyzing and assessing the interface between business and society. They have come to realize that as part of society they too will suffer from society's problems and therefore must work to find solutions. As a result, some corporations have created their own staff of experts and techniques for assessing and monitoring social issues. This, in a nutshell, is the significance of the "social responsibility" movement.

Once the social consciousness function is institutionalized within the company, it can be systematically planned for, analyzed, and, in some cases, the effectiveness of social-action programs can be assessed and measured. Top management, as well as division managers and the planner, must decide the intensity of the company commitment, as well as the shape and form it should take.

There are a handful of very large corporations who are social planning trail blazers: for example, Chase Manhattan Bank or IBM or Cummins Engine, where topmost management—sometimes a single powerful chief executive officer—has decided, *a priori,* that the company should make a maximum feasible commitment to social problems and social therapies. These companies have gone far beyond the requirements of the collective corporate conscience, or of the law. Frequently they have let business decisions be influenced by considerations not traditionally regarded as part of business: as when, for example, IBM built a plant in New York's Bedford Stuyvesant ghetto.

Ordinarily corporations make a more restricted interpretation of their responsibilities. Their top management tends to be less politicized. They want to comply with human rights laws and pollution control regulations, but within the time-tested framework of shareholder-oriented profit maximization.

In both the leaders and followers there are changes of procedure apparent. The old, unanalyzed procedures for charitable distribution and minority hiring are being shelved. And in their place a new set of methodologies is emerging. These methodologies call for new types of information gathering; new awareness of the highly complex and not-at-all-well-understood interreaction between the corporate state and the public state. What's more, as this technology emerges and is refined, the entire field of social responsibility will be increasingly amenable to long-range planning, to systematic analysis and evaluation.

Already there have been a number of new and valuable techniques developed. One of these is the corporate Community Audit—a process wherein large corporations examine the environment around their major facilities. The purpose of the Community Audit is to isolate and define community problems and corporate opportunities for social action. With this data it is then possible for the corporation intelligently to structure specific approaches, policies, and programs—targeted to genuine needs, not just traditional institutions.

One company with extensive experience with the Community Audit is Babcock & Wilcox, a manufacturer of power generation units, which owns 30 plants in the United States. At Babcock & Wilcox, nine different Community Audits were completed in 1972 and 1973. They ranged from large cities to towns of 14,000. The information developed from these audits provided local plant management with data upon which to base programs. It also provided corporate management with a macro view of society in general, thereby providing it with trends data to plan corporate programs.

The man in charge of Community Audits at Babcock & Wilcox is George C. Valli, head of Corporate Community Relations. The intense but affable Valli has thoroughly sounded the *zeitgeist* of Middle America—principally in the South and Midwest.

His findings often reverse preconceived notions. For example, it is widely recognized that drugs can present a problem for industry. Yet most businessmen share the belief that drugs are a big city problem. Not so, says Valli. "Drugs are a national problem. In one town in the South, with a population of under 30,000, a town which is in the middle of nowhere, there are many very sophisticated drug users. Nor is crime a big city problem alone. Psychologically the effect of real or imaginary crime is ubiquitous. In many small towns people feel that they are living in the middle of a crime wave. Women won't go out and shop at night. But if you look at the statistics, there's hardly any crime at all in many cases."

The fundamental purposes of the Community Audit, however, is not to arrive at generalized truths about the pulse of the nation. It has a more modest and palpable objective: namely, to discover in a town, or a borough, or a county, the underlying social structure and community climate as they affect the corporation's interests.

An initial problem commonly faced by those directing the new corporate social responsiveness is to convince senior management of its long and short-range importance: to spell out how a company can be adversely affected by a poor social environment. For example, senior management must be convinced that heavy drug consumption and alcoholism in the community can spread to plants and offices. Within the corporate borders, these pathologies can then cause an increase in accidents. They may also affect the quality of production. And they certainly undermine discipline.

Moreover, higher accident rates eventually mean higher medical payments by the corporation or higher insurance premiums, workers' compensation, indemnity bills. The effects of a poor local school system can be just as devastating in the profit and loss column. Poor schools ultimately saddle the company with hiring less than adequately qualified personnel. This in turn affects the quality of production. Or the company has to pay for additional and remedial training to bring these under-educated workers up to standard.

Housing discrimination can adversely affect a company's capacity to hire minority executives—or to freely transfer minority member executives between company locations. More broadly, a declining community eventually will result in the imposition of higher taxes. Services will decline: roads, local health institutions, etc. The cumulative effect of this is that a company can find its capacity to recruit professional and management personnel seriously diminished.

These examples also point to another change in the way some corporations look at social responsibility. Rather than approaching the solution of social problems through a philosophy of philanthropy or charity, the attempt here is to provide a profit motive to their solution. Simply stated, the social responsibility policy of Babcock & Wilcox is that the company's long-term profitability is dependent on a continuing healthy social, economic, and political environment.

Given the complexity and scope of such challenges, it's clear that the traditional methods used by corporations to relate to their local communities are not adequate anymore.

The actual procedures in a Community Audit are simple and easily explained to senior management. First, the corporate community auditor studies selected published data on the town. Valli reads the newspapers of that community for three months to determine the major visible problem areas and identify people who might be knowledgeable about them. He then sits down with company personnel and interviews them on their views about the community—positive and negative—and asks them to identify persons in the community who could address themselves to these major issues. In addition, the auditor-investigator selects his own interview candidates within the community. Since it is essential that all levels of the power structure be given a hearing, and that all special interest groups be contacted, Valli's list of interviewees includes bank presidents as well as hourly workers, teachers, students, and the superintendent of schools. In these interviews he takes a comprehensive check list that details the most likely problem areas, such as general economic conditions, housing, drugs, alcoholism, transportation, leadership, race relations, taxes, education, pollution, recreation, poverty, employment, youth, health, the aged, crime/police relations, cultural affairs, and civic and charitable organizations.

As part of its investigation, the corporate auditor also makes an internal survey of resources, including the contributions, budget, manpower, and facilities which are available for use in helping to solve community problems.

At an early point in the investigation, the auditor will have to determine the parameters of the community being studied, whether it's the immediate neighborhood, the city, or the county. This act of definition is crucial to the method of investigation and will, in turn, influence the kinds of problems that surface and the kinds of remedies the corporation should take. For instance, a plant could be in the inner city or in a suburb. In the former case, the company could define the community of the plant as either the immediate neighborhood, or as the city as a whole.

The Community Audit's practical goal is to obtain a true social topography of the community. To get this, Valli usually conducts between 25 and 50 interviews—depending on the size of the community and the problems raised. He then authors a report for the local management's community relations program. Subsequently, local policies and programs are monitored from corporate headquarters.

Aside from the possibilities of its generating new strategies and approaches, the Community Audit can be useful in preventing mistakes. For example, in one municipality local management was busy nurturing a black enterprise. But the Community Audit revealed that there was in reality very little black unemployment in town, and that the project had little sponsorship support within the black community. The biggest problem identified by the Community Audit was black *under*employment. Accordingly, a more useful approach was to upgrade jobs within local factories.

In several smaller towns the Community Audit showed that the drug education program was naive. Local adolescents needed no lessons on drug use. In fact, there was some evidence that drug education only accelerated drug use. This project has been scrapped in favor of a more promising and realistic drug prevention effort. In yet another town, Valli discovered that alcohol abuse was a serious social problem: not just in homes and bars, but within the company itself. The answer: an in-plant alcohol abuse program. In a Canadian town, the Community Audit revealed that few company personnel were involved in community affairs. This now is being remedied.

Perhaps the best way of understanding a Community Audit is actually to see the results of one. The following much-abbreviated report, dated Spring of 1972, is taken from the Community Audit at a large, industrial Midwestern facility. Babcock & Wilcox is the dominant employer in the region and has a high visibility. The town was undergoing crises on many fronts. According to Valli, the interviews with 53 community leaders had two main objectives:

1. To identify social, economic, and cultural needs of the community which have not been met.

2. To highlight specific needs which Babcock & Wilcox can help meet—either directly, or in concert with other local leadership.

Both objectives were developed in an effort to comply with our corporate policy of social responsibility.

The Community Audit developed some strong recommendations of a general nature, as follows:

SHORT-TERM RECOMMENDATIONS

1. *Consideration should be given to some form of intensive education program concerning drug abuse and alcoholism—both in the plant and in the community.*

2. *Attempts should be made to determine the skill needs of the underemployed, both black and white. The intent would be to become involved in a total community effort to reduce poverty by preparing people for local jobs.*

LONG-TERM RECOMMENDATIONS

1. *Efforts should be made to provide the city with effective leaders, both in and out of government, both from B&W and from other organizations.*

2. *A new concerted effort should be made by industrial and commercial interests to stem the economic deterioration of the city.*

3. *The Governor and the State Legislature should be made aware of the transportation difficulties faced by the area. B&W should organize the effort to get necessary highways and bridges built.*

4. *B&W should take a more active role in local, county, and state politics and government relations.*

In support of these recommendations, the Community Audit offered an extensive analysis of the problems of this town, and the interface between corporation and community. Highlights of this report are:

BABCOCK & WILCOX IN THE COMMUNITY

Babcock & Wilcox is the major influence in the community. As might have been expected, there are two conflicting opinions about B&W's role in that community. Some interviewees indicated that B&W was influencing events and "running" various civic and social groups.

The opposite opinion was shared by a greater number of those we talked with: that while B&W is actively involved in the community we do not contribute our share, nor do we wield our "power" in the best interests of the community. These contradictory opinions were sometimes expressed by the same person.

Opinions were often given that B&W should use its influence with state government to obtain programs and money for the area, for example, in transportation and downtown revitalization matters. Others pointed out that even by doing little or nothing, B&W was allowing the city to die as a commercial center.

It should be noted that several people interviewed stated that B&W management was the most capable of any similar group in the country. The assumption was made that if B&W became committed to solving some of the area's problems, B&W had sufficient expertise to develop solutions.

One interviewee stated that "Anything that happens in this community will be put at B&W's doorstep. You employ over 5,000 people. The next largest employer is under 500. If you fellows really get involved, some will say that you are trying to run everything. But it's the only way real improvement can be made.

And you will get even more criticism if things don't improve. You really can't ex-pect to win."

As will be shown in the sections of this report which follow, problem areas were discovered in almost every topic explored. We also discovered that there were B&W people involved in each subject area. What we uncovered was the request of community leaders that B&W management get more deeply committed and involved, and—in many case—assume direct control of community efforts.

The greatest problems facing this community are: a loss of employment and a resulting deterioration of the economic base of the area; inadequate housing; poor transportation systems; a leadership vacuum; racism; and drug and alcoholism problems.

Although drugs, alcoholism, and racism are the only areas which have a direct effect within the plant, any priority criteria for establishing new programs should include the long-term implications that economic deterioration, inadequate housing, poor transportation, and lack of leadership must have upon B&W.

GENERAL ECONOMIC CONDITION

The downtown business or shopping district of a city often determines the "character" of the city and its surrounding communities. For decades, this town was a major shopping area. This is no longer true.

The deterioration of the downtown area ranks as one of the most important problems the community faces. This fall from economic and commercial vitality directly affects and adversely contributes to the community's drug traffic, poverty and unemployment, youth problems, rising crime rates, racism, higher taxes, and other problems affecting the area.

There are several reasons for this decline of the downtown area. Undeniably, a major factor is the Mall which opened outside of town last year. Another such mall, already proposed, could cause more serious economic hardships on the town. In the downtown area, absentee landlords are reluctant to concern themselves with needed building improvements and maintenance. In addition, many shopkeepers are elderly and refuse to invest large sums of money to expand or modernize. The traffic problem mentioned in another section of this report is also a major contributor to the decline.

Although numbers of storefronts are vacant and the prices of real estate properties along the main retail area are significantly depreciated, two construction projects in the downtown area are presently underway.

A redevelopment program has been authorized by the county and state for a portion of the south end of town. The redeveloped area will most likely include several middle-income housing units and a small area for industrial development.

A Charter Study Committee was organized by the local Chamber of Commerce and endorsed by the voters last fall to recommend to the voters alternative forms of city government. The committee's studies will be completed in June and the voters will vote on the recommendations this fall.

TRANSPORTATION

In the last six months a transportation problem has escalated into a situation of very serious proportions. The following has occurred: (1) The Motor Coach Company has discontinued its routes through the area. (2) The State Highway Department has informed the community that a main artery to and from downtown will be closed to all traffic for a three-month period for repairs. (3) The only new four-lane highway proposed for the area is running years behind schedule. It has been learned from state officials that it will not be completed through the town until the 1980's. (4) A By-Pass, which was proposed to eliminate through-traffic from the downtown area, will not begin construction for a six-year period. (5) Parking facilities are inadequate in town and it was learned that the City Parking Authority has become a serious financial liability. It was stated that parking meter receipts are low and if they reduce further the City will be forced to use General Funds to more extensively subsidize a service which is not now very well utilized.

HOUSING

Most of those interviewed stated the belief that there are shortages of housing and apartments and that the middle class is leaving the older, more established urban centers and moving to the suburbs. Statistics support these opinions.

EDUCATION

The major problem in the local school districts is one of overcrowding and old facilities. Both school systems are in the process of building new high schools and reorganizing existing facilities.

The drug problem in both school districts is serious. Lately muggings and extortions have taken place within the schools and these can be directly related to the drug problem.

Racial tensions have increased in the schools resulting in one major outbreak which occurred in the downtown business district last year and continuing skirmishes, particularly among junior high school students. These tensions are expected to increase.

A significant segment of the people hired for the bargaining unit at our plant do have educational deficiencies. Some have completed only a few years schooling. Others have more schooling but have not completed all the requirements for a high school diploma.

The Manpower Development Department has had a program designed to help employes obtain high school diplomas for several years. Also, employes are encouraged to further their education at the expense of the company through the Educational Refund Plan.

There is at present a group attempting to gain support for a vocational high school. Their response from the local Manufacturers' Association was almost totally negative. Although management has not yet taken a position on this issue, the general consensus appears to be that various internal education programs are meeting our needs.

RECREATION

Reaction toward the adequacy of recreational facilities in the community was mixed. Among those people interviewed who had a direct involvement with various recreation programs (Little League, Boy Scouts, YMCA, etc.) the overall feeling was that the facilities were barely adequate. Where ballfields and parks exist, they are ill-kept with a minimum of equipment.

These people identify the following as problem areas: the one local swimming pool is too small to handle the crowds; the YMCA is old, unattractive, poorly located and does not attract a sufficient number of users; there is no adequate facility or area available for teenagers at night with the result that poolrooms, hamburger stands, and the library steps have become "hangouts."

B&W, whose workforce makes up about 30 percent of the "heads of households" in the area, provides sporting facilities and programs for employes. These include softball teams, bowling leagues, Children's Christmas Party, employe picnic, golf tournament, etc. They are not available to the general public.

RACE RELATIONS

In the general population, basic race relations problems exist in housing, schools, and employment. In housing, most blacks live in ghetto areas, some of which can properly be called slums. Most of the unpaved streets to be found in town, for example, are in the area which is predominantly black.

It was indicated in several conversations that it is more difficult for a black, regardless of financial considerations, to obtain mortgages or credit from local banks.

Local realtors indicated willingness to have blacks as customers and professed to practice no discrimination—due primarily to fear of loss of license. However, some form of discrimination is obviously being practiced.

The major concern of the black community was identified as poverty. While unemployment is approximately 6 percent (accurate figures were not obtainable), the level of jobs available and advancement opportunities appear quite limited for minority members. There was some concern that vocational education was inadequate, especially for black girls in the clerical field, and that remedial training would be beneficial.

There is no single effective black group. The black community was unable to sustain a Community Action Program. The Neighborhood Youth Corps appears to be doing more counseling than job training or placement.

DRUGS

The problem is centered in the schools with an estimated 50–60 percent of junior-senior high school students having at least experimented with some form of drug other than alcohol. During the past 12–18 months drug usage was found almost exclusively in the high school; however, the current concern now among law enforcement, health officials, and educators is that drug abuse is spreading to students in the 7th, 8th, and 9th grades.

The predominant drug is marijuana. The use of LSD—which at one time was used extensively—has declined appreciably during the past year to the point where it is now almost non-existent. The abuse of amphetamines and barbituates among more affluent students is now widespread.

The most important change in the drug scene (aside from the growth in numbers of users) is the introduction of heroin to the area. It is estimated that there are approximately 50–75 heroin addicts in the area.

One of the most important side effects of this increased drug usage is the rising crime rate which is discussed in the section on crime.

Health services appear adequate to handle detoxification of addicts.

Babcock & Wilcox has taken the lead in recognizing the dangers of the drug problem. Most of those we talked with mentioned the B&W program which began last fall.

As a result of B&W's educational effort, community groups and leaders interested in doing something to curb drug abuse come to B&W for opinions and advice.

There appears to be no major drug problem in the plant although there are reports of several employes who are suspected of being drug users or are associating with known users. There have been no drug-related incidents in the plant and no indication that drugs are used in the plant.

However, if a large portion of the school population is using drugs, then this problem must eventually surface in the plant.

ALCOHOLISM

Alcoholism appears to be no greater a problem in the area than in other similar areas. The vast majority of arrests are for drunk and disorderly conduct.

POLLUTION

The major pollution control activity in the area is the $14,000,000 expenditure by B&W for air and water pollution control equipment. Most of those interviewed made mention of this program and were impressed and gratified by B&W's commitment.

CRIME

There is a general increase of crime in the area, which in some cases is quite dramatic. House burglaries have increased rapidly in the past year, especially in the more affluent areas. These are generally attributed to the increased use of drugs among young people.

The biggest problem identified by the Police Department is the youth problem. Fights, vandalism, and rowdy behavior in the district are increasing.

In response to this complex of interrelated problems, local management has become more active in the community. It is aggressively seeking new solutions to the main issues, and is especially active in trying to find answers to the fundamental and chronic leadership problem. Needless to say, the Community Audit cannot take credit for all new initiatives or for identifying all the essential problems. The problems in the community were known to local management before it ever heard of the term Community Audit.

The central usefulness of this managerial device is twofold. One, it brings all the problems systematically into focus—after which options can be more clearly analyzed. Two, it makes it evident to local management that corporate headquarters will measure and assess its interaction with the community and make this assessment a formalized part of its performance appraisals. Thus, in a sense, the Community Audit broadens local management's area of accountability, and encourages it to widen its horizons and to use corporate power more effectively.

WALTER P. BLASS

Corporate Governance— What's Ahead

THE CHIEF EXECUTIVE OFFICER is speaking:

The FTC is threatening to go to court against our toy division for false adver-
tising—on toys, mind you. The city fathers are about to convince some judge in
Wisconsin that we are killing people with our paper factory. The management
people in our own headquarters complex not thirty miles from here are talking
about "flexible hours." The head of some women's organization wants to know,
obviously for publication, how many female officers we have, so she can go to
EEOC I suppose and drag us into court. Who's running this company? Am I or
are all these kibitzers?

This report deals with the answers to that question. For the mythical
CEO in the above paragraph is not so mythical; each of the president's
trials has been endured by a real person in the past two years. The man
is actually rather prescient in his final question, rather than merely a
male chauvinist, a polluter, rigid, or too lightly involved in social responsibility. He is asking a question as basic as those asked by Berle and
Means,[1] Schumpeter,[2] and Burnham.[3] Who is running a capitalist corporation, on whose behalf, and with what limitations on his power?

Within the past decade we have seen in this country, and to a lesser
degree in Europe, a growing awareness of a diffusion in the purpose of a
corporation. Contrary to Milton Friedman's dictum[4] that the purpose of
business is to make a profit, period, a growing sentiment has been
expressed, accepted, and gradually enshrined in administrative and civil
law that corporations have other duties, other responsibilities, and may
be measured by criteria other than dollars on the bottom line.

J. P. Morgan and Andrew Carnegie, not to mention Cornelius Van-
derbilt, would have smirked at the notion of a monthly journal called
Business and Society Review and guffawed at the idea of being interviewed by it. But two leading bankers, Walter Wriston[5] and David
Rockefeller,[6] have been interviewed by such a journal and have articu-

lated their views on what business owes society. A movement for social accountability is growing, even as the definition of what that means is in dispute. Directors have been sued both for failing to disclose sufficient information about their firms and for failing to exercise sufficient diligence in discovering information, particularly when damaging to stockholders. Customers, workers, citizens of communities where corporations exert influence, fellow businessmen (outraged at the "bad name" of American business abroad), congressmen, and bureaucrats, all are proving to be effective forces in limiting the freedom of action of the chief executive officer and his corporation.

STYLES OF GOVERNING

In studying the subject of what constrains the CEO, it may be useful to distinguish four quite different styles of governance. I am using this more general term, rather than the usual simpler synonyms of "running a corporation," "directing," "presiding over," etc., because I wish to stress the potential lessons from other domains. Table 1 illustrates these different styles.

Table 1. Governance forms.

Character	Military	Market	Political	Systems Analysis
Organizational structure	Line-staff functional	Market group, management by objective, profit centers	Constituencies block tradeoffs	PPBS corporate planning, eclectic
Power	Absolute	Checked by competition	Majority vote; minority obstruction	Logic, as defined by analyst
Redress	Through chain of command	Exit from vendor, buyer, or market	Election; recall or impeachment	Better logic; better feedback loop; action after failure
Direction of authority	Downward	External	Upward, except as agreed to by law, or manipulated	Downward from analyst

Most business readers will not have difficulty identifying the cells in this table into which their companies fit. A few corporations still run largely on military lines, but as William Irwin Thompson[7] points out, some of the lineal descendants of the warrior are much more refined in their exercise of power. The market-oriented organization, rather than seeking its goals from within, takes its cue, more or less, totally from outside, maximizing only the bottom line, regardless of other factors. The political form stresses its accountability downward and corresponds to the character of the make-up of its constituencies ("A people deserves the leadership it gets"). The "scientific approach" of systems analysis (McNamara, International Minerals and Chemicals[8]) is elegant, easily and neatly described in a logical diagram, but currently under a cloud due to major errors in the perception of the less quantifiable factors in society (nationalism, "people power," price elasticity of supply).

THE CHANGING CORPORATE ENVIRONMENT

Such a taxonomy may help us to understand what business' reactions to major changes in the environment have been. I use the term "environment" in its widest context; Chairman Mao's phrase comes to mind, with corporation substituted for Party: "We in the Party are like fish in the sea; we must depend on the people for breath, food, and protection." This environment has changed appreciably in the past three decades. Some of the changes that have occurred are listed in Table 2.

Change, thus portrayed, bears heavily on the role of the chief executive. He can no longer expect to rule from the apex of a pyramid, isolated in his wood-paneled office, choosing his principal officers with care, and leaving the operational responsibilities to them. Increasingly he is exposed more to the external world, however large or small his company or nonprofit organization. Increasingly his personal style of governance is subject to the exigencies of the world. Indeed, a statement often used in historical studies is applicable to corporations: Times shape the man.

What Lies Ahead?

Let us test this hypothesis by prophesying the future. If Table 2 is correct, what lies ahead for the governance of corporations? I will make four predictions of what the future will hold for corporations, and then point to five areas where they are likely to fail.

1. There will be an increased emphasis on the board of directors, with specific goals set and public accountability and personal responsibility for meeting them established.

When a debate erupts in the pages of the *Harvard Business Review*, one can generally assume that within five years the average Fortune 500 firm will be applying, rightly or wrongly, the conclusions reached. In 1974 there was a rash of articles dealing with how the CEO ought to work with his board of directors. Fewer articles start from the other end and ask what the role of the directors should be. Much of the discussion is still vague, but the following issues seem to be emerging.

Table 2. Changes in the corporate environment.

Then (1920–1930)	*Now (1970–1980)*
Tasks	
Fixed technology	Rapid change technology
Fixed/limited market	Much larger/smaller markets
Fixed production functions (no productivity growth; no technological change)	Requirement for improvement in productivity to overcome cost squeeze of inflation
Obedient work force	Militant unions
	Equal opportunities for minorities and women
	Self-actualizing demands of employees
Product/service acceptance	Consumerism
	Naderism
	Safety
	Truth in advertising
	Quick changes in values and tastes
Environment	
Local/federal government passivity	Government activism
	Ombudsman
	Consumer spokesman in White House
	EPA
	Congressional Office of Technology Assessment
	Economic jawboning
	Cost of Living Council/incomes policy
Regional and national factor or product market	Multinational work force, capital, products, information
Stability	Periodic change
Highly structured	Ambiguous
	Ad hoc
	Taking advantage of temporary resources
Organizational Response	
Total dependence on information from below and within organization	Heavy emphasis on outside feedback or validation
Accountability specified at lowest level, vague at top	Directors, CEO objectives set and publicly accountable

(a) The board has the ultimate responsibility for determining the future course of the company. It is the directors who choose the chief executive and who must remove him for nonfeasance or misfeasance.

(b) Representation on the board, especially in large national corporations, not only will be based on ownership, but will also reflect major inputs to that company's factor markets. Bankers have sat on corporate boards for a long time, but "public" figures such as Leon Sullivan at General Motors and Arthur Goldberg formerly at TWA will appear more often, and so will union leaders, militant churchmen, activist foundation chairpersons, and—lo and behold—consumerists. It is not unlikely that governments also will appoint directors.

(c) Specific goals will be set by the board for the company, whether by broad areas of business, profit targets, employee make-up including upward mobility, or social responsibilities by major categories.

(d) Audit committees of the board not only will be concerned with the post hoc audit of the books of the company by the company's hired auditors, but will present to the board their conclusions on whether and to what degree the goals stated above have been met, and if not, who is responsible. Task forces commissioned by the board will most likely be formed with subpoena-like powers to make this provision effective. These moves will be even more probable as a preventive measure to forestall increased governmental intrusion on such accountability of major corporatons.

2. The need for increased sensitivity to externalities of the firm will be recognized and acted on at the highest levels by emergent organizations.

Several years ago the increased impact of government on corporations was acknowledged by the creation of the Vice President's Public Affairs/Government Relations or VP/Washington Office. *Dun's Review*[9] featured an article in which these functions were described in detail and their importance weighed in the usual American coin: salary levels of the individuals concerned. But externalities do not end with Washington. A corporation the size of General Motors, General Electric, Exxon, or American Electric Power, with hundreds of thousands of employees, capital budgets in the billions, and wage-setting patterns that sweep across the nation and overseas, must become aware of many other areas of concern.

(a) Pollution needs little further headlining. The case of Reserve Mining Company on Lake Superior suggests only that every company of any consequence must reassess its effluents and their impact on both human communities and uninhabited areas.

(b) Employee welfare is another area of broad influence that has surfaced in recent years, with a major emphasis not merely on the present company work force, but on the future work force both inside and outside the company. We may expect to see even greater demands on corporations for substantive impacts regarding labor mobility, training, and broadly defined education, hours of work, work content, and equal treatment of males and females, nonwhites and whites, citizens and immigrants, affluent and disadvantaged youths. Many companies will discover that further improvements in productivity lie less in more capital per se than in major changes in how employees use capital resources, for example, team-size batch processing versus assembly lines and computerization for fewer reports.

(c) Community impact of the corporation is an area of growing concern. Nowhere is this more clear than in the area of housing. A landmark case is the city of Petaluma, California, which seeks to enjoin further building on its boundaries. Although the plaintiffs are not large corporations but primarily small builders, the issues involved have a heavy bearing on the rights of the community to regulate corporate influence. In France closing a plant is very difficult; in Japan layoffs are unheard of. This is an area in which the United States might follow rather than lead, and therefore it may be easier for businesses to learn from others' mistakes.

(d) Societal values are changing and few corporations seem to be aware of these changes. Whether the issue is permissiveness, zero population growth, privacy, or changing lifestyles, few of the larger companies seem to take these changes into account or to know what impact they may have on their basic way of conducting business.

3. The impact of these changes, outside and inside the firm, will lead to more multidimensionality in appropriate measurements.

It is interesting to note how many companies make changes in their organizational structures but leave the basic measurements which their officers study untouched. Often the direction of change in measurements is toward more detail rather than toward a broader spectrum of possible measurements. The concern with the speed of change is usually expressed in the desire to get the existing measurements sooner ("fifth working day after the end of the month") rather than in looking for measurements of the broader institutional or secular changes.

(a) Earnings per share will no longer be the sole measure of corporate performance. As inflation's ravages continue to be felt, real rates of return after inflation, discounted cash flow calculations in real dollars, and opportunity costs, rather than earnings per share, will reflect a company's success.

(b) Beyond profitability, however measured, investors will demand indications of future performance. Market size and share, degree of technological innovation and cost savings, and regard for customer opinion, especially on newer products or services, will be insisted on.

(c) Employees will have a larger role in the new measurements. In addition to looking outside for validation of their marketing or technological strategies, companies will ask employees directly or indirectly for their "vote of confidence."

(d) The secondary consequences of technological change will be studied in terms of their impact on company measurements. Are we competing with ourselves in order to forestall outside competition? Are we anticipating labor force needs three to ten years ahead, considering simultaneous changes in technology and management thinking? Are we acting in time on predicted changes in available energy, land, trained work force, or societal reactions to new possibilities?

(e) With this plenitude of possible measurements, management will have to guard against a broad diffusion of purpose of the corporation. As politicians have discovered, trying to take advantage of every shift of the wind can get you nowhere. The corporation may have to learn to be far more aware of many dimensions but to retain a firm grasp on a limited purpose.

4. Governance by agreement is likely to become more evident in business as it has in universities and government.

One of the oldest political forms, the coalition government, is slowly making its way into other domains. When electorates were unable to make decisive choices among competing philosophies or programs, representative government leaders found it necessary to make temporary, sometimes lasting alliances with other parties to form governing coalitions that could muster majority votes in parliaments.

After the troubles in American universities and colleges in the 1960s, many schools experimented with a technique that had proved effective for many years in some Quaker colleges: the consensual decision-making body. Students as well as faculty and administrators were queried, and the agreement of all was obtained before action was taken. Cumbersome as this may seem it is more effective than a school torn by rioting, a government overthrown by a repressed opposition, or a business ruined by rigid union demands for work rules and wages that are economically unfeasible.

(a) The concept of the office of the president, executive policy committees, and even a chief executive as *primus inter pares* will spread in large corporations. As the requirement for representation of various interest groups becomes more acute both from above (boards of directors) and below (employee groups), as markets change the whole composition of a firm within a single decade, as technology revolutionizes production or distribution methods, the whole concept of the role of the chief executive will change. The traditional hierarchy of command will begin to fade and roles will be redefined. Robert Greenleaf's suggestion[10] of a CEO as merely a first among equals reflects both a recognition of the limitations of any one individual and the conviction that a group composed of dissimilar individuals can achieve diversity within unity. This is not leadership by committee, but a sharing of responsibility without a weakening or obscuring of roles.

(b) The military concept of holding a single general accountable for results regardless of outside factors is no longer widely held. Similarly, the old comfortable baronies, such as a legal department, African and Asiatic operations, or even personnel, where no one interfered so long as nothing disastrous occurred, are fading. Today's corporation unit, whether business, university, or even semi-governmental, has to pull its weight as a whole, lest by its failure the whole goes down. Decisions still need to be made, risks taken, and leadership exerted, but policies must be formulated on the basis of shared kowledge, shared assumptions, and shared risks. Thus the organizational model of the firm in the latter part of the decade will reflect both the *stiffer goals* of the board and the *team responsibility* of the decentralized or functional unit.

Failure to Adjust

Finally, I should like to point to five areas where corporations are likely to fail to heed these lessons.

1. *Political insensitivity.* ITT, Howard Hughes, and several airlines are probably not the last fish to be caught in a lake of anonymity and darkness that is rapidly drying up. More and more firms will learn that every significant action will be as exposed as the politician's act, will be covered in a specialized press if not in the general media, and may even be exposed by insiders who are disaffected. Large corporations don't just make the equivalent of the GNP of smaller governments: they are governments and, more often than not, in the future they will be held accountable to the population at large just as governments are. Corruption, internal strife, gross abuse of individuals, and failure to give due process to grievances will be as damaging to firms as they are to governments.

2. *Refusal to take into account changing social values.* Despite what I suggested previously about the desirability, nay the necessity, of surveillance of the outside environment, many firms still have policies that discriminate in the hiring, promotion, or cross-training of women and social deviants such as ex-criminals or drug users; insist on internal procedures that violate the privacy of the individual ("Do you intend to have children?"); and rely on absolute managerial judgment rather than on internal or external consensus. The increasing diversity of values will complicate corporate decision-making no end, but the regarding of social values as fixed ("That's the way we've always handled that problem") or as interpreted internally probably will be one of the most frequently made errors.

3. *Disregard for the Equal Employment Opportunity Commission.*

One corporation continued to fight an EEOC action after being notified by its general counsel that out of 115 cases litigated, 107 had been decided in the plaintiff's favor. I do not yet see a substantive acceptance by corporate America of the reality of this organization or what it stands for.

4. *Failure to set up adequate environmental surveillance units* (as a corollary to the first point). Although some corporations have already instituted such units with great success in terms of operational changes, cost reductions, or in less quantifiable terms related to political and institutional vulnerabilities, most probably never will attempt such measures. Too often companies are able to digest only information that is generated through the normal channels of the personnel, marketing, legal, or finance departments. They can maintain activity, but not initiate it.

5. *Hearing, seeing, and smelling danger, but not acting on it.* This final failure is the most ironic. The clear and present danger doctrine of Justice Holmes appears to be held even more vigorously in corporate board rooms than in law courts. Twenty years after the fertility rate began to decline in the United States, the Gerber Company, according to *Business Week,* is reeling from the dearth of babies. Similarly, 30-odd years after the evolution of the supermarket, drug companies are discovering that the old-fashioned drugstore is no longer an important vehicle for their products. Fifteen years after the Japanese government created a measurement of the ratio of new or advanced technology exports to standard commodity exports, firms in the United States and Europe are still running to their governments for tariff relief on shoes, textiles, cement, and the simplest iron and steel products. What will it take to convince these companies that their demise is foreordained if they do not act?

SUMMARY

In summary, I have tried to suggest in this contribution that the old-fashioned style of running a corporation is likely to result in great perils. The changes in the requirements for worker motivation, increased sales in zero population markets, rapid technological change, and increased political and social sensitivity to corporate actions all point to the need for changes in top management style. Persons both above and below the CEO are involved. Indeed the concept of the chief itself may give way to the group, and the bottom line may give way to a multifaceted set of measurements that represent the past and future of a company rather than merely a snapshot of a butterfly in flight. Unfortunately, failure to adjust to these changes is likely, and the consequences will be serious.

What does all this activity affecting the CEO mean to the corporate planner? First, it suggests that the planner should keep an eye on the societal and organizational developments mentioned above. Often he can do so more systematically and comprehensively than the CEO. Second, the planner, "if he is to get closer to the chief executive and has some tendency even toward becoming a peer of the CEO,"[11] must make sure his supervisor acts in awareness of these developments. The CEO shouldn't find himself booby-trapped by "instinctive" reactions learned in bygone days of greater freedom of action. Finally, if the failures pointed to here are to be avoided, the corporate planner will have to find his voice in executive councils. He will have to find a coherent, convincing way of bringing together amorphous warnings and forecasts or disparate facts. And he will have to find the courage of his convictions, to be willing to stake his professional reputation on his advice as much as the product manager or the general counsel.

REFERENCES

1. Adolf A. Berle and Gardiner C. Means, *The Modern Corporation and Private Property*, rev. ed. (New York: Harcourt, Brace, Jovanovich, 1968).

2. Joseph A. Schumpeter, *Capitalism, Socialism and Democracy*, 3rd ed. (New York: Harper & Row, 1950).

3. James Burnham, *The Managerial Revolution: What Is Happening in the World Today* (New York: The John Day Company, 1941).

4. Milton A. Friedman, with the assistance of Rose D. Friedman, *Capitalism and Freedom* (Chicago: University of Chicago Press, 1962).

5. Walter Wriston, "World Corporations: Saints or Sinners?" *Business and Society Review/Innovation*, Winter 1973–1974.

6. Theodore Cross, "The Dilemma of Corporate Responsibility and Maximum Profits: An interview with David Rockefeller," *Business and Society Review/Innovation*, Winter 1973–1974.

7. William Irwin Thompson, *At the Edge of History* (New York: Harper & Row, 1971).

8. Robert McNamara was Secretary of Defense under President Kennedy and introduced the Program-Planning-Budget System to the Pentagon during his term of office. International Minerals and Chemicals is a private enterprise that made use of a highly sophisticated mathematical model of world fertilizer supply and demand in the early 1960s.

Note: The views expressed in this article do not necessarily reflect those of the New York Telephone Company.

9. Gerald R. Rosen, "Washington's Corporate Ambassadors," *Dun's Review*, April 1971, pp. 48–76B.

10. Robert K. Greenleaf, *The Institution as Servant* (Cambridge, Mass.: Center for Applied Studies, 1972).

11. George Steiner, *Proceedings of the International Conference on Corporate Planning*, December 1971, Montreal, Canada.

LEE E. PRESTON AND JAMES E. POST

Public Responsibility— An Answer to the "Corporate Dilemma"?

IT IS NOW generally acknowledged that the business corporation is involved in, and must therefore accept some responsibility for, planning and executing a matrix of social relationships extending far beyond its specific economic functions. But the recognition of social involvement—both its reality and its critical managerial importance—complicates rather than resolves the "dilemma" of the modern corporation. The more seriously one takes the basic idea, the more carefully one then tries to sort out the significant questions and to search for operational answers. It is evidently not possible for individual corporations, even very large ones, to take active roles in every sphere of economic and social life. Indeed, a "do whatever you can" principle is essentially unworkable because it provides no real guidance for identifying specific goals and assigning priorities. And, being unworkable, "do whatever you can" becomes a justification for doing nothing at all, or—at best—for uneven and unrelated endeavors, based on transient and personal enthusiasms, rather than long-term organizational plans and commitments.

On the other hand, what are the alternatives? Let us suppose that the top management of a corporation sincerely acknowledges the reality and responsibility of broad social involvement. Furthermore, the management realizes that "do whatever you can" and ad hoc responses to crises and pressures are no more satisfactory guides for managerial action in this area than they would be in production, marketing, or finance. How can the management decide which areas of social involvement merit first attention and greatest effort? What goals are to be pursued? How will it evaluate performance, or even distinguish success from failure? If there is to be a bonus for the division or manager achieving the highest level of social performance, in addition to the usual bonuses for profit contribution or sales growth, how will top management decide who should get it, and how will it explain that decision to the rest of the organization?

The problems of scope and goals for corporate social involvement are intimately linked. The more narrowly the scope of responsibility is defined, the more precisely the goals can be stated and the criteria of success specified. If it were true, as Milton Friedman insists, that "the social responsibility of business is to increase its profits," then inspection of routine accounting reports would settle the entire matter. If, on the other hand, as Kenneth Andrews suggests, corporations are to be made "moral" in some general sense, then the scope of responsibility is virtually unlimited, and attempts to identify specific tasks, establish priorities, and sort out the successes and failures will probably generate more argument than action. Lectured at from both these extremes—and confronted with an avalanche of criticisms, demands, and prescriptions—the business community is understandably confused and defensive. The "corporate dilemma" is real.

After reading, teaching, talking, and writing about this set of interrelated problems for a number of years, we are prepared to offer a new approach, which we call the principle of public responsibility.[1] Our thesis, briefly stated, is that the corporation's role and purpose in society is defined both by market forces and by public policy. Market forces determine the scope of corporate activity (that is, its range of principal functions and their consequences), and within that scope public policy supplements market considerations to determine the goals.

Public policy provides, in fact, the initial basis for a corporation's existence, since the corporate form itself is a privilege established by law. Moreover, corporations can be put out of business just as surely for failing to follow public policy guidelines—for example, for violating EPA standards or engaging in illegal activity—as for failing to attract customers. The principle of public responsibility extends these familiar notions into the broader area of corporate social involvement. It offers a middle position between an exclusive concern with profit and market performance, on one hand, and an unlimited commitment to solve all the problems of society (as seen by whom?) on the other. Furthermore, the principle of public responsibility leads directly to a set of goals, priorities, and evaluation procedures articulated by society itself through the public policy process.

To borrow Daniel Bell's terminology, the traditional official framework of corporate management has been the "economizing mode," that is, the search for optimal combinations of costs and results, sacrifices and benefits. Alongside this official framework there has, of course, been a second and personalistic mode of decision-making based on rank and prerogative, particularly for persons in high-level positions. The personalistic mode has been the major factor in the historic response to social involvement, corporate philanthropy. The principle of public responsibility augments the first of these and partially replaces the second by explicitly introducing Bell's concept of a "sociologizing mode," involving "the effort to judge a society's needs in a more conscious fashion, and . . . to do so on the basis of some explicit conception of the 'public interest.' "

Although the public interest is scarcely as precise a notion as the momentary time and temperature, it is a less amorphous conception than may appear at first glance. The public interest in any particular community or society at any particular time—and certainly in our society and our time—is identified and articulated through the process of public policy formation and implementation. This process generates both the public policy agenda, the set of key topics and issues on which attention is focused, and the specific policy goals and strategies that are adopted. National defense is on the public policy agenda in most developed societies; styles of dress generally are not. The prohibition of specific policy in some areas—such as the practice of religion—is, of course, itself a matter of public policy.

The most important and far-reaching aspects of public policy development are the changes that gradually take place in the policy agenda itself. An historic agenda item now largely forgotten is the protection of the civilian population from mistreatment by the military establishment. The Third Amendment to the Constitution, which limits the quartering of soldiers in private houses, reflects the high priority once given to this issue. Perhaps the most significant recent change in the agenda is the increasing attention being paid to societywide health and medical care standards and costs, matters formerly left primarily to individual citizens.

Public policy is dynamic. Issues are brought onto the public policy agenda in many ways, and specific policies adopted, altered, and repudiated over time. The policy-formation process reflects a changing social environment, and therefore provides an appropriate guide for individual and organizational activity within that environment. Effective policy may take many different forms, from widely understood and accepted standards to specific laws and requirements, including newly emerging viewpoints and issues. There may be ambiguity, or even conflict and inconsistency, with regard to particular policy guidelines and directives. There may be honest differences of opinion as to the particular guideline or criterion to be applied in some specific situation. At the same time, ambiguity and variety within the policy framework permit a considerable amount of individual variation and experimentation among firms, industries, localities, and situations. Hence it is not inconsistent to say that public policy in many areas includes an emphasis on adaptation and modification in individual cases, within a broad guideline as to the desired direction of change or character of performance.

Public policy differs from unspecified "good behavior" and moralistic guidelines for corporate performance in several important respects. Although there is plenty of room for disagreement, with respect to both the policy agenda and the substance of specific policy measures, public policy can never be thought of as something which each individual can have his own unique vision of, something whose character varies—like most ethical and moral judgments—from person to person and case to case.

An appropriately broad orientation toward the complexity of standards, norms, and expectations involved in the relationship between corporate management and other elements of society, individually and collectively, is suggested by the term "rules of the game." One may be surprised to discover that the "rules" of the socioeconomic game being played by private business units in the U.S. economy are nowhere comprehensively stated. On the contrary, they consist of a great variety of statutes and programs in a context of general economic and social traditions and values. Corporate management is concerned not only with the current content of the rules—what activities are involved and what performance is required or prohibited—but, perhaps more importantly, with the directions in which the rules are changing and the processes by which such changes are brought about. Indeed, like a constitutional provision for amendment, a procedure for changing the rules is an essential part of the rules themselves. (Societies in which the rules of the game can be changed only by revolutions have revolutions.)

In sum, the "rules of the game," as reflected and modified within the broad framework of public policy, provide a guide for managerial behav-

---

What Is a Public Policy?

A policy *is a principle that governs action.* Public *policy is the set of widely shared and generally acknowledged principles that direct and control actions having broad implications for society at large or major portions thereof. Public policy includes the spirit as well as the letter of the law. Indeed, the letter of laws that are not implemented or enforced is not part of effective public policy, and some very important underlying principles of social life—such as the preference for private ownership of economic resources—are not part of formal law at all. Moreover, a broad conception of public policy includes principles of policy formation as well as specific content, that is, means as well as ends.*

ior more objective than individual moral or ethical insights, and more general than the literal text of laws and regulations. Public policy includes the spirit as well as the letter of the law. Furthermore, policy exists even in areas of social life in which there is no specific letter of the law for reference. (The preference for the market economy is perhaps the outstanding example.) Clearly, there are many areas of social concern in which formal statutory requirements, judicial interpretation, and executive enforcement are expensive, largely ineffective, and perhaps even repugnant. It does not follow, however, that these areas of concern are excluded from the reach of public policy or the scope of corporate responsibility.

Not only is public policy different from individual moral judgments and personal concepts of "what's good for people," it is also different from the specific goals and interests of narrowly defined interest groups and special publics. Hence emphasis on public policy as a source of managerial guidelines and appraisal criteria contrasts sharply with superficially similar suggestions based on an "interest group" analysis. For example, one recent proposal contends that "the best strategy for the corporation is to develop a systematic mechanism by which to measure the preferences of various groups for corporate actions and the relative strengths of these groups to affect corporate welfare." Although we would agree that opinion monitoring is an important element in an ongoing program of environmental scanning, we doubt that corporate social involvement and impact can be accurately appraised through an "interest group" approach.

Special publics—both inside (employees, stockholders) and outside (customers, neighbors, autonomous action groups) the corporation—are real enough, and the spontaneous and often surprising objections and demands from self-appointed spokesmen for such groups have frequently been the first indications of dissatisfaction with managerial performance. A conventional initial response was to question the "legitimacy" of such expressions and viewpoints. A more modern perspective recognizes any and all such reflections of social dissatisfaction as "our problem, whether we like it or not." In a sense, the latter response is realistic and essentially correct. It leads, however, to two serious pitfalls. One is the tendency to define corporate social involvement only in terms of the complaints of those elements of society that have been heard from, that is, to take managerial cognizance only of criticisms and demands brought forward by particular special publics. The second pitfall is the view that any and all such expressions of opinion are equally valid and deserving of attention. Both these pitfalls can be avoided if primary emphasis is placed on the broad framework of public policy itself, not simply on the specific complaints and proposals and to reject some of them as inappropriate, without falling back on discredited ideological or legalistic arguments. Most of the approaches suggested to date have been ad hoc in character, and have involved the tracing of particular corporate activities to discover their impact somewhere in society. (Alternatively, in some of the best-known instances corporations have not taken notice until concerned citizens were breaking down the doors to present complaints. These incidents stimulated the growth of the new corporate consciousness.)

The corporate–community audit reported by John Thackray[2] suggests a more comprehensive and continuous approach. As carried out by Babcock & Wilcox, this type of audit involves an initial survey of the community itself along basic outline dimensions—economic conditions, transportation and housing, recreation and education—and then an analysis of the role of the firm with respect to each of these areas and their critical aspects. The resulting report (only summarized in *Planning Review*) is very similar to corporate performance summaries based on a "social indicators" approach, which we have been experimenting with elsewhere. Other firms using some variation of this approach include Quaker Oats, First National Bank of Minneapolis, and CNA Financial Corporation. The grandfathers of this school of thought are probably the long-range environmental scanning activity at General Electric and a less widely publicized but similar approach (now discontinued) at American Telephone & Telegraph.

One particularly attractive feature of a community-based approach to corporate analysis and planning with respect to social involvement is that it should also encourage the development of greater comparability of social performance reports among corporate units. Firms reporting their experiences against a common set of goals and concerns will gradually generate a set of corporate performance reports that will be comparable among themselves. Of course, some of these reports will show "zero" entries with respect to those areas of community life that are untouched by the activities of the specific reporting company. However, over time, reports of corporate performance in terms of community concerns and public policy guidelines—rather than in terms of current enthusiasms of management or the concerns of the most vocal pressure groups—should generate data only slightly less comprehensive and comparable than current accounting reports (which, after all, are not all that comparable anyway!).

No matter what approach is taken to the problem of analysis and reporting with respect to corporate social involvement, another critical issue remains: How and by whom is corporate management to be held responsible for performance in the wide range of issues covered by public policy? In our view, the notion of managerial responsibility is to be understood in these areas, as in all others, in the strict dictionary sense: "answerable with respect to cause, motive or effect; chargeable or accountable for results." Hence management is responsible in relevant public policy areas in precisely the same way it is responsible in areas governed by the market mechanism and covered by conventional accounting procedures and reports. For example, management is routinely responsible for money, plant, employee safety, and product quality. The notion that "it all comes down to profit" is nonsense, if the reported "profit" results from over-commitment of working capital to inventory and sales promotion; deterioration of facilities due to neglected maintenance; inadequate safety protection followed by accidents, fines, and lawsuits; or one-time sales made to unsuspecting purchasers of defective merchandise. All these tactics can be converted into "profit" in some accounting report, but they are rarely associated with competent or successful management over the long term.

The problem of balancing multiple performance objectives is not a new one, nor is it unique to concerns with social involvement. On the contrary, corporate management is almost invariably concerned with both profitability indicators and volume or market share goals. Yet additional volume and market share can often be "bought" at some sacrifice of profitability, and, conversely, a slight reduction in market share and sales goals can often generate a short-run increase in profits (by dropping high-cost services and customers, for example). Management routinely balances these and other competing or noncomparable objectives, including, particularly, the achievement of different performance levels over different time periods and the maintenance of an organizational environment that is at once harmonious and strongly motivating. Hence the notion that managers cannot be held responsible for performance in terms of multiple objectives, or that "it all comes down to profit" in any strict sense, is a naive oversimplification and always has been.

One concluding remark: The principle of public responsibility, which relates the direct and indirect impact of corporate activity to the major goals of society reflected in public policy, is a particularly appropriate response to the overwhelmingly important characteristic of the world in which we live—rapid and pervasive change of every kind. The attempt to define either the scope or character of managerial responsibility in terms of specific tasks and roles—even with very broad guidelines such as "be a good citizen" and "do what is right"—can be taken seriously only within a stable environmental context. If the larger social environment were in fact stable, then we might indeed be able to define particular roles and responsibilities for individual managerial units and expect these standards to be applied year in and year out. But our environment is conspicuously unstable, and therefore our guidelines and appraisal criteria have to be stated in terms of the process by which they are determined and changed, not in terms of specific rules, standards, or goals. Hence recognition of the public policy process as the source of guidelines and standards for managerial performance serves to resolve the problem of goals and criteria more clearly than a specific list of "do's and don'ts." Any specific set of tasks and guidelines will, in our rapidly changing environment, quickly become obsolete. The process by which problems are identified and guidelines developed, however, is central and continuing. Therefore, in defining the scope and role of responsible management, we require neither a list of specifics nor a series of moral exhortations, but rather a reliable framework for adaptive and constructive behavior in a changing world.

REFERENCES

1. Lee E. Preston and James E. Post, *Private Management and Public Policy* (Englewood Cliffs, N.J.: Prentice-Hall, 1975).
2. John Thackray, "Audits Aim Social Strategy," *Planning Review*, October–November 1973 (this volume).

Part IV
BUSINESS STRATEGY

MICHAEL J. KAMI

Revamping Planning
for This Era
of Discontinuity

HARD TIMES inevitably make a planner's job more hectic. During the recent downturn and recovery in both the U.S. and world economies, many corporate plans have been disrupted. In addition to facing bad economic news, corporations are having to cope in a period of dramatic social change. These two factors have taken their toll on planners, and it would not be an exaggeration to say that planning is in the midst of its gravest professional crisis.

To counter the twin problems of economic uncertainty and rapid change, planners should be reacting vigorously, stepping forward with opportunistic, strategic programs for companies hard pressed by hard times. Unfortunately, though the times demand imaginative entrepreneurs, most planners have become accustomed to a very different role. This is understandable if we consider the history of planning. During the 1950s a planner had to be a salesman, selling the concept of planning. During the 1960s, after planning was more established, planners concentrated on making the process systematic. During the past five years the tools and techniques of planning advanced a quantum jump. It became difficult to keep abreast of new technology, and many planners withdrew into the task of optimizing management information systems. Too many planners wrongly assumed that their elegant and expensive computer models would provide reliable portals to the future.

But when the economic situation became more erratic, as Peter Drucker warned it would in his 1968 prophecy, *The Age of Discontinuity*, the computer models, no matter how sophisticated, began to spew out nonsense. Short- and long-range projections, based on assumptions for normal times, have proved embarrassingly inaccurate.

The new factors of rapid change, discontinuity, and unpredictability of what used to be simple and proved ratios and trends, make our favorite approach of simulation and modeling a very difficult task. More than 1,000 corporations have developed corporate simulation models, as

Thomas Naylor notes in "The Politics of Corporate Building," published in *Planning Review*'s January 1975 issue. There are hundreds of econometric models to predict the future of world and national economies. In December 1973 a famous econometric team of a large corporation, armed with a mammoth computer program and a 185-sector input-output Leontiev matrix, made a 12-month economic forecast. The results were astronomically off on profits, 71 percent off on consumer prices, 26 percent off on prime rate, 67 percent off on year-end interest rates, and 940 percent off on real GNP. Unless we can produce models that can easily and rapidly be programmed whenever we discover new factors, new relationships, and new variables, we will discredit simulation and modeling for years to come. That would be a pity, because the concept is sound and the techniques are valid; but the execution has suffered from the rigidity of the structure in a period of rapid changes and unforeseen discontinuities.

The role of the planner must change if this current period of discontinuity is to be dealt with effectively. If I were hiring a planner, I would look for a gutsy realist, a person who could be a brutal pessimist on occasion. During the past era of continuous growth too many planners got in the habit of optimism. Frequently, optimism was the only attitude tolerated by the corporate hierarchy. The planner of today needs to be suspicious of the future and ever ready to make quick adjustments for the unexpected.

The theoretical understanding of discontinuity, the so-called "break point" on a continuous curve, is neither new nor difficult. We discussed it for years, calling it the key clue of change. But most planners were mesmerized by constant growth and consequently dismissed the repetitive signals of discontinuity as unimportant wiggles on the charts.

Some of the most astute corporate managements took the same blind trail. For example, Sears Roebuck and Company, considered by many as the leading organization in its excellence of strategic and tactical planning, made this error. Much was written about the unerring acumen of the world's largest retailer and the country's second largest insurer of cars and homes. But in 1974 the sales growth was far less than inflation growth, and profits slumped for the first time in 13 years. Sears missed several turning points and kept going in the wrong direction. Sears stores were growing through the strategy of "upgrading"—increasing the value of their wares. Through extensive television advertising, Sears promoted its house brands as name brands, pushed its higher-quality and higher-priced lines. Soon higher markups meant that all prices crept up, and whole segments of lower-price merchandise were surrendered to discounters and other competitors—even to Montgomery Ward.

The Sears strategy of "Trade up America" was natural under the premise of a steadily increasing affluent society. With considerable foresight, in September 1974, *Forbes* compared this approach to the hypothetical situation of MacDonald's introducing the sirloin steak, raising the price of the Big Mac, and completely withdrawing its plain hamburger.

Sears chose to ignore the fact that the University of Michigan Consumer Confidence Index had reversed its long-term upward trend in 1965 and had zigzagged downward ever since to its lowest point in December 1974. The Conference Board's similar but independent index confirms the steep downward slope since the end of 1972.

Sears and many other consumer-dependent organizations ignored another significant advance warning signal: The per capita disposable personal income, converted to real dollars, had continued to move upward for the past 35 years, almost without a trace of hesitation, until the third quarter of 1973, when it reached $2,952. It coasted through the fourth quarter of 1973 and then moved steadily downward to a low of $2,775 before resuming a zigzag trend in 1975. The historic age of continuous growth of U.S. affluence and rise in standard of living ended in September 1973, but many still refused to believe it. Did Sears change its strategy, its policies, or its operations? Apparently not, since the "upgrading" continued and Sears increased its inventories. In September 1974, a full year after the beginning of the standard-of-living decline, Sears projected a highly optimistic rebound in the fourth quarter. It turned out to be one of the worst quarters and projections in Sears history. After 75 years of planning leadership, the giant had faltered by refusing to recognize change, because it was not to its liking.

Certainly, Sears was not an isolated case. As another example, the Chairman of the Board of General Motors confidently predicted in September 1974 a 10-million-car year for 1975. Any car owner in the country would have told him that the 9-million-car annual rate at that time was due to customers' buying defensively as a protection against 1975 price increases. The U.S. car industry had the sharpest one-year sales decline in its entire history in 1975; its domestic production has been set back 20 years; the consumer has decided since the beginning of 1973 to end his love affair with the car as a status symbol by cutting his car budget as a percentage of his total expenditures by 27 percent over two years. But one of the highest-paid executives in the world has not yet discovered, and no planner has yet been able to convince him, that there may be a need for a new strategy at General Motors!

The planning lessons to learn from such rapid social changes are not how to foresee or predict better, but how to react faster. This can be achieved by the examination of "clues" of change rather than solid facts. A "clue" is an isolated event which may, however, have serious consequences if repeated often enough to become a "fact." In the past we had enough time, because of a slower rate of social change, to delay acting on social clues until they became established and recognized factors. Even then we often massaged the data to the point of "paralysis through analysis." Today we certainly cannot afford paralysis; we may not be able to wait for factual analysis; we may have to learn to act on incomplete and unclear signals, which vaguely indicate future trends. Any type of social change costs money because of the disruption of routine and the effort necessary to adjust to a new situation.

Social changes create new discontinuities in costs of crime and fire insurance, liability insurance, medical plans, consumer class suit protection, and legal fees in general. A planner can no longer calculate historical expense ratios of various categories to gross sales and merrily project them five years forward. Innovative, continuous, and penetrating thinking is needed on every phase and every facet of operations.

Pollution abatement, for example, continues to be a major expense, and there is no sign that the energy crisis, inflation, or other economic problems will significantly change the cost trend and enforcement of federal, state, and local government regulations. The overall growth in capital expenditures for pollution control was 21.3 percent from 1971 to 1972, 29.1 percent from 1972 to 1973, and 54.9 percent from 1973 to 1974.

Also, equal opportunity and nondiscrimination are not new concepts or unfamiliar terms. They are part of our heritage, part of our Constitution. The past 20 years gave us plenty of clues, data, facts, laws, and regulations on equal opportunities for blacks. We had to readjust our personnel policies, hiring practices, and training programs. We even planned correctly the extension of these policies to Puerto Ricans and Chicanos. We were caught by surprise by the demands of the American Indians, but probably rejected the clue as statistically nonsignificant. However, it took a militant women's liberation movement and a $40 million court-imposed settlement by American Telephone and Telegraph to suddenly make us realize that women represent 51.3 percent of the population and 40 percent of the total labor force and that equal pay and equal opportunities for women are not going to be minor and insignificant budget items. And how about the Occupation Safety and Health Act? What are its real future costs and consequences?

Have we learned to heed the clues of change? In 1975 a large oil company lost an age-discrimination suit filed by a 61-year-old retired employee. His claim, upheld by the courts to the amount of $750,000, was that his early retirement was not voluntary. Are we seeking a precedent that may change all our plans for "rejuvenation" of our personnel and reduction of personnel through retirement and pension plans, early or otherwise? Was the case an isolated incident or the "clue" to a costly new trend?

The complexity of planning in this era of discontinuities has increased since the United States lost its position as an absolute leader that other nations had to follow if they wished to prosper. When the world became a global village, when the OPEC nations taught us a practical lesson in international interdependency, we lost our traditional world hegemony.

The combined 1974 GNP of seven European countries was within 20 percent of that of the United States. If you add Japan to the first group, the GNP exceeded ours by 20 percent. In fact, the combined GNP of ten Western countries exceeded our GNP by more than 30 percent, while that of the Soviet Union is still 50 percent behind ours. Germany has twice as many liquid assets as we do. A tabulation of the richest countries in GNP per capita places the United States in fifth place. It's a new ball game, and we had better learn to play it because we no longer can change the rules at our convenience. Our strategic and operational plans must now consider global economics even if we operate in only a small area of the country.

The energy crisis looms paramount. Few predicted the event; none that I know claim to have actually planned and prepared for it. It is more threatening now than it was in the fall of 1973. Two years after the embargo and the 547 percent global increase in the price of oil, we produced domestically 10 percent less oil than in 1973. During these two years our dependence on imported oil increased from 40 to 43 percent, and this figure is climbing, despite a $25 billion annual price tag on our total oil imports.

Remember that we were dependent on imported sources for only 26 percent of our oil in 1971. We must be extremely careful with assumptions on future availability and costs of energy. We must evaluate oil, coal, and other equivalents at various high price levels. We can probably make one safe assumption: Energy costs will be higher, not lower, in the years ahead.

Important suppositions must be made on the future costs and availability of some 40 raw materials and commodities that are indispensable to our industrial production and must be imported from abroad. Short-term, extreme fluctuations are possible and probable as economics become inexorably intertwined with politics.

The new breed of planner has to stimulate throughout his organization a new integrated system of rapid and continuous analysis, action, and control. The following should be emphasized:

• Innovation rather than improvement. A 5–10 percent steady improvement will not make much difference in today's multidigit change. We must innovate, do things differently, forget the good old days and good old methods.

• Action rather than perfection. We must act fast, or by the time we develop and prove a new method, conditions will have changed and the method will be obsolete.

• Tougher schedules and standards. Whatever our performance period was two years ago, we must cut it in half.

• Flexibility rather than fixed policy. Formal policies are the antithesis of flexibility. The days of formal and rigid planning processes are gone. Policies may become dangerous constraints that will delay the decision-making process beyond its useful peak.

• Fast, correct, and intelligently chosen data feedback as an integral part of the planning, acting, and checking system.

• "If" scenarios and alternatives. The multiple "ifs" and hypotheses are now a routine part of planning. The concept should be used daily and for short decision-making processes. What we need are not the long-range (year 2000) scenarios instituted by think tanks, Herman Kahn, and the Club of Rome, but short-term alternatives from which we can select operational action plans according to external conditions.

But above all, we have to use common sense. We have to maintain a sense of proportion and a strong rationale, and we have to convey these to other members of our organizations. We live in an era of multiple crises. Each crisis requires organizational adaptation. Planners and planning can and should facilitate this process.

PETER P. PEKAR, JR.

Matching Action Plans to Market Development Stage

INTRODUCTION

Uncertainty is the norm of our time: uncertainty with the U.S. economy, uncertainty with continuing oil supplies at a reasonable price, uncertainty with continued economic growth. American industry stands at the threshold of a new era. Perhaps never before has industry had at one time so many problems and such promise for the future. Superior planning, management, and research will be required to solve the problems ahead and to realize the prospectus for the future.

There are effective ways to manage change, and these will call for new skills in organizational planning. The main points are (1) identifying business areas that comprise a multiunit corporation, and (2) developing what the commixture of these units can and should be.

A multibusiness company seeks to maximize performance by achieving the best fit of the diverging units. Each possible permutation has its own characteristics and capabilities. While the multibusiness company seeks to maximize its leverage, balance, and diversity, the single-product company seeks to do things in the one best way. Unfortunately, too many companies still try to treat a diversified operation as if it were a single-product firm.

Our purpose is to present a new approach to planning for maximizing change. This approach enables management to control change without either sacrificing heterogeneity or agreeing on some common filter for all units. The key steps in applying the approach are as follows:

1. Defining the distinct business areas in which the company is involved.
2. Identifying the positions of these areas in terms of their product life cycles.
3. Characterizing their competitive positions.

4. Developing strategic goals and objectives.
5. Analyzing financial and managerial liquidity.
6. Determining strategic risk.
7. Designing a managerial structure.

DISTINCT BUSINESS AREAS

In a multiunit corporation, a distinct business area would comprise independent products or product lines which divorce themselves in terms of price, quality, and competition from other units in the firm. It is around these business areas that information is collected and from which strategic goals and objectives are formed. It is more difficult to define such business units than it appears at first. In many corporations, distinct business areas are found to exist at different organizational levels. The accepted principles of categorizing organizational units into cost, profit, and divisional centers further hinders such identification. However, it is imperative that distinct business areas be identified in order to achieve maximum utilization of the planning process.

Many operating managers find themselves managing two or more business areas. The differing requirements of the business areas may impede planning.

In the plant nutrient business, for example, companies have tended to view nutrients in terms of the farmer, yet many nutrient product lines have extended themselves into the consumer homeowner area. For management to accept the notion that these new products make up a distinct business area is difficult when the consumer business end of the market is still a relatively small portion of the total business.

PRODUCT LIFE CYCLE

After the natural business areas have been classified, the next step is to determine where the product lines of each business area fit in a normal competitive life cycle. In general terms, business areas should be classified into four stages of development: the initial, growth, mature, and decaying stages. A business in the initial stage (for example, electronic measuring devices) can be characterized by fluid motion, rapid growth, and volatile market shares. This type of business needs flexible and risk-taking management. A growth business (for example, mini computers) is one in which market size is growing but markets, share, and technology are defined and barriers to entry are beginning to be established. A mature business (for example, steel) is generally characterized by stability in size, market share, and technology. A decaying business (for example, automobile convertible tops) is best characterized by narrow profit margin, falling demand, and declining competition.

For instance, the medical supply industry exhibits all the characteristics of a growth industry as contrasted with a mature industry, such as plant nutrients. Planning in this environment is longer range. Management style is more leadership dependent and flexible than in the plant nutrient business, which tends to be fixed. Growth for medical products and services is greater than the GNP growth rate, whereas growth for plant nutrients is closer to it. There are fewer policies and procedures than in a mature business area. Communications are more informal and less uniform. Control is less fixed and more flexible. In essence, because of its growth position in the product life cycle, there is more freedom of movement and action in the medical industry than in a mature business.

COMPETITIVE POSITION

Once a business area has been classified into its developmental stage, the next critical step is the appraisal of its competitive position. It is useful to think of the competitive position of a business area as being either prevalent, powerful, advantageous, vulnerable, or insignificant. Having a sense of where one stands with respect to the competition is essential for determining the strategic options available. A business in a prevalent market position can influence the behavior of its competition and has a wide range of options open to it. A business with a powerful position can maintain an independent stance or action without loss of share. The factors that have to be evaluated in determining market strength include: market share and position, pricing policy, type and degree of integration, financial position, product mix, technological capability, and marketing capabilities.

Twice a year each operating business area manager should position his business area into the competition grid shown in Table 1. The indicators given in the table are only a sample of the factors examined. As can easily be seen, business area A is in a vulnerable competitive position, while business area B is in a prevalent position.

STRATEGIC GOALS AND OBJECTIVES

The results of the competitive position analysis are a guide for helping business areas select strategies that are appropriate, that is, those that are reasonable in terms of likelihood of successful implementation given a particular competitive position.

An examination of the data collected for the product life cycle and

Table 1. Competitive positions.

Competition Indicators	Major Competitors				Business Environment
	A	B	C	D	
Market position	Vulnerable	Prevalent	Strong	Vulnerable	Attackable
General trend in market position	Steady	Steady	Up	Down	Down
Profitability (low, average, high)	Low	Average	Average	Average	Low
Financial strength (low, average, high)	Low	High	Unknown	Low	Low
Product mix (broad, narrow, extensive)	Narrow	Broad	Narrow	Narrow	Extensive
Technological capability (strong, weak, average)	Average	Strong	Average	Weak	Average
Cost outlook (favorable, unfavorable)	Unfavorable	Favorable	Favorable	Unfavorable	Unfavorable
Quality (good, satisfactory, minimum)	Minimum	Good	Satisfactory	Minimum	Satisfactory
Product development (good, satisfactory, minimum)	Minimum	Good	Satisfactory	Satisfactory	Good

competitive position provides a framework for selecting a strategy based on competitive position. Possible strategies include:

Contraction
Maintenance
Replacement
New venture

The selected strategy provides a basis for the development of detailed action plans and for commitment of the necessary management skills and associated program expenditures, as outlined in Table 2.

FINANCIAL AND MANAGERIAL LIQUIDITY

Once the action plans have been identified and selected, specific directly related program expenditures should be developed. Since the entire planning process is an interactive communicative process involving appropriate key production, marketing, financial, and R&D people, it is essential for these individuals to meet periodically to evaluate the course

Table 2. Strategies.

Strategy (New Venture)	Course of Action	Program Expenditures	Critical Issues
Increase profitability of existing products by entering new markets	Begin site selection in 1980	New plant full production by 1981: $8.0 million 1982: 2.0 million	Governmental approval Capacity level
	Start up advertising and promotion in fall of 1981	1981: 3.0 million 1982: 1.5 million	Account commitment and extent of orders

of action.

The following example is offered as a general guideline to assist in clarifying this process of linking strategies with action plans and the related program expenditures.

After all program expenditure requests—including expenditures for fixed assets, working capital, and major operating expenses—are developed, these should be classified into contraction, maintenance, replacement, and new ventures expenditures. Contraction involves reduction of the current configuration to a more profitable form. Maintenance expenditures should be limited to those necessary to meet proper guidelines of health, safety requirements of governmental agencies, and the replacement of equipment needed to continue operation. Replacement expenditures permit improvement of an existing operation, including the replacement of an entire facility with a new more efficient kind. New venture expenditures are directed toward increasing the scope of present business operations through expansion of marketing and/or manufacturing capabilities and acquisition of existing businesses or assets. After the expenditure classification is made, *pro forma* income, balance, and cash flow statements should be compiled for each program expenditure by business area. These may be recapped into four summary sections plus a corporate consolidation: Return on Investment and Net Present Value, coupled with probability using Monte Carlo techniques, accompany each major program expenditure.

Consider this example. A company composed of three distinct business units had planned to distribute 10, 35, 30, and 25 percent of all new committed expenditures to contraction, maintenance, replacement, and new venture projects. The expenditures necessary to implement these strategic action plans were developed from more than 100 plans which ranged from simply meeting EPA and OSHA requirements and replacing worn-out equipment to increasing market share and entering new markets. This type of planning allows management to determine the funds necessary to continue, improve, shrink, or expand each business area given the product life cycle and competitive position. On the basis of these findings, internal negotiations are instituted with strategies, expenditures, and the targets at which to aim agreed upon.

A one-page summary containing the following condensed data dealing with all the planning years is also drawn up. These ratios help management notice any inconsistency with its plans and financial structure.

Net income	Orders received
Sales	Orders on hand
Total assets	Number of full-time employees
Total capital employed	Sales per employee
Sales per 1,000 square foot	Net income per employee
Receivables	Percentage return on sales
Inventories	Percentage return on assets
Plant, property, equipment	Percentage return/capital employed
Capital expenditures	Percentage receivables to sales
Provision for depreciation	Percentage investments to sales

STRATEGIC RISK AND MANAGEMENT STRUCTURE

Certain risks are associated with any particular venture. For example, offshore drilling involves greater risks than does the retail liquor business. The past predictability of performance of each business area is a convenient guidepost on the proposed strategies and results. An understanding of where to place money and the realization of the odds against success are essential. For instance, top management should be aware that in a young business the general manager should have the characteristics of an entrepreneur, while in a growth business he or she should be more of a market manager. A mature industry calls for a controller-type administration. Communication should be more informal and personal in a new business than in a mature business where a formal and more uniform type of communication is appropriate. Procedures in the former should be few, in the latter, many. If management is not aware of or is blind to the strategy risks and managerial styles necessary to operate on the appropriate product cycle, then the predictability and profit performance indicated by strategic plans will be marred.

SUMMARY

The objective of the planning process is to allocate resources against strategies. The planning process described here is intended to help planners assess plans in terms of business area, strategy, finance, and risk. The process begins with collection of information about business areas and product life cycles. From this information each business area assesses its competitive position and selects one or more strategies that are appropriate. Each strategy can serve as a framework for developing specific action plans and for specifying associated program expenditures and risks.

BRADLEY T. GALE

Planning for Profit

ONE HUNDRED AND NINETY of the world's largest and most diversified companies have added a new capability to their arsenal of planning tools. They have tapped into a new and unique collection of strategic experiences of product-line businesses now maintained by The Strategic Planning Institute (SPI). Member companies use information derived from this data base as one additional input to:

Identify key success factors
Quantify a business's strengths and weaknesses
Establish ROI benchmarks
Estimate probable consequences of alternative strategic moves
Review portfolios at the group or company level
Screen acquisition candidates
Size up competitors

This contribution offers a brief overview of The PIMS (Profit Impact of Market Strategy) Program of SPI. It describes a multi-company effort to develop a factual, scientific basis for strategic planning. It also indicates how SPI's member companies capitalize upon this new basis in order to enhance their return on investment and their cash flow.

FINANCIAL PERFORMANCE OF BUSINESS IN A COMPARABLE SITUATION

Often, the task of explaining why low-profit businesses fail seems more difficult than trying to explain why profitable businesses succeed. Poor profits may result from a variety of factors, including too much specialized equipment in the production process, or attaining only a small market share in a high-growth market, or spending too much on marketing, or producing a nondifferentiated product. While the decision to initiate most of these ill-fated strategies may have seemed sensible, each of these actions increases the chances of bad financial performance.

The tap root of these planning mistakes is that the experiences of many businessmen are excessively narrow. Experience will tell a businessman which factors are critical for his particular industry. For example, electronics manufacturers appreciate how important it is to keep a careful watch on research and development expenditures and new-product introductions. Soap companies learn the importance of monitoring their competitors' advertising campaigns. Distribution businesses focus on the flow of sales per square foot of store or warehouse space.

While knowledge gained from one's own industry can be very helpful, it can, at the same time, be incomplete or even misleading. For example, it may well be a mistake for a business which is ranked number two or three in the industry to follow the strategies of the industry leader, who could be twice as large. Rather, one should search the strategic experiences of businesses in other industries to discover empirical evidence as to how a number two can compete against a much larger number one and make profits in the process. The trick is to examine the strategy experiences of businesses outside one's industry that have similar characteristics and face a comparable competitive situation.

PRACTICAL GUIDANCE IS NOW AVAILABLE
Evolution of PIMS

Until a few years ago it was nearly impossible to obtain empirical data on the successful and unsuccessful experiences of businesses outside one's own industry. Such data had not been systematically assembled and analyzed. Planners were forced to work with highly aggregated data collected by government agencies or trade associations. During the last five years, however, The PIMS Program has assembled a unique business data base, and has developed a research program and planning service specifically designed to help corporate managers and planners select and implement strategies that promise a higher return on investment. This data base is cross-sectional, that is, it comes from product-line businesses in many industries.

The PIMS data base was developed in response to economic pressures of the time period.[1] During the 1960s, some diversified manufacturing companies were confronted with severe cash-flow problems, which forced them to be very selective as to which of their businesses to expand. Unfortunately, many top-management teams did not have first-hand experience in each product-line business. Others felt that their experience was not relevant to their future environment. Managers began to search for a systematic way to analyze the strategic options advanced by their different operating units. This basic need for factual information on individual business units was intensified by the general cash-flow crunch which hit many companies during the early 1970s.

In 1972, The PIMS Program was established as a developmental project at the Harvard Business School.[2] Three dozen large, diversified companies agreed to contribute the strategy experiences of some of their product-line businesses to a new and shared data base. The intent was to discover in this cross-sectional data base the "laws" of the marketplace. Next, PIMS was to produce reports for the managers and planners of each business unit in the data base which they can use as a basis for decision making.

PIMS Now

By 1975, more companies had joined The PIMS Program. The data base contained almost 600 product-line businesses. Many of the participating companies wished to broaden the range of planning services available from researchers on the PIMS staff. Accordingly, The Strategic Planning Institute was formed in 1975 as the permanent home of The PIMS Program. It is a nonprofit, tax-exempt corporation governed by its member companies in the United States, Canada, Europe, and South America. Thus, The PIMS Program is now a multi-company, multi-country activity. Its primary goal is unchanged, namely, to provide a factual basis for the business-planning efforts of its participants.[3]

As of this date, the PIMS data base contains detailed information on the strategy experiences of more than 1,000 product-line businesses. These businesses are owned and operated by a diverse group of companies operating in many different industries. The PIMS staff analyzes these experiences to discover the general "laws" that determine what business strategy, in what kind of competitive environment, produces what profit results. The findings are made available to member companies in a form useful to their business planning.

The PIMS research program has identified about 30 factors which, taken together, can explain about 75 percent of the differences in profitability reported by these businesses.

It is interesting to note that these factors do not include the name of the product, industry, or technology. Rather, they pertain to (1) the structural characteristics of the industry (for example, the rate of growth, the degree of customer and seller concentration); (2) the business's competitive position within its industry (market share, product quality relative to leading competitors); and (3) the productivity of capital and labor, regardless of what they produce.

PIMS research findings of this type are disseminated to member companies in two forms. First, they are issued as general reports on the principles of business strategy. A few examples are included at the end of this article. Second, PIMS produces specific reports on each business in the data base, that is, PIMS applies the general findings to a particular business. It diagnoses the complex relationships between key factors and financial performance. Each business receives a detailed analysis of its strategic position based on what one would expect from other similar businesses (that is, those with the same business characteristics, though not necessarily those operating in the same field of goods and services). This analysis helps to insure that strategic decisions are made neither on a hunch nor solely on the basis of an individual company's past practice in one industry, but with the knowledge of what other managers have achieved with businesses having similar characteristics.

But My Business Is Different

When first introduced to PIMS concepts, most general managers will insist that their business is different or unique. They imagine that experiences of businesses in other industries are irrelevant to their strategic planning effort. It is true that each business has a particular market share, a particular industry growth rate, a particular level of marketing expenses, and a particular investment base. Yet one must also recognize that businesses in other industries may have the same market share. Thus, while each business is unique, one can gain strategic insight by focusing on the factors which are common across businesses, rather than on differences. It is the relative importance of each of these common factors that is unique. Recall that some 30 factors explain about 75 percent of the variability in profit performance. Other things that make a business unique explain only about 25 percent. Indeed, PIMS research indicates that much of this unexplained 25 percent is due to transitory factors.

Medical practitioners would find the above methodology quite familiar. They appreciate that each patient is unique. Yet they insist on focusing on characteristics common to everyone (pulse rate, blood pressure, body temperature, weight relative to height, smoker vs. nonsmoker, and so on).

HOW MEMBER COMPANIES USE PIMS
Identify Key Success Factors

Member companies use SPI reports and resources for a variety of planning purposes. Most begin by using PIMS concepts to provide a common language for discussion of business strategy. They review research findings to isolate key factors which influence profitability and cash flow. During their first year with SPI, most companies use PIMS as a vehicle to generate key questions about the current position and future prospects of their businesses.

Par Report: Quantify Strengths and Weaknesses, Set ROI Benchmarks

Each business receives a set of reports based on its own characteristics. The "Par" ROI Report specifies the return on investment that is normal (or "Par") for a business, given its market attractiveness, competitive position, degree of differentiation from competitors, and its production structure. The report also quantifies individual strategic strengths and weaknesses, as indicated by the impacts of key profit-influencing factors. These strengths and weaknesses explain why the Par ROI is high or low. The Cash Flow Par Report provides similar information, but with a focus on factors that influence cash flow (expressed as a percentage of investment).

Some companies use PIMS Par Reports to establish reasonable objective profit or cash-flow benchmarks for each of their businesses. Others use these reports to diagnose major strategic strengths and weaknesses. For example, what factors tend to drain cash, or produce large profits? In some cases, the strategic weaknesses far outweigh the strengths. Although inputs to a divestment decision come from many sources, PIMS reports appear to have clinched the difficult decision to exit in several cases.

Estimate Probable Consequences of Alternative Strategic Moves

SPI's Strategy Report offers a product-line business a computational pre-test of several possible strategic moves in the business. It indicates the normal short-term and long-term consequences of each such move, based on the experiences of other businesses that have made similar moves, from similar starting points, in similar business environments in the past. The report answers the following questions: (1) If this business continues on its current track, what will its future operating results be? (2) What changes in market share, investment intensity, and vertical integration are likely to produce better results?

Member companies also use SPI's Strategy Report to estimate the future consequences of specific strategies under management consideration. For example, when management is getting ready to make a strategic decision for a particular business, there will frequently be a flurry of activity to generate strategy reports based on several different sets of strategic moves and different scenarios about the future market environment.

SPI's Optimum Strategy Report nominates that combination of market-share, investment-intensity, and vertical-integration moves which promises to optimize a given performance measure (for example, discounted cash flow over 10 years, return on investment for the next 5 years, or short-term dollar earnings). This nomination is also based on the experiences of other businesses operating under similar circumstances. Some companies use the Optimum Strategy Report as a catalyst to nominate strategies with a better yield than the current business plan for detailed exploration.

Portfolio Review

A recent capability has been developed by SPI researchers. Member companies can now assess the strengths and weaknesses of portfolios of businesses. This analysis can be done for the entire company, a group, or a division. Using PIMS research findings, as assessment of the strengths and weaknesses of a portfolio can begin with an examination of the portfolio's position with respect to several key profit determinants. In some cases, a key weakness such as heavy investment intensity or low product quality may affect the entire portfolio of businesses.

Companies analyzing portfolios use PIMS to answer the following kinds of questions:

- Has the strategic position of the portfolio improved over the last few years?
- Is the portfolio performing well or badly given its strategic position?
- Will proposed business plans strengthen the portfolio? How much?
- Which plans deserve the most detailed review?
- Which businesses are potential divestment candidates?

Special Topics

While the bulk of PIMS' activity focuses on the major businesses of member companies, PIMS has also developed tools to help managers address specialized planning problems in other areas. For example, the Start-Up Business project has assembled a new data base to provide a factual basis for planning decisions pertaining to new business ventures. Member companies use SPI's Start-Up Business Report to help decide whether to continue, alter, or close down a start-up business. SPI has also developed a tool for screening acquisition candidates and sizing up competitors. This limited information tool is used in circumstances when it is difficult to assemble detailed information. A recent probe has been launched to discover strategic or tactical remedies for businesses in profit trouble.

Interface Between SPI and Member Companies

To help member companies make effective use of these planning tools, SPI assigns a staff member to each participating company (as a service coordinator). The service coordinator works with member companies to plan their PIMS activity, explain general research findings, define business units, interpret reports on individual businesses, organize presentations, and perform a variety of other service tasks.

Each member company designates an individual to act as the liaison between its business unit and SPI. In many cases, this individual represents the corporate planning staff. Typically, division-line people know more about their particular industry than the planner. By drawing on the PIMS data base, however, the planner can usually provide additional information and strategic insights which complement the hands-on knowledge of division managers.

SOME RESEARCH FINDINGS

The PIMS staff has built a number of empirical models to explain why profitability and cash flow differ from business to business. These models contain factors which affect financial performance. Some representative findings are summarized in the following exhibits. PIMS participants find these exhibits especially interesting when they imagine the position of a particular business, or a portfolio of businesses, in the exhibit.

Marketing Share Helps Profitability

It is now widely recognized that one of the main determinants of business profitability is market share.[4] Under most circumstances, businesses that have achieved a high share of the markets they serve are considerably more profitable than their small-share competitors. Figure 1 shows average ROI (pre-tax) for groups of businesses in The PIMS Program, highlighting their profit enhancement from successively larger shares of their markets.

There are several reasons why a high share of the market causes high profitability. First, large-share businesses usually enjoy scale economies in working capital, marketing, research and development, and in certain other cost components. Second, they also enjoy economies of cumulative volume which reduce unit costs via the experience-curve effect, and by spreading set-up costs over a longer production run. Third, those

Figure 1. Market share helps profitability.

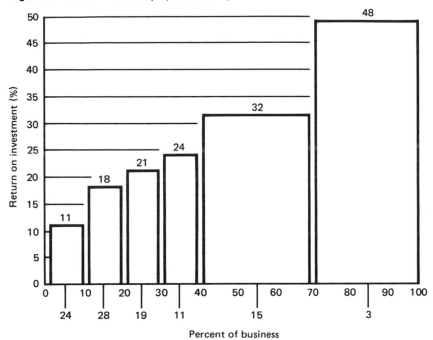

anxious to minimize the risk of making a wrong choice may favor a large-share business. This customer behavior gives dominant suppliers a share-based product-differentiation advantage. Finally, large-share businesses often have a greater bargaining power over customers and suppliers, and frequently they are able to take the initiative over their competitors.

Unionization Reduces the Effect of Share on ROI

While the PIMS data base clearly demonstrates a strong general relationship between ROI and market share, it also indicates that the importance of share can be amplified or attenuated by other factors. For example, when a large fraction of a business's labor force is unionized, the effect of market share on ROI is reduced (Figure 2). In the graphic portion of Figure 2 (and in Figure 3) the PIMS sample of businesses is divided into three approximately equal groups on the basis of two factors. The figure shown in each of the nine boxes represents the average ROI of the businesses in that subgroup. Figure 2 includes both a plot and a matrix of the relationship of ROI, market share, and unionization, both high and low.

Figure 2. Unionization reduces effect of share on ROI.

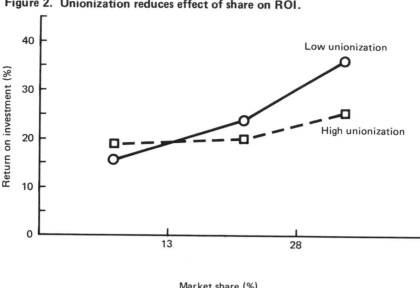

Market share is more important to businesses that are not unionized than it is to unionized businesses. Put differently, unionization hurts ROI when market share is high. Unions appear to dissipate much of the potential unit-cost advantage of large-share businesses. This failure to achieve lower unit costs may occur (1) because of the restrictive work rules which reduce productivity, or (2) because union bargaining results in a larger fraction of value added ending up as wages and a smaller fraction as profits.

Strong businesses have a high ROI potential so they can tolerate some restrictive work rules and practices or concede some bargaining points

Figure 3. Unionization hurts productivity.

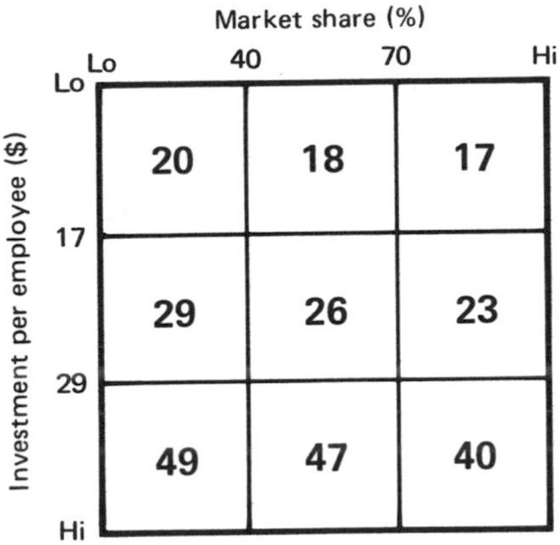

and still earn an ROI sufficiently above average to satisfy corporate management. Small-share businesses have a low ROI potential. They cannot and apparently are not forced to tolerate cost-inflating work rules and practices, as shown by the insignificant profit difference between low and high unionization when market share is low. Of course, the data reflect only those businesses which had both small share and high unionization and survived.

These research findings suggest that large-share businesses should be especially concerned about the adverse effects of becoming unionized. Strong businesses which are already unionized should seek union cooperation to avoid work rules and practices that may reduce productivity, raise unit costs, or dissipate a potential cost advantage. For businesses with a small or medium level of market share, the profit benefits of obtaining a large market share are greater if the industry (or business itself) is not unionized. But competition for share and the cost of building share may also be greater for the nonunionized businesses.

Part of the reason why unionization reduces the profitability of large-share businesses appears to be the negative effect of unionization on productivity. Specifically, Figure 3 shows the joint effect of unionization and investment per employee on value added per employee. As one would expect, productivity (as measured by "value added per employee") increases dramatically as investment per employee increases. By contrast, value added declines as unionization increases.[5]

Gaining Market Share Tends to Drain Cash

High-share businesses generate more cash than low-share businesses, but the process of building market share absorbs cash. Figure 4 shows

Figure 4. High market share generates cash, but building share absorbs cash.

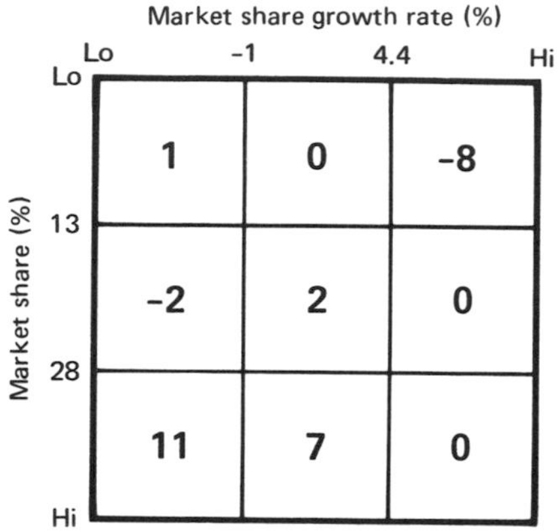

Market share growth rate (%)

the joint effect of market share and market-share growth rate on the ratio of cash flow to investment.

Cash flow in a particular year is defined as cash generated by after-tax earnings minus cash absorbed by any increase in working capital or by an increase in new investment in plant equipment. The ratio shown in Figure 4 is average cash flow (1971–1974) expressed as a percentage of the average level of investment tied up in the business during this four-year time period. Investment is defined as the level of net book value of plant and equipment plus working capital.

Small-share businesses which are gaining share absorb a good deal of cash because they are building their productive capacity. By contrast, large-share businesses which are losing share tend to generate vast amounts of cash.

Figure 4 reports cash flow before dividends. With an after-tax ROI of about 10 percent and a payout ratio of 50 percent, the after-dividends pattern of cash flow would be about five points less than the figure in Figure 4. Such an after-dividends pattern of cash flow dramatizes the cash crunch faced by many businesses.

SUMMARY

Before the advent of diversified companies, competition in the marketplace determined which businesses were shaken out of the industry. In a modern, multi-business company, management must decide which businesses to liquidate and which to expand. Managers can serve both their companies and society at large by making investment decisions which reduce the probability of wasting scarce investment resources. To make these decisions, managers need detailed information on the competitive position and the expected financial performance of each business in their portfolio. They also need to know what strategic and tactical courses of action typically succeed and which typically fail. Given such information, they can minimize the risk of making investments in unproductive areas.

The PIMS Program has developed a strategic planning service designed to satisfy these management needs. Information on strategic actions, market and industry situations, and results achieved has been compiled and organized into a multi-purpose data base. The analysis of this data base has shown which business characteristics are the important determinants of profitability and other success measures. Executives of the participating companies are using SPI findings, reports, and services in a variety of ways to develop and appraise strategic plans for individual business units and to balance their portfolios of product-line businesses.

REFERENCES

1. Prior factual, scientific programs had also been developed in response to the economic pressures of their time periods. The depression of the 1930s led to the development of macroeconomic theory, national income accounting data, and macroeconomic models and forecasts. World War II brought about supply bottlenecks caused by dramatic changes in the composition of final demand by industry in the United States. This led to detailed input-output data (information on interindustry sales and purchases) and the estimation of output targets by industry.

2. From 1972 to 1974 PIMS was located at the Marketing Science Institute, a research organization affiliated with the Harvard Business School.

3. For an overview of PIMS during its developmental period see Sidney Schoeffler, Robert D. Buzzell, and Donald F. Heany, "Impact of Strategic Planning on Profit Performance," *Harvard Business Review*, March-April 1974.

4. For additional empirical evidence on the share-ROI relation, see Bradley T. Gale, "Market Share and Rate of Return," *Review of Economics and Statistics*, November 1972, and Robert D. Buzzell, Bradley T. Gale, and Ralph G. M. Sultan, "Market Share—A Key to Profitability," *Harvard Business Review*, January-February 1975.

5. Unionization is especially damaging to productivity when investment per employee is high.

HAROLD W. HENRY

Report Card
for Planners

CORPORATIONS are continually under pressure to improve performance. Many different indexes are used to evaluate performance by various groups with legitimate concerns; these include stockholders, customers, employees, suppliers, communities, and governmental units. Return on investment is a basic index, but the quality of products or services provided and contributions to the welfare of society in general are also evaluated. Thus corporations must periodically measure their performance on various indexes and compare the results to accepted standards.

When performance does not meet expectations, corporate executives seek ways to improve performance through better management of available resources. During the 1970s many corporations have sought to manage better by redesigning their corporate planning systems. Since results are not likely to be better than the plans they are based on, attention to the planning function of management is primary and essential.

To determine how corporations are planning to achieve corporate performance goals, I conducted personal interviews with top executives and planning specialists in 29 large corporations in seven industries over two years. Most of the companies visited had made major changes in their planning systems in the early 1970s in an effort to improve corporate performance. Notably more emphasis is now being given to strategic planning than when I conducted a similar study in the mid-1960s. Furthermore, top managers are involved to a greater extent in formulating corporate strategy.

Several specific types of changes have been introduced by these companies in the past few years in an effort to plan more effectively. Most important are:

Better selection and training of managers and planners
New organizations for planning

Formal evaluation of plans and the planning process
Managerial incentives to plan better
More systematic product and market analyses
Company-wide portfolio analyses
New external monitoring systems
Forced contingency planning

PERSONNEL SELECTION AND TRAINING

Many companies have made deliberate efforts to select better qualified personnel to be strategic planners and managers of strategic planning units. They have also provided formal training for such persons to increase their understanding of the planning process, as well as of the overall structure, goals, and philosophy of the corporation. In selecting staff planning specialists, companies have sought individuals with outstanding capabilities and the potential to move into higher management positions. The best qualified individuals available have been sought because such planners "put knowledge at the disposal of power"—a critically important function. These planners often do move into higher management positions later. One company has used weighted selection criteria for strategic planners including personal characteristics (40 percent), knowledge of planning methodology or technology (40 percent), and knowledge of the business (20 percent). Personal characteristics such as toughness and determination were considered essential.

A new dimension has also been added to the selection of key operating managers, namely, matching the manager to the strategy adopted. Thus a manager with the experience, philosophy, and operating style considered best for implementing a particular strategy is assigned to head the unit in which the strategy is employed. This approach contrasts sharply with the traditional practice of keeping a manager in one position for many years merely because he served effectively there in the past. The logic that underlies the newer approach is that an organization may become the major impediment to changing the strategy, so the organization must be changed to carry out a new strategy properly.

Formal training programs also have been introduced in many companies in an effort to make their planning systems more effective. For example, at Electro, Inc.,* planning specialists received a two-week course and general managers, division managers, and department managers received a 3½-day course. In addition, several thousand section managers and subsection managers received a one-day audiovisual pre-

---

* Fictitious identifying names are used for all companies cited in this contribution.

sentation on planning. In turn, they were given a package of visual aids to take back to their units for training of lower-level personnel. Most of the formal training was conducted at a location remote from operating centers, and extensive use was made of planning specialists from universities and consulting firms. At Computer Corporation regular managerial training classes, which include sessions on planning and control, are held for supervisors down to the second and third levels.

At Electrical Equipment Corporation an innovative new planning system was introduced which combined managerial training by noncompany leaders with an internal company evaluation by participating managers. The setting was the annual management conference, and the theme selected by the chairman was "strategic planning and programming." Invited external speakers presented and discussed new ideas about planning to stimulate the thinking of participating company managers. Many informal discussion sessions on planning were held after the conference, and this process of "educating" managers was viewed as essential for formalizing and improving the planning efforts in the company.

ORGANIZATION FOR PLANNING

Several unique organization designs have also been introduced in the past few years. One of the most interesting was found at Electro, Inc., where more than 40 units called "strategic business units (SBUs)" were designed strictly for planning purposes. These SBUs resegmented or recombined the basic structure of groups, divisions, and departments in the company. In most cases each SBU was either a group, a division, or a department (see Figure 1), but only about 40 percent of the existing division managers were designated as general managers of these planning units. Each unit developed strategic plans and received resource allocations just as if it were a separate business. In addition to grouping interrelated activities for planning purposes to improve performance, this plan avoided major disruptions and inefficiencies which would have resulted from a major organizational change. In time, perhaps the planning units (SBUs) will become the basic structure of the company through an evolutionary process. Other features of this system included a new executive staff with primary responsibility to look at the future rather than the day-to-day operating activities. Also, each SBU had a designated strategic planner.

Another structural innovation is found in the corporate planning staff of Computer Corporation. This unit, located under the vice-president of planning, consists of three basic subunits. One is concerned with the

Figure 1. Basic structure and strategic business units in Electro, Inc.

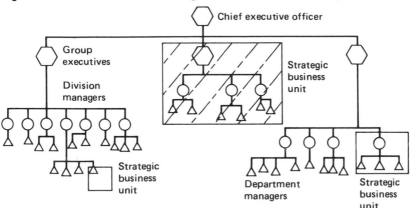

design of the planning process, one with implementation of this process, and a third with assessing the quality of the output or the substance of the plans which are generated in the process. Thus the basic managerial functions of planning, execution, and control are the basis for the planning staff structure. Certain key executives are assigned dual roles, such as manager of planning for a major division and for the corporation.

In most companies the primary responsibility for seeing that the planning function is carried out is vested in a staff vice-president at the corporate level, and this pattern of organization has prevailed since formal planning systems were introduced in many U.S. companies in the 1960s. A small planning staff usually exists under the planning executive with the primary role of coordinating the planning process and advising operating managers. However, the role of the planning staff has been broadened in some companies in recent years to include the development of alternative strategies for review by top management and assistance in setting performance standards for operating units. Thus planning staffs may be used effectively as an extension of the chief executive's office.

EVALUATION OF PLANNING

Several companies are evaluating plans and the planning process as soon as they are completed, instead of waiting until performance results are available. For example, at Electro, Inc., a formal rating system is used to evaluate the plans submitted by the managers of each SBU. Twenty criteria are used, including such factors as consistency, clarity, and understandability. The consistency criterion is used to determine the match between the numbers and the basic plan. Each plan submitted is rated on each criterion as either high, medium, or low. In 1973 several teams of five persons each were formed to evaluate the strategies of each planning unit. Each team was headed by a vice-president and included representatives from finance and planning as well as a technologist. Most were staff people, and they were expected to identify key issues and inefficiencies. The teams reviewed the plans individually and as a group and met with the top corporate planning executive to discuss issues, problems, or concerns about the plan under review. Then they prepared a formal report and sent it to the head of each SBU one week before his review meeting with an executive board composed of top executives. The dual review by a staff committee and by top executives indicated to each SBU manager that the planning effort was considered important and improvements were sought before plan implementation.

MANAGERIAL INCENTIVES

A serious, continuing problem in achieving better performance through better planning is that most managers are evaluated and compensated on the basis of the current year's performance. Many companies, especially the larger corporations, have stressed the importance of a manager's developing effective long-range plans as well as performing well in the current year. However, it is difficult to evaluate the soundness, completeness, and payoff of long-range plans, so the most expedient action is to compensate managers for performance in the current year.

Diversified Electronics, Inc., established an executive bonus plan in which 25 percent of the bonus was tied to actual performance relative to certain factors in the strategic plan. These factors included five or ten targets which were considered most important. However, performance was measured for the first year of the plan, and subsequent years did not get the attention they deserved, even though financial goals were established for each of the next five years. The development of long-range plans was used as one performance criterion, even though it was procedural rather than performance based. In 1975 the incentive plan was linked more closely to planning by careful goal selection and program administration. In addition to the executive bonus plan for top executives, each division received a bonus to be allocated to divisional executives. This program is viewed by insiders as an effective motivating device.

At Office Machines Company division managers are evaluated on their performance relative to several key financial goals that are established by corporate management after negotiation and agreement with each manager. These standards pertain to sales growth, profit margin, capital turnover (sales over capital), return on capital employed, cash flow, and operating income. However, these targets are established each year, so here too the focus is on performance during the current year.

At Computer Corporation top management establishes specific targets for each division before strategies and operating plans are developed within the divisions. Difficult targets are established because top management believes that people are more highly motivated to achieve difficult targets. One executive said, "People can crank up and really produce if there is a goal to shoot for; if retrenchment is needed, they cannot do that as well." Thus the management system in this company seeks to motivate managers by providing challenging goals. Recognition and tangible rewards apparently follow goal fulfillment.

PRODUCT AND MARKET ANALYSES

A fundamental part of planning in any business is to determine those products and markets which offer the greatest potential return. More and more companies seem to be evaluating existing and potential products and markets in a more systematic way. One popular approach used by many firms in recent years has been to classify each company product by share of the market held and market growth potential (see Figure 2). In this way, products are segmented into four major categories:

Heavy cash providers
Heavy cash users

Figure 2. Product line–market matrix.

Market Growth Rate	Market Position		
	Leading	Major	Minor
10 percent and over	Self-sustaining growth		Maximum cash need, uncertainty
6–9 percent			
5 percent and under	Maximum cash generation		Minimum profit potential

High growth and profit potential
Low potential return

This method of classification, segmentation, and evaluation of each product allows for better decisions on the allocation of resources for future product and market development.

In one company where the chief executive officer is a strong believer in strategic planning, a goal was set to grow faster than GNP and the strategy selected to achieve it was to use a differentiated approach to resource allocation. Basic marketing strategies were determined by identification of those product lines which offered the highest leverage for earnings growth and then allocation of the maximum level of required resources to those products. The method outlined above was used for this purpose. Another important benefit of such a systematic analysis of products and markets was to obtain a balance in the product line between those products which provided cash and those which demanded cash for development. In this way, cash flow analysis was directly linked to investment decisions.

As part of this product-market analysis, companies also analyze their entire investment portfolios. The assets allocated to each line of business are determined, and past as well as projected future returns are evaluated. A priority of investment opportunities is determined, and resources are allocated to those products with the greatest potential for growth and profitability so that the return on total assets employed can be maximized.

Most companies establish a target return on equity and return on sales, but they recognize that in diversified companies there is a wide range of businesses and the return on each one might vary quite widely. The discounted cash flow method of investment analysis is still used to evaluate the worth of incremental investments, but it is not considered as important as in the past. Instead of ranking investment opportunities by potential return, companies have substituted a planning methodology for evaluating alternative investments. The focus is on the strategy to be employed in a given business, the cost of implementing the strategy, and the long-term benefit to the company.

EXTERNAL MONITORING

Until recent years external monitoring by corporations consisted primarily of forecasts of product demand and GNP. Today firms recognize that many important changes occur which are not economic in nature.

These include changes in the social, political, technological, and physical segments of the environment. To establish better planning premises, in recent years several companies have made efforts to monitor social and political changes. For example, at Electronic Equipment Corporation an ad hoc committee at corporate headquarters looks worldwide for social and political trends which might affect the corporation. The committee's findings are given to the operating divisions for use in the planning process.

At Kopy Company a strong corporate market research unit provides data on social changes for corporation-wide planning. Also, many inputs on the external environment are provided by various market-information service organizations and from forecasting specialists. This company has employed private consultants to study political and social forces which could affect the economy in 1980, and the study is to be updated periodically.

In Computer Corporation a Washington office under the communications staff is responsible for tracking the legislative scene. In addition, various staff personnel follow legislation which pertains to their functions; for example, the personnel staff follows pension legislation and union matters.

Office Machines Company subscribed to some group studies on social changes. One of these focused on changing attitudes and lifestyles among college youth. Another study which was being planned in 1974 required several corporation clients which would each contribute several thousand dollars. A modified Delphi study was planned which would provide social, political, and economic forecasts by approximately 150 experts in various fields of study. Clients could add a few questions of special interest to them.

Technological forecasting is not performed in a systematic way by the companies studied, but the research and development units in each company are generally expected to follow developments in each scientific discipline which might affect the company's products or performance.

CONTINGENCY PLANNING

In the past decade one of the more serious problems encountered in corporate planning systems has been that assumptions used as the basis for plans proved to be invalid. Many companies now realize that forecasting is an inexact art and that premises based on any forecast may become invalid quickly. Therefore, companies have started to develop more than one set of premises and various scenarios to use in developing strategic plans. Some have required contingency plans which are based on a different set of premises than those used for the primary plan.

One company recently added a section to each strategic plan on contingencies in which each manager was expected to explain the conditions under which his plan might fail. The managers in another company were asked to develop contingency plans in the event of an economic downturn in which GNP and revenues dropped by a fixed amount. Managers quickly recognized the operational and performance impacts of these assumptions and were able to track actual conditions more closely and thereby provide better control and quicker responses when changes did occur. The probabilities of occurrence of certain economic downturns were estimated, and this type of performance-risk analysis caused managers to be more cautious in implementing plans. Contingency planning dampened the enthusiasm of young managers who had grown up in a "go-go" environment in which performance was always good and growth had been steadily upward. Contingency planning compensated for the overly optimistic psychology of these managers and introduced a higher degree of caution into their decision-making efforts.

Another company imposes a requirement to develop a contingency plan for investment priorities, established by a segment of the market. Other companies use simulation models for answering "what if" questions. They assume a change in one key variable and determine the impact on other variables. This type of contingency analysis helps managers realize the sensitivity of certain variables to changes and enables them to recognize the implications more readily.

SUMMARY

The changes in formal planning systems which have been introduced by large corporations in the United States in the past few years have the potential for producing significant improvements in corporate performance in coming years. *Business Week* pointed out that some evidence exists that performance has already improved in the companies that have made the greatest efforts to improve their planning systems ("At Potlatch, Nothing Happens Without a Plan," November 10, 1975). Those changes which pertain to the personnel who are involved in the planning process are very important. Most organizations have access to the same resource markets, the same financial institutions, and in many cases the same technology. The key difference in the performance of corporations rests primarily with the personnel who manage them. Thus any effort to select, train, organize, evaluate, and motivate top executives, operating managers, and planning specialists has to be a step in the right direction in the improvement of corporation performance. In addition, the procedural changes which involve a more systematic evaluation of every product a company sells and every market served, as well as an evaluation of the investments required for selling each product and serving each market, will reveal those areas in which performance is unsatisfactory and those in which potential improvement is greatest.

Efforts to monitor changes in the social, political, economic, technological, and physical segments of the external environment of a firm will provide information essential in the planning process for identifying threats and opportunities. Those companies that do the best job of monitoring, interpreting the results, and applying the findings in the planning process should improve performance the most in future years. The discipline of making alternative assumptions about future conditions and developing contingency plans based on those alternative premises should pay dividends in future performance. In a world in which change seems to be the only thing certain, the use of more than one scenario or set of assumptions about the future will provide managers and planners with a much broader perspective and much greater flexibility as they plan for the future. Changes in direction and reallocation of resources can be made much more quickly under these conditions than when one set of assumptions and one plan are developed.

By adopting the attitude that formal, systematic, corporate strategic planning is a continuous process which enables managers to make sounder, quicker decisions, any business firm can improve the effectiveness of its managers. The results will be reflected in improved long-term corporate performance.

MELVIN E. SALVESON

Pinning the Blame for Strategy Failures on the CEO

COMPANY PRESIDENTS frequently have short memories, if we judge by their annual report messages. All too often a project touted in the Message from the President one year as an exciting new venture is "forgotten" by the next annual report. Every corporate success has a proud father, but failures are doomed to bastardy. Some annual reports try to draw attention away from failures by highlighting a category called Profits from Continuing Operations. Thus a president can discreetly abandon the venture that failed by categorizing it in the annual report as a Discontinued Operation—a seemingly unimportant item. Such public relations devices may salve the chief executive officer's conscience, but they make fair assessment of his performance difficult. Discontinued operations are also a product of the CEO, and are an end result of his strategy. As failures, they deserve careful examination by directors, stockholders, employees, and press. And for the CEO, analysis of past mistakes is his best way to prevent future strategy failures.

It is on the doorstep of the CEO that strategy failures must be laid, since he or she is the "chief strategist." The success of the enterprise is largely determined by the CEO's skill in initiating and managing strategy. In this contribution we examine the anatomy of corporate success and failure in strategy formulation and implementation.

STRATEGY AND GROWTH RATE

Excellent proof of the importance of the CEO's strategy can be found in the different rates of growth during an 80-year period in the history of the General Electric Company. Under five different chief executives, G.E. adopted five very different strategic concepts and experienced five different rates of growth.

Employing these five different strategies, G.E. grew at five different sustained rates, which ranged from -1 percent to $+8.5$ percent, compounded annually, after adjustments were made for differences in rate of inflation and growth in GNP. Over the 80 years, G.E.'s annual sales grew from $13.5 million (1892) to $10 billion (1972), over 740 times its original size (if we take into account the change in the value of the dollar). During this period there were five different sustained CEO "teams" (individuals or pairs who jointly occupied the office of the CEO), and each adopted different strategies, each with different results.

These measurements allow for a two-year carryover between successive administrations. During these two-year interregnum periods, the rate of growth under a new CEO tended to continue at the rate characteristic of the preceding CEO. Thus each new CEO required at least two years in which to discontinue his predecessor's strategy and to make his own strategies effective. In this study adjustments have been made for this lag, and other adjustments made for the different rates of growth in GNP and for the different rates of inflation.

Table 1 summarizes the strategy, rate of growth, and size of G.E. during the administration of each CEO team. Analysis of each CEO's strategy was made by review of his writings and such documents as his annual reports. The reliability of equating a CEO's "words" and "deeds" is not perfect. But two historical facts are clear. First, each CEO publicly focused time, money, and energy on certain issues and concerned himself with definably different ways in which to direct G.E. Thus each set different goals to accomplish and measured off different milestones for management. Second, there were differences in the results from one CEO to the next, even though the company structure and product did not change significantly from one to the next, at least until each successive CEO had had a chance to implement his strategy.

The fastest growth of G.E. or any of its antecedent companies was under Thomas A. Edison, whose strategy focused on new-product invention and innovation. Edison is included for comparison in this study of the corporation because, though he was never CEO of G.E., he founded one of G.E.'s principal antecedents: Edison Lamp Company. G.E. itself never grew so quickly. Edison, as much the strategist as the inventor, developed a conscious, deliberate plan for introducing the incandescent lamp, which made the arc and gas lamps obsolete.

The second fastest rates of growth were under Charles Coffin (1892–1921) and Charles Wilson and Phillip Reed (1939–1950). Each of these CEO teams pursued strategies that focused on motivating employees to implement the technologies developed under predecessors and demanded by the market place.

The third fastest growth took place under Fred Borch (1963–1972). A marketing executive, Borch focused on balanced or rationalized central-

Table 1. Comparison of chief executive effectiveness at General Electric Company, 1892–1972.

Name of CEO	Dates	Total Tenure (Years)	Annual Sales ($)[a] Beginning	Annual Sales ($)[a] Ending	Focus of Strategy	Raw Growth (%), Annual Sales	GNP Growth (%)	Net Adjusted Growth (%), Annual Sales
Edison (Edison Lamp Company)	1881–1891	10	13.7 K	11 M	Invention, innovation, market penetration	95	0.5	94.5
Coffin/Thomson/Rice	1892–1921	29	13.5 M	200 M	Market penetration of prior technology	9.6	0.9	8.5
Swope/Young	1922–1939	17	251 M	259 M	Control, centralization, internationalization	0.01	1.0	−0.99
Wilson/Reed (Swope 1943)	1939–1950	10	396 M	1,600 M	Implementation of prior technology to war/personnel development	11.5	4.0	7.5
Cordiner	1950–1962	11	3,500 M	5,000 M	Reorganization, professional management	3.3	3.3	0.0
Borch/Jones	1963–1972	9	4,900 M	9,400 M	New markets, products, ventures	9.6	4.3	5.3

[a] K equals thousands; M equals millions.

ization versus decentralization, as well as a more aggressive approach to new ventures and to rebuilding the staff organization. He had problems, however, in maintaining profit growth.

The second slowest growth was under the strategy of Ralph Cordiner (1950–1962), who advocated the development of the "professional manager." Cordiner decided that "professional management" would fulfill G.E.'s needs for continued growth. Unfortunately, he provided too little strategic direction for the 170 general managers he created, and they did not produce the results he envisioned. By rigidly requiring all of them to achieve returns of 7 percent on sales and 22 percent on investment (and using these goals for computing their incentive compensation bonuses), Cordiner forced emphasis on short-term profit and eliminated most "growth" projects.

The slowest growth took place under Gerard Swope, the international marketer, and Owen Young, the financier (1922–1939). Swope and Young followed Coffin, and their strategy was to consolidate the strong advances made by their predecessors. They increased centralization, and reduced the emphasis on new-product development. Financial goals became paramount, and the company became less innovative. Efforts toward penetrating international markets were made, but were unsuccessful.

Keeping this G.E. history in mind, let us sidetrack for a moment to differentiate between "corporate-level" and "product-level" strategies. At the corporate level, the concern is with such questions as:

- Which products/markets should the company pursue?
- What will be the allocation of resources among the alternative product opportunities?
- What will be the corporate capital structure and sources of funds?
- What will be the methods of motivating product operating personnel?
- What are the continuing objectives and the measurements for determining their achievement?

At the product level, important considerations are:

- Given the features of product A, will it be successful against competitor X?
- When should product A be introduced? At what price?
- When should product A be phased out and product B introduced?
- Should the manufacturing be highly automated, or should the product be produced in a job shop?
- Where should dealer's reserve stocks be located?

• How is competitor X vulnerable? Can we outperform competitor X in the area in which it is most vulnerable?

The concerns of corporate chief executives are to formulate corporate strategies that move the company in the direction of opportunity and to assure that the strategies adopted by the operating/product-level managers are well conceived and likely to succeed.

G.E.'s Cordiner, for example, because he understood the appliance industry well, conceived of and promoted the Appliance Park manufacturing facility in Louisville, Kentucky. This created a major new facility for G.E. that greatly increased capacity and reduced costs. Cordiner's daring thrust gave G.E. a major cost and price advantage over any of its appliance competitors. The advantage was permanent for G.E. and devastating for the competition. Appliance Park was built in 1954, and by 1974 G.E. so dominated the industry that even Westinghouse was forced to withdraw from appliance manufacturing and to sell out to White Appliances.

Thus in Cordiner's actions we see exemplified the differences between "corporate-level" and "operating-level" strategies, and the great differences between skills required to formulate and to implement successfully. A former washing machine salesman, Cordiner understood what needed to be done in appliances. Unfortunately, he lacked the conceptual skill to see a framework of strategies by which he could lead his newly created 170 general managers. Also, he lacked proven canons of strategy by which to test and appraise strategies proposed by the managers. Furthermore, he denied himself the support of a corporate staff to assist in the analysis of strategies of subordinates or in the formulation of corporate strategies.

Under Fred Borch (1963–1972) and Reginald Jones, G.E. reversed much of Cordiner's strategy. The number of profit centers has been reduced from 170 to 43; a corporate staff for strategy analysis and planning has been reinstated; and focus is on the development of viable, superior strategies for both the corporate and operating levels.

INVENTOR VERSUS FINANCIER

Two of the most striking executive records to compare are those of Edison and Owen D. Young, the financier who served as chairman of General Electric during the 1920s. Young summarized the strategy of his stewardship as follows:

Fifteen years is about the average period of probation, and during that period the inventor, the promoter, and the investor, who see a great future for the invention, generally lose their shirts. Public demand, even for a great invention, is always slow in developing. That is why the wise capitalist keeps out of exploiting new inventions.*

Since Edison was a vigorous promoter, as well as one of the greatest inventors in American history, his strategy was diametrically opposite to Young's. To test which strategy was more effective, Edison's or Young's, we evaluated the various strategies of 48 different G.E. product lines. The data are summarized in Table 2 and shown graphically in Figure 1.

Table 2. Summary of data for the 48 G.E. products in the sample.

Product's Ordinal Position	Market Share			Profitability		
	Number	Mean	Standard Deviation	Number	Mean	Standard Deviation
1	12	0.0985	0.040	13	0.105	0.041
2	11	0.081	0.044	9	0.084	0.042
3	9	0.059	0.035	10	0.058	0.050
4	8	0.055	0.037	7	0.062	0.041
5	4	0.035	0.035	5	0.037	0.039
6	4	0.019	0.040	4	0.015	0.040

The Note at the end of this chapter gives a full analysis of the data.

Let us define the following terms:

The entrepreneurial investment: The dollar amount invested by G.E. in any product's development prior to the product's first appearance in the market, either by G.E. or by a competitor.

The relative investment: The ratio of the entrepreneurial investment (I) in the product to the total annual dollar sales (S) of the product and its competitors five years after introduction of the product; that is, relative investment $= I/S$.

The relative success of the product: As measured by both the ordinal market position—the standing of G.E.'s product, that is, first, second, etc., in the market place—and the ordinal profit position—the relative return on investment of the product compared with the profitability of competing products. (In the present study, the profitabilities of competitors' products were estimated.)

The results charted in Figure 1 show that G.E. enjoyed first place in the market place and the highest return on investment in those areas in

---

* In W. Rupert Maclaurin, *Innovation and Invention in the Radio Industry* (New York: Macmillan, 1949).

Figure 1. Ordinal market and profit positions for 48 General Electric products.

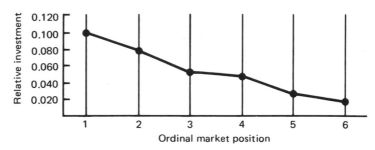

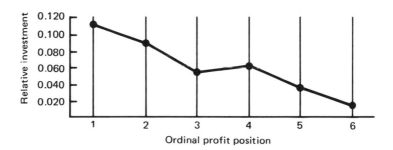

which it had spent the most on product development prior to the product's introduction into the market place. In other words, the results show that Owen D. Young's anti-innovation stance was wrong, at least for G.E.

The same indexes were measured for two of G.E.'s competitors. These are plotted in consolidated form in Figure 2, and the data are given in Table 3. (Again, see the Note at the back of this chapter for fur-

Table 3. Summary of data for the 26 products from G.E. competitors in the sample.

Product's Ordinal Position	Market Share			Profitability		
	Number	Mean	Standard Deviation	Number	Mean	Standard Deviation
1	4	0.045	0.03	4	0.070	0.03
2	6	0.075	0.03	7	0.085	0.04
3	5	0.048	0.015	5	0.051	0.03
4	4	0.039	0.031	5	0.042	0.025
5	4	0.042	0.02	3	0.030	0.02
6	3	0.03	0.02	2	0.016	0.01

ther details.) The competitors did not derive the same success from their enterpreneurial investments. They showed a lower average return on investment and a lower return on sales than G.E., and fewer products in first place in the market.

There are companies in other markets—for example, Procter and Gamble—that are noted for "never innovating" in product or in R&D. Procter and Gamble prefers to copy and imitate. Yet is has a very successful track record, including a good return on investment and a good growth rate. As another example, King Electronics is also reluctant to innovate, yet it is a solid No. 2 in the aviation electronics field.

Through Project CASE (Comparative Analysis of Strategy Effectiveness), we at Corporate Strategies International have found preliminary results which show that the likely success of a strategy is related to a number of factors. Some of these and their effects are:

- Companies with proportionately large investment in R&D and with high overhead and general and administrative rates, coupled with innovative marketing, tend to experience satisfactory gross margins and to be viable and profitable.

Figure 2. Ordinal market and profit positions for 26 of General Electric competitors' products.

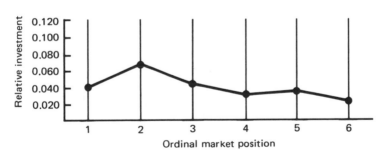

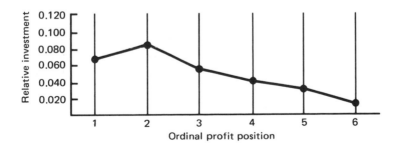

- Companies with high rates of investment in R&D and with the tendency to be imitators or followers in marketing tend to have lower gross margins and to be less profitable.
- A strategy of low R&D spending, coupled with attempts to pioneer a market, also tends to fail.

Corporations that design an overall consistent strategy tend to be most successful. In addition, the data show that there is a significant relationship between the success of one corporation and its strategy and the interaction of that strategy with the other corporations and their strategies, in the arena within which they compete. That is, three different strategies may "coexist" with profitable results to each of the three different enterprises. For instance, one enterprise may adopt the "pioneering" strategy of investing first and most in order to lead the market. A second may adopt the follower strategy and may always be second, with a lower overhead and a lower-priced product. A third may specialize successfully, for example, in a high-quality, high-styled product in a narrow niche in the market.

OPPORTUNITY KNOCKS TWICE

The strategies of two CEO entrepreneurs, Edison and William Painter, the inventor/cofounder of Crown Cork and Seal Company in 1892, deserve comparison in order to illustrate the differences in the ways that business people may perceive opportunities and develop and implement strategies to exploit them. On the one hand, Edison adopted a strategy of supplying the full incandescent lighting system, including generator, transformer, meter, apparatus, and lamp. Under the protection of the lamp patent, Edison had an opportunity to develop the full line of products necessary to supply and install the electric systems. In turn, the full line pre-empted competitors who would supply only one or a few of the needed products.

Painter revolutionized the beverage industry by inventing the metal Crown seal (named after its shape) that is still used today for bottles. But Painter's strategy focused only on selling the seal. He manufactured seals and machines for applying them. His customers, in turn, supplied their own bottles and contents, and marketed the end product. Painter could have emulated Edison's strategy and used his patent on the metal crown to supply a full "beverage system," including the bottle, the contents, and even the marketing. Given the competitive advantages of his patent, he could have achieved a dominant position in the industry for many beverages, such as beer, soft drinks, juices, and oils. Painter's

Beer might have been as much a household word today as Hires Root Beer.

Instead, when Painter's patents expired, Crown lost market position, since it had no identity with the end consumer. Painter's seal customers soon adopted and used his process without buying seals from him. Crown now has sales of about $600 million per year, versus G.E.'s $14 billion. Crown is the "follower" in the container industry; G.E. is the "pioneer-dominator" in the electrical industry. John Connelly, current president of Crown, has adopted by necessity an effective "imitator" strategy.

The two dominant container corporations, Continental Can and American Can, are each several times the size of Crown. But Crown not only stays viable by occupying a special niche, it is growing more rapidly than either competitor, and it has a higher price to earnings ratio and return on investment. American Can and Continental Can could be described as two lions feasting on one antelope, with neither lion fully sated. Crown, to continue the analogy, is a vulture feasting richly off the remains left behind by the lions. However, recently Crown has faced new reversals. The narrow niche Crown occupied, selling hard-to-contain aerosols powered by fluorocarbons, was affected when scientists voiced concern about the potential harm to the ionosphere caused by fluorocarbons. In a classic example of the vulnerability of narrow product lines, Crown will have to go through a change of strategy. At such perilous times the drama of the CEO's strategic moves are clear to one and all.

NOTE

The data* and relationships shown in Figures 1 and 2 yield conclusions that may be useful for strategy formulation.

First, within G.E. product lines, those products in No. 1 market positions had a mean relative investment of 0.0985, and those in No. 6 market positions had a mean of 0.013—a range of 500 percent. Thus for a "standard" market size, when G.E. enjoyed a No. 1 market position, it had invested an average of 500 percent more in the product than it had invested for a product in sixth position. G.E.'s competitors had invested an average of 150 percent more in first- versus sixth-place products.

Second, within the same product line, products that were most profitable in their respective markets had a mean relative investment of 0.105, and those that were sixth had a mean of 0.015. Thus for a "stan-

---

* Data have been scaled to prevent use by competitors.

dard" market, when G.E. enjoyed No. 1 profitability, it had invested an average of 700 percent more in the product than when it was in sixth position. G.E.'s competitors had a similar relationship: They had invested an average of 437 percent more in their first-place products than in their sixth-place products.

Third, G.E. enjoyed a higher percentage of its products in No. 1 market positions than its competitors, and G.E. had made a higher relative investment for those No. 1 products than its competitors had made for their No. 1 products—0.0985 versus 0.045, or a factor of 218 percent. This suggests that when G.E. elected to enter a product line through the R&D route, it cost G.E. over twice as much to do so as it cost its nearest competitors. In spite of this greater investment, the percentage of G.E. products that were first in profitability was almost twice as great as that of its nearest competitors.

Fourth, G.E.'s average relative investment for new products in a "standard" market was 140 percent of that of its competitors. Yet G.E.'s net profit on sales and on investment was, at the time of the sample, 148 and 162 percent of those of its two nearest competitors.

Clearly, strategic decisions are not easy. As the market and competitive situation changes, modifications in basic strategy may be imperative. The wrong decision may bring difficulties or a disaster. The right decision will avoid "discontinued operations" and prove that the CEO has successfully fulfilled his function as chief strategist.

MELVIN E. SALVESON

Examination of
a Strategy Failure

DURING THE 1960s AND 1970s A large number of corporations focused on rapid growth and diversification. Within a few years, almost all of them experienced severe growing pains when they attempted to manage their diversified stable of companies. Many have found that such pains can wrack and sometimes even destroy an organization that otherwise seemed to be quite strong. The following case history of Teledyne/Packard Bell outlines some of the problems and results in one instance of diversified growth. It also examines the process of planning and achieving growth and suggests strategies for avoiding the kind of failure that the Teledyne subsidiary, Packard Bell, experienced.

TELEDYNE'S RISE

In 1972 Teledyne/Packard Bell pursued a dynamic, new program to "go national" and to gain a larger share of both the American and foreign television markets. A new group vice president was hired to supervise Packard Bell; he organized the company into six autonomous divisions: marketing, manufacturing, financing, service, export, and advertising. To promote sales, new "distributing sales companies" were set up around aggressive salespersons. This eliminated the existing "two-step distribution" method and increased dealer incentives while reducing the dealer risks. A new solid-state chassis, designed to be competitive with the best on the market, was put into production.

Thus geared to compete with the television industry on a national scale, Packard Bell's $20-million sales doubled within one year.

TELEDYNE'S FALL

In May 1974 Teledyne announced that Packard Bell TV was closing down and operations were being discontinued. The estimated loss was $50 million.

THE WHY'S

Were the human relations bad? Was the product deficient? Was the marketing incompetent? Were financial resources inadequate? Was the engineering of the product not actually competitive? The answer to all these questions is "No." In short, the defect at Packard Bell was in its strategy. This company could be productive today, serving the needs of all: the public, its former employees—now discharged—and its stockholders—who lost an estimated $3.00 per share.

The demise of Packard Bell was due to the failure at the highest level to grasp the separate elements of the strategy which had been developed and implemented for that company. This incident illustrates the necessity that the chief executive of a corporation be a "master of strategy" if the firm is to effectively serve all those who depend on it for goods and services, employment, or earnings.

SITUATIONAL ANALYSIS

How might a chief executive avoid the pitfalls encountered by Packard Bell? What should he look for in a situation requiring strategy decisions? How does he make a situational analysis for strategy? Can he test such decisions in advance? What are the canons of strategy to guide him? What were some of the danger signals in the Packard Bell situation?

Consider the following elements of the Packard Bell situational analysis:

Product maturity. Television was a mature product; it had passed its zenith in sales and rate of growth many years earlier. The technology was not novel, and the product was essentially a "commodity." Price was a key factor in competition.

Competitor maturity. The number of survivors of the fierce competition in television production was small. From a high of 110 companies, eight were surviving at the time of Packard Bell's decision and only six remained in 1975.

Market maturity. National and international markets were dominated by a few large high-volume producers. Their channels of distribution were well developed and highly efficient. Their volumes of production gave them relatively low cost bases for pricing. And the death throes of the 102 competitors had caused discount selling which pushed prices lower and lower.

Dealer immaturity. Teledyne's new dealer "distributing sales companies" were relatively immature, in comparison with established houses. When added to their freedom from inventory risk, this made them willing to take risks and promote sales, with the failures going to the manufacturer and the gains, if any, to the distributor.

Market sharing. Since the market was mature, competition did not strongly increase the total market, but redistributed it among the surviving competitors. Gains by one competitor came from decreases in the market share of others, and the companies reacted violently to each other's thrusts and ploys.

Having considered this situational analysis, we can now analyze the effects of Packard Bell's decision to "go national." Previously, Packard Bell had occupied a small niche in the television market, selling high-quality high-style sets in the 11 western states. When it ventured out of its sheltered niche, Packard Bell confronted the major producers such as Sony, RCA, General Electric, and Zenith.

STRATEGIC ANALYSIS

With facts of the situation at hand, the chief executive's task is to think through the implications of the chosen strategy, to avoid such pitfalls as those that caused the demise of Packard Bell. What might have been the Teledyne chief executive's analysis of the Packard Bell strategy?

Lacking any new capability, such as improved technology, Packard Bell could have achieved its national objectives only by reducing the market share of the well-established giants, and its only competitive advantage was reduced prices, margins, and profits. Packard Bell reduced prices by increasing incentives and decreasing risks for dealer-distributors. But the high-volume competitors had lower costs, which Parkard Bell could have achieved only with a massive investment (of $250–500 million). Even if the funds had been available, the combination of lowered costs and lowered prices would have yielded profits insufficient to satisfy normal "return on investment" criteria.

Furthermore, at about the same time that it was embarking on a strategy which required massive funds for its success, Teledyne was engaged in the repurchase of about $200 million of its common stock. At first the chief executive used cash and borrowings for such repurchase; then he issued bonds. Thus Teledyne was simultaneously engaged in two different and conflicting major thrusts of strategy. Probably as a result the price of the firm's stock did not increase. Then Packard Bell failed.

What effective action could the chief executive have taken to avoid such results? With the advantage of hindsight, how can we reanalyze the strategies, and how should the analyses have been carried out? What are the proper qualifications for such analyses, and how does a chief executive officer succeed at them?

In a company with a narrow product line, the chief executive officer usually has progressed to the top within that product/market environment. He has direct experience in it; he knows the competitors and their capabilities from direct observation. He knows how they will counter each other's moves. He should then consider the outcome of many different strategies and accept the one which has the best chance to survive and succeed.

But in highly diversified companies, such as Teledyne, it is beyond reason to expect the chief executive officer to have direct personal knowledge of the many markets/products in which the company is competing. So he must rely on other methods of analysis in order to assure winning strategies. He could, for example, employ a larger corporate staff including persons trained in strategic analysis and planning who could extend his reach.

Another method is the "school of fish" approach to product line management. Under this method, instead of engaging in a single large-volume business, a company engages in many small ones. Any one may fail, and the parent will survive. Teledyne has 160 companies averaging $10 million in annual sales which must be managed. General Electric has 43 companies to be managed, averaging $250 million each.

A third approach is for the chief executive officer of a large, diversified corporation to recognize that he must be a master of the art of strategy. Such mastery is difficult to achieve. Unlike the strategy of war, which has been well analyzed and developed, the strategy of business has not yet been reduced to canonical form. Hopefully, through the examination of errors of strategy, such as the present article, we will move toward such a canon.

These guidelines, together with the ability to analyze strategy proposals, will enable the chief executive officer to extend the range and scope of the business which he guides and controls.

This last approach gives the chief executive officer greater power and requires of him greater involvement than do the alternative approaches. It also promises greater gains. And, considering the relatively small size of the corporate staff and implementing system required to pursue a sensible strategy analysis, surely the cost is less and the gain is greater for the corporation than the "school of fish" approach—even with its sparse corporate staff.

THE CHIEF EXECUTIVE OFFICER AS A MASTER OF STRATEGY

The maxims of war articulated by Caesar and von Clausewitz were learned through experience and through the analysis of countless successes and failures. It is in a similar pursuit of useful knowledge that we examine here the specific errors of strategy committed by Teledyne's chief executive officer.

• The chief executive officer failed to prevent his company from entering an arena in which the price-volume-profit squeeze would intrinsically work against the firm in its attempt to gain volume taken from its competitors.

• The chief executive officer structured, or allowed the structuring of, Packard Bell into six highly interdependent divisions, violating the "strategic business unit" concept. This structure caused a diversion of energy from competition with other companies in the market to competition with other divisions within Packard Bell. As a result, all divisions suffered.

• The funds needed to succeed, if success could have been achieved at all, were withdrawn from the company in order to repurchase stock. Thus the full set of resources was not provided, and Packard Bell was allowed to adopt a strategy which required funds and resources not available within the corporation.

• If the venture had succeeded, the amount of funds required would have been so large that miscalculation would have embarrassed or even bankrupted the parent corporation. In general, the chief executive officer should keep such risks or ventures directly under his personal surveillance.

• The chief executive officer allowed the corporation to undertake a risky venture, with important consequences to the survival of the company, without having direct experience in and personal understanding of the industry and markets into which his firm was venturing. He placed the company's survival in the hands of a subordinate executive.

• He committed resources to a venture which, competitively, would not allow a return on investment of even as much as the prevailing interest rates. That is, he could have invested more securely and profitably in bonds of other companies.

• He permitted one-sided incentives to be given to the group vice president and the "distributing sales companies." They could gain through sales, stock options, and profit improvements, but they did not suffer proportionately on the "downside." As a result the distributors went further in accepting risk than was prudent for the company.

• The chief executive officer allowed Packard Bell to change from a viable approach to a new strategy without empirically testing all elements and the full strategy in the new environment before committing substantial resources to it.

• He allowed Packard Bell to undertake a venture without the firm's having a strong competitive advantage over competitors who had many advantages.

ALTERNATIVE STRATEGIES

The value of examining alternative strategies is that the chief executive officer can discover the weaknesses and advantages of various approaches without having to commit himself to one until he has tested it and affirmed its worth. What might have been the alternative strategies for Packard Bell?

First, Packard Bell could have stayed in its profitable niche selling high-quality high-style television sets in the western United States where it was known, accepted, and respected. To maintain its product competitiveness, it could have updated its chassis by purchasing technology from another manufacturer.

Second, Packard Bell could have moved into the national market slowly, starting with test marketing outside its western arena. If it had found that its product was competitive, it could have expanded its market area by small steps, without inviting direct competitor counteraction.

The third alternative, the one it followed, involved high-growth rates and high risks, and brought on vigorous reaction from competitors who did not like Packard Bell's attempt to gain market share at their expense.

The least likely approach would have been for Packard Bell to develop a unique advantage, such as a new technology, which would have given it a stronger position in the market. This would have insured a greater share of the market, higher returns on investment, and other advantages. But this strategy would have involved an investment and a longer lead time which management probably would not have accepted.

DISCONTINUED OPERATIONS

The phrase "Profits from Continuing Operations" is now a standard phrase in 90 percent of corporate annual reports. The failures are abandoned, written up as "discontinued operations." This is not an accurate representation of the facts. These discontinued operations are part of the output of the company's chief executive officer, and those that go unexamined are likely to breed more in the future.

The loss in market value to Teledyne stockholders from the Packard Bell adventure was about $500 million. U.S. economic problems arise partly because of the cumulative effects of many similar corporate failures. Teledyne's losses in the demise of Packard Bell affect us all.

MILTON LEONTIADES

A Case History of
Strategic Planning

THERE IS a certain ambivalence between the theory of corporate planning and a case history used to illustrate it. On the one hand theory must generalize and capture enough of reality to explain it. It must be simple enough to be useful yet complex enough to be relevant. But a case history deals only with specific facts. It need not reflect practices which are right for any other company. Consequently it invariably questions theory since no formula can capture all the variations of a particular case.

For corporate planning the position of theory is especially tenuous. Systematic planning efforts are of a relatively recent origin. As one well-known commentator on the state of industrial planning has observed, "until the end of World War II, or shortly thereafter, planning was a moderately evocative word in the United States. . . . For a public official to be called an economic planner was less serious than to be charged with Communism or imaginative sexual perversion, but it reflected adversely nonetheless."*

Such a charge aimed at business planners may not have been made so strongly but it would have been accurate in principle. It was only after the war that the acceptance of formalized business planning gained momentum. Since its emergence, the transitions in planning theory have been rapid with a building cascade of learned articles and books on the subject. This torrent of advice, however, has tended to outrun the time required to absorb it. As yet no single unifying theory, or even standard definition, of strategic planning suffices. Where one is needed, many are available.

The current evolving and unsettled status of strategic planning makes it particularly important to continually probe those theories put forth to determine which are relevant and which are merely provocative. In this

---

*John Kenneth Galbraith, *The New Industrial State* (Boston: Houghton Mifflin, 1967), Chapter 3.

vein it is helpful from time to time to test what is claimed against what is practiced. Provided with a sufficient number of case histories, one can judge how carefully theory respects reality, and thus strive to bring the two into better harmony.

The case history presented here provides some insights that hopefully aid such a process. It concerns a large diversified company well up in the Fortune 500 rankings that decided to extend an existing position in wholesaling into completely new markets. The methods were tailored to the particular circumstances, but many of the lessons should have broad application.

One lesson early imparted, for example, might qualify as the first law of corporate strategic planning: "No theory can operate without management's tacit approval but management need not plan according to any theory." In this case, top corporate management knew it wanted to diversify and subjectively selected wholesale distribution as the preferred area. The underlying logic was not made available to the planning staff. Thus the trigger point initiating the planning process was a unilateral decision by management. This is obviously not the textbook approach, which is typified by a systematic evaluation of external and internal approaches to reaching corporate goals and, if the external approach is indicated, weighing alternate avenues of diversification.

Although management short-circuited a logical approach in order to concentrate on an area of their preference, this did not prejudice the remainder of the analysis which employed more systematic decision techniques. However, it obviously narrowed the task of the planning group. A brief investigation of wholesaling was undertaken ex poste to give some respectability of analysis to management's decision. This review unearthed some positive reasons for supporting management. But it is probable that whatever the objective findings, management would have pursued their chosen course, demonstrating that truth is not always stronger than conviction.

A second qualification to a textbook approach was an internal dispute over which department would control the project—a situation typical enough to constitute a possible variant, if not a second law, to planning theory. The Corporate Planning Department, in charge of coordinating planning by the divisions, was on one side; Corporate Planning Development, which was responsible for acquisitions and divestitures, was on the other. In contention was the use of a computer model to simulate a typical wholesaler's operation versus analysis of specific industry segments within wholesaling. The former approach would have relied on collecting sample data from a single retail center, using the data to simulate an improved distribution system, and building a company wholesale distribution business around such improvements. The industry approach envisioned a much broader look at actual data by wholesale product lines and individual firms, and successively narrowing the field to the most promising segments into which the company could then build or acquire a position. In essence the difference was between developing a novel wholesaling system (a better mousetrap) and finding the best niche within the existing system. Ultimately the more pragmatic industry analysis proved persuasive.

After this internal dissension was resolved, certain early decisions were made which shaped the type of analysis which followed. First, it was decided to use outside consultants. Although the company was in certain parts of wholesaling, it lacked the expertise and personnel to survey the rest of the field. Second, management wished to reach a minimum volume goal of several million dollars in five years, which precluded small market-size opportunities. There was no attempt to prejudge the task of selecting market opportunities in the initial stages other than with this broad guideline.

With this background we can now proceed to the decision flow diagram in Figure 1. In order to follow the steps in the diagram there are numbers in parentheses that are keyed to appropriate numbers inserted

Figure 1. Decision flow diagram.

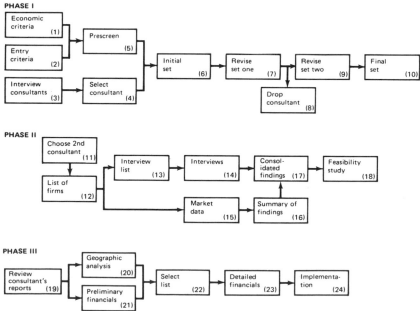

Table 1. Phases of strategic planning.

Phase	Primary Mission	Primary Responsibility
I	Selection of wholesale product lines for Phase II	Company/consultants
II	Field survey and feasibility report	Consultants
III	Detailed analysis of field survey findings and implementation of the strategic plan	Company

in the text. Outlined in Table 1 are the three major phases of the study.

Underlying the project design was the intent to interlock the efforts of the corporate planning staff tightly with those of the consultants. This meant that the staff would do as much of the work as was efficient; they would provide specialization of effort, but primarily they would maintain close working control over the project so as not to be surprised at the end with what would be essentially "a consultant's solution." Incidentally, this approach also allowed close supervision of costs and operations.

PHASE I

The first step was undertaken by the company: to conduct a rough screening of potential product lines. Bureau of Census Industrial Classifications of over 100 wholesale product lines were used to define the possible alternatives to be screened. Against this array certain economic (1)* and entry (2) criteria were tested. These criteria, indicated in Table 2, were in turn determined partly by the available data.

Table 2. Criteria for strategic analysis.

Economic	Entry

Size of markets
    Merchant wholesaler's value of shipments by product line
	Concentration
	    Buyers
	        Percent of total shipments accounted for by 8 largest manufacturing firms

Forecast growth of markets
    Percentage growth in output of major markets served: 1970–1985
	Sellers
	        Percent of wholesale sales accounted for by firms with over 5 establishments
	        Percent of wholesale sales accounted for by firms with over 25 establishments

Leverage
    Sales/per employee
    Fixed assets/net worth
    Sales/net worth	

Profitability
    Profits before tax/net worth
    Income/operating receipts	

* All numbers in parentheses in the discussion of Phases I–III correspond to those in Figure 1.

The data were not of equal consistency for all wholesale product lines. However, while additional data may have permitted a more refined screening procedure, there are seldom enough data in a study of this nature, and industry product lines which tended to be skimped were those so small as to fall short of management's desired volume goal.

Ratings were developed to rank each product line by the economic and entry criteria established, with a total rating used to indicate the overall potential for that product line. Because of some arbitrariness of numerical rating systems of this type, all questionable decisions were made in favor of retaining the product line for additional evaluation.

Involvement of the company in this early research aspect of the study was very helpful. It kept the initiative with the company and enabled it to better evaluate the qualifications and expertise of the consultants. Also, this preparatory work would need to have been done by the consultants in any case, at a significant cost if done thoroughly, and it was potentially an area the consultants might short-change if costs had to be contained. In this case, consultants were used to thoroughly review the company's approach, to insure that cost savings were not at the expense of faulty research. As it turned out the company's methodology was enthusiastically endorsed with approval in principle of the fourteen industry product lines which passed the company's prescreen (5).

Retracing a bit, the company was interviewing consulting firms (3) as it was conducting the prescreen. After interviewing six firms with heavy experience in wholesaling, the decision was down to two choices (4). Both firms were asked to evaluate the prescreened industries, with their performances to determine which one was to be retained for subsequent phases of the project. The rationale was to assure maximum expertise in this critical early phase. The added cost seemed a small price for the additional insurance. With a very significant eventual contract for the winner as a carrot, the company was confident of the best efforts from both candidates.

As indicated, the result of the prescreening was to narrow from more than 100 product lines to 14. This residual list was then discussed in a meeting between the company and both consultants, with preliminary notice to the consultants to come prepared to criticize, add to, or eliminate from the list. During the meeting a minimum of comment was directed at the selection process which determined the fourteen product lines. However, the list was narrowed from fourteen to six, with consultants' recommendations eliminating some product lines that had shortcomings the prescreen could not capture, as well as joint agreement to drop some marginal inclusions which failed to gain any additional support from the consultants.

Emerging from this meeting was an initial set (6) of six product lines. Both consultants were given this initial set with instructions to examine it in greater depth and were encouraged to further test the selection criteria using their internal data sources and presumed expertise in wholesaling.

The first revision which came back from the consultants (7) reflected very little analysis or change and was disappointing to management. The consultants appeared satisfied to accept what was basically a management list of wholesale product lines and get on with the study. But management clearly had intended the prescreen as only a first selection process which the consultants would use as a starting point for refining the list. It was put forcibly that if they could progress no further than the company's own efforts, other than some cosmetic changes, there was no need to continue the relationship.

This message motivated one of the two firms and the other was dropped (8). In meeting with the chosen consultants, the importance was again impressed for original thinking and fresh contributions at this stage of the project. Using specific criticisms directed by management to the first revision, the consultant prepared a second revision (9). One of the contributions of this revision was a look at the synergy potential of grouping together several product lines which served similar markets. This was a core market concept suggested by management in order to optimize the use of resources and achieve economies of large scale. Figure 2 illustrates how this concept was visualized in building a network of related products to serve a single core market.

In addition, the second revised list expanded the possibilities from six to fifteen product lines. New data were supplied on each area and a rationale developed for its consideration. In essence, the original list had been recycled after the consultants had taken a fresh look at the entire field.

The company endorsed this new perspective but with reservations about the results. First, another pass seemed necessary to arrive at a more manageable number of product lines for an in-depth study. Also, to avoid missing opportunities because of a too dependent focus on product lines, the company had decided to ask for a special analysis of a selected few markets (for example, distributing products to a fast growing market such as health care, in addition to looking at separate product lines which might or might not lead to serving this market in a significant way).

Management's change of heart to encompass this broader sweep of possibilities was discomfiting to the consultants. In effect the rules were being changed while the company was simultaneously sitting very

Figure 2. Multiple product lines to single market.

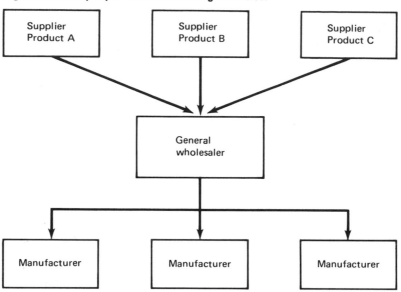

tightly on the original cost estimate for the project—a not uncommon tactic for consultants to encounter. In the end a compromise was reached which was short of the additional dollars the consultants wanted but which offered a narrower scope of investigation from what the company had asked.

After several consultations, a set of four wholesale product lines distributed to two major markets was selected (10). There appeared potential for merging three of these product lines into a single wholesaling network initially serving one primary market. The other product line represented sufficiently large volume to be considered on a stand-alone basis.

The company felt satisfied that a thorough review of feasible alternatives had been made and a good foundation established for the beginning of Phase II. In addition, a wealth of information on different wholesale product lines was available for future reference as well as valuable insights on the structure of wholesaling in general. (Eventually the information from one consultant alone filled four large binders.)

PHASE II

Now Phase II was ready to begin. This was to be the guts of the study—primary data collection and field interviews—to be conducted by the consultants. As indicated by Figure 1, a second consulting firm had been added for this phase (11). This addition was made in order to obtain a proprietary data base on wholesalers. The additional cost was quite modest and access to such data was expected to combine in a synergistic way with the main consulting effort. In retrospect this was a mistake. The data files were not reliable for a variety of reasons and in most part information had to be rechecked or duplicated by the lead consultant. As a result, little synergy arose; this aspect of the project, if repeated, would probably be assigned to the primary consultant.

As an aside, if more than one consultant is used, accountability for the total effort should be assigned to only one. This conforms to most consultants' own preferences, at least those designated as the lead firm, and it would clearly have been more efficient here.

Once a list of companies to interview had been determined (12, 13), a total of about 10 weeks was spent in the field. The in-field interviews were the basis for the study recommendations and the rationale for the use of consultants familiar with wholesaling. Many companies which diversify are satisfied with primarily a financial analysis conducted from corporate headquarters. Partly because of the many small wholesalers with less than adequate records, and partly due to a preference for the added information gained from personal interviews, this option was believed an unsatisfactory way to go.

More than 100 personal interviews were conducted among wholesalers, customers, and manufacturers (14). Because of the large number of firms within the scope of the study, four regional areas containing the greatest concentration of firms were selected for the interviews. Choices within these regions were in part influenced by the willingness of firms to cooperate in the study. Thus, the sample was not scientific although a sufficient number of large firms was included to assure the company of representative data for this important segment of the survey.

A set of questions was developed so that certain standard information could be tabulated for all interviews. In addition, there was leeway for the consultants to probe deeply in any interview where the respondent volunteered relevant information. The objective of these field interviews was to:

- Build a profile of each class of wholesaler
- Identify the critical functions within each class of wholesaler
- Determine the improvements possible (a) in present operations, (b) through economies of scale, and (c) through additions to the product mix

In a few interviews the consultants were accompanied by members of the planning staff. Progress meetings were also held periodically throughout. It was deemed important to maintain continuity and control of the different study phases by frequent contact between consultants and the company.

Also, part of the input to the main survey was to be provided by the secondary consultant (15). This included certain characteristics of individual firms, such as the information contained on a Dun & Bradstreet card file, and was supplemented by phone contacts to more than 100 firms. As noted previously, the net benefit of such information was not great. The difficulty was in integrating the information from one source with what was being derived from field interviews. In the end the company got a lot of data from the second source (16) for a very modest outlay which was, unfortunately, reflective of what it was worth.

The consolidated findings were than bound in a large volume and presented to management (17). This included detailed information on the structure of the two major markets plus composite data on firms, by size, serving these markets, in the four selected wholesale product lines. Essentially this presentation was a progress report to adjust for any company feedback prior to drafting the final report.

In reviewing opportunities, the consultants had relied on four general criteria, in addition to adequate size, developed with management during the course of the study:

Above-average growth
Opportunity to improve performance
Opportunity to expand product/market participation
No serious problems of entry

In the final feasibility study to management (18) all four product lines surveyed were considered to represent potentially attractive opportunities, and diversification into these fields was recommended. At this point it should be admitted that a build or buy option to diversification had always been a visible part of the strategic plan, primarily for reasons of internal review. Yet the staff felt before beginning that only a buy decision was feasible. This instinct was supported by findings on several corporate disasters where large companies had tried to build their way into wholesaling. They had overlooked the difficulty of changing customer relations developed by existing firms over a period of many years. Also, there was a tendency to overestimate the efficiency of large size compared to a no frills and a low overhead operation typical of local wholesalers.

PHASE III

In reviewing the final report (19), management paid particular attention to detailed financial and descriptive information that was supplied on a number of companies by product line. This information aided in developing two supplemental analyses conducted by the company. One identified companies above a minimum size by location and contrasted this information with the location of major volume markets by product sales (20). In addition, a preliminary financial analysis was performed on selected companies which seemed to fit criteria of geography, size, and potential growth (21). Based on a number of financial analyses, the most promising firms began to emerge as a select candidate list of companies for acquisition (22). Using these companies as a base, more detailed financial workups were begun, including pro forma forecasts of profit and loss statements, balance sheets, and consolidated "fit" with the buying company (23). Finally the company entered active negotiations and acquired a number of firms in the desired industry product lines (24).

POSTSCRIPT

The final stages of the study were strongly influenced by management's urgency to begin acquiring companies. Consequently, the concept of achieving an overall strategy of multi-product lines serving core markets lost much of its validity. Availability and size of potential acquisitions seemed to become the primary criteria once negotiations began.

In general, the trigger and terminal aspects of the study were the least methodical. In between is where the planning staff and the consultants exercised primary responsibility, and by nature of their technical expertise, took a more systematic approach. In theory, a systematic approach should pertain throughout the strategic planning process. Perhaps it should, but in the end method must give way to action. A continuing point of debate is likely to remain about when this point is optimally reached. In this case, a lingering doubt remains on the quality of management's judgments.

Thus far the company is apparently on target in meeting volume and profit goals. However, there is no evidence that the acquisitions followed the strategy for integrating outlined in the study. If so, the long-range prospects should be geared primarily to the prospects for the particular wholesale lines. Once an adequate post-acquisition period has passed, allowing for certain inital operating and accounting changes, time will tell if the company has been able to reach significantly higher goals than the firms could have been expected to achieve on their own.

Finally the study provided some insights into the selection and use of consultants. For instance, it is difficult to judge the value of a consulting firm by its credentials. Firms the company interviewed were very enthusiastic about this kind of study because it was challenging and broad-gauged instead of narrow and specialized like most bread and butter assignments. For the company the routine done-it-a-hundred-times type of specialization is what it thought it could get. Instead, consulting firms' industry expertise was found to have minimum application to a strategic planning project of this sort. A presumed depth of experience from multiple studies of this type did not exist. Thus, in lieu of highly specialized consultants, a company may have to settle for qualified personnel and hope they will quickly develop a steep learning curve. To assure quality performance, a company should insist on interviewing the persons who will actually do the work in addition to those contacts made with the generally senior consultants who sell the proposal. Also, close monitoring of the project is advised. Without supervision, the consultants may be put in the position of anticipating what direction the study should take and come out in the end with what I have termed a "consultant's solution."

MICHAEL G. ALLEN

Diagramming GE's Planning for What's Watt

THE AGE OF DISCONTINUITY had just dawned when General Electric started its strategic planning process in 1970. The Corporate Executive Office sought stronger planning at all levels in our decentralized Company, because it foresaw volatile environmental conditions, intensifying competition, and a growing scarcity of resources. Sure enough, things got worse. From 1971 to 1975, the world economic boom-bust became obvious to everyone. However, less perceptible, but more fundamental, structural changes were also impacting most industries in which the Company participated. Each major sector of General Electric underwent a transformation in its outlook (Figure 1) from what had seemed a strong future potential in 1971 to the harsh realities of late 1974, among them:

Eroding corporate liquidity (for example, of electric utilities).
Mushrooming capacity excesses (for example, in airlines).
Differing industry performances in coping with inflation.
Increasing synchronism of the world economic cycle.
Surging energy costs—both fuel and capital.

Regular planning reviews of these environmental problems revealed their hereditary, pervasive, and interacting character. These crises were not separable transients in the level of economic activity. They represented structural forces that would change the outlook for many of our businesses permanently.

We concluded that a timely strategic response to this restructuring of our environment would require restructuring several basic management methods. Specifically, we improved our approach to resource allocation, tied control of operations to strategic priorities, and reinforced these thrusts with appropriate managerial leadership and motivation. The results of this program of sustained strategic management are visible not only in the Company's results, but in the manner of their achievement.

Figure 1. The changed outlook for each sector. (Top) Strong future potential. (Bottom) Harsh present reality.

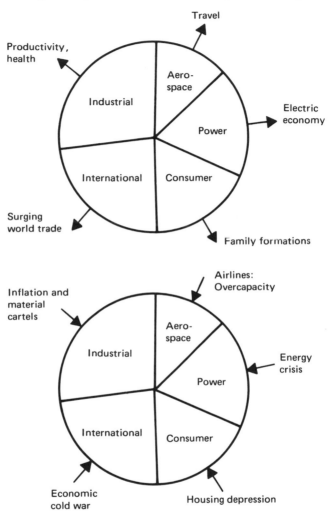

IMPROVED APPROACH TO RESOURCE ALLOCATION

General Electric's results in the sixties showed a pattern of "profitless growth." Many investments were yielding sales growth, without commensurate earnings gains, causing return on investment to decline. This profitless growth pattern (Figure 2)—experienced by many companies at

Figure 2. Pattern of profitless growth.

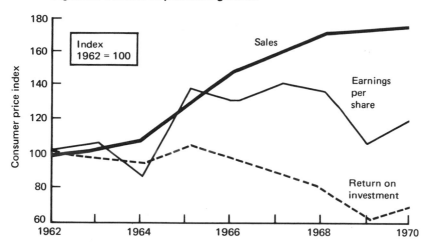

that time—was amplified by the stagflation conditions of the early seventies.

The profit disappointments from our investments suggested that flaws existed in our approaches to investment decision making and resource allocation. Correcting these flaws was a major objective of the new strategic planning process.

In 1971, the "business screen" (Figure 3) was developed to differentiate the potential for future profit in each of our 43 Strategic Business Units (SBU). Its use has been described in a number of publications.* It differs from most other methods of evaluating investment priority in three important ways:

• It uses multiple factors to appraise "industry attractiveness" for investment profitability and measure our "business strengths" to compete successfully. Other approaches rely heavily on single numerical measures (for example, market growth, market share) that fail to describe the different structure and potential of different industries.

• It lays stress on analysis of the structural forces affecting industry performance—such as the role of new technology. This reduces management dependence on deterministic results forecasts (for example, of Discounted Cash Flow Rate of Return), which have proved highly unreliable in recent years.

---

*For example, "Corporate Planning Piercing Future Fog in the Executive Suite," *Business Week*, April 28, 1975; and "Business Strategies for Problem Products," Report No. 714, The Conference Board, New York, 1977.

Figure 3. Business screen for resource allocation priorities.

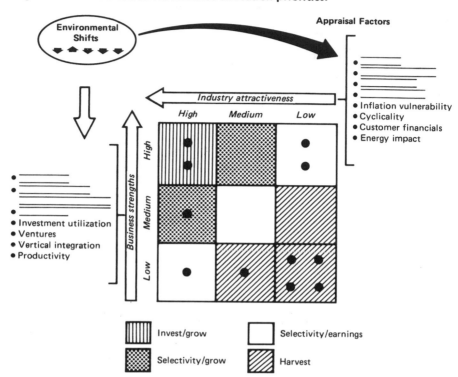

• It combines analytical staffwork with managerial experience and judgment. It does not try to replace management decisions with a set of computer-derived investment criteria.

From 1971 through 1976, this "business screen" has been used at many levels in General Electric—from the Corporate Policy Committee to the sales division planner—in order to differentiate resource allocation priorities.

As the environment shifted and our perceptions of the forces affecting industries changed, managers at all levels adapted the appraisal factors. Understandabily, increased attention was given to such factors as the impact of inflation, cycles, or the energy crisis—and business strengths such as investment utilization and new ventures capability became more critical. The planning process itself became a dialog on the changed prospects for product lines for entire SBUs in the light of new environmental prospects. Businesses or product lines shifted their "matrix" positions, and with these changes went changes in resource allocation priority (Figure 4). Investment increases were largest in the invest/grow category, which contained our strangest business opportunities. Investment allocations increased less for the lower-priority business categories.

During the period under review, the General Electric Company placed great emphasis on cash management and investment utilization in response to the liquidity crisis of late 1974. However, while striving for improvements in working capital utilization, account was taken of the ability of our stronger businesses to use working capital more productively than those businesses in weaker situations. Thus, investment increases were greatest where industry conditions and business strengths allowed achievement of good returns on investment.

In sum, a very real differentiation of investment resource allocation occurred—aided by pervasive application of the "business screen" approach to defining strategic priorities. Importantly, introduction of the selective investment strategy in 1971—as the economy turned up and resource demands of all businesses rose—proved to be effective timing in relation to the economic cycle.

Figure 4. Investment increases concentrated on the stronger business opportunities (1971–1976).

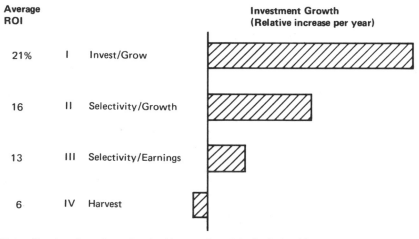

Note: Numbers have been disguised but retain original relationship.

STRATEGIC CONTROL OF OPERATIONS

The second thrust of General Electric's strategic business planning program was to link operations control with strategic priorities. Management of annual profit results has a large bearing on the strategic development of General Electric businesses. The reason is that technology, marketing, and facilities programs for future business benefit represent large current expenses and a drain on near-term profit. When annual profit budgets are set, our scarcest resources are effectively allocated.

This "strategic jugular vein" of technology-intensive industrial businesses became vulnerable to the intense operating pressures of the last several years:

1970, 1971	Domestic and foreign competition intensified, labor costs inflated, excess-capacity conditions existed—pressuring prices and market share.
1972, 1973	Rising inflation, coupled with price controls, squeezed margins—pressuring overhead.
1974, 1975	Energy and liquidity crises led to market collapses—pressuring volume and overhead.
1976	International recession, surging imports—pressuring volume recovery and market share.

At times of "operating crises" such as these, both our planning sessions in midyear and our budgeting sessions in November/December were intensely involved with margin improvement, price-share trade-offs, breakeven point control, and control of employee overhead. One measure of the tightness of this operating control is that average GE employment worldwide dropped from 398,000 in 1970 to 380,000 in 1976—while sales increased 80 percent.

Notwithstanding this broad pressure on cost of operations, the "all-levels" resource allocation philosophy enabled strategic priorities to be preserved. For example, near-term cost controls on employee numbers and breakeven points were applied most heavily in the categories of business with lower priority for future growth (Figure 5). The stronger businesses in more attractive industries were protected. The tendency is often the opposite—to pressure the strong to compensate for the weak. Our strategy positioned the stronger businesses to lead Company recovery in the economic upturn of 1976/1977. Such strategic control of operations has prevented operating crises from undermining longer-range investment strategy.

Figure 5. Cost and breakeven controls reflecting strategic priorities (1971–1976).

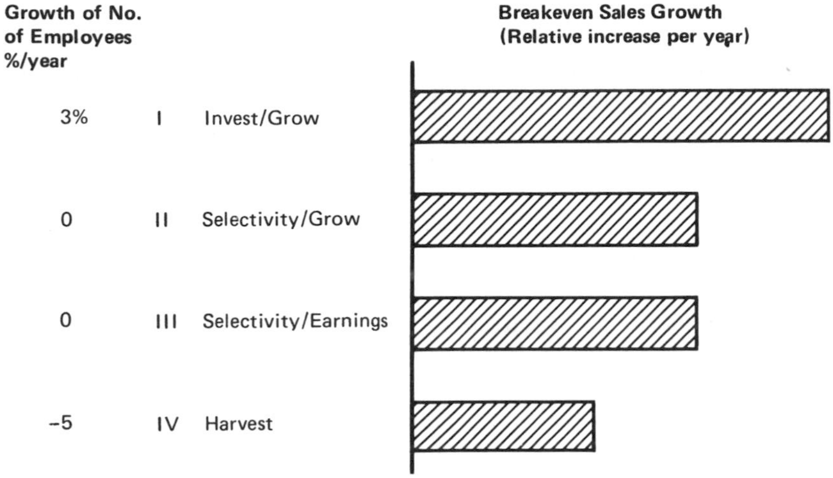

| Growth of No. of Employees %/year | | | Breakeven Sales Growth (Relative increase per year) |

Note: Numbers have been disguised but retain original relationship.

MANAGERIAL MOTIVATION

Management motivation that stresses present-day results can also undermine longer-range strategic plans. Proper managerial motivation proved vital to the implementation of our differentiated resource allocation strategy and to the effective strategic control of operations, in three ways:

1. *Top management identified itself with strategic priorities at the most critical times.* This was well illustrated in the first quarter of 1975—when Company earnings fell 39 percent. In 1974, the Corporate Policy Committee had selected 12 venture opportunities for accelerated funding and mantained and added to that support through the tough conditions of 1975. Also in 1975, Corporate Research and Development expenditures were budgeted to grow while other staff overhead shrank. These actions enabled the chairman to write in his annual report for the year, "Faced with a continued economic downturn and a continued cost/price squeeze, General Electric's managers cut back expenses rigorously but in ways that, in the judgment of management, will not impair the company's potential for future growth or long-range strategic planning."

2. *Managerial capabilities were aligned with business strategy.* Executive Manpower planning increasingly reflected the investment strategy

for each business. Within the constraints of availability, the more entre-preneurial managers—skilled in leading change—were matched with our invest/grow businesses. The most experienced managers were as-signed to handle the tough problems of cost control and investment reduction in weak businesses—while treating employees and communi-ties well. Finally, our most sophisticated, critical managers were asked to tackle the businesses requiring selectivity between strong and weak products—and simultaneous management of both.

3. *Bonuses were weighted according to strategic business objectives.* A different balance was applied in awarding bonuses to the management of different categories of business, as shown in Figure 6. Low emphasis (40 percent) was given to current financial results in the growth busi-nesses, and higher emphasis on performance that would yield future benefits (48 percent). The weighting was skewed more heavily to cur-rent financial results in harvest businesses.

Our experience with these motivational actions reconfirmed a basic axiom of management through the business cycles: that performance in good times or bad is determined by decisions made when conditions were just the opposite—at a different phase of the cycle. Such "counter-cyclical" strategic decisions only occur if management motivation is also one step ahead.

Figure 6. Bonuses weighted to match strategic priorities.

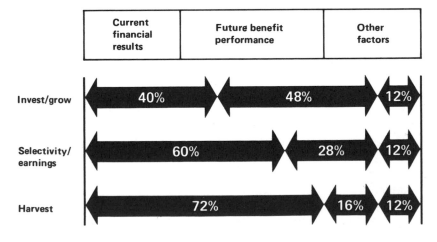

THE RESULTS OF SUSTAINED STRATEGIC MANAGEMENT

There are three bottom lines of General Electric's strategic business planning program of the last five years; they are the same lines as those shown in Figure 2 (Sales; EPS; ROI), brought up to date in 1976 (Figure 7).

The "strategic management" combination of improved resource allocation, strategic control of operations, management leadership, and motivation has brought about an improved trajectory of results.

- Profits are now growing in line with sales.
- A collapse was prevented in the 1975 recession, and a strong rebound was achieved in 1976.
- GE cumulative profits (ex-Utah) were 84 percent higher in 1971–1976 than in 1965–1970, compared with an advance of 39 percent in total U.S. corporate profits.
- Return on investment has been rebuilt to the highest level in ten years, ensuring continuing ability to finance future growth.

These bottom line results are important—but so is their manner of achievement. The Company's ability to continue this improved performance trend in the future is indicated by the performance characteristics of business units in each strategic category of the "business screen."

The businesses receiving investment priority not only achieve high

Figure 7. Improved trajectory of results.

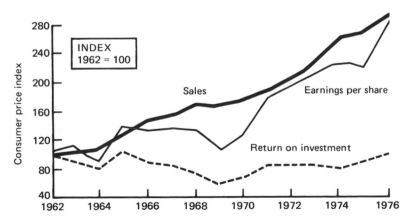

sales growth and market share gains, but also are more effective in dealing with inflation, with higher energy costs, and with tougher international conditions. Multifactor appraisal, therefore, gives investment priority to businesses with depth of capability. Management's judgments that such capabilities will yield profitable business results have been vindicated by the relative category returns on investment—averaged through good times and bad.

Such times of discontinuity and uncertainty as we have experienced in the last five years provide a searching test of strategic planning effectiveness. They are times that we will undoubtedly experience again; they are times of basic change in a company's prospects and performance. . . . They are Times for Strategy.

ABRAHAM KATZ

There's No Room
for Guesswork
at IBM

NATURE OF BUSINESS

The IBM corporation develops, manufactures, markets, and services a wide variety of information-handling products. Most of these products fall into three business areas: data processing (DP), the products making up the larger-scale data-processing systems, such as the System 370; general systems (GS), those for the smaller-scale data-processing system, such as the System 3, as well as sensor-based systems, such as the System 7; and office products (OP), including typewriters, copiers, and other products used in the office. The remaining IBM activities deal with advanced technology and special systems to meet the needs of the U.S. government; with disk packs, data modules, and supplies used in information-handling systems; and with educational materials and services for schools and industry.

IBM does about half its business outside the United States. The scale of our operations worldwide is reflected in these 1976 data:

Gross income from sales, rentals, and services	$16.3 billion
Total assets	$17.1 billion
Number of employees	292,000

Organizational Philosophy

Insofar as planning is concerned, IBM's philosophy of organization is implemented as follows:

• IBM activities are grouped into a number of operating units which, where feasible, have profit/loss responsibility. These units are differentiated by business area and geographic region, and have the range of functions needed to conduct their assigned missions as autonomously as practical.

• Operating unit management is responsible for development and implementation of its plans. Prior to implementation, plans are reviewed and approved by corporate management. Performance against plan is measured and controlled by operating unit management, and monitored by the corporate staff. Periodically, the results of operations are reviewed with corporate management. Plan changes, as necessary, are also reviewed and approved by corporate management.

• Business policies are controlled at the corporate level, and provide the broad framework within which all operating units function.

• In its review and assessment of the operating units' plans and performance, corporate management is assisted by the corporate staff which provides counsel and performs certain centralized services.

IBM Organizational Structure

The organizational structure of IBM is depicted in Figure 1. Six operating units involved in the three major business areas have been assigned missions as follows:

Data Processing Complex (DPC). For the DP business area, DPC has responsibility for coordination of market requirements and development of products worldwide, and for manufacturing, marketing, and service within the United States.

General Systems Division (GSD) and Office Products Division (OPD). For the GS and OP business areas respectively, GSC and OPD have responsibilities worldwide and within the U.S. which are analogous to those of the DPC.

Europe/Middle East/Africa (EMEA) and Americas/Far East (AFE). For the DP business area, EMEA and AFE have responsibility for manufacturing, marketing, and service within their respective geographic regions. For the GS and OP business areas, they have responsibility for marketing and service in the smaller countries.

General Business Group International (GBGI). For the GS and OP business areas, GBGI has responsibility for giving functional guidance for manufacturing, marketing and service within the larger countries outside the United States.

There are strong dependencies among these six units and some degree of overlap among the three business areas. Consistent with our philosophy of decentralized management of operations, the planning and control system requires the designated units to develop and implement their separate but coordinated plans within an integrated corporate framework.

Figure 1. Organizational structure of IBM.

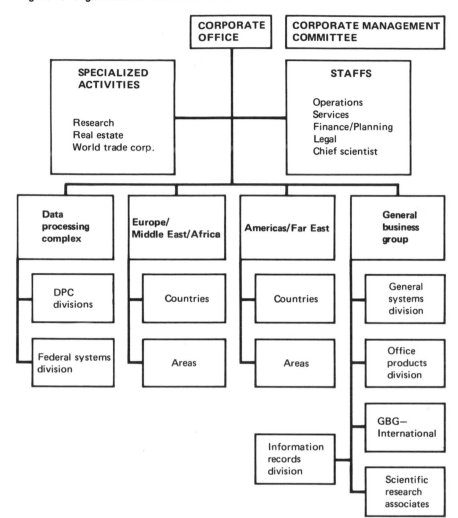

THE BASIC PLANNING PROCESS

Information-handling products are used across the entire spectrum of human activity and in every part of the world. The number and scope of product applications are expanding rapidly, being limited only by the creativity which the users and firms like our own bring to bear on solving information problems.

Dealing with Change

Continuing and rapid change is, therefore, inherent in our business. Technology is advancing rapidly; competition is intense; the world economy is in flux; governmental actions often affect the business environment; and societies everywhere are moving through an "age of discontinuity." Expecting change and recognizing that it may take many forms, IBM scans the environment through two organizational mechanisms—one being the operating units affected and the second, the corporate staff.

Operating unit management maintains an awareness of emerging problems or opportunities which may affect its business. Concurrently, within their respective areas of functional expertise, the various corporate staffs are also monitoring change. When an event or trend of potential significance is detected (for example, slackening of economic conditions in a country we serve), the operating unit affected will alert corporate management as to the magnitude and timing of the expected effects. In some cases, the unit is joined by the corporate staff in developing and recommending a course of action. Once accepted, these recommendations are then built into the unit's plan by its management. Where a problem is of major and continuing importance (for example, energy), a joint council involving affected units and staffs will be created to monitor and recommend action on a regular basis.

Organizing for Planning

As indicated at the outset, planning and implementation are line management responsibilities. However, planning staffs to support line management exist at the corporate, operating unit (and where these are large, at the divisional or country), and plant/laboratory levels. The size and functional mix of these staffs depend on the specific responsibilities of the line managers they support. At the operating unit level, the executive will normally have finance and planning, as well as functional skills needed to develop a properly balanced profit plan. For example, his technical staff will review and assist in integrating the various product plans into the unit plan. The unit executive makes the final judgments as to business volumes to be achieved, resources required, and risks to be accepted.

At the corporate level, the line executives also have finance, planning, and other functional staffs to assist them. For example, among the responsibilities of the Corporate Business Plans staff are design of the IBM planning system, establishing the plan guidance and data requirements, managing the plan schedule, recommending profit targets for the various operating units, and reviewing and assessing their strategies and plans.

Program and Period Planning

There are two distinct but interactive kinds of planning within the IBM system, as shown in Figure 2 (light outline for program planning; bold, for period planning):

• Program planning (for example, a program to develop a product or improve the productivity of a function) is characterized by the following: The program plan generally has a single objective, but may involve several functional elements. Its time horizon is determined by the nature of the specific program objective and the work processes required to achieve it, by its cycle for review and decision making, and by the inherent dynamics of the program.

At any point in time, each operating unit has a large portfolio of product and functional programs in various stages of planning and implementation.

• Period planning complements program planning and is characterized by the following: The period plans balance among multiple-program and other objectives to achieve the profit targets assigned. Its time horizons are fixed by corporate management, being two years for the operating plan and five years for the strategic plan. The cycle for review and decision making is tied to the calendar to assure the availability of an operating budget for each unit at the beginning of each year.

Clearly, decisions made as part of the period planning process affect the program plans—accelerating some, terminating others, and so on. The converse is also true—some program decisions require changes in the period plan of an operating unit. It is the responsibility of operating unit management to establish and maintain the proper balance among its objectives and resources.

PROGRAM PLANNING
Product Management

Program planning may be directed toward a system product, industry (that is, a specific class of customers), or functional objective. To illustrate the process, consider the planning associated with a product program. Such planning generally proceeds in two distinct stages: defining the market requirements and, once the requirements have been accepted, translating them into products.

Figure 2. Period and program planning at IBM.

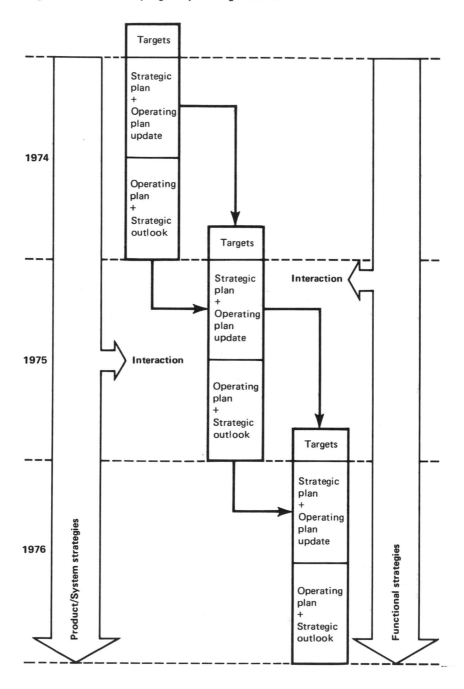

In most cases, the market requirements relate to an existing IBM product, one for which there has been a continuing need. As part of his normal activities, the manager within an operating unit having responsibility for a certain product will periodically measure the performance program versus program plan for the product he currently has in the field. Concurrently, he will be proceeding with the development of advanced techniques and devices for the next generation product. Depending on the sales performance of the current product and the availability of new technology, he will recommend to his management whether and how to enhance or replace it. Since many of our products work together within a data-processing system, the product manager's recommendations must always be considered within the total system's framework, since system integrity must be maintained.

In some cases, a customer's needs may be basically new, lying beyond IBM's current skills and experience. Product planners will then work with the marketing force on case studies, interviews, and questionnaires to determine the user's requirments, the functional characteristics needed in the new product, and its expected mode of use. Depending on the prospects for an economically sound program, the product manager will make his recommendations as to proceeding with it.

At its discretion, operating unit management initiates programs which fall within the assigned missions, approved strategies, and negotiated organizational budgets of the unit. Once a program is initiated, management periodically reviews performance against plan. These reviews typically occur as the product program moves from one phase into the next (for example, from study into design). The product manager reviews all aspects of the program (forecasts of business volumes, cost estimates, technical problems, schedules) with the operating unit management and with all functions and operating units having an interest in the program. Prior to product announcement, there must be agreement as to its economic soundness, and commitment from each organization to do its part. After announcement, there are periodic reviews of performance against plan, with corrective action taken as necessary.

Forecasting

IBM relies on in-house econometric models to forecast both the U.S. economy and the demand for certain of the company's products. The same techniques are now being used for international forecasts. Economists in the major countries work with the Corporate Economics Department to assure proper reflection of the local situations.

The company uses two national income and expenditure models in its forecasts of the U.S. picture. The quarterly model produces forecasts for use with the company's two-year operating plan; the annual model produces forecasts for use with the strategic plan. IBM also uses an input/output model to project industry supply and demand patterns. The first two models each contain about 50 behavior equations, each one relating to some economic variable such as the consumption function of durables. The programs are written mainly in FORTRAN and run on 370/155s and a 360/91.

Product forecasters in each operating unit use a wide range of forecasting methods, including analyses of growth and replacement patterns for new product or systems; extrapolation from a sample of case studies selected to represent industry, size, or application distribution; interviews or questionnaires for new products; and projections based on sales or backlog analyses for products already announced. Through the use of typical system configuration ratios, systems forecasts are decomposed into forecasts of the individual products they comprise.

PERIOD PLANNING

An overall planning system is necessary to meet the business needs of the corporation and its operating units. In this system, each IBM operating unit annually performs both strategic and operating planning. The purpose of strategic planning by a unit is to establish its business direction; that of operating planning, to implement the direction within budgeting requirements and to commit the unit to achieving planned results.

Strategic Planning

Key elements in strategic planning are corporate targets, operating unit goals, product/system and functional strategies, and a strategic plan. The five-year time horizon for strategic planning lies sufficiently beyond the two-year operating period so that sound and timely decisions on business direction can be made. The strategic process is as follows:

Corporate targets and operating unit goals. Corporate management assigns targets (profit and profit margin) to each operating unit. In response, each operating unit management develops and assigns goals to its product/system and functional managements to guide their strategy development.

Strategies. Operating units with development responsibilities prepare and maintain product/system strategies to serve as the foundation for their marketplace offerings. All units prepare functional strategies to assure that the most effective organization and business approaches are used to achieve increasing productivity of resources. As part of its marketing strategy, a unit may assign industry goals and develop strategies to meet the needs unique to specific customer sets.

Strategic plan. The strategic plan integrates the several product/system and functional strategies of the units, presents the financial results over the plan period, and compares planned results against corporate targets. This plan (and selected strategies) is submitted to the Corporate Management Committee (CMC) by the operating unit executive. The plans are reviewed by the corporate staff and, prior to CMC review, their assessments are forwarded to the CMC and the operating unit. Among the bases for these assessments are:

Consistency with approved strategic direction.
Balance between objectives sought and resources required.
Relationships to plans of other operating units.
Excellence in each functional area.

Certain staffs also write short critiques as to the strengths, weaknesses, or risks associated with the individual plans. On the basis of these staff inputs and the operating unit presentation, the CMC approves the unit's proposed business direction, resolves nonconcurrences, reevaluates its targets, and reassigns them.

To support this planning work, the operating units with product development responsibility generate product assumptions; Corporate Economic provides the economic and environmental assumptions; and the various corporate staffs issue functional guidance as necessary. Other factors and trends are monitored and analyzed to determine their possible implications (for example, environmental issues, consumerism, privacy and data security, and international political and economic relationship).

Using the product and economic assumptions, the forecasting department of each operating unit produces an overall set of business volumes by integrating the individual product forecasts previously developed with the results of the supply–demand balancing against the order backlog. These volumes provide management with a projection based on explicitly defined and quantifiable factors. Management then applies judgment to take into consideration the unquantifiable considerations previously mentioned, and the adjusted business volumes are distributed to the various functions as the basis for their plans. Based on historical experience, each function then uses its own planning factors and models to translate these volumes into workload, resources, and cost/expense. Computer models are widely used at both the operating unit and corporate levels. For example, all manufacturing activities use computers extensively for balancing supply against demand and determining plant loading; engineering, for design automation; Marketing and Service, for territory analysis and proposal preparation. The unit staff then integrates the several functional inputs into a properly balanced plan, which the unit executive approves and submits to corporate management.

As one approach for dealing with the problems of uncertainty, corporate management may request contingency analyses to test, for example, the effect of a more extreme set of economic assumptions on unit plans. Corporate Economics will then issue two outlooks—one for the base plan and a second for the contingency plan. Operating units will then develop two plans and review them with corporate management. This approach has proven useful in improving the speed and flexibility of our response to unanticipated conditions.

OPERATING PLAN

Based on the business direction in the approved strategic plan and including changes as necessary, the unit then develops an operating plan which focuses on implementation over the current year plus two. This plan contains detailed business volumes and workload forecasts, as well as functional resources and financial plan commitments. These data are developed through planning processes similar to those for the strategic plan described earlier. The operating plan is used to establish budgets and other objectives for the next year. Certain units provide selected revenue and resource items in a long-range outlook at the time of the plan submission to show the probable extended effects, risks, and exposures of the proposed plan. After approval by the operating unit executive, the plan is submitted for corporate review and assessment (as for the strategic plan). The CMC resolves nonconcurrences and approves the unit plan.

When significant deviations occur in actual results vs. plan, a unit may request approval for changes in its operating plan. All requests are coordinated by the IBM Director of Budgets (and, indeed, may be initiated by him); those requiring CMC approval are reviewed and assessed by appropriate corporate staffs.

ACKNOWLEDGMENT

This contribution was adopted from "Longe-Range Planning" prepared for the Sub-Committee on the Environment and the Atmosphere of the Commission on Science and Technology, U.S. House of Representatives, 94th Congress, Second Session, by the Congressional Research Service, Library of Congress, Serial BB, May 1976.

Part V
ACQUISITIONS

PARMANAND KUMAR

Profit Planning Through Acquisition

INDUSTRIAL COMBINATION AND ACQUISITION has been a common corporate activity throughout the past 75 years. There has been a transition from a predominance of large, horizontal, multiform consolidations to an emphasis on conglomerate acquisitions of relatively smallers firms. The historical series of corporate mergers is portrayed in Figure 1. This figure features three peaks. The first occurs around the turn of the century, the second in late 1920, and the third begins after World War II, continuing into the 1960s. In the early 1970s, mergers and acquisitions were still a growing phenomenon. Some have suggested that this is the corporate form for the twenty-first century,[1] others have forecast impending disaster.[2] A study of 74 corporations concluded that growth

Figure 1. Annual disappearances through merger of manufacturing and mining firms.

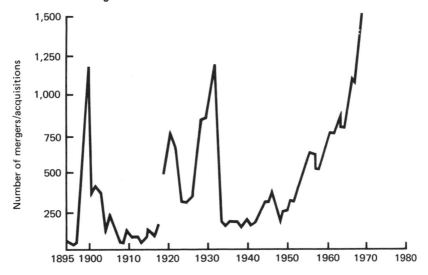

through merger and acquisition was about $6.2 billion or 22.3 percent of total growth of $28.0 billion, with the remaining $21.8 billion or 77 percent through internal growth.[3]

ADVANTAGES

The corporation is a complete economic creature. Its performance is influenced by many variables which are basically interrelated. These factors are presented in Figure 2. The immediate interest of a corporation engaged in acquiring another company is to increase profits or earnings per share. Some have suggested[4,5] that there may be a feedback effect operating on the market prices of firms actively engaged in using their common stock for the acquisition of other firms with lower price-earnings ratios. The result of such acquisition is an immediate increase in the earnings per share of the acquiring firm (Table 1). If the acquiring firm

Table 1. Immediate increase in earnings per share of the acquiring firm. Acquiring firm (A) acquires a firm having lower price-earnings ratio (B) for stock-for-stock.

	Firm A	Firm B	Combined Firm A & B	Net Effect After Acquisition (%)
After-tax earning	$ 100	$ 100	$ 200	+100
Outstanding shares	100	100	150	+50
Earnings-per-share	$ 1	$ 1	$ 1.33	+33
Share market price	$ 20	$ 10	$ 27	+33
Price-earnings ratio	20	10	20	−0
Market value	$2,000	$1,000	$4,000	+25

The market value of firm B, $1,000, is equivalent to 50 shares of firm A ($20 × 50 = $1,000). Hence, the outstanding shares of A after acquisition are 150, an increase of 50 percent. However, the combined earning is $200, which gives the new earnings-per-share of $1.33 ($200/150), an increase of 33 percent. If we assume that the price-earnings ratio of firm A remains the same after acquisition, then share price increases from $20 per share to $27 per share and market value $4,000, an increase of 25 percent.

repeats the same process continuously, the firm will show a growth pattern in earnings per share which, in turn, places the common share of the acquiring firm at a still higher price-earning multiple. It will result in an increase in the market value of the acquiring firm without any change in its economic value (Table 2). There is no creation of wealth, only a redistribution of wealth. However, this kind of feedback relationship is only possible if the acquiring firm maintains a market value advantage over those acquired.

It is generally recognized that increased diversification makes a corporation more valuable to shareholders because variations of returns in different fields of activity cancel each other and reduce the overall level

Figure 2. Sources of earnings-per-share growth through aggressive, diversified acquisition.

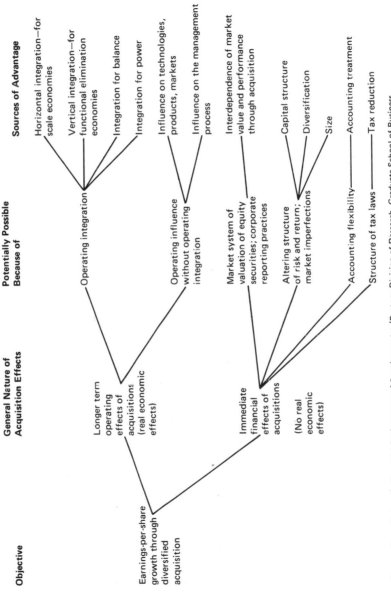

Source: Harry H. Lynch, *Financial Performance of Conglomerates* (Boston: Division of Research, Graduate School of Business Administration, Harvard University, 1971).

Table 2. Increase in market value of the acquiring firm (A) without changing its economic value by acquiring lower price-earnings ratio firm (C) and increasing its price-earnings ratio from 20 to 25 (25%), showing growth in earnings per share of 20%.

	Firm A	Firm C	Combined Firm A&C	Net Change After Acquisition (%)
After-tax earning	$ 200	$ 100	$ 300	+50
Outstanding shares	150	100	187	+25
Earnings-per-share	$ 1.33	$ 1	$ 1.60	+20
Share market price	$ 27	$ 10	$ 40	+48
Price-earnings ratio	20	10	25	+25
Market value	$4,000	$1,000	$7,480	+87

Market value of firm C, $1,000, is equivalent to about 37 shares of firm A ($27 × 37 = $1,000). Hence, the new outstanding shares of firm A after acquisition are 187 while combined earning is $300. The earnings-per-share after acquisition is $1.60, an increase of 20 percent. The growth of earnings-per-share resulted in raising the stock price to $40 and the new market value to $7,480, an increase of 87 percent without change of economic value.

of variability. The other side of the argument may be that diversification does not increase real economic value. However, acquisitions do create a firm of larger size which has a better resistance to failure, more marketable securities, more accessible and less expensive sources of financing. There is evidence that the shares of the large corporation will be valued more highly than those of the smaller corporation, other aspects being the same.[6] Furthermore, it is well known that acquisitions have contributed significantly to profit and growth of acquisitive conglomerates such as Gulf + Western, Teledyne, Nytronics, Litton Industries, Textron, Whittaker, and others.

Some other advantages of acquisition stem from accounting flexibility and the tax laws. It is difficult to conclude that acquisitions have contributed significantly to profitability through the accounting treatment of various items in acquired firms and through the mechanics of pooling interest transactions, but both have provided some advantages in many cases. On the other hand, tax provisions have provided many advantages for the acquiring firm, including the benefit of tax loss carry forward and the ability to balance development costs in one division against the profits of another. However, this cash flow advantage does require an acquisition of a firm operating at a loss, which has an unfavorable immediate effect on earnings per share. Because a large corporation generally has more resources, another positive result of acquisition is better operating performance in the acquired company.

Traditionally, acquisitions do not involve completely unrelated firms. There are some common factors within the two companies—technologies, products, or markets—and integration is relatively easy.

Horizontal integration of purchasing, production, marketing, and other functions provides larger activities in those areas, resulting in reductions in cost and better performance. Vertical integration of advertising, selling, and transportation may also offer economies. Complementary integration, particularly those specialized functions which small companies cannot afford, may provide the balance of resources needed for future progress and add to profitability and future growth. Finally, these integrations may increase market power in buying and selling which will lead to greater profitability. However, this process is quite complex, and many factors will be against it, including the rapid pace of acquisitions, the diversity of operations, and the need to retain previous operating management. On the other side, some advantages can be achieved easily, including combining knowledge, expertise, funds, personnel, and other resources that will benefit both companies.

REASONS FOR ACQUIRING

The Federal Trade Commission has prepared several reports[7] on corporate merger and acquisition activities. These reports show six major reasons for mergers in U.S. manufacturing and mining industries (Table 3). Several interesting conclusions can be derived from different studies on U.S. mergers[3,8,9] and European acquisitions.[10]

Table 3. Relative importance of reasons for merger: U.S. mergers in manufacturing and mining industries.

Reasons	Percent
1. Expanded existing markets	32
2. Product diversification	21
3. Lengthened product line	21
4. Backward vertical integration	10
5. New market	8
6. Forward vertical integration	8
Total	100

SOURCE: Federal Trade Commission. "Reports on Corporate Mergers and Acquisitions," U.S. Government Printing Office, Washington, D.C.

1. On the average, the acquiring company is much larger than the acquired company. The average assets of the acquiring company are about $70 million against $2 million for the acquired company.
2. The average acquiring company growth through acquisition and merger is about 20 to 25 percent.

3. The minimum risk acquisitions are horizontal acquisitions (expanding existing market).
4. The smaller acquired companies usually have serious management problems.
5. In general, growth and profitability resulting from acquisitions is three to five years faster than by other routes.
6. Acquiring companies are basically interested in growth potential companies for acquisition.
7. Acquiring companies are willing to pay a premium price if they can determine the growth potential of the acquired company.

CONCLUSION

There is great interest in the results of corporate acquisitions and mergers. However, mixed conclusions are evident in the little data that has been gathered to date. Some studies report that aggressively merging firms are markedly unprofitable while other studies conclude that actively acquiring firms are neither more nor less profitable than comparable firms in a similar industry. The major disagreement in these conflicting conclusions is the question of how to measure the profitability of a merger. While this strategy is subject to risks which are not common in internal growth, acquisitions can be profitable and the acquiring companies can enjoy better growth through acquisitions.

REFERENCES

1. George D. McCarthy, *Acquisitions and Mergers* (New York: The Ronald Press Company, 1963).
2. M. L. Mace and G. C. Montgomery, *Management Problems of Corporate Acquisitions* (Boston: Graduate School of Business Administration, Harvard University, 1962).
3. *Mergers and Acquisitions, Planning and Action* (New York: Financial Executives Research Foundation, 1963).
4. Sydney Prerau, ed., "How to Buy and Sell a Business," *J. K. Lasser's Business Management Handbook* (New York: McGraw-Hill, 1960).
5. Charles A. Scharf, *Techniques for Buying, Selling and Merging Businesses* (Englewood Cliffs, N.J.: Prentice-Hall, 1964).
6. H. B. Maynard, ed., *Handbook of Business Administration* (New York: McGraw-Hill, 1970).
7. Federal Trade Commission, *Reports on Corporate Mergers and Acquisitions* (Washington, D.C.: Government Printing Office, June 1968).

8. J. Linter and J. K. Butters, "Effect of Mergers on Industrial Concentration," *Review of Economics and Statistics* (February 1950).

9. John Shad, "Higher Premiums in Corporate Acquisitions," *Harvard Business Review*, July–August 1973.

10. John Kitching, "Winning and Losing with European Acquisitions," *Harvard Business Review*, March–April 1974.

DARRYL J. ELLIS AND PETER P. PEKAR, JR.

Acquisitions—
Is 50/50 Good Enough?

OVER THE PAST 90 YEARS, 50 percent of all mergers have been judged failures by the executives responsible for them.

Often acquisition failure is the result of inexperienced operating management which devotes little thought to objectives. While there have been successful acquisitions on gut feel, most such attempts have been unsuccessful.

Fortunately, there are fundamental procedures that can minimize the risk. Proper planning tends to lead to prosperity.

HISTORICAL PERSPECTIVE

There have been three identified movements in diversification activity in recent U.S. history. (A fourth one appears to be started.) The first was from about 1898 to 1903, when vertical combinations and horizontal mergers were designed to secure domination in particular fields. These mergers were a direct outgrowth of a previous long period of bitter competition. The next thrust of activity took place in the period from 1918 to 1929. This movement was characterized by the growth of large holding companies, considerable product differentiation of a primary line, and combination to exploit the expanding American and world markets.

A third movement covered the decade of the 1960s. It emphasized less vertical and horizontal integration, and more concentric and conglomerate integration. Since 1974, however, we have seen extensive interest in acquiring onstream facilities to expand existing product lines and market representation. This phenomenon was a direct outgrowth of inflation and governmental programs (OSHA, EPA) which have reduced profit margins and diverted the use of capital. While diversification is as old as business history, the question remains: "How successful has it been?"

A study[1] analyzing 409 companies participating in business combinations during 1888 to 1905 revealed that 50 percent of these acquisitions had been failures. The "failing" category did not necessarily mean they had failed in the legal sense, but had failed to show adequate earning power, had been reorganized, or had made several capital adjustments. A more recent study conducted by Booz, Allen & Hamilton in 1960, covering 128 acquisitions, and focusing on managerial appraisals of the acquiring companies, revealed that 50 percent were felt to have resulted in less than favorable results.

The National Bureau of Economic Research made an extensive study of diversification from 1929 to 1954 and came to the conclusion that only a mild, positive correlation existed between diversification and company growth during that period of time. Nevertheless, one encouraging fact revealed by Booz, Allen & Hamilton was that by the time companies had gained experience in making five or ten acquisitions, the results were rated good, with 62 percent of those surveyed implying favorable results. It is evident from this record that experience teaches.

Summarizing the historical data, despite all the good intentions, the record of corporate mergers has not lived up to expectations. Table 1 shows that during 1971 to 1975, earnings and P/E ratios for acquisition oriented companies (comprised of corporations recognized and followed by industry analysts at leading investment houses as growing through acquisition) have not, on the average, outperformed the Dow-Jones Industrials. Although individual companies have done well, as a group the companies have not outperformed the Dow-Jones 30 Industrials.

It thus appears that acquisitions, while never considered low risk ventures, are chancier than anticipated and call for careful planning prior to and during implementation.

When we reviewed unsuccessful merger ventures, we found these prime reasons for merger failure:

- Lack of knowledge of both the history and the market potential of the industry into which diversification will occur.
- Failure to fully investigate all aspects of the seller's business, including motives for selling, the contribution required of management (for success), financial arrangements necessary for successful operation of the business, technological expertise required, and depth of personnel (both in the acquired company and the acquiring one).
- Failure to determine the fit of the acquisition into the combined enterprise. Unrealistic expectations of profit contribution and of the participation required of management, marketing, production, and other corporate functions.
- Failure to develop and follow an extensive checklist to review all

Table 1. Comparative earnings and common stock performance.

Diversified Group	1971 EPS	1972 P/E Ratio	1972 EPS	1973 P/E Ratio	1973 EPS	1974 P/E Ratio	1974 EPS	1975 P/E Ratio	1975 EPS	P/E Ratio
Beatrice Foods	2.39	17.3	1.34	16.4	1.52	14.6	1.69	9.2	1.79	12.2
Consolidated Foods	2.38	20.2	2.49	16.0	2.61	10.8	2.35	6.0	0.30	57.9
Gulf + Western	2.69	10.0	3.48	10.4	4.91	3.1	6.64	3.2	4.91	5.8
ITT	3.39	16.8	3.70	14.7	4.10	7.7	4.13	4.1	3.05	7.1
Litton Industries	1.28	19.7	0.30	42.9	1.04	8.2	(1.34	—	0.87	8.6
LTV	(5.42	—	(1.94	—	3.00	3.3	6.40	1.5	3.18	4.0
Northwest Industries	3.29	9.1	3.80	8.1	5.18	4.0	8.65	2.2	11.21	2.8
Teledyne	1.58	13.9	1.62	12.0	2.52	5.2	2.68	4.3	3.35	6.2
Tenneco	2.18	11.5	2.52	10.4	2.72	8.4	4.20	4.8	4.03	6.3
Textron	1.96	15.0	2.23	14.9	2.58	8.3	2.81	5.3	2.48	8.9
U.S. Industries	2.10	12.3	2.40	8.9	2.35	4.8	1.25	3.6	(0.31	—
Average of these companies	1.61	13.25	1.99	14.06	2.95	7.12	3.58	4.01	3.16	10.8
Average D.J. Composite	1.84	16.2	2.24	15.2	2.87	9.9	3.30	6.2	2.52	11.3

The EPS represent the latest 12 months reported earnings as of December 31 in each year. The price/earnings ratio is based upon the 200 day moving average stock price. EPS are not restated for stock splits or stock dividends. However, for comparative purposes, it is important to remember that the Dow-Jones Average is automatically adjusted for stock splits and dividends.

aspects of the seller's business, particularly nonfinancial areas. These kinds of checklists have been developed by several sources.[2]
- Overeagerness to make a deal.
- Making sweeping changes in management, personnel policies, market procedures, and tactics upon consummation of the transaction, but prior to determination as to why the acquired company was successful.

When business combinations are so risky, how do we improve the odds?

PLANNING FOR DIVERSIFICATION

Judging from the historical data, we have concluded that a planned acquisition program is more likely to be successful. In a planned diversification program, the sequence of steps is more or less governed by a timetable of events. The first stage in this cycle is the realization that an acquisition program is needed and the company is currently able, financially, to support such a program. This recognition is usually an outgrowth of:

- The perception that in the near term the company will not achieve its strategic objectives (either financial results, market penetration, or the development of new products).
- Belief that there are not enough ongoing internal projects to provide acceptable returns.
- Awareness that in the not too distant future, major business units or product categories will either stagnate, enter into a stage of decline in the life cycle, or face severe constraints through government or competitor market-oriented actions (or both).
- Suspicion that competitors have developed new technologies which cannot be quickly reproduced internally.
- Confidence that earnings and cash generation are more than adequate to finance all present businesses.

This leaves managers with several alternatives: pay down debt, buy back the company's stock, increase dividends, expand the investment portfolio, develop new internal projects, or initiate an acquisition program.

Once corporate management has recognized the need for action and has decided to embark upon an acquisition campaign, prudent planning should be emphasized. Planners should recommend actions similar to the following tactical acquisition planning sequence of events.

Phase I Identification of Objectives Including Recognition of One's Own Strengths and Weaknesses

Whenever any company decides to embark on an acquisition program, the first step should be to define its objectives. This can be done by an executive committee, chief executive officer, or by the board of directors. Regardless, it is difficult to see how a diversification program can be successful without a clear definition of objectives. A company's objectives may vary greatly, ranging from expansion of capacity, product diversification, improvement of competitive position, economic protection, acquisition of management or technical personnel, or merely acquiring an operation for tax considerations.

The consequences of not identifying strengths and weaknesses can have significant consequences. Consider Esmark (formerly Swift & Co.) whose objective was to move from a cyclical meatpacker to a diversified, growth-oriented corporation. It appears that in choosing to participate in diversified businesses, management decided not to exploit its basic strength—that of providing human nutrition. The results have been a precipitous slide in Swift & Co.'s industry position while only one of numerous acquisitions has performed beyond expectation. A reflection of this attitude can be seen in management's explanation of performance. When performance was favorable, management touted its success in creating a well-balanced, diversified company and downplayed the food division's contribution (which, incidentally, was a major factor). However, when results turned unfavorable, it was the recently overlooked food business upon which blame was placed, despite poor performance in other recently acquired businesses. The lesson is that, in the rush to diversify, don't forget your basic strengths.

In determining objectives and in devising means to achieve them, the strengths and weaknesses of the company must be honestly and penetratingly set forth. There is no substitute for indentifying one's own particular capabilities and limitations for each business area. These, in conjunction with objectives, will provide invaluable insight useful in the determining of the appropriate industries from which candidates should be selected.

Phase II Evaluation of One's Own Company

To uncover strengths and weaknesses, the evaluation should cover thoroughly a company's traditional elements such as marketing programs (including unique skills), technical talent, managerial capabilities and depth, financial strength (cash availability, reporting and control, credit lines, etc.), channels of distribution, and risk attitude. Among the more esoteric skills requiring scrutiny are capability in dealing with unions, ability to cope with unstable prices, exploitation of new product ideas, and sensitivity to consumer needs.

However, management should not assume that strengths are easily transferable. For example, consider the plight of GATX. Company management thought of itself as being expert in the field of rail car leasing. Logically, management assumed this expertise to be transferable into all fields of transporation leasing—especially shipping (supertankers). Unfortunately, the composition of these markets is different and the capital cost for building one supertanker versus that of one rail car is hardly comparable ($38 million vs. $38,000). In addition, the United States is no longer dominant in shipbuilding, and foreign governments have subsidized competitors. The sum of these factors has resulted in unfavorable performance by the GATX acquisition.

Given your company's strengths and weaknesses, objectives for the corporation and each business unit, and some indication of the characteristics a candidate should exhibit, the next step is the formation of a working acquisition group.

Acquisition Group

Unquestionably, the committee approach is overdone in many cases. However, in the acquisition area, because of the wide divergence of information required, it takes the judgment of more than one person to reach a sound conclusion. Hence, the creation of a working acquisition committee brings together all the disciplines necessary for a comprehensive analysis. This committee should be directed and chaired by an operating officer who has been given the responsibility by the board of directors to guide the activities of the committee which result in affirmative action rather than staff reports.

Horizontal Extension

If the acquisition is intended to complement an ongoing operation, then it is useful to have members from each of the following internal functions represented on the committee (not necessarily on a full-time basis).

Members from the Corporate Staff	*Members from the Operating Company*
Economics and planning	Marketing
Market research	Production/Engineering
Finance	Distribution
Research and development	

Concentric Addition

However, if the candidate is to come from outside the present scope of one's business, the committee should include outsiders with industry expertise, thus augmenting internal capabilities. The committee should meet periodically and review progress. Tasks, timetables, and responsibilities should be assigned to each member.

With a strong committee, a carefully developed statement of objectives, and identification of strengths, weaknesses, and guidelines for candidate characteristics, the company should be in a strong position to find appropriate target enterprises.

Consider Mobil Corporation. Management recognized that the company had developed tremendous financial talent but was crude poor and thus vulnerable to any interruption of supply. The company created an acquisition committee that for several years reviewed industries in search of a horizontal acquisition. The objectives were simple: Identify a firm that was unrelated to oil, not dependent on natural resources, could use constant inflow of capital, and in which Mobil's marketing expertise could be applied. One industry which met all the criteria was the retail industry. Mobil's acquisition of Marcor has proven to be a good marriage.

Phase III Outline of Desired Acquisition Characteristics

Once the evaluation process has been completed, a general statement outlining basic characteristics of acquisition prospects should be developed. The statement should contain at least the following pertinent information:

Size of companies. Profit ranges, returns on equity, capital assets, P/E, estimated purchase price, and type of purchasing arrangements.

Property. Preferable plant, equipment, office uses, and locations.

Product lines. Industrial or consumer product lines sought, along with identified major products.

R&D. Type of engineering, research, and development desirable.

Marketing. Whether active management would be required to continue or whether it would be necessary to supply management from in-house.

Growth potential. Whether it is to be stable or erratic, and what market share would be of interest.

Ownership. Will minority owners be necessary? (This is of particular importance in international negotiations.)

Phase IV   Finding Acquisition Prospects

Rather than limiting itself to certain companies that happen to come to attention, the acquisition group should identify companies that may be considered good prospects. This can be accomplished by:

• Review of the Thomas Register of American Manufacturers, the classified industries section of Moody's Industrial Manual, the SIC code classification, or similar directories.

• Confiding in one's bankers, the company's independent public accountants, legal counsel, and others who often know of companies that might be interested in a sale.

• Encouraging suggestions from managers in the operating divisions (especially sales personnel) with repect to interesting companies.

• Engaging investment bankers, business consultants, or brokers.

After identification and analysis of potential candidates, a prioritized list (including projected merger terms, costs, and financial arrangements) should be submitted by the committee to senior management for review and final approval. Once this is completed, negotiations can begin.

In at least one company which arrived at this stage in the procedure, the next step was for the chief executive to reach agreement on the company's first acquisition on the golf course, during 18 holes with an old friend who wanted to sell out. The acquisition was not related to the parent company's goals, did not fit the acquisition criteria, and was, not surprisingly, a dismal failure.

When the acquisition is more orderly, remember that thoroughly planning a follow-through is as important during consolidation of the acquisition as during the pre-merger procedure.

SUMMARY

Chance has played and will continue to play an important role in successful diversification. In the long run, however, the "luckiest" will be those managers whose program is based on thoughtful and soundly conceived planning. By identification of the company's reasons for acquisition, careful selection of candidates, and thoroughness in execution, planners can improve the success rate of these ventures.

Examine the records of acquisition oriented companies. Those that have planned, such as Tenneco, Beatrice Foods, Mobil, Bayer of Germany, Robert Bosch, ITT, and Northwest Industries, have fared well. Those that have chosen the "pot luck" approach, such as Jimmy Ling's

LTV, Litton Industries, U.S. Industries, Apēco, and IU International, have found the acquisition path to be a maze of trouble.

REFERENCES

1. Shaw Livermore, "The Success of Industrial Mergers," *Quarterly Journal of Economics,* November 1935.
2. George D. McCarthy, *Acquisitions and Mergers* (New York: The Ronald Press Company, 1963), p. 46.

Part VI
THE PLANNING PROCESS

FINN E. JERSTAD

An Administrator's Manual of Planning

ALTHOUGH there is no shortage of literature on subjects dealing with the content of plans, little has been written about those issues which are of more direct interest to planning administrators. Their key tasks are to set the planning process in motion and to keep it moving. There are certain prerequisites to this process. First, strong support is needed from the corporate chief executive, and indirect power that follows such support. Second, continuous cooperation and real involvement in the planning process are required from division and profit-center management. Such conditions are normally mutually dependent on one another, but the planning director must keep the support and interest constantly alive through communication, education, and sometimes badgering.

A third factor important to the success of planning is the review and revision procedure that must take place at regular intervals, sometimes as often as every quarter, depending on the type of industry and fluctuations in markets or in economic circumstances.

Fourth and most important of all is the planning director's ability to understand all essential aspects of the corporation's activities and to reflect them in the rules he or she sets for the planning game. This is the most important, yet the most difficult, task for corporate planners, and one that is often underestimated.

The reason formal rules are not normally described in literature or discussed in planning seminars is probably that the subject is too mundane to excite anyone. But guidelines for corporate planning are, in fact, the laws that govern the planning process. They give the planners their direction and constrain the plan contents. Rules cannot be written in sufficient detail to cover all business situations adequately, and they will necessarily be interpreted differently by planners. Rightly so, because all laws are subject to individual interpretation and all undergo modifications as the circumstances of our environment change. Planning guidelines are important for several reasons.

• They constitute the common framework which tells the person doing the planning what is expected of him or her. They create a shared context for the writing of plans.

• They explain planning concepts and introduce a terminology which, once it is understood, makes it easier to plan.

• They set the standards for judging plans. The plans, in turn, make it possible to judge the quality of the guidelines. Poorly conceived guidelines produce inferior planning.

• They are the base from which a corporate planning director establishes his or her dialog with planners throughout the corporation.

• They give the director of planning leverage with division and profit-center management. In essence, the director is setting the rules, and is responsible for the implementation of the rules and, therefore, of corporate strategy.

If it is true that the corporate planning administrator derives indirect power from issuing rules to planners, and if he or she can rely on them as judges rely on rules of the legal system, then it follows that the administrator's chief responsibility is to produce good guidelines.

Good guidelines are flexible to fit changing circumstances, externally and internally. As a corporation matures and its executives become familiar with planning ahead, the system changes. Plans often become shorter, but they contain more relevant facts and depth in thinking. Guidelines can encourage such progress.

Good guidelines apply to varying circumstances in markets and environment. In a highly diversified corporation, the awareness of this need is greater. Inflation, recession, cyclicalities, and other economic forces have different effects in Minnesota, Texas, and Maine, even in similar types of businesses. It takes time and hard work to appreciate the complexity of these variances; but if the guidelines allow for them, the plans will improve.

Good guidelines help the division and profit-center planners develop operational plans that are within the constraints set by corporate strategic decisions. Operational plans that point in a direction that is not consistent with the overall corporate direction or that require resources that are not available, or are otherwise inconsistent with corporate strategies, indicate that the planning director has failed to communicate through the planning guidelines and through ongoing dialog with the organization's planning units.

A key to successful performance by the corporate planning director is the dialog he or she is capable of establishing with line management. In a diversified corporation, the planning specialist, regardless of how bright, experienced, and educated he or she is, cannot fully understand all the critical aspects of several different businesses by observing them from a distance. The specialist must go through the learning process which only an active ongoing dialog will make possible. This two-way communication is centered around the guidelines, and it becomes essential to the improvement of the quality of planning.

Examples 1 and 2 illustrate for a service industry the difference in detail required in guidelines for planning. Example 1 is relatively detailed. However, the introduction of the concept of "strategies" in Example 1 was not well accepted by the planners as it proved to be difficult to respond to. Accordingly, on the next plan cycle we tried the terser and simpler approach shown in Example 2.

Note that the full version of these guidelines also includes a time schedule for planning and explanation of some planning concepts. A financial section with forms requiring detailed quantitative goals in the three-year period is also included in the guidelines. These address themselves strictly to operating management for single companies and require strict coordination with the steps and goals described in the strategic section of the plan. Special guidelines exist for division plans, with the key focus on long-range strategic planning.

EXAMPLE 1: THE 1975 PLAN GUIDELINES

I. Unit's present position
   A. Business purpose and description
      1. *Present business purpose of the unit*
         Describe the nature and scope of the unit's current business activities. Include the following:
            Services offered
            Other customer benefits offered
            Key markets by segments
            Basic policies
      2. *Unit's present internal resources*
         Describe the unit's human, physical, financial, and other resources or capabilities, and explain why they are important. Summarize the unit's most distinctive competitive strengths in the areas of:
            Management
            Marketing
            Merchandising
            Finance
            Personnel

3. *Present internal weaknesses of the unit*
Include important resources and capabilities that are not present in the unit at this time but that are possessed by competitors, or are important to develop or strengthen for other reasons.

B. Unit's external environment
   1. *Social, economic, technical, and political trends*
   Describe the present climate and those major changes you expect to see taking place in your environment in the next three years which will significantly affect the unit's performance. The assumptions you make with respect to market decline or upswing, inflation ratios, regulatory legislation, political trends, consumer attitudes, disposable income, etc., form the information base on which your objectives and strategies are established. Your assumptions must be specifically and quantitatively defined to be useful for planning.
   Example
   Nonquantified assumption:
   "Trading stamp use will increase in supermarkets."
   Quantified assumption:
   "Supermarket use of trading stamps will increase 'X' percent through 1977."

   2. *Competition in the industry*
   This should include an assessment of the market structure with respect to:
   The three largest competitors with market shares
   The characteristics of strong competitors
   The degree of concentration and dominance of major companies
   Describe those critically important factors in the industry which must be kept under surveillance in the plan period in such marketing areas as:
   Selling/merchandising methods
   Service
   Service competitiveness
   Service innovation
   Promotion
   New trends and developments
   Describe also those major trends that are now affecting the industry and will influence future volume, pricing structures, costs, and earnings. Include any significant competitive moves expected to take place in the next one to three years.

II. Performance against previous plan
   A. Comment briefly on the unit's performance in 1975 to date, and explain fully any significant deviation from the 1975 Plan.
   B. Describe how the unit is progressing toward the most important objectives included in the 1975–1977 Plan.

III. Business objectives

All objectives must be designed to move the unit toward achieving its overall Business Purpose as stated in I.A.1.

A. Financial objectives

The forms determine those strictly financial areas in which goal setting is required. These include targets in areas of:

Profitability (profit percentage of sales)

Growth (sales and earnings)

B. Other objectives

Specific and measurable objectives are needed also in such key areas as:

Market standing (share of markets, company image, customer loyalty)

Innovation (new services)

Productivity (sales per man, cost per unit)

Staffing (personnel training)

Social responsibility (community programs)

Such objectives must be stated in a manner that makes it possible to control progress toward their attainment.

IV. Business strategies

The strategies must explain, in a broad sense, how the objectives will be achieved. They should not be detailed programs. The base for strategies is:

Internal strengths (capabilities) and weaknesses

Assumptions made with respect to the future environment

It may be helpful to ask:

Which new services should we add?

What should we do to improve services presently offered?

What new business should we pursue?

To what markets should we pay particular attention?

How should we best allocate our management, financial, and other resources?

Strategies are made up of those major moves and changes that will enable the unit to make the best possible use of existing opportunities and to strengthen its position in the industry. There are two types of strategies:

A. *Innovative strategies.* The key types are:

Risk: involves risk-taking decisions, a departure from status quo

Resource allocation: usually involves major reallocation of the unit's physical, human, and financial resources

Future oriented: concerns the future and is creative

B. *Operating strategies.* These are concerned with "doing more of the same better."

Describe those major strategies that you have established in order to attain the objectives in major functional areas in the plan period. For example:

Service strategies

Merchandising strategies

        Pricing strategies
        Promotion strategies
        Sales-force strategies
        Customer strategies
        Productivity strategies
        Buying strategies
        Distribution and warehousing strategies
        Staffing and training strategies
        Other

Those strategies described in the plan should all be concerned with improving the performance of the unit's existing business in a significant way. Innovative strategies are of special importance.

V. The key steps

One of the secrets of success in operational planning is identifying, ranking, and concentrating on the few truly significant issues and factors of the business. The action plan must include only those key steps that make important contributions to the implementation of strategies and progress toward objectives. Insignificant items will only obscure the key issues and waste management's time.

List and describe briefly those major key steps that unit management will take to attain the objectives set for the plan period 1976–1978. The key steps should be listed and described by functional areas of the unit. For example:

A. *Marketing*
        New accounts
        Geographic coverage
        Consumers/savers
        Selling rates
        Services
        Sales forces
        Operating procedures
        Consumer outlets
        Distribution/warehousing
        Purchasing
        Suppliers
        Inventory
        Other

B. *Personnel*
        Management replacement
        Personnel management
        Recruiting and training
        Salary costs
        Turnover

C. *Finance and control*
        Controls

Improvement of procedures
Credits/collections
Account financing
Reporting systems
Management information
Data processing
Cost-reduction programs
Other

VI. Contingency planning

In a rapidly changing economic environment, one can only make educated guesses about the future. Contingency planning will enable the unit's management to switch its strategies and actions to adjust to new situations more rapidly than competitors and, if need be, to change the unit's objectives. Contingency plans must exist before events start to take place.

For example, one assumption made in the unit plan is that the recession in the food retail business will level out at year end 1975, and pick up rapidly through 1976. If, by November 1975, it becomes apparent that the recession will continue through the first half of 1976, a contingency plan ready for implementation must exist.

Describe briefly what other strategies you must implement and what other key steps you are ready to take if a substantial change occurs in your markets or industry which creates an immediate threat or an opportunity for your unit. Contingency planning involves several possibilities.

A. *Changing objectives*

If the changes in the future environment are substantial, they may cause you to change the unit's objectives in the plan period. In Section I.B.1, you have described those changes that may occur in the plan period. How will they affect your objectives if and when they do occur? Describe briefly what alternative strategies and key steps you must implement in order to attain the revised objectives.

B. *Maintaining objectives*

Objectives may be attained in more ways than one. If, under changing conditions in the marketplace, the economy, lifestyles, etc., you still think the unit's stated objectives can be reached, state those changes you must make in:

1. Major strategies
2. Key steps

Such changes can be made by:

Increasing sales force
Developing new markets
Adding new services
Improving productivity
Improving purchasing procedures
Increasing prices
Advertising more effectively

Getting more mileage out of facilities, equipment, personnel
Cutting costs in any area

VII. Ten years hence
This section deals with those long-range concepts and developments that you would like to see implemented under given circumstances.
A. Describe briefly those major trends and conditions that you now see in your industry and your markets as much as ten years ahead.
B. Describe briefly what you now believe your unit's business will look like in ten years.

After we completed the 1975 plan it was clear that our managers—the planners in each business unit—were ready for a new stage in the development of our planning cycle. They understood the concept of strategies and they knew the basics of the planning guidelines. It was not necessary to repeat the work done in developing 1975 plans, or to update the routine figures. Instead, we looked for changes that would be significant to each business unit. The next set of guidelines was shorter, but required more creative thinking. As the team of managers develops competence and familiarity with planning, plans should emphasize important changes and contingencies rather than repeating basic strategies.

EXAMPLE 2: THE 1976 PLAN GUIDELINES

I. Assessment of unit and its environment
A. *Present purpose*
1. Give an updated and brief description (200 words or less) of what the unit is setting out to accomplish.
2. Internal resources: Summarize those most distinctive competitive strengths you now have in all areas of business activity.
3. Internal weaknesses: What are the most important problems you are presently experiencing as a result of shortcomings?
4. Performance factors: What factors are most critical to success in your type of business?
B. *General market and environment situation*
1. Give an updated description (150 words) of the economic, technological, social, and political climate in which you are now working, and list those factors that have significant impact on your unit's performance.
2. Competition in the industry: Describe briefly any significant changes that have taken place in your industry since your last plan. What, if anything, has happened to your competition which calls for new measures of performance on your part?

II. Performance against previous plan
  A. Comment briefly on the unit's performance in 1976 to date, and explain fully any significant deviation from the 1976 Plan.
  B. Describe how the unit is progressing toward those most important objectives included in the 1976–1978 Plan.

III. Business objectives
  A. *Financial objectives*
  State the unit's financial objectives in the financial forms in accordance with the instructions given.
  B. *Nonfinancial objectives*
  Describe briefly and as specifically as possible those objectives the unit has established with respect to:
    Markets (response to needs and wants)
    Services offered
    Management organization
    Personnel (staffing, training)
    Information, control, research
    Other
  Emphasize significant areas of innovation or change from earlier planning. Comment on priorities of objectives and timing of expected achievement. If it is not self-evident, explain how the objectives fall into a coherent overall unit strategy.

IV. Key steps
  Describe briefly those essential key steps that you will take to achieve your objectives. The key-step descriptions must be placed under those objectives to which they apply. Where key steps are related to each other in support of one or more objectives, this should be explained. Include the following in your description of key steps:
  1. Timing of actions
  2. required organization
  3. Person responsible
  4. Cost of action

V. Contingency plans
  Describe briefly how you would modify your objectives and key steps if it becomes clear that significant and unanticipated changes occur in your industry, in your markets, or in your environment. What are those most significant lead indicators that would cause you to make such changes in objectives and key steps?

VI. Ten years hence
  Describe briefly what you foresee ten years from now in terms of the size and structure of the industry you are in. Also describe its profitability, services, distribution, consumer attitudes, needs, and wants in terms of technology and other significant characteristics. How will your unit compare to its leading competitors? What kind of organization and resources will you need?

JAY S. MENDELL AND W. LYNN TANNER

Process Is
More Important
Than Product
Throw Out the Plan and Keep the Planner

THE MYTH OF RATIONALITY

To prepare a technology assessment is to engage in a struggle between openness and closedness. This is the inherent struggle of planning and forecasting, since one's objective is to include the significant and exclude the complicating. In technology assessment, this struggle is particularly awkward, since in principle the assessment should be open to the consideration of side effects and ricochet effects and to alternative future environments. Yet in practice there are limitations on time, personnel, and funding, and limitations on the willingness of decision makers to assimilate a complicated, differentiated equivocating analysis. So closedness is imposed where there might be openness.

Among decision makers there exists a myth of rationality. They like to believe that their decisions can be justified in terms of fact and valid theory. They feel compelled to give scientific reasons even for hunches and acts of imagination, often preparing after-the-fact rational explanations for nonrational decisions. They do not want to talk about, indeed they often do not want to know about, the uncertainties, contingencies, discontinuities, and competing theories that are swept under the carpet in preparing an assessment or plan. The ideal assessment would look far enough into the future; side effects would be considered in sufficient depth; the interdisciplinary team producing the assessment would not only represent relevant academic disciplines, but also all of the conflicting values, interests, and ideologies; and the assessment would include the best policy recommendations that could be inferred from the analysis, based on judgment and imagination. The team would have long enough to get the job done while delivering a timely report.

No assessment can be made to meet such naive expectations. We are not talking about a temporary inadequacy, but an inherent limitation on planning, decision making, policy making, dialoging, and futurizing.

Maybe we had better learn not to hide our uncertainties but to structure them.

Consider a forecast of the future social–technological–economic–political situation. Of the forecast one may ask: Why did you use this method and not some other? Can you justify the particular social theory used, or the particular data? Do you know how your competitors will react to the strategy assumed by your policy? Most importantly, how can you predict inventions unless you make these inventions yourself? If you are not yourself inventive and creative, how can you forecast in any area where invention and creativity may be a critical factor?

Of a plan or strategy, one may ask the above questions and others, such as: How do you know what you want, unless you know what you can get? And how do you know what you can get, unless you know how badly you will want it when the time comes? How may we know you have not consciously or unconsciously suppressed unpleasant possiblities about the future? (Maybe your institution has no future in the future.) Remember: Your assumptions are assumptions not because you know they are true, but because you do not know. If they were true, they would be facts.

The questions above barely begin to hint at the threatening and confronting ambiguities and issues of creativity implicit in futurism and planning/forecasting.

"THROW OUT THE PLAN AND KEEP THE PLANNER"

A strong case can be made that the client who buys a forecast or plan is actually paying an analyst to educate himself or herself at the client's expense. The client may or may not be educated by the process or product.

The analyst, immersed in the process, does the following (and more). He/she (hereafter referred to as "he") defines an area of interest; he searches for pertinent data, pertinent theory, pertinent (and impertinent) interpretations of fact and theory; he struggles with his conscience to decide which internal and external factors have to be simplified out of the analysis; he engages his critical and creative faculties; he finds the language to explain his concepts; and, in the end, he writes a report to his client which imparts about 1 percent of what he has learned.

The client can never learn all that the analyst learned because of the problem of tacit knowledge—understanding that cannot be imparted to someone who has not shared the learning experience.

Under the circumstances, it might make more sense to consign the final report to a wastebasket and concentrate on letting the planner educate the client. In other words, throw out the plan and keep the planner.

This illustrates another one of the generally neglected value issues of planning: Process is more important than product.

LIVING WITH AMBIGUITY

The dictionary has several definitions for ambiguity. There is, first, "doubtful or uncertain"; then, "capable of being understood in two or more senses." But we prefer to go back to the root, *ambigere*—"to wander about."

Ambiguity thus conveys the notion of refraining from unjustified decisions, conclusions, and exclusions. In other words, an assessment should retain (indeed should highlight) uncertainty, ignorance, and risk; and decision makers should learn not only to work with these factors but to use them creatively. Here are some of the faces of ambiguity:

1. There is never exactly the right information to justify a decision.

2. For any social policy or decision, there is no unique social theory from which one can proceed with assurance.

3. No significant piece of reality is sufficiently described by a finite number of indicators. Thus, it is not true that "if you can't count it, it doesn't count."

4. Though the input knowledge to any assessment can ostensibly be identified as a certain body of methods, theory, and facts, the assessor, before he uses the methods, theory, and facts, must first assimilate a vast amount of background knowledge whose relevance to the assessment in hand is not apparent.

5. Conversely, a considerable amount of theory and data may be brought into the assessment process because the decision maker thinks he needs it or because the analyst thinks the decision maker will want to see it. But this information, possibly acquired at great expense, will be ignored if the decision maker feels he should decide based on his values rather than his information.

6. Any prediction about the future development of a technology or the future social environment in which the technology will be diffused is at best a surprise-free prediction, contingent upon identifiable events which may or may not come to happen; upon willed actions which competitors and other actors may or may not subsequently take; upon the success or failure of willed events; upon surprises which were completely overlooked in the analysis; and upon unknown unknowns (factors unidentifiable at the time of planning).

7. In futurism it is often useful to invent concepts, postulate alternative futures, and propose goals and strategies as straw men (to elicit general or specific criticism), as ideal cases (baselines for discussion and thought), or as provocations to the imagination. Sometimes futurism is done just to see how it looks when it is done, that is, as an exercise with no clear-cut purpose other than an instinctive desire toward action. Likewise, a completed plan, though seen by its sponsor as authoritative, may be more useful as a straw man, a departure point, or a provocation. Further, any part of the planning process or the planning report may serve such a purpose by triggering a creative process.

8. In setting goals and objectives, you never know exactly what you want because you are never sure exactly what you can get. And you do not know exactly what to aim to get, because you do not know how badly you will want to work for it at some future time.

CREATIVITY IS NONRATIONAL AND INDISPENSABLE

Richard Davis was in charge of technological forecasting for the Whirlpool Corporation. Responding to rumors of a new delayed cure process for resins, Davis realized this would be a basis for the manufacture of permanent press fabric (hence garments). To perform the assessment, Davis had to conceptually invent permanent press garments, after which he was able to confirm that permanent press was indeed the goal of the resin process. Because of Davis's anticipatory thinking, Whirlpool was the only manufacturer of clothes dryers with a cycle ready for timely introduction upon the appearance of permanent press garments.[1] To achieve the required engineering lead time, Davis first had to experience the creative act of conceptually inventing permanent press fabrics.

A proper job of forecasting and planning should ideally include a strong component of inventing the future. The forecaster should anticipate the kinds of discontinuities that can come only from creative acts.

To conceptually invent the future is probably beyond the capabilities of most forecasters. Society may not adopt the future that the analyst invents; or, the analyst may fail to invent conceptually the future that eventually occurs.

This problem is not often mentioned in connection with technology assessment and planning because it introduces ambiguities and allows an irrational factor, creativity, to be dragged to a central position in a supposedly rational process, planning.

A creative perception can change our view of a technology. One of the authors (J.S.M.) has adapted and developed imagination-stretching techniques to change a client's perception of his business. Employees of a large business machine company were asked to define their dominating concept of the computer. "Giant brains" was soon identified. Later the clients were asked to view the year 1974 from the vantage of the year 2020 and then comment on an absurd feature of 1974. One employee remarked on the absurd amount of useless information being retained by society; then he reflected that "computers ought to be used as giant kidneys: you know, to help us excrete useless information from our systems." Can we predict, through current methodologies, creative shifts of perception? Perception shifts like these are influential in shaping our technologies, and hence our assessments and plans.

Edward deBono, a leading researcher and teacher, pointed out that the truly creative person is the one who cares least about being right all the time, who makes mistakes and turns them into useful concepts, or who thinks nonlogically when strict logic would impede progress toward new insights.[2] To admit that this kind of non-logic-bound thinking has a place in planning is difficult for anyone claiming rationality as the most important foundation of the discipline.

There is an irreducible role for insight and creativity. You simply cannot interpret the signals of change mechanically; you must proceed imaginatively. Ambiguity, too, cannot be made to go away. Different people will arrive at radically different pictures of what will happen, what might happen, and what might be made to happen. The differences are rooted in differing theories, differing data, differing time depths of perception, differing social breadths, differing perceptions of how the society will react to changes, differing normative values, differing vested interests, and differing abilities/preferences for unpleasant views of the future. And again, to differing degrees of insight, outsight, curiosity, creativity, and courage.

THE NEED TO DEAL WITH INDIVIDUAL CONCEPTIONS, OUTLOOKS, AND COMPETENCIES

There is no use denying that technology assessment and other analytical frameworks for planning and policy making have contributed enormously to our ability to integrate forecasting and planning; to process information; to include important steps which might be carelessly or ignorantly omitted; to parcel out work among generalists and specialists; to iterate and integrate analytical steps; to gain acceptance for plans and policy; to control execution. But such highly expensive, carefully conceptualized, intellectually elaborated, painstakingly executed attempts to cope with the rapidly changing environments are only attempts. Expense, conceptualization, elaboration, and execution, no matter on what scale they are undertaken, are no guarantees of success in coping with environmental changes. They may simply be the best effort possible short of actually changing the outlook and competencies of a substantial number of individuals involved in analysis and decision making.

Planners and policy makers have for many years operated under a paradigm which says that the changing environment is basically manageable. By increasing the planning effort, processing additional information, and using sufficient services of experts, the future environment can be analyzed to a satisfactory level for planning and operations to proceed. So the paradigm indicates. The whole institution, its mode of organization, its purposes, and its future viability do not have to be rethought in their entirety since the environment is not seen as so turbulent or revolutionary as to be incomprehensible and unplannable.

Also part of the paradigm is the notion that our ability to handle the future will improve rather than deteriorate. This is to say that the future will become more forecastable and plannable as our tools improve. The paradigm is seldom stated explicitly.

But there is now reason to believe that within a few years, turbulence (complicatedness accompanied by rapid change) will produce such pressure on the organization that some sort of process of planning, replanning, questioning of purposes, and upheaval will be continuous. This implies the need for total responsiveness and adaptability, which implies the de-expertizing of futurism since no one will escape the force of change. Planners will have to acquire a new consciousness, new outlooks, and new competencies. The increasing pace and complexity of society may cause formal planning to wither away in favor of a continuous process of monitoring and adapting to the changing environment.

REFERENCES

1. Richard C. Davis, "Organizing and Conducting Technological Forecasting in a Consumer Goods Firm," in James R. Bright and Milton E. F. Schoeman, *A Guide to Practical Technological Forecasting* (Englewood Cliffs, N.J.: Prentice-Hall, 1973), pp. 601–618.
2. Edward deBono, *Lateral Thinking for Management* (New York: American Management Associations, 1971).

MALCOLM W. PENNINGTON

Why Has Planning Failed and What Can You Do About It?

EVERYBODY TALKS about formal planning. Everyone reads the literature. And most people agree that the concept is compelling and logical, and that planning is a thoroughly grand and sensible thing to do.

But if you talk to top managers and planners, you will find that planning usually fails. That is to say, formal planning is abandoned, or it does not change the organization's way of making decisions, or top management is not satisfied with the results. Why is it that most of the time planning fails?

The basic reason is that, despite all the talk, planning is not really woven into the fabric of management. True, plans are made and approved, but too often they are then put aside, not to be looked at for another year. Meanwhile, they have little impact on the way the company actually operates. They have little influence on current decisions that may affect the company one, five, and ten years from now.

Most people in top management are not comfortable with planning. They do not want to be involved in planning, and once the planning has been initiated, they do not use it as a regular tool. Often this is because they are not satisfied with planning.

Planning does, of course, have its advocates, people who believe it is possible to look into the future and make reasonable forecasts, and to make moves now that will affect the future environment. These people believe that a good forecast will allow them either to react effectively to the changes in the environment as they occur or to make changes in that environment. In practice, companies that plan will succeed well. IBM, a staunch advocate of planning, is a classic example.

IBM tries to foresee changes in the business environment and control them. Its competitors will attest to its success. While IBM does a better job than most, many companies like the idea of being the hunters instead of the hunted. Hunters do not wait for crises to force a response. They anticipate crises. They attempt to shape their environment and to do things in their markets to which their competitors can only react. They let their competitors be the hunted.

Why, then, when planning can do so much, does it fail so often? And how can this situation be reversed?

Problem 1

People are basically conservative, resistant to change, and usually accept change only when it is forced on them. A planner, of course, is an agent of change. How can this problem be overcome?

Sell like hell. The essence of the planner's job is to sell management on planning as a concept and as a part of the management function. This means getting managers involved.

Keep the planning staff small. In most cases the ideal planning staff is one planner, one secretary. The job of the planner is to cajole, to provide information, to coax people along, to help them with deadlines, to talk to managers, to get them thinking about problems before building plans. If the planning staff is large, it will tend to do the planning. But if the staff does the planning, the managers will not feel involved, and planning will have no effect on the way the company operates.

Stay away from jargon. It's easy for planners to talk about algorithms, but managers do not want to talk about algorithms, even if they are able to. They want to talk about next week's production or next year's marketing. Jargon makes them resistant. Talk the manager's, not the planner's, language.

Be wary of fancy techniques. True, they give the illusion of science and precision. And they are very useful in certain applications. Delphi techniques, decision trees, and matrix analysis, for example, are worthwhile in many areas. But they may not be useful in practical planning. They are difficult to explain, difficult to understand, and difficult to justify. The most successful figuring in the real world is done with a pencil and paper.

Start small and build up. Several years ago an old-line specialty paper company decided it needed planning. It hired a planner who tried to get people to sit down and talk about the future, what they needed, what they should do; in short, to do planning. But these managers were dying of today's problems. The planner got nowhere.

One day, however, he did get a responsive glimmer from the manager of research and development who wanted to know what directions he should be taking in his research. They began to work in R&D planning. In developing these plans, they used inputs and direction from the marketing division. The results were positive.

About a year later, the marketing vice-president looked at R&D's improvement and went to the planner. Soon they were making marketing plans. Eventually the entire company became involved in planning. But it all began with one department.

Remember that each company and organization has its own individual characteristics. Each has its own history, its own management, its own style of doing things. What's good for Company A is not necessarily good for Company B. The planning approach that will work for General Electric will not necessarily work for Pacific Gas and Electric. Furthermore, a planning approach that works beautifully this year may no longer work next year. General Telephone & Electronics International changes its planning format annually. This allows its overseas managers to look at their problems from a different point of view each year. After looking at their operations from several different angles over a period of years, the managers understand their own operations a great deal better. And they do not get bored.

To get ongoing change, you must have the support of top management. One way to get this is to be successful in your first endeavor. Even if it's a modest success, it may get management interested. Another approach is to make sure that, once you have begun, you place a minimum demand on top management's time. In other words, get top management involved in planning, but only at those critical points where it's needed most. You can't get a man like Bob Six at Continental Airlines to sit down for a three-day planning session. But you may get him to sit down for one day to go over with his division chiefs the broad direction of planning for a given period. When the plans are put together a month or two later, you may ask him to spend another day reviewing the division plans and fitting them together. And a few weeks later, when the sorting between divisions is done, you may have to spend a third day with him to approve the final plan. This is a system that works well with the personalities and the history of Continental Airlines, and it takes a minimum amount of the chief executive's time. If you value a man's time, and use it carefully and well, you are likely to get much more support from him.

Problem 2

There are no perfect planning systems. We Americans tend to look for the ideal system, the one right answer. But life is too complicated and too changeable these days to get away with a "let's set it up now and compare results at the end of the year" approach. The world changes, and so must the plans. You have to have a planning system that works for your company and that changes when your company changes. IBM, for instance, used to do annual planning. But their market was changing so rapidly that they switched to quarterly planning. It worked, but it took too much time. So they switched again, to their present system of replanning every time a significant environmental change throws their plans out of kilter. It's still a lot of planning, but it has proved successful.

Problem 3

It is difficult to predict the future. Worse, the news may be bad. And as we all know, it is difficult to face bad news. In the old days, when a messenger brought bad news the custom was to cut off his head. The spirit of the custom has survived in modern business. People still do not want to hear bad news.

Even good news can present problems. One airline had a projection of a big increase in business. As a result it was going to need a big increase in mechanics and reservations personnel. This, in turn, meant a big—and immediate—increase in the personnel department, so it would be ready to hire and train new employees when they were needed. One top executive said, "If you hadn't brought this up, I wouldn't have had to worry about it for six months." Yet six months from then, when they needed the help, they were not faced with a crisis. They were prepared. What can be done?

Develop contingency plans. Don't tell top management that you see bad news ahead. Say, "What if such and such happens? We'll work out a contingency plan that will cover it." One company, for example, had a situation in which one customer represented 40 percent of its market. No one thought of this as a hazard, but still the company developed a contingency plan in case it lost that 40 percent customer. In order to assess the odds on losing the customer, the company's planners first figured the impact of this customer's integrating vertically to supply himself. Then they approached the customer with the economics of integrating vertically. The customer, as it happened, had been planning just such a move. But the supplier's presentation of the economics persuaded the customer to drop the project. Contingency planning can be a way either to avoid bad news or to avoid stating it outright.

Get the top man to say it himself. Some years ago I worked for an organization in which the president felt that ideas that came from subordinates could not be good ideas. We vice-presidents held our own meetings before we met with him. When we did meet with the president, we'd say, "Boss, how about doing such and such?" and he'd give us 20 good reasons why we couldn't. We'd wait six months, at which time he would say, "Gentlemen, I've come up with a brilliant idea: we're going to do such and such." We would give him back his same 20 reasons, and he would have a good answer for each one.

The chief executive of another company had some unfortunate experiences with planning and was bitterly opposed to planning. His vice-presidents, however, did not share his views. They would meet by themselves every month away from the office and, working with a consultant, would do their own planning. Then they would gradually sell their plans to the chief executive in their regular staff meetings. The chief executive might resist an idea for awhile, but eventually it would emerge as his idea.

SUMMARY

Change is difficult, a source of anxiety, and often unpleasant. As agents of change, planners have chosen a difficult profession. Their approach to the problems of their profession must constantly vary because there are no proven techniques that work in all (or even most) cases. And they are constantly working in an unknown and unknowable future.

Nevertheless, most of us believe that good planning is an essential ingredient of effective management. If planning is to be an effective management tool, planners have to do more than just plan well. They have to sell the concept and practice of planning within their organizations, and they have to persuade managers to plan well.

A. GEORGE GOLS

The Use of
Input–Output in
Industrial Planning

AN INFORMAL SURVEY conducted by Arthur D. Little, Inc., in 1972 showed that there were 200 corporations in the United States that, at one time or another, have used input-output in some form in their corporate planning work. Of these 200 corporations, all of which have sales in excess of $500 million annually, 60 firms indicated that they used input-output regularly and intended to continue to do so. From some other informal questionnaires that ADL circulated among some 50 or so major U.S. corporations for whom it had undertaken input–output studies, it was found that input–output analysis was typically used in connection with forecasting work. A few other types of application have been made that tie directly into corporate planning.

INPUT–OUTPUT ANALYSIS APPLICATIONS

The four principal types of input–output analysis applications that are distinguishable are:

Forecasting
Sensitivity testing
Flow and structural analysis
Sorting and screening

To some extent, these applications overlap or are interdependent, but for purposes of discussion, let us consider them separately.

Forecasting

Forecasting seems to have been the mainstay of past input–output analysis applications in corporate planning. Most likely, it will remain such. Some of the early applications here originated with work done in the early 1950s at the Western Electric Company. Later ADL, the University of Maryland, the Battelle Institute, and other organizations launched more ambitious and comprehensive research efforts in this area. This was done by assembling groups of corporations to jointly sponsor forecasting studies.[1,2]

At ADL, input-output application work during the last five years has progressed to the point where an input-output model is used every year to provide, on a regular basis, forecasts of the U.S. economy to a group of 30–40 corporate clients. The forecasts are made to cover 214–230 individual industries for the year ahead (in current and constant dollars) and in constant dollars for five to ten years. The key job here is not only to update and project the final demand and/or the exogenous variables that feed the input-output model, but to update and forecast the structure of the coefficient matrix. It is also necessary to interpret results in a way meaningful to the average corporate planner who may be unfamiliar with input-output definitions, data, and methods, and to help apply them in the planning work.

Input–output forecasting has been useful in several areas of corporate planning, but its prime application has been in corporate opportunity search. The information is used to assist corporate planners to identify acquisition, diversification, and general investment opportunities. This is done by screening industry growth or decline forecasts derived with the input-output model, and by determining which industries are likely to grow at a more or less rapid rate than the economy as a whole over the long term. If realistic forecasts are to be obtained, it is essential to develop quantitative estimates of the likely structural shifts that will take place in the input–output matrix over time. These shifts represent the expected changes in the size and position of individual industry markets. We determine what these shifts are likely to be by assessing likely changes in technology and competition of various products in different industry sectors via surveys of specialists and by undertaking specialized analysis work.

One-year, or even quarterly, input–output forecasts can be made to help the planner focus particular attention on more immediate business problems arising from unexpected alterations in the business environment. The alterations may emerge from a suddenly announced new goverment policy or a business cycle change, or some external event, like the energy crisis. The results of this type of input–output forecast become useful in setting up or changing corporate work schedules and programs. Input–output forecasts can also be useful in the performance monitoring and controls function where corporations evaluate profit centers in terms of how actual results compare with planned results.[3] Input–output forecasts, if detailed enough, can be used to adjust actual performance measures of profit centers to reflect actual changes in the

business environment, to more objectively measure the *real* performance progress of profit centers.

Sensitivity Testing

This type of input–output analysis is, in some respects, simply a
variant of forecasting work. However, it is geared to test the consequences of alternative hypotheses or scenarios concerned with changes
in the economic environment. Specifically, it deals with "what if" questions, such as: "What if the growth of the economy goes this way or that
way?" "What if the structure of an industry shifts along this direction instead of that direction?" "What happens if we have, or do not have, the
introduction of a specific new product in an industry next year—What
difference does it make?" Here, input-output analysis can help to draw
the boundary lines of the likely effects on industry and company growth
of alternative scenario developments. Such scenarios may set out different final parameters of GNP growth or GNP component mix, or alternative hypotheses about changes in the market structure or changes
in technology. For example, a few years ago, the North American Rockwell Company, a major aircraft producer, wishing to understand the impact on U.S. industry of the introduction of a space shuttle in the United
States, undertook an input–output analysis to better define the dimensions of such an impact.[4]

In sensitivity testing, input–output is particularly useful in demonstrating the indirect effects of specific changes. For example, a change in
the mix of a nation's exports, due to a currency revaluation or devalua-
tion, obviously directly influences the growth of corporations that export
goods and services. But the change in exports also affects the growth of
corporations that import their materials and supply products to either
the corporations that do the exporting or the enterprises that are major
suppliers to the exporting corporations. In such a case, input–output
analysis can reveal hidden but significant indirect effects. Similar questions about impacts arise when a change in an industry's production
technique changes the input patterns of another industry that is not directly involved in this change. The energy shortage in the United States
provides a good example. The materials and components inputs to the
mining equipment, shipbuilding, and transportation equipment building
industry have to be changed to respond to changing equipment needs of
the mining sector that arise, for example, as mining activity shifts its emphasis from onshore to offshore oil drilling.

With the profusion of seismic tremors that seem to be reverberating
through the world and domestic economic environment these days, and
the increasing number of multinational companies that are involved in

all types of activities all over the world, input–output's greatest potential use will lie in quick evaluations of the likely industry impacts and ramifications of international and complex events.

Flow and Structural Analysis

The input–output concept provides one of the best frameworks for analyzing some of the key flow patterns of goods and materials and services in the economy. The determination of flow patterns or the identification of the network by which goods move through the economy can provide insights into possible bottlenecks, strategic connections, and ways in which specific markets are coupled to each other. For example, in carrying out plant and product feasibility studies for corporations, patterns of materials input hierarchies and input mixes of different industries can be used in determining which particular material supplies should be given priority attention.

How useful the analysis of the pattern by which products and materials flow through the economy is to corporations is still to be determined, but at least one recent event has proven it a very useful tool. When energy developments pointed out a possible lack of petrochemical feedstocks for the chemical industry, input–output analysis was used to determine what petrochemical inputs the chemical industries directly require, and what industrial and employment repercussions would occur if these imputs proved to be in short supply.[5] The knowledge of the flow network of the petrochemicals industry in the United States was obviously one of the most essential ingredients to carry out such evaluation work. But it was necessary to do the evaluation within the framework of all industries operating in the national economy to determine how dependent the overall economy was on this industry.

There is, in addition, the possibility that flow analysis along input–output lines can also be carried out for an individual enterprise in identifying flow patterns of materials between different entities within a given corporate enterprise. This is being looked at by some very large chemicals corporations that have substantial intracompany product flows. It may yet turn out to be an important application for input-output analysis as more corporations move toward highly vertically integrated operations.

Sorting and Screening

Here, input–output serves primarily as an ordering tool by which markets and industries can be arrayed according to size, category, and other criteria. We have arrayed industries on the basis of their energy-intensiveness or usage. Similarly, we could array key markets of the metal-producing, chemical, or food processing industries on the basis of size or categories of suppliers, or we could order industries on the basis of their similarity of principal materials inputs [which to some extent is the basis of the U.S. Standard Industrial Classification (SIC) Code]. At ADL we can array more than 40,000 markets by perhaps as many as 20 different key configurations. The possible different ordering configurations are theoretically almost limitless. This type of information can be a key to determining the priorities that should be given to different markets or material supplies. It can enter into determining manpower needs within production units in corporations or in sales departments. It can be useful in corporate planning to demonstrate how or why management has reached certain decisions about allocating resources or establishing priorities.

OVERCOMING BARRIERS

Why, with all these possibilities for using input–output in the corporate planning process, has there not been more widespread use of the input–output analysis tool by businesses? There are at least three major barriers that must be overcome:

Better information. Unless input–output can work with more detailed up-to-date information, it will remain an academic exercise and useless to the highly specific information needs of the planner.

More work on nitty-gritty applications. There is a reluctance of the input–output analyst to deal with details of applying input–output to business problems. Input–output specialists will also have to learn more about the decision-making and planning process in corporations.

Better interpretation. There is a need to translate the abstract and theoretical formulations of input–output into operational terms that the average business planner, indeed the average businessman, can understand.

A Concrete Illustration

The above statements are best understood by referring to concrete illustrations. So let us briefly consider at least one scenario of a planning situation confronting a typical major manufacturing corporation.

A manufacturing corporation in the United States has diversified interests in various business areas and a yearly sales volume of around $1 billion. The individual divisions of the corporation are engaged in manufacturing products in three key areas: plastics, metals, and electronics. These products are sold to various markets, but in the main to the automotive, appliances, and machinery industries. The management of the company is very venturesome and aggressive. It wants to expand—possibly, but not necessarily, into new products. Obviously, it wants to avert a contraction in profitability and sales. It feels there is a need not only to enlarge its share of existing markets (which financial analysis shows leads to higher profits or return on investments) but also to look for opportunities in new areas where risks are high, but potential returns are also better.

The planning department has been asked by the management to systematically investigate future growth opportunities in the economy to determine how they might be tied into existing operations and the resources and experience of the company. This is typical of the kind of opportunity search work that is carried out by thousands of individual companies in the United States periodically, if not continuously. How does input–output enter into the process?

The Company Seeks Opportunities

The planner starts by drawing up a business environment scenario of the U.S. economy for the next 10–15 years. This will, he hopes, provide him with some of the key ingredients to determine the economic environment and the assumptions needed to undertake more detailed opportunity search work. He consults with the company's economist, who provides some of these inputs, such as long-range GNP forecasts, population trend forecasts, and market forecasts in key industries and products. However, this does not prove comprehensive enough for the planner. He also wants to identify opportunities in key areas with which the internal staff and in-house economists are relatively less familiar and lack the overall analytical framework by which to crosscheck the consistency of the analysis results. The planner tries to consult the literature and collect various articles; he can interview various marketing managers and marketing research staff inside and outside the company, but he has a problem linking it all together.

As the matter comes to a head, his information search confirms a suspicion already held by the management—namely, that a small compact car will perhaps soon replace the full-size vehicle that has been traditionally produced by the auto industry. This would, at first glance, imply substantial decreases in the demand for the company's plastics and metal products. But how much impact will it have, and what offsetting opportunities may arise? The corporate divisional market research managers also have become increasingly aware of this threat, but they have done little to analyze the industry-wide or company-wide repercussions.

The planner knows he needs to do this. He goes back to the economist. The economist now indicates that it is necessary to develop a rather elaborate framework to determine all the possible repercussions that might arise from such a fundamental change in the company's markets. Particularly tricky is the problem of arriving at quantitative estimates of the impact, particularly if one wants to measure not only the direct but also the indirect effects on materials demands, since it appears that the production of the small car will involve not only the substitution of materials for each other, but also the introduction of new technologies (pollution-control and electronics equipment) into the car. This obviously raises the possibility that new markets will be created for electronics and other components. It raises the question of whether other industries and materials needs will evolve as a consequence of these more direct changes that are now anticipated.

The economist, a resourceful woman, well-informed about the new tools of her trade, recommends the use of input–output analysis. She reasons that the planner can thereby not only forecast the impact of economic and technological change, but also learn something about how and to what degree other industries are affected, and to what extent these effects represent opportunities for the corporation.

The Company Analyzes

Because the corporation's in-house economic research capabilities are inadequate to handle this kind of study, the corporate planner and the economist decide to contract with an independent research organization to provide long-range forecasts to help analyze the problem. It is thought that the information would be most meaningful if the change could be analyzed by using in the input–output analysis the GNP forecasts which the corporation's economist has already developed. The research organization concedes this can be done, but also points out that there is a need also to have at least reasonably up-to-date detailed data on present materials usage in cars, and to forecast new materials usage patterns in the auto and related industries. This requires engineering and survey data from many industries. The research organization therefore proposes a more significant exercise than had earlier been anticipated by the planner or the economist. The planner and the economist reconcile themselves and their budget to this situation, but their real problems have only begun. When the first forecasts are generated, the planner compares the results with data with which he is familiar. He finds inconsistencies having to do with reconciling information of different sources. This is not necessarily peculiar to input–output, but it complicates the assessment work.

A more fundamental problem is to determine what it is precisely that the planner wants to know about materials demand. Does he want to measure demand in physical or value of output terms? Does it make a difference to him? Why is it critical? It so happens that the engineering data show that the small car or compact car will be structurally quite different from the large car. It will contain significantly more plastic and significantly less steel. It will contain new types of pollution-control components and electronic devices that have never existed before to improve the braking, warning signal, and motor operations of the vehicle. The auto will cost the same, but weigh only half as much as the traditional large-size car. Now, should the input–output analysis measure plastics, electronics, pollution-control components, and steel demand in tons, dollars, capacity, or what? The planner wants to know them all. The input–output analyst must decide whether to run a constant dollar or current dollar model, or both; short-term or long-term model, or both. Also, he must decide how to measure coefficient changes.

Table 1 outlines a hypothetical computation of alternative input–output coefficients of steel usage in the average automobile and in the auto industry as a whole. The table first shows steel usage in cars before any change takes place. The average car uses 1 ton of steel. Coefficients are given in physical and value terms as 0.5 and 0.1, respectively. That is, if 10 million tons are used to produce 20 million tons of cars, or 1 ton to produce a 2-ton car, the physical coefficient measures 0.5. On the other hand, if the total cost of steel used in 10 million vehicles (at $200 a ton) is $2 billion, and if the average vehicle cost $2,000 and 10 million vehicles are produced, the industry's total value of output equals $20 billion. The value coefficient is thus $2 billion divided by $20 billion, or 0.1. We therefore have a choice of using a value or physical coefficient and this, in turn, depends on whether the planner wants to measure demand changes in physical or value dimensions.

Let us further analyze this by looking at the situation where there is a substitution of plastic for steel, but no changes in the size of the car. Usage of steel per vehicle drops to 0.8 ton; plastic is substituted for steel (not shown on the table). Cost per ton of steel was formerly $200 and is now $250 because a new higher tensile-strength and more corrosion-resistant type of steel is used. But this increases the price of steel by 25 percent. If we now use only 0.8 of a ton of steel, which costs 25 percent more, the input of steel in cost terms remains the same at $200. The price of the car also does not change significantly because, while there is an increase in plastic usage, plastic prices decrease proportionately more than plastic usage increases.

Thus, neither the value coefficient of plastics nor the value coefficient of steel changes. But the physical input of steel and plastic changes. The

Table 1. Hypothetical computation of alternative input–output (I/O) coefficients (steel inputs to cars).

In Physical Terms		*In Value Terms*	
Before Substitution and Technological Change			
Steel usage per vehicle	1 ton	Cost per ton	$200
Total weight per vehicle	2 tons	Cost of steel per vehicle	$200
Total amount used (in 10 million vehicles)	10 million tons	Total cost of steel (10 million vehicles)	$2,000 million
Total weight of all cars	20 million tons	Total cost of 10 million vehicles	$20,000 million
I/O coefficient (1/2 = 0.5)	0.5	I/O coefficient ($2 billion/$20 billion)	0.1
After Substitution of Plastic for Steel and Price Changes in Standard-Size Car			
Steel usage per vehicle	0.8 ton	Cost per ton (25% price increase)	$250
Total weight per vehicle	2 tons	Steel cost per vehicle (0.8 × $250)	$200
Total amount used (in 10 million vehicles)	8 million tons	Total cost of steel (10 million vehicles)	$2,000 million
Total weight of all cars produced	20 million tons	Total cost of vehicle	$2,000
I/O coefficient (0.8/2 = 0.4)	0.4	Total cost of 10 million vehicles	$20,000 million
Physical coefficient change	20% decr.	I/O coefficient	1
Total steel demand change	20%	Value coefficient change	0%
		Total value of demand change	0%
After Introduction of Electronics and Pollution-Control Equipment and Plastic Substitutes in Compact Car			
Steel usage per vehicle	0.3 ton	Cost per ton (25% price increase)	$250
Total weight per vehicle	1 ton	Steel cost per vehicle (0.3 × $250)	$75
Total amount used (in 10 million vehicles)	3 million tons	Total cost of steel (10 million vehicles)	$750 million
Total weight of all cars produced	10 million tons	Total cost of vehicle	$2,000
I/O coefficient (0.3/1 = 0.3)	0.3	Cost of 10 million vehicles	$20,000 million
Physical coefficient change	40% decr.	I/O coefficient	0.04
Total steel demand change	70% decr.	Value coefficient change	60%
		Total steel demand change	62.5%

steel usage has dropped to 0.8 and steel demand now stands at 8 million tons. The total weight of the car has not changed since the plastic which displaces the steel is equally heavy, so the physical input coefficient of steel has now dropped to 0.4 or by 20 percent. This is important for planning, because physical demand changes affect plant capacity utilization rates in both the steel and plastics divisions of the company.

But the problem has only started. The design of the car is changed radically, as the size of the car is significantly reduced. Because of this, even more plastic and less steel is used in the compact car. The physical coefficient of steel drops to 0.3 or by 40 percent. The value of steel input is now $75. But the cost of the car stays the same because of the additions of high-cost electronic and pollution-control equipment. The value coefficient of steel drops to 0.04 or by 60 percent. In physical terms, the demand for steel has dropped from 10 million tons to 3 million tons or by 70 percent. In dollar terms, it has dropped from $2 billion to $750 million or by 63 percent.

The planner really needs to know all these things. He needs to know the steel usage in physical terms because it influences plant capacity utilization rates, and he needs to know the value of steel sold because it affects the corporation's revenues and cash flow profits. But he also needs to know the demand for electronic and other components in physical and value terms, because they promise new opportunities. He wants comparable information for all the other industry sectors that make up the input–output model. But the problem of measurement can get even more difficult there. What do we do about measurement in the electronics and other sectors, such as machinery, where perhaps performance capacity, instead of weight, has to be used to lend a meaningful physical dimension to coefficient changes?

Emerging from all of this is the insight that perhaps the key stumbling block to input–output use in corporate planning is that the assumptions and definitions concerning technological change, structural change, pricing and demand sensitivity, on which the input–output coefficient changes are based, are of great interest to the planner and of perhaps least interest to the input–output analyst. In fact, most input–output analysts tend to sweep these assumptions under the analytical rug, because they interfere with the mathematical elegancies of the input–output model or the simplicity of the analysis task.

THE OUTLOOK

If the input–output analyst cannot demonstrate a full understanding and sympathy for what is important to the corporate planner, the latter is not likely to accept the results of any input–output analysis. The kind of analysis problem illustrated above is duplicated and magnified in the application of input–output analysis in almost all the various stages of corporate planning.

Widespread acceptance of input–output in corporate planning thus awaits better solutions to dealing with the nitty-gritty, vexing, but very real problems attending the practical use of input–output analysis. Some progress is being made by those who have the interest and patience to tackle these problems; but it is not the most fashionable pursuit among input–output analysts. So progress is slow in coming, but very rewarding when attained.

REFERENCES

1. *The Growing Use of Input/Output Models*, EDP Analyzer, Vol. 7, No. 7, Canning Publications, Inc., Vista, California, July, 1969.

2. Staeglin, Reiner, *Zur Anwendung Der Input-Output Rechnung Kanjunktarpolitik*, Vol. 16, 1970.

3. Yost, S. W., and C. E. Stowell, Using Input/Output Analysis for Evaluating Profit Center Performance. Paper presented at the Institute for Management Sciences XVIII International Conference, London, July 1–30, 1970.

4. Gibson, T. A., and C. M. Merz, *Impact of Space Shuttle Program on the Economy of Southern California*, Space Division, North American Rockwell, September 1971.

5. Ficcaglia, V., and Hegeman, G., *United States Petrochemical Industry Import Analysis*. A report to the Petrochemical Energy Group, Cambridge, Massachusetts, November 1973.

ROBERT D. SMITH AND JAMES G. MORRIS

Simulation—
When All Else Fails

INTRODUCTION

Traditionally, corporate planning was, and sometimes still is, a curious blend of aspiration, perspiration, and inspiration. In this age of Future Shock these virtues are admirable but not sufficient. Nor do simple trend projections deal effectively with external conditions related to consumer behavior, federal reserve policies, energy uncertainties, stock market fluctuations, and technical innovations such as computer networks and time-sharing. Fortunately, a relatively new tool, made possible through electronic computers, improves the planner's capability to cope with accelerated change and the increasing risks associated with planning for such change.

The approach is referred to as simulation and, while not a panacea, does permit the planner to test numerous assumptions about the environment and their potential impact upon planned strategies. Our purpose in this report is to (1) define simulation, (2) suggest when it should be used for planning, (3) point out its advantages, (4) provide some cautions in its use, (5) describe the computer programming languages most often used for simulation, (6) provide brief examples, and (7) identify some of the best sources for more in-depth study of this vitally important planning tool.

WHAT IS SIMULATION?

Consider the typical "mess" found in many job shops: orders are received sporadically; raw materials are overstocked in anticipation of possible needs; costly in-process inventories are maintained to absorb slack in the flow of batched orders; machine maintenance is performed after a breakdown occurs; and, frequently, the purchase of high-cost equipment and the expansion of facilities occur when the plant manager screams loud enough to be heard in the corporate board room.

Simulation, which aids in the smoothing of production demands and the planning for future maintenance, inspection, inventory, space, and equipment needs, is an invaluable tool for financial planners who wish to reduce the decibel level of line management's cries for last-minute help. Simulation requires the use of a model which imitates important aspects of a real-world problem or system. The model may be physical (such as a wind tunnel for evaluating the performance of a proposed new airplane) or symbolic (such as the econometric models now being applied to long-range financial planning). In this contribution we are concerned with the symbolic type of simulation model.

Business organizations, recently hurt by unanticipated change, are turning in large numbers to simulation as a replacement for intuitive and informal trend projections for planning. Many firms are using national economic and financial data banks to develop smaller, more useful models of their own markets, cash flows, costs, and profitability.

Computer time-sharing services provide external data on gross national product, employment, interest rates, profits, investment, consumption, steel production, bond rates, and so forth. Individual firms then introduce proprietary statistics on sales, costs, and profits to form a combined base of data which is the foundation for building a simulation model.

The broad base of internal and environmental data is integrated so that relationships among the variables in the base are defined. For example, simple or multiple regression analysis can be used to indicate the interaction among costs, prices, demand, and supply. Once a model or set of equations has been developed, planners using computer terminals may then input their own assumptions about public policy changes (such as money market, energy, grain sales) and private sector conditions (such as automobile sales, bond prices, and planned capital expansion) in order to develop financial forecasts.

The impact of changing the size of a wing upon aircraft stability can be studied in the wind tunnel. This same form of analysis, called sensitivity analysis, is one of the most important benefits of simulation modeling as applied to financial planning.

Simulation also assists planners in developing useful estimates of future activity based on past results and personal judgment of environmental changes. After the model is constructed, it may be used for financial statement projection; analysis of product strategies in relation to aggregate economic conditions; evaluation of acquisition alternatives; development of inventory, quality control, maintenance, and scheduling decision rules; evaluation of corporate performance with respect to industry performance; and other vital organizational applications.

In sum, a computerized simulation model is a "laboratory" for experimenting with change. It provides understanding about how a system operates, predicts behavior of the system under various and changing conditions, and assists in the evaluation of alternative courses of action before implementation of a decision in real life. The computer, by compressing several years of simulated experience into minutes, permits many experiments to be run at a tolerable cost without the need to wait months or years to determine the impact of a particular decision.

A RELEVANT EXAMPLE

A specific type of simulation approach, called the Monte Carlo model, uses historical information to describe the frequency of occurrence of important variables in a problem such as arrivals per hour at an unloading dock, customer demand for each product by week, or the amount of crude oil pumped per well per day. From these historical facts, the model-builder generates "future" data about the problem and analyzes what happens as changes are made in the model.

For example, suppose an oil producer wishes to change his manpower scheduling policy from "work a normal week of 40 hours when refinery demand is 1 million barrels per week or less" to "work on extra four-hour shift each time refinery demand increases by 50,000 barrels a week over a base point of 950,000 barrels." What would be the effect on payroll costs of such a change in decision rules? On cash flow? What would happen to these two variables if the base point were shifted to 975,000 barrels? To 1,050,000? The reader can readily conclude that countless alternatives are possible, many of which could be tested without altering the real-world system given a representative simulation model of the important variables within the system.

In building a model to imitate the oil-producing system illustrated above, the planner can describe historical data by a frequency distribution. For example, during a 100-week period, demand from all refineries may have ranged between 800,000 and 1,300,000 barrels. A frequency distribution for the demand is given in Table 1. During 30 of the 100 weeks, demand was 800,000 barrels. Thus the probability of 800,000 barrels being ordered in any single week was 0.30.

Once the probability is calculated for each important variable, the Monte Carlo technique is used to generate future history from past probability distributions. In this manner, a planner can, for instance,

Table 1. Frequency distribution.

Demand (Barrels)	Frequency (Weeks)	Relative Frequency
800,000	30	0.30
900,000	20	0.20
1,000,000	15	0.15
1,100,000	15	0.15
1,200,000	10	0.10
1,300,000	10	0.10

test the impact of increased investment in dock facilities upon total shipping costs under various demand conditions.

ADVANTAGES OF SIMULATION

Every important management tool has a unique set of advantages and limitations or caveats. The most important advantages of simulation are the following:

1. It permits direct consideration of the dynamics of problems and processes too complex to be represented by mathematical models.
2. A simulation model allows for a reduction in the number of simplifying assumptions required, in contrast to highly mathematical approaches which in many cases assume the problem away in order to "solve" it.
3. It is a versatile technique that can be applied to a wide variety of problems.
4. It allows exploration of many more strategies than is possible with intuitive thinking.
5. It helps to identify variables to which system efficiency is more sensitive.
6. It indicates serious flaws in systems design before implementation takes place.
7. Simulation models can be constructed to permit intermittent examination and evaluation of outputs at various stages of analysis before advancement to subsequent stages. This feature provides for the reinforcement of the planner's intuition or, on the other hand, abortion of the experiment as a result of failure of the outputs to coincide with political realities.
8. Simulation provides a mechanism for verifying theoretical predictions in cases in which experimentation on the actual system would be impossible or excessively expensive.

9. Results of simulation analyses can usually be presented in the form of a few compact, easily understood, and nondetailed tables.
10. Building a simulation model tends to educate the model-builder about the system under study more effectively than do alternative tools for corporate planning.

LIMITATIONS OR CAVEATS OF SIMULATION FOR BUSINESS PLANNING

1. A simulation model, in providing a great deal of data compression, brings about a loss of resolution. (For example, in a logistics simulation of sales districts, individual customer identity may be lost by the time aggregate sales data are obtained. That is, grouping of transactions often distorts individual customer characteristics related to such variables as sales volume, credit ratings, and timing of purchases.)
2. Outputs of a simulation model are limited in quality by the quality of the input data. Much of the accounting information in a typical data base has been generated for transaction processing, tax reporting, and transfer pricing purposes. Before simulation is applied for internal decision analysis, a good financial data base designed for internal planning and decision making must be available.
3. Simulation studies may be significantly more expensive and time-consuming than expected at the outset.[1,2]
4. If a simulation model incorporates probabilities, optimization of system performance, while possible, is never guaranteed.

SIMULATION LANGUAGES

Building computer simulation models using a general-purpose computer programming language such as FORTRAN is more costly and time-consuming than using a simulation programming language. Emshoff and Sisson[3] report that it is common to reduce the time to prepare a simulation model by a factor of 10 by employing a special-purpose computer programming language rather than a general-purpose language. Simulation languages, unlike general-purpose languages, automatically provide such aids as random-number generation, event control, file storage and retrieval, statistical calculation, and printing of output reports. Many simulation languages are available, the most popular being GPSS, SIMSCRIPT, and GASP. These are described below for comparison purposes.

1. GPSS[4] is a highly structured, complete language for simulation and uses "units of traffic" called transactions which move through and thereby activate a series of information-processing blocks which make up the logic of the model. GPSS is, therefore, oriented toward problems which require the modeling of interactions among processes. The language is relatively easy to learn, even with little previous computer experience, and is less general than SIMSCRIPT II.5 or GASP IV. It is machine dependent since use of GPSS requires a processor which will differ depending on the computer used (that is, each processor supports a different dialect of language). However, most dialects are compatible with GPSS/360.[4]

2. SIMSCRIPT II.5[5] is a complete event-oriented simulation language for simulation, relatively comprehensive in scope with aspects similar to PL/1. It is less problem oriented (that is, more general-purpose) than GPSS. The language is more adaptable to large-scale simulations than is GPSS/360 and allows more flexibility in the use of statistics. SIMSCRIPT is not as easily learned, even with previous computer background, as is GPSS and requires the user to be concerned with more programming detail. It has evolved, sometimes with drastic changes, to the most recent form, SIMSCRIPT II.5.

3. GASP IV[6] is a set of FORTRAN subroutines which enables the user to carry out discrete-event, continuous, or combined continuous-discrete simulations. The language is event oriented, modular, easily extended and modified, independent of the computer used, and can be implemented directly from ref. 6. The language offers a great deal of flexibility but is less structured and involves more programming detail than GPSS. GASP IV requires no special translator program and can be made to run on any digital computer having a FORTRAN IV compiler. The user must know FORTRAN.

Which language is more suitable for a simulation depends on whether the system is to be modeled continuously [use CSMP,[7] DYNAMO,[8] GASP IV], discretely [use GASP IV, GPSS, SIMSCRIPT II.5, SIMULA[9]], or in the combined fashion (GASP IV). If simulation is an infrequently used tool of analysis, then perhaps a general-purpose language such as FORTRAN or PL/1, which the analyst already knows, will be most appropriate.

Choosing the most appropriate language requires familiarity with each of the alternatives. However, suitability is also related to the skill of the programmer in using a language. A thorough understanding of several languages extends their usefulness and reduces the opportunity cost of not having chosen the "most appropriate" one. We have developed a table for the reader who may wish to read more about this important planning tool called simulation (see Table $22^{-4,10-15}$).

WHEN TO USE SIMULATION

Problems that are large and complex are good candidates for solution by a simulation method, especially when more analytical tools such as linear programming are not appropriate. Even if a mathematical programming approach were applicable, simulation, because of its relative ease of explanation to line management, could well be the more practical approach. There is much truth to the saying that a manager would rather live with a problem he cannot solve than accept a solution he does not understand. Simulation, because of its avoidance of heavy mathematical symbolism, is understandable to intelligent but nonmathematical executives.

Simulation is also useful when the system being studied is dynamic and risky (that is, probabilistic). When the riskiness must be accounted for in planning, it is an impossible dream to hope for the one best solution. Rather, a set of good (acceptable) alternatives provided by simulation is a more realistic and practical goal.

We heartily disagree with those[16] who claim that simulation should be used as a tool of last resort. Since simulation is a relatively simple modeling technique, the user (that is, planner, manager, decision maker) can more easily evaluate the result of the analysis. In fact, the planner can actually take part in the development of the model. We say "take part" because we do not believe that a good simulation model can be developed and used without the assistance of a technical specialist skilled in model-building, systems analysis, and computer programming.

We emphasize that if the analysis underlying a solution is not understood but is accepted by the decision maker, he is in effect delegating decision making without delegating the responsibility for the results of the decision. Therefore, the use of sophisticated mathematical approaches has the potential to separate decision making from decision responsibility—an undesirable feature if successful implementation is to take place.

SUMMARY

Simulation is a critically important, relatively easy to learn tool for improving planning effectiveness. It requires a technician/model-builder to interface with management and can be costly. The tool will more than

Table 2. Annotated references to selected digital simulation texts.

Source	Level of Exposition	Concepts and Methodology	Statistical Considerations	Design of Experiments	Simulation Languages	Major Applications
Chen and Kaczka[10]	Introductory/ intermediate	Discussed	Discussed	Briefly discussed	None	Operations management, marketing, finance, personnel administration
Emshoff and Sisson[3]	Introductory/ intermediate	Discussed	Discussed	Briefly discussed	GPSS, DYNAMO, and general discussion	Computer center operations
Fishman[11]	Advanced	Discussed	Extensively discussed	Extensively discussed	GPSS/360, SIMSCRIPT II, SIMULA, and general discussion	None
Meier et al.[2]	Introductory	Discussed	Discussed	Briefly discussed	General discussion	Production/distribution system
Mihram[12]	Advanced	Briefly discussed	Extensively discussed	Extensively discussed	None	None
Naylor[13]	Intermediate/ advanced	Discussed through examples	Discussed	Extensively discussed	General discussion	Economic and management models
Reitman[14]	Introductory/ intermediate	Discussed	Not treated	Not treated	GPSS V, SIMSCRIPT II, and general discussion	Railroad transportation system, production management, computer system design
Schrieber[15]	Introductory	Not explicitly discussed	Not treated	Not treated	None	Corporate simulation models
Schriber[4]	Introductory/ intermediate	Discussed	Not treated	Not treated	GPSS/360	Production/inventory and service facility problems

pay for itself, however, if it is carefully designed and effectively implemented with top management involvement.

REFERENCES

1. Goldie, J. H., "Simulation and Irritation," in *Supplement to Corporate Simulation Models,* edited by A. N. Schrieber (see Ref. 15).

2. Meier, R. C., W. T. Newell, and H. L. Pazer, *Simulation in Business and Economics* (Englewood Cliffs, N.J.: Prentice-Hall, 1969).

3. Emshoff, J. R., and R. L. Sisson, *Design and Use of Computer Simulation Models* (New York: Macmillan, 1970).

4. Schriber, T. J., *Simulation Using GPSS* (New York: Wiley, 1974).

5. Kiviat, P. J., R. Villaneuva, and H. Markowitz, *The SIMSCRIPT II.5 Programming Language,* rev. ed. (Santa Monica, Calif., CACI, Inc., 1973).

6. Pritsker, A. A. B., *The GASP IV Simulation Language* (New York: Wiley, 1974).

7. IBM Corporation, *CSMP III General Information Manual,* GH19-7000 (White Plains, N.Y., 1971).

8. Pugh, A. L., III, *DYNAMO II User's Manual* (Cambridge, Mass.: The M.I.T. Press, 1970).

9. UNIVAC, 1106/1108 *SIMULA Programmer Reference,* UP-7556 (Blue Bell, Pa., 1971).

10. Chen, G. K. C., and E. E. Kaczka, *Operations and Systems Analysis: A Simulation Approach* (Boston, Mass.: Allyn & Bacon, 1974).

11. Fishman, G. S., Concepts and Methods in Discrete Event Digital Simulation (New York: Wiley, 1973).

12. Mihram, G. A., *Simulation: Statistical Foundations and Methodology* (New York: Academic Press, 1972).

13. Naylor, T. H., *Computer Simulation Experiments with Models of Economic Systems* (New York: Wiley, 1971).

14. Reitman, J., *Computer Simulation Applications* (New York: Wiley, 1971).

15. Schrieber, A. N., ed., *Corporate Simulation Models* (Seattle, Wash.: College on Simulation and Gaming of the Institute of Management Science, Providence, Rhode Island, and Graduate School of Business Administration of the University of Washington, 1970).

16. Wagner, H. M., *Principles of Operations Research with Applications to Managerial Decisions* (Englewood Cliffs, N.J.: Prentice-Hall, 1975).

WAYNE DRAYER AND STEVE SEABURY

Linear Programming— A Case Example

THE OPERATIONS RESEARCH (OR) project described here involved an application of linear programming to help plan a major expansion of the Babcock & Wilcox Tubular Products Division (TPD) at Ambridge, Pennsylvania. Project Ambridge, the largest facility expansion yet undertaken by Babcock & Wilcox, will require a capital investment of about $49 million. This project will enable TPD to compete successfully for an expected increase in customer demand.

A supplier of specialty steel products, tubular and solid extruded shapes, welding fittings and flanges, and specialty forgings, TPD also supplies carbon, alloy, and stainless specialty steel tubing to its Power Generation Division, as well as to its competitors within the steam-generating equipment industry. Miles of specialty tubing of various sizes and material grades are used to manufacture both fossil-fueled and nuclear-reactor steam-generating systems. Specialty tubing is also used in oil and gas exploration, in refining, and in petrochemical production, as well as in the manufacturing of bearings.

Management Problem

The production process consists of three basic operations:

Producing steel billets in the steel mill.
Converting the solid billets into pierced hollows in the hot mill.
Forming the hollows into finished tubes in the finishing department of the tubing mills.

TPD management predicted as early as 1971 that demand for its products would exceed division capacity by 1976. As customer demand continued to increase, hot mill operations in particular became a major bottleneck in the production process. Having decided in 1971 that additional hot mill capacity was needed, TPD management acquired a portion of the Armco Steel Plant at Ambridge, Pennsylvania, with adequate floor space for a new hot mill and associated finishing equipment.

Purchasing a new hot mill is a crucial management decision in terms of both the capital investment required and the effect of the acquisition on the division's long-range ability to compete in future markets. The cost of the new hot mill will account for a significant portion of the total $49 million required for Project Ambridge and, in one increment, this addition will expand the production capacity of the division to a level which should satisfy future customer demand for many years.

A major problem facing management was that of determining the best design for the new hot mill. A new hot mill would have to be managed as an integral unit with the three existing hot mills. A management team visited domestic and foreign steel companies to determine the production capabilities of newly built hot mills. Several different hot mill designs were identified as good choices for TPD's needs. A method for analyzing each design was needed and was the motivation for OR participation in the project.

The Operations Research Problem

The objective of the study was to arrive at the optimum hot mill configuration by adding a new hot mill to the existing complex of three mills. To do this, the study needed to identify the optimum design parameters for the new mill from among the variety being considered. To accomplish this task it was necessary to develop a model of the hot mill facilities that would provide a means of measuring its performance under many different combinations of market demand and operating conditions.

Detailed data were required on customer demand, the actual production rates and costs for each product, and the production capabilities and operating constraints of each of the three existing mills as well as of the proposed new mill. All these factors were incorporated into a linear programming model of the hot mills.

Demand forecasts were supplied by the marketing department for seven basic grade categories. To analyze hot mill operations, it was necessary to develop detailed forecasts for each of 600 products. In addition to the seven grades there were 17 variations in outside diameter and many wall thickness combinations to consider. Historical sales data were used as a basis for expounding the aggregate market forecast into individual product requirements.

Operating costs for each mill were established for each of the products within its capability. Although each mill was different, many products could be made in several mills, although with different rates of efficiency and cost. No mill could make all the products.

The cost per ton for making each product on each of the existing mills was computed from predicted production times, historical cost, and production delay factors. Production times were obtained from a set of regression equations developed to predict production times for the existing mills.

In addition to performance data obtained from the three existing hot mills, expected operating characteristics were developed for each potential new mill design. Initially, seven basic new mill designs were to be analyzed. Eleven additional mill design variations were defined following the analysis of model results. Ultimately, through an iterative procedure, a total of 18 designs were evaluated.

It was important that the practical operating constraints for running a hot mill be taken into account. For example, costly setup, maintenance, and manpower scheduling procedures make it uneconomical to operate a hot mill less than 40 hours per week. Another operating consideration was investigated to determine the consequences of closing down an existing mill when a new one comes on line.

The Model

The hot mill model is a linear programming formulation. The model logic determines the least-cost allocation of products to mills. With this technique it is possible to examine the economic tradeoffs and the interactions of products with existing and new hot mills, all functioning under many operational as well as management policy constraints.

The mathematical formulation of the linear programming model was as follows:

Objective:
$$\text{Minimize operating costs } Z = \sum_i \sum_j C_{ij} X_{ij}$$

Subject to Constraints:
$$\text{Meet demands } \sum_i X_{ij} = D_j, j = 1, 2, \cdots, N$$
$$\text{Stay within capacity } \sum_j T_{ij} X_{ij} \leq H_i, i = 1, 2, 3, 4$$

where C_{ij} = cost of producing 1 ton of product j on mill i
X_{ij} = number of tons of product j produced on mill i
D_j = number of tons of product j required
T_{ij} = number of hours to produce 1 ton of product j on mill i
H_i = number of hours available on a yearly basis for mill i

In the mathematical formulation, the objective was to minimize the total operating costs while meeting demands for the various products subject to operating constraints such as limiting the maximum number of hours available annually on each mill. The model consisted of approximately 600 constraints and a total of 1,600 variables.

The analytical results included three performance measurements that were important to TPD management:

The total annual operating costs for running all four hot mills.
An economic determination of the mill selected to process each product.
The utilization percentage for each mill.

Model Usage

Many of the 18 different mill designs had to be evaluated under multiple product demand and operating conditions. The decision to expand would involve commitments for many years during which forecasts of demands would vary widely. The possible results of pessimistic sales forecasts as well as some optimistic forecasts needed to be examined. Management was concerned about what would happen if the product mix changed in size or grade. In addition, some of the practical trade-offs involving methods of operating the new and old machinery were explored. For these reasons, over 100 cases were studied.

The model was utilized in an iterative fashion. Several candidate designs were studied under a standard set of assumptions. In the course of analyzing the model results, the better designs were identified and then examined under varied assumptions. Some designs were discarded after one evaluation as being clearly inferior to the other designs or suggested entirely different alternatives to be studied.

Analytical Advantages

Many of the usual advantages of using modeling techniques were apparent in the Ambridge project:

• It became feasible and economical to conduct a large number of detailed analyses. With many other methods, only a few studies could reasonably have been performed.
• Since the new hot mill had to be managed as an integral unit with existing facilities, the capabilities of the new and existing mills had to be considered simultaneously. The numerous variables precluded making even gross approximations by any manual or less comprehensive mathematical method.
• The model results provided a much better projection of the production capacity of proposed new hot mill designs. The mill ultimately

selected was originally estimated to have a capacity of 100,000 tons per year; however, model results, later verified by plant engineers, indicated its capacity would be over 140,000 tons per year. The implications of this difference had a significant impact on both manufacturing and financial considerations.

• The model allowed management to measure the effects of relatively small changes in hot mill design. For example, even changes such as an increase of one-half inch in the outside diameter capabilities of the mill were often evaluated. This sensitivity to small changes is possible because the model is extremely detailed. Without the model to assimilate and structure the information, there would have been no practical way to reach this level of detail.

Results Used by Management

In addition to providing accurate measurements of expected mill operating performance, the analytical results obtained from the linear programming analyses were used by management in the following specific ways:

• The cost data generated by the model were used in the financial calculations made to support requests for the necessary expansion capital.

• The model allocation of the product mix for the hot mill facilities formed the basis for planning how the new mill as well as the existing mills would be loaded with products. Therefore, the model not only helped establish the new mill configuration but also provided guidelines on how the new mill and existing mills should be jointly operated in the future.

• The model allocation of products to mills was also used to design space and supporting equipment requirements for the Ambridge billet storage area. In this facility steel billets are stored and cut to proper length prior to the hot mill piercing operation.

• The detailed product forecast used in planning the new mill was also used as a basis for planning the production of steel in the company's melt furnaces and the rolling of appropriate quantities and sizes of steel billets.

• The new Ambridge plant is 15 miles from the other plants at Beaver Falls. The allocation data from the model were used for transportation studies conducted by division industrial engineers. During these studies requirements for truck, rail, and material handling facilities were developed.

Conclusion

The linear programming model developed by OR played a significant role in Project Ambridge. It provided division management with a quantitative framework for making a crucial management decision concerning the design of a new hot mill. In addition, the model output was used to make related facility decisions as well as to provide financial justification for Project Ambridge.

SURENDRA S. SINGHVI

Financial Plans
That Are Tempered
to Bend

THIS CONTRIBUTION discusses some concepts related to planning for financial flexibility used at Armco. The planning process and concepts are equally applicable in other industrial firms.

COMPANY BACKGROUND

American Rolling Mill Company was founded in Middletown, Ohio, at the turn of the century by George M. Verity, grandfather of C. William Verity, Jr., the present Chairman and Chief Executive Officer. In 1947 the name of the company was changed to Armco Steel Corporation. Today Armco is the fifth largest steel producer in the United States, in terms of steel shipment. It has a steel-making capacity of 10 million tons per year and eight plant locations.

Nevertheless, the steel group's contribution to total profits was only sightly over 50 percent in 1974. The remaining profits came from our nonsteel business in the Enterprises Group: International Division has manufacturing plants in 23 countries; National Supply Company, acquired in 1958, manufactures drilling rigs, hydraulic pumping units, and seamless pipe; Metal Products Division serves the construction market and installs pre-engineered buildings; HITCO, located on the west coast, specializes in the reduction of nonmetallic composite materials and serves mainly the aerospace and defense industries; Bellefonte Insurance Company operates principally in the reinsurance market; Armco Leasing provides general equipment finance leasing in the United States, Canada, Australia, and Europe.

Armco has grown substantially in terms of its revenues, net profits, and total assets, as shown in Table 1. Armco is now the third-largest steel company in terms of total revenues, and is one of the top 50 industrial corporations in the United States.

Armco adopted formal long-range planning in the late 1960s in consul-

Table 1. Armco's growth: 1964–1974.

Cash Factors	Growth (millions of dollars) 1964	1969	1974	Compound Annual Growth Rate (%) 1964–1974
Revenues	1,218	1,584	3,218	10.2
Net profits	84	96	204	9.3
Total assets	1,144	1,852	2,545	8.3
Shareholders' equity	820	1,036	1,275	4.5

tation with the Stanford Research Institute. In 1974 the corporate strategy function was created at the recommendation of the Boston Consulting Group. This function assists the profit-center managers in defining various businesses and developing business strategies. Figure 1 shows the place of the financial planning function in the overall organization. The financial planning group works very closely with the corporate strategy group and finance people at various profit centers.

FINANCIAL PLANNING ACTIVITIES

The long-range financial planning horizon has varied from a minimum of three years to a maximum of seven years, depending on general economic conditions and our needs. Presently, the financial planning horizon is limited to five years including the current year. However, the planning horizon is much longer for capital expenditures.

Each year the corporate strategy function develops a planning calendar for the entire corporation. In the third quarter, the financial planning group asks each profit center to provide its annual objective for the following year. The annual objective, which is due in December, is established in the form of an income statement and balance sheet broken down by quarters. Once it is approved by top management, the annual objective becomes a benchmark for evaluating performance throughout the year. In 1975 we adopted a flexible objective approach, whereby profit centers were allowed to revise their annual objective upward or downward at the end of each quarter to adjust for variables beyond their control, such as changes in investment tax credit, surtax, and industry shipment.

During the first quarter, the corporate financial planning group requests each profit center to provide its five-year financial plan. The annual objective becomes the first year of the five-year plan. During the second quarter, profit-center financial plans are reviewed, analyzed, and consolidated by the corporate financial planning group, and then presented to top management for review and comments. After necessary revisions are made in line with the overall corporate strategy and man-

Figure 1. Place of financial planning function.

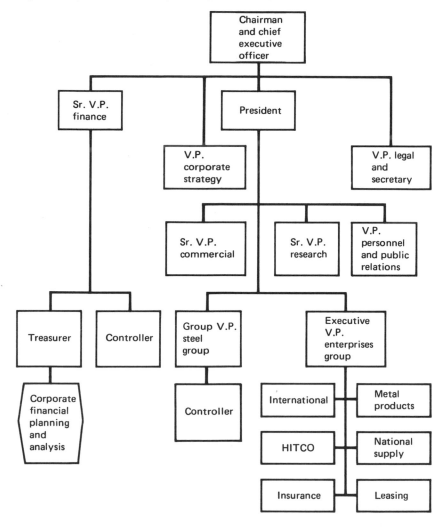

agement judgment, the long-range financial plan is submitted to the board of directors for approval. The plans are updated for known changes and reviewed by top management and the board of directors each quarter.

Financial planning activities commence at the profit center level in response to the corporate financial planning group's request during the first quarter. Each profit center begins with a forecast or set of assumptions on what conditions in the economic and political framework, business environment, and industry will be for the next several years. The economic research group, which is a part of our company's commercial function, assists profit centers with this forecast.

In addition, each profit center analyzes its cost-volume-profit relationships for the recent past. Such analysis, along with managerial judgment, provides a valid basis for forecasting sales volume, prices, and costs.

Each profit center's financial plan includes a sales forecast based on specific plans covering anticipated new products, projected penetration of existing and new markets, changes in product mix, and other related matters. The sales forecast is expressed in both physical volume and monetary terms, when possible.

Key assumptions underlying these financial plans include sales price increase, labor cost increase, raw material cost increase, working capital as a percentage of sales, and tax rates. Profit centers are required to spell out these assumptions so that the validity of their financial plans can be determined by corporate management.

In addition, profit centers are required to provide their forecasted income statements and balance sheets by year for five years, based on capital expenditures and investments already approved and committed by top management.

The corporate financial planning group reviews long-range financial plans for internal consistency as well as reasonableness with respect to the key assumptions underlying these plans. Using a computer program, which was developed in 1973 on a time-sharing facility by our group, we consolidate forecasted financial statements for five years.

Some of the profit centers also use computers for preparation of forecasted financial statements. In the late 1960s we used a canned computer program developed by one of the major commercial banks for financial forecasting and planning. It enabled us to play "what if" games with respect to the key assumptions. However, with increased complexity of our businesses, we had to discontinue use of the canned program. We are presently developing a computerized financial planning model that could be used at the corporate level as well as at the profit-center level. This program will allow us to consolidate financial forecasts of profit centers and will enable us to undertake various sensitivity analyses.

The objective of planning for financial flexibility is to quantify the financial resources and various demands on those resources so that we can reexamine our financial constraints, assist top management in allocating our financial resources for continued profit growth, and plan for raising external funds at a reasonable cost and under acceptable terms.

Three financial constraints critical in planning for financial flexibility are:

Dividend payout
Debt ratio
Equity capital

The first constraint determines how much cash out of earnings is available for reinvestment in the firm for expansion and growth. The last two constraints determine how much cash is available from external sources for growth and at what cost.

CASH FLOW FORECASTS

On the basis of consolidated forecast financial statements, we project annual cash flows for five years, as shown in Table 2. Our major cash inflows consist of net income, depreciation, and deferred taxes. Net income, of course, is the most difficult to forecast by year. For example, in 1970 we projected earnings for 1970–1974 that were significantly off (either higher or lower) each year compared to our actual results. How-

Table 2. Cash flow projection (in thousands of dollars).

Cash Factors	19X1	19X2	19X3	19X4	19X5
Beginning cash balance	200	45	20	30	60
Cash inflows					
Net income	160	195	210	225	240
Depreciation	100	105	110	115	120
Deferred taxes	20	30	30	30	30
Divestments	5	5	10	10	10
Planned borrowings	—	—	—	—	—
Total	285	335	360	380	400
Cash outflows					
Capital investments	200	220	215	200	180
Dividends	55	65	70	75	80
Debt repayment	65	30	30	30	30
Reinvestment of earnings	15	18	20	23	25
Increase in adjusted working capital	100	30	20	20	20
Others (net)	5	(3)	(5)	2	0
Total	440	360	350	350	335
Cash balance	45	20	30	60	125
Less operating cash required	(20)	(20)	(20)	(20)	(20)
Surplus cash cumulative	25	0	10	40	105

ever, actual earnings for the five years combined were below the projected level by only 5 percent, which is not unsatisfactory. The problem lies in forecasting business cycles over a five-year period.

A minor source of cash, but an important business activity, is divestment. We manage our businesses as a portfolio, and aim to have a balanced portfolio. Businesses with low market share and low growth potential are divestment candidates. All potential divestment candidates require financial justification similar to that needed for new capital investments.

The major cash outflows consist of capital investments, dividends, debt repayment, reinvestment of earnings in unconsolidated subsidiaries and associated companies, and increase in adjusted working capital. Adjusted working capital equals receivables plus inventories minus current liabilities, excluding the current portion of long-term debt.

In a capital-intensive industry such as ours, capital investments represent the most significant use of cash. Only those projects that have been approved or committed by top management are included in the cash flow projection. Uncommitted capital investments are optional, and these are not included in the cash flow projection. Our approved/committed capital investments consist of these projects:

- Normal capital expenditures for routine replacements, minor pollution control, safety, morale, and the like are approved once a year by the board of directors. The amount is substantially below our depreciation expense.
- Special capital expenditures for major expansion, major replacement, major pollution control, and the like are generally approved once a quarter.
- Investments in joint ventures and unconsolidated subsidiaries, as well as in acquisition of existing business, are generally approved once a quarter.

All discretionary projects must earn an after-tax 15 percent discounted cash flow return over the project's life. This hurdle rate is based on the overall cost of capital.

Debt repayments are mandatory but easy to forecast. In a company such as ours, with approximately 80,000 shareholders, some dividends must be paid, but the amount is optional. We do have a target payout ratio which is used in financial planning as well as in quarterly dividend decision making.

Once we have projected our cash inflows and outflows, we determine any surplus cash or deficit for each year. For this purpose, we estimate a minimum operating cash required. This has been less than 1 percent of our sales. We can run our business with $20–30 million of cash because of our revolving bank credit agreement for $100 million. In brief,

$$\text{Surplus (deficit) cash} = \text{beginning cash balance} + \text{cash inflows}$$
$$- \text{cash outflows} - \text{operating cash required}$$

FINANCIAL FLEXIBILITY

A year-end capital structure projection is made for five years, as shown in Table 3. Debt ratio is a relationship of long-term debt to long-term debt plus shareholders' equity. We calculate our additional debt capacity from the following formula:

$$\text{Additional debt capacity} = \frac{E}{1-TDR} - (E+D)$$

where E = year-end equity
$\quad D$ = long-term debt, year-end
$\quad TDR$ = target debt ratio (in decimals)

Table 3. Capital structure projection (in thousands of dollars).

Cash Factors	19X1	19X2	19X3	19X4	19X5
Stockholders' equity	1,200	1,330	1,470	1,620	1,780
Long-term debt	400	370	340	310	280
Total capitalization	1,600	1,700	1,810	1,930	2,060
Debt ratio (%)	25	21.8	18.8	16.1	13.6
Additional debt capacity at 25 percent of target debt cumulative	—	73	150	230	313

For example, at the end of 19X2, we derived additional debt capacity as follows:

$$\text{Additional debt capacity} = \frac{1,330}{1-0.25} - (1,330 + 370)$$
$$= \$73.3$$

For each $1 increase in equity, the additional debt capacity will increase by $.25, $.33, and $.50 if the target debt ratios are 20, 25, and 33⅓ percent, respectively.

Surplus (deficit) cash derived from cash flow projections plus additional debt capacity derived from capital structure projections equals financial flexibility. This financial flexibility represents the financial resources, at a given time, that top management can allocate tentatively to various projects under consideration by profit centers.

We use the word "flexible" to convey to top management that these resources could increase if our projected earnings increased, dividends and working capital decreased, target debt ratio were raised, and vice versa. As mentioned earlier, we update our financial plan each quarter to determine any change in financial flexibility, and then we alter our behavior accordingly.

Once we have determined our financial flexibility for the entire corporation, we make tentative allocation of this flexibility to various projects submitted by profit-center management. These allocations are tentative and are for planning purposes only. Each project with tentative allocation of resources must be justified with complete details and approved by top management at a later date. Since demand for financial flexibility is in excess of the availability of such flexibility, we must allocate four financial resources to various projects under consideration in the following priority:

Certain pollution-abatement projects
Major replacement and modernization projects
Cost-reducing projects
Capacity-expansion projects
Acquisition of new businesses

Profit centers are not required to provide any engineering study or return-on-investment calculation to include a project for tentative allocation. It is also recognized that the capital-required estimates could be higher or lower than shown in the tentative allocation.

We consider the impact of projects approved and under consideration on our profit picture over the planning horizon. A bunching of major projects in a limited time frame severely affects our profit, with higher interest charges, higher depreciation, and start-up costs occurring before any benefits of the project develop, despite high discounted cash flow return on each project. In addition, bunching of projects places a strain on our ability to control the projects efficiently. A leveling or balancing of projects over the planning horizon produces much more satisfactory results in the short as well as in the long run.

On the basis of financial flexibility and tentative allocation, we prepare a tentative financing plan. The annual financing requirement is determined by tentative allocation less surplus cash (or plus deficit cash). Depending on the anticipated cost of capital, we may raise additional funds earlier or later than indicated by the plan. If we decide to delay raising external funds because of capital market conditions, we defer some of the projects included in our tentative allocation.

SUMMARY

Planning for financial flexibility is a system designed to quantify the financial resources and to assist in allocating such resources so as to maintain and improve Armco's profitability and liquidity. It is a self-imposed discipline developed by management, and used as a tool in decision making.

WILLIAM F. CHRISTOPHER

Computing
Who Deserves
the Gold Stars

BUDGETARY CONTROL SYSTEMS measure organization performance in financial terms, by accounting standards. The assumptions on which such budget structures and reporting systems have been built have gone unquestioned, and perhaps even unrecognized, for too long. And as the years have passed, these assumptions, unexamined, have become less and less valid, while at the same time the budgetary control systems based on them have become more and more complex. In many businesses today, precisely interrelated financial models are constructed, reporting procedures developed, and budget variances analyzed in many dimensions, and in great detail. While this effort provides many hours of work for accountants, computer specialists, and managers, its contribution to business operations is often minimal.

In times of rapid change and restructuring, we can no longer expect adequate guidance from a budgetary control system based on the following assumptions:

Standards of performance can be expressed in financial terms.
Accomplishment against standards can be measured financially.
Totals for an accounting period are significant.
Currency valuations are predictable.
Business conditions are predictable.
Budgetary control is a responsibility of top management.

In any business such a budgetary control system is a major effort. In a large diversified enterprise, it is monumental. In a multinational enterprise working in many countries, in many currencies, and in a variety of businesses, it often becomes more burden than benefit. Perhaps we should alter our historical assumptions and, on the basis of a new set of assumptions, do some creative thinking about our budgetary processes in the light of contemporary experience. I suggest these new assumptions:

1. Objectives for performance can be determined for all the key performance areas that determine the success of the enterprise.
2. Progress toward these objectives can be measured in terms appropriate for the performance area.
3. Such objectives and feedback can be developed for total company, components, and work units to the point of individual jobs.
4. Change, trends, and changes in trends in progress toward objectives are what is important, not aggregates for an accounting period in comparison with a budget standard.
5. Environmental impacts on the enterprise, such as business conditions and currency valuation, are not reliably predictable but can be input to business management through scenario development and monitoring methods.
6. This kind of budgetary control is a responsibility of all jobs.

Financial reporting provides evaluation of yesterday's profitability. A reporting system based on this different set of assumptions focuses on the future. It measures achievement in all areas important to the success of the enterprise, and provides feedback for decisions and actions to achieve tomorrow's goals. I call this kind of a reporting system, based on the assumptions above, achievement reporting.

Achievement reporting begins with a conceptual approach to business management. I define the conceptual approach as a search for the fundamentals on which the success of the enterprise will be built. These are usually some combination of products and services to be offered, markets and segments to be served, the geographic area of operation, the competences that provide unique advantages to the firm, and the implementing strategies that relate all of these to the relevant environment. An enterprise may be conceptualized as one business or as several. A large company may be a whole portfolio of businesses and countries or areas organized into appropriate units, each with its own goals and strategies relating its resources and position to the business and the relevant environment.

A major weakness of financial reporting systems is their dedication to annual data. A twelve-month fiscal year is compared with a subsequent twelve-month fiscal year. Ten such fiscal years are lined up side by side in the annual report. Any student of economics will quickly recognize the tyranny imposed by the fiscal year reporting period. Aggregates are not a mark of performance. Trends and changes in trends are marks of performance, and they are developing continuously. Business does not work by annual aggregates; it works by daily, weekly, monthly achievement and change. Reporting rules required by taxing authorities and regulatory agencies need not prescribe the reporting system used in the decision process throughout the company to manage operations. A different perspective and a different content will be required.

Our reporting system will be designed to provide performance feedback to all company people so they will see the results of their work and be able to take effective action to achieve goals.

MARKET STANDING

Market standing objectives become specific goals for marketing, product management, and sales. Market standing achievement also becomes an important input to resource strategy and resource commitment that is a major concern of top management. At the top management level, the following feedback on market standing is useful:

Report	Frequency
Definition of the business by strategic business unit or segment	Every two years plus whenever there is a change
Total company sales and sales of major units or segments	Monthly plus time-series trend and changes in trend
Market share for major business segments	Monthly or quarterly time-series trend and changes in trend
Sales to target accounts	Monthly plus trend

PROFITABILITY

I have found two ways of reporting income to be very useful in defining problems and opportunities and determining appropriate decisions and action programs: time series and income statement by marginal income accounts. As with sales volume, it is important to see a moving picture, not merely monthly snapshots, and we must see the picture in terms relating to action.

We are accustomed to income statements reported from a full-costing system. We are so accustomed to them that we may overlook other possibilities. For the businesses that I have worked with, I find marginal income accounts far more useful than the others for providing the intelligence needed for sound business decision and action. For top management reporting, a very useful monthly summary is provided by a monthly income statement by marginal income accounts. One format for that kind of income statement gives average monthly performance for previous years along with each month's results for the current year. That provides a visual check on changes and developing trends. For key accounts in the income statement it is also useful to maintain a time-series chart over several years, tracking changes. Useful charts are:

Sales, twelve-month moving totals
Marginal income percentage, three-month moving average
Fixed costs, three-month moving average
Breakeven, three-month moving average
Breakeven percentage of sales, three-month moving average
Value-added percentage, three-month moving average
Value-added, twelve-month moving total
Operating income, twelve-month moving total

Setting up the income statement by marginal income accounts helps us find opportunity for income improvement. There are three and only three possibilities:

Increase sales volume.
Reduce fixed costs.
Increase marginal income rate by increasing price, reducing variable costs, or improving mix.

OTHER KEY PERFORMANCE AREAS

For the other key performance areas, no generalized reporting system can be followed. Each enterprise will have unique needs, and its objectives will determine what reporting of achievement it will require. The specifics for each business will have to be worked out individually. They will not remain the same; as objectives change, the needed feedback reporting will also change.

We do not want a procedural system of reports; we want feedback that will help us achieve our objectives. One way to keep those key objectives always in mind is to list them in a monthly operating report along with a telegraphic comment on recent achievement or current problems. An example of this kind of report is shown on the next page.

An achievement reporting system is not only simpler than the financial model kind of budgetary control system; it requires the enterprise to function differently in two important ways:

1. Reports provide informational feedback needed for goal achievement. The enterprise acts on the basis of the reports.
2. Achievement reporting provides a time perspective. The enterprise manages its affairs by predictive control rather than by after-the-fact management by exception.

January	1977		XYZ
MONTH	YEAR		COMPANY NAME

KEY PERFORMANCE AREA OBJECTIVES

Key Performance Area Objectives   Progress

Market standing

1. Maintain leading market position in product lines A, C, and D

2. Improve market position in product line B from 3 to 1 in 5 years

3. Improve market position in product line E from 10 to 5 in 5 years

1. A, number 1 position, strengthening
   C, number 1 position, steady
   D, number 1 position, steady

2. New marketing program to be launched at March 12 sales meeting

3. Product line audit to be completed March 31

Innovation (technical, commercial, organizational, financial)

4. Develop standardization program for product line in this year

5. Produce and commercialize new _____ equipment by November

4. Task force appointed

5. On schedule

Productivity

6. Maintain total fixed costs, within 27 percent of net sales

7. Improve sales productivity by a target account program

6. January, 24.8 percent

7. All salesmen have target account objectives. Performance reported monthly. YTD January, 89 percent of YTD goal.

Physical and financial resources

8. Optimize manufacturing operations in the two plants

9. Reduce slow-moving inventory to $_____ by _____

8. Task force appointed to set objectives and program

9. January inventory, $_____

Profitability

10. Achieve net income after tax of $_____ this year

11. Raise marginal income percentage to 40.0 percent by June

10. January YTD, $_____

11. January, 36.4 percent

Manager performance and development

12. Develop managers through financial and technical professional seminars

13. Conduct operations through management by objectives program

12. Management by objectives workshop scheduled for February 5

13. Objectives set for top management staff; will be extended to other levels after February 5 workshop

Worker performance and attitude

14. Improve human relations with labor and salaried employees through seminars and sports programs

15. Improve internal communications

14. Program not yet developed

15. Company newsletter in development

Public responsibility

16. Cooperate with authorities to develop regulations for pollution control

16. Regular contact by plant manager

Predictive control, through achievement reporting, becomes an essential part of the way of life for the achieving enterprise. With achievement reporting we will still have all the financial measures we need, and we will understand them better than we do from other systems. For we will at all times see the moving picture—past, present, and future—and not just snapshots in a frame of official expectations. In addition, we will have measures and understanding of all the other key performance areas that determine the success of the enterprise: profitability, innovation, productivity, physical and financial resources, motivation and organization development, public responsibility. In short, we will have the feedback system we need to move the enterprise toward the achievement of its goals. There need no longer be an annual ordeal of budget planning. There need no longer be a periodic ordeal of official long-range business planning. The achieving enterprise can have the action-oriented equivalent at all times through: identification of the fundamentals on which it will build its success, determination of key performance area objectives to achieve that success, and achievement reporting to provide feedback on progress. The system will be simpler. And the achievement will be greater.

FRED E. LEE

Planning the Picking Order for the Company Totem Pole

"PEOPLE are our most valuable asset" is a common expression used by most chief executives. Yet how much is really spent keeping track of this "most valuable asset"? What kind of resources are allocated to determining the company's management needs, and to developing manpower plans that match the company's growth? What controls are in effect that will trigger action when there is a variance from the plan? To what extent should the board of directors be involved? Does the chief executive officer allocate as much time, effort, and resources to the company's human resources development as he or she does to sales, finance, or production?

To what extent is a management manpower planning, audit, and review system utilized? It should include at least the following:

- Information to determine organizational management manpower needs and individual development needs.
- A planning and organization chart that visually portrays present status, future needs, and problem areas—both individual and organizational—and serves as a constant check on actions that need to be taken.
- Managerial review of organizational manpower needs, strengths, and weaknesses, with final review by the chief executive officer. Objectives are established, accountability defined, and follow-up status determined at regularly scheduled review meetings.

To investigate these questions, I surveyed a cross section of 386 large, medium, and small companies, in all types of industries, throughout the United States. Responses were received from 204 or 53 percent of these companies. Table 1 shows the results with respect to personnel planning systems.

One executive vice-president wrote, "It is with some embarrassment that I reveal how little we are doing with respect to Management

Table 1. Personnel planning systems.

System	Percentage
Complete, three-part formal system (inventory, audit, review)	46
Partial system	23
No system	31

Manpower Planning, Audit, and Review. . . . I hope that your survey will act as a spur to our taking positive steps with respect to Manager Manpower Planning."

Not everyone believes in a formal system. In response to the section on Manpower Inventory, one president said, "No, I develop it on yellow notepaper that I keep with regular reviews with Group V.P.'s. . . ." To the section on the Audit Chart, he stated, "A bureaucratic waste of time."

The vast majority of replies indicated a great deal of interest in a total system with built-in accountability and follow-up procedures. Undoubtedly, this interest is a result of problems such as not having replacements available to fill vacancies.

Perhaps the most important advantage of a formal system is ensuring that needed replacement actions are taken. Replacement planning is most difficult and it is human nature to sidestep it: leave it alone and maybe it will go away. It does not go away, and eventually it emerges as a severe problem.

Of the 94 companies that have full systems, 89 percent have given the responsibility to the Personnel Department, 7 percent have separate functions, and 4 percent didn't answer the question. The sizes of the companies with full systems are given in Table 2.

Table 2. Size of companies having full three-part systems.

No. of Employees	Percentage
1,000 and below	15
1,000–2,000	9
2,000–5,000	10
5,000–10,000	5
10,000–20,000	19
20,000 and over	42

The smallest company *with* a full system has 475 employees. The largest company *without* a full system has over 150,000 employees.

Managerial Manpower Inventory

Manpower inventories have been used by 53 percent of the 94 companies with full systems for five or more years. The oldest system was started in 1940.

Three-fourths of the 94 companies include the manager's career choices. During a discussion with executives of one company that has a highly successful program, they mentioned that they will add the element of career planning and personal choice to their inventory. They felt strongly that it is necessary to adjust their system to reflect the emergence of a high degree of personal satisfaction needs expressed by today's younger generation. Table 3 indicates the sources of information in the inventory, while Table 4 shows the type of data included.

Table 3. How information is obtained in the inventory.

Source	Percentage
Regular performance appraisals	96
Personnel records	93
Special planning appraisals	70
Personal interview with appraisers	59
Personal interview with manager being evaluated	54
Assessment centers	17

Table 4. Information on each individual.

Item	Percentage
Title	81
Age	77
Job grade	54
Years to retirement	29
Years–present position	71
Quality of performance	69
Promotability	76
Time before eligible for promotion	46
Replacement name	60
Time before replacement eligible for promotion	30

Audit and Planning Chart

Most companies (66 percent) portray the individual manager profile on an organizational audit and planning chart. The remainder use a variety of presentation techniques, such as computer readouts by position and overlays on organizational charts. One company goes so far as to list executives from outside the company as possible replacements for people in its top three levels.

Management Manpower Planning Review

How often does the chief executive officer participate in the review process? A final review is held between the chief executive officer and the vice-presidents in 66 percent of the companies. Most of the other replies indicated at least vice-presidential level as final review. A few said two levels above the individual participated. In 41 percent of the companies these reviews are held in conjunction with salary reviews, while 59 percent keep salary considerations out of the discussion.

To ensure action and accountability, subsequent follow-up must be built into the system. Answers to questions concerning this vital area were:

- When reviewing their staff, are managers asked to make recommendations on:

	Yes (%)	No (%)	No Reply (%)
Replacements?	88	12	
Promotions?	95	5	
Demotions?	80	14	6
Lateral move for development?	84	8	8
Additional training?	94	3	3

- Are notations made of these recommendations in the form of objectives to be achieved? (Yes, 88 percent; no, 11 percent; no reply, 1 percent.)
- Is accountability established, and at subsequent review meetings are these objectives reviewed and status determined? (Yes, 74 percent; no, 16 percent; no reply, 10 percent.)

Note the fall-off in terms of the follow-up to the objectives. Of the companies that establish objectives, 16 percent do not hold the manager accountable.

System Effectiveness

Of the companies with total systems 62 percent feel that the system is moderately effective, 33 percent feel that it is exceptionally effective, and 5 percent feel that their system is of little use.

The final question on the survey dealt with visibility of the system within the company. The results were as follows:

- Highly confidential, desire very low profile, little known about the system except for those involved (17 percent).
- No attempt made to either publicize or hold down knowledge about the system; information about individuals very confidential (46 percent).
- Encourage visibility of the system; information about individuals

very confidential; view the system as a plus toward developing high morale based on career growth opportunities (37 percent).

The Payoff

Is the payoff sufficient to justify the time and effort put forth by companies that have successful total programs? Personal interviews with executives from many companies indicate an unqualified "yes." Comments such as, "We couldn't operate without such a system" were common. Endorsement was high, but it was pointed out that it takes a long time to make the system function in an exceptional way. Like all other management tools, it has to be tried and modified to fit the tone of the company. After some trial and error the system will become a way of life.

DENNIS A. HAWVER

Management Potential— The Gap in Your Plan

CORPORATE PLANNING has recently been faced with extreme changes in methodology and scope. Planners report that more variables than ever before must now be considered in both long- and short-term projections. Alternative sets of plans are becoming the mode, partly in recognition of the unpredictable aspects of many of these variables. Protectionism, environmentalism, consumerism, and social concern are all impacting on plans already confounded by severe changes in economic conditions, balance of trade, energy usage, and foreign affairs. Planners are increasingly turning to computer systems for assistance in manipulating these large numbers of complex variables.

THE ROLE OF HUMAN RESOURCE PLANNING

Coincident with the advent of these new factors is an intensified concern about one of the basic elements in organizational planning: the utilization of human resources.

The importance of human resources has been recognized for many years. The necessity of obtaining and developing highly qualified people and encouraging them to develop their own resources is so well accepted that it generally goes unspoken.

Part of the current revitalization of concern is a result of recently introduced human resource accounting methods. These methods tie dollar figures to employment decisions with disquieting effects. It is one thing to proclaim, "People resources constitute our single greatest investment and asset." It is quite another to learn that replacement of a press operator is costing you $3,000, replacement of a trained salesman over $80,000, and the expected investment in a single manager hired at age 40 is well over $2.5 million.

Figures such as these direct attention to the executives who, charged with maximizing the utilization, conservation, and development of corporate assets, are naturally interested in the controls established for their human asset management. Because both the investment and expectation are highest for managerial assets, attention frequently focuses there. And many organizations are becoming aware that there rests the investment over which they have least control.

MANPOWER PLANNING: SOME DOUBTS ABOUT ITS BASIS

Manpower planners consistently request ratings of potential and/or promotability along with quantitative needs projections. These ratings are used for promotion, transfer, and termination decisions. They determine the management control over each of these multi-million-dollar assets.

Because such ratings have been supplied and used for some time now, it is frequently taken for granted that they are accurate, reliable, fair, and systematically derived measures. But are they?

The events of recent years have raised severe doubts that managerial performance and potential ratings meet any of these criteria. A radically changing economy has tested their utility under extreme conditions. The federal government has initiated challenges to their accuracy and fairness, and research has surveyed critically their bases and systematic application.

The Boom

The first show of concern occurred in the sixties, when many companies became involved in mergers or acquisitions. Executives were dismayed to find that information available about the potential of specific individuals was limited to their present and next probable positions. Moving a person into a different career ladder evoked a great deal of anxiety, requiring considerably more risk-taking than should have been necessary. Some of these trial-and-error tests of potential proved costly.

Many of these acquisitions are now being reevaluated. It is still an easier decision, based on known and projected quantities, to divest than to attempt to improve performance through a speculative process of appraisal and reassignment of managers.

The Government

As the boom turned to decline, another source drew attention to the quality of human resource management. The federal government, under the Civil Rights Act of 1964 and Executive Order 11246, began reviewing all employment decisions for their business relevance and consistency of application. The impact of this action on American industry has been enormous. Many organizations, upon critical investigation, found that they really did not know whether they were recruiting, selecting, developing, training, and promoting people in the best interest of either the organization or the individual.

The more discerning corporate planners and personnel executives have watched the pattern of enforcement quite closely. The initial emphasis was on hourly-level recruiting and selection practices. As these began to improve, the emphasis shifted to training, promotion, and termination. Because the enforcement agencies view and evaluate the entire employment process as a continuing system, more enlightened companies began integrating their own procedures into a more manageable and efficient system framework.

Recently, the regulatory thrust has been turning more to entry-level management positions. A key interest has been in the promotion of nonexempt females and minorities into lower or middle management. Concerned people are recognizing the difficulty of measuring a secretary's potential for management when the dimensions of managerial performance and potential have not been clearly identified, let alone measured in a reliable way.

It does not take much forecasting skill to predict that review of managerial development and promotion methods is forthcoming. Nor does it require more than an elementary comparison of those methods against current government standards to see that much work needs to be done.

The Recession

With a drastic change in the economy, the cardinal and continuing importance of sound systems for the evaluation of managerial performance and potential is underscored. More candidates are available today for almost every position. There is more opportunity and more pressure to select the most qualified. But final decisions still tend to rest on such amorphous predictors as "gut feelings."

These same economic conditions have forced an examination of the other side of the coin. Many organizations are now faced with the necessity of making "out-placement" decisions. It is extremely uncomfortable to select which executive should be terminated, armed with less solid evaluation data than one would need to fire a clerk.

The Research

There has been dissatisfaction with managerial evaluation methods regardless of the economy. The government is concerned about the methods currently in use and is prepared to share its concern. The social, political, and economic climates are demanding increased attention to the quality and fairness of decisions. And any organization handicaps itself when it relies upon managerial decisions based on anything less than the best information that can be developed.

Recent research has begun to focus on managerial evaluation and to lay the necessary groundwork for change by establishing the rationale of present assessment procedures. Surveys, questionnaires, and comparative organizational studies confirm that evaluation procedures are slow to change and that no single method has reached general acceptance. Some insight is also offered into the trends and apparent direction of managerial appraisal.

It is well beyond the scope of this paper to review all of this research, but a few of the more consistent findings bear mentioning.

More firms today are using some sort of formal appraisal system at lower and middle management levels. Most performance evaluation systems use rating scales, written paragraph-style evaluations, or global judgments. Their relationship to the appraisals used for selection or promotion (interviews, tests) is usually remote.

Many sets of criteria are used for performance evaluation. Across organizations, little similarity is found in scope, number, ease of measurement, position specificity, or definition. Some firms attempt to judge traits (intelligence, leadership); others rely on measurement of objectives (profits, costs); and many try both. Again, the criteria to be used to evaluate a manager's performance are rarely related to those used for his or her selection.

Interviews with managers uncover their frustrations. They feel that enough information is available to fairly and clearly evaluate their performance. If the criteria were established and known to them, in most cases managers could improve their performance. But now, they say, they work against a model constructed by their own reading of what is probably expected. Thus, they may be downgraded, not for lack of capability, but for a misperception.

SYSTEMS FOR CONTROL OVER INVESTMENTS

One fault is common to most procedures for evaluating managerial performance and potential. Although some criteria have been established, some measurement tools are in use, and the difference between performance and potential is recognized, only rarely are all these components integrated into a meaningful system.

If we lease a new office copier, we activate a system designed for controlled investment and maintenance of equipment. Copying needs, present and future, are analyzed. Various machines are assessed against known relevant criteria, such as speed, quality, cost, and special features. Servicing and preventive maintenance are considered, as is the potential for expansion as needs change. Careful analysis of all of these variables, and more, is considered a necessary prerequisite to the investment.

Upon selection of a machine, its support staff is assigned, a preventive maintenance schedule created, responsibility for monitoring its reliability and performance determined, and a projected time for updating programmed. Such decision and utilization systems have long been operational as controls over capital investments.

Similar systems, detailing all the information necessary for proficient decision making, are in effect for other organizational investments. The purchasing of raw materials, components, services, and capital equipment—as well as acquisitions, mergers, and divestments—are all based on information systems.

But when you hire or promote a manager—look for the list of specified criteria against which his or her performance will be measured. Look for the description of characteristics, traits, and special features he or she should possess to meet those criteria. Try to find the systematic, detailed method for comparatively evaluating candidates. Upon "selection," look for the career path counseling provided, the scheduled and systematic performance reviews, the feedback and developmental programs, and the measurement and utilization of potential for expansion.

In most organizations, you will find some of the above. There are isolated bits and pieces, but there is no true system designed to maximize the effective use of this significant investment.

Compare, if you will, the efficiency and specificity of your own system for leasing a machine in the $250 per month range with your methods for selecting or promoting a manager whose overall expected investment is 10,000 times that. It is disturbing to realize that the manager who will make the decision on the copier was probably selected with less care than was the machine.

A MANAGEMENT RESOURCE SYSTEM

Application of systems principles to employment procedures has proved successful in a number of companies. Although this concept has not been widely used at managerial levels, early reports look encouraging. The benefits, in terms of communication, understanding, acceptance, efficiency, and manageability, far outweigh the costs and problems of implementation.

A generalized, and somewhat simplified, model for a management resource system is presented in Figure 1. This model adopts the "objectives" approach for performance appraisal. Organizational (or departmental) goals determine the objectives of the position. These should not be vague verbalizations, but measurable achievements which can be accepted by company and manager alike as a sound basis for performance review.

Given the objectives, the resources available to the position should be outlined. This "how" box in the model includes the formal responsibilities and authorities, the prescribed working relationships, controls, restrictions, and options of the position. It is the bag of tools which will be given to the manager.

From the "how" factor may be derived the "person specifications." These detail the knowledge, experience, skills, traits, and characteristics necessary to use the given "tools" to achieve the established goals.

Parallel to the "person specifications," the model recognizes "change" factors. These are the variables which are most subject to controlled or

Figure 1. Production model for management resource system.

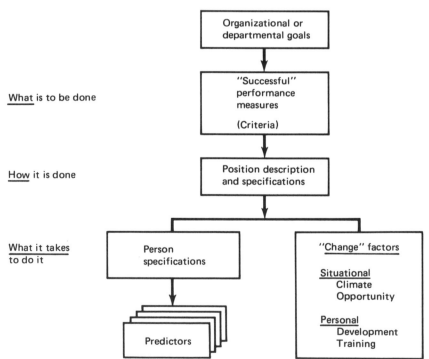

uncontrolled change, and which may affect performance. To the extent that these variables are controlled, they also affect the person specifications.

Once the person specifications are established, it becomes possible to seek measures and/or predictors. Evaluative measures are appropriate when the candidate has had an opportunity to display a given characteristic either on the job, avocationally, or in simulation. Predictive measures are used when one or more performance characteristics must be extrapolated.

Note that, if the derivations required by the model are correctly performed, the predictors are oriented to the ultimate performance appraisal, even though they are directly related to the present set of person specifications. Because both predictors and criteria are measures, they provide a continuous feedback loop, permitting timely evaluation of predictive efficiency. The feedback loop also simplifies alteration of the predictive set when the criteria are changed.

Although the system must be developed from the top down, it works from the bottom up. Any candidate for a position may be matched against the person specifications. These provide a standard, fair, and comprehensive set of standards.

Because the position description and the performance criteria are known to both incumbent and superior, communication, understanding, and the setting of goals are facilitated. All parties involved know, in advance, how the individual manager's performance will be judged.

Knowing the sets of characteristics required for various positions permits the comparison of two or more sets to provide valuable information for transfer and promotion decisions. Most managerial positions in a given organization have a great deal of overlap, but the specifics are difficult to judge or use because the required characteristics have not been identified.

This system responds to all the objections and dissatisfactions described earlier. It provides a fair, reliable, and valid measure of both performance and potential. The system has a logical appeal which makes it far more acceptable than most procedures. It provides its own cross-check to avoid outdating. It is designed to meet the demands of the organization, the individual manager or candidate, and the government.

There are too many truly uncontrollable variables affecting corporate planning. There is little excuse, therefore, for accepting the extreme error variance which may result from inadequately controlled managerial resources. The risk is too great, the solution too near.

JOHN C. CHAMBERS AND
SATINDER K. MULLICK

Forecasting
for Planning

QUALITATIVE TECHNIQUES

Uncertainty about the future has forced the planning of many corporations to become more flexible. *Business Week* stated that, instead of relying on a single corporate plan with perhaps one or two variations, top management at more and more companies is getting a whole battery of contingency plans and scenarios. For corporate planners, and even more for the senior executives who must act on their advice, the problem is not so much that some day they will have to deal with a future that is cataclysmic, but that they must plan today for a future that has never been more uncertain."[1] Brice A. Sachs, corporate planner at Exxon, states that "a lot more is thrown at top management because planning assumptions are not pinned down."[2] Accordingly, as a minimum, forecasts should contain some consensus of experts relating to assumptions and basic direction.

Alvin Toffler, author of *Future Shock,* notes that "economists are like generals. They're busy fighting the last war. Their price controls and economic policy is like a cobwebbed economic version of the Maginot Line, a mighty fortress with guns pointing in irrelevant directions." He blames the current economic predicament on what he terms Ecospasm, defined as "a combination of inflation and unemployment, all frightfully complicated by technological upheaval, ecological breakdowns, breakup of service, disruption in the family structure, and rapid value change."[3] Toffler indicates that growth patterns will be different, due to natural resource availability, and suggests that there will be a shift to human services as a partial solution to problems resulting from Ecospasm. If his analysis and projections are accurate, they must be considered in market, economic, and other types of forecasts.

The Delphi method is one qualitative technique that has been used extensively to predict future technology, customer preferences, industry changes, and the like. Developed at the Rand Corporation in the 1940s, it is a method for soliciting unbiased expert opinion and obtaining consensus through a sequence of questionnaires utilizing controlled feedback. Many articles describing the Delphi method and its applications under corporate, government, and academic sponsorship have appeared in the *Harvard Business Review* and various technical journals.[4] Delphi studies can range in size from those relying on three or four experts to technological forecasts where companies have 25 to 200 of their scientists participating. One of the largest was undertaken in Japan, involving approximately 4,000 experts over a six-month period. The study developed technological, sociological, and political projections for a ten-year period.

Significant improvements in the Delphi method reportedly have been made in recent years. These may counteract the recent criticism of H. Sackman of the Rand Corporation who authored a report entitled "Delphi Assessment: Expert Opinion, Forecasting, and Group Process." Sackman's analysis concludes that "conventional Delphi is basically an unreliable and scientifically invalidated technique in principle and probably in practice . . . it is suggested, but not proven, that the results of most Delphi experiments are probably unreliable and invalid. Even variations of conventional Delphi should not be encouraged unless they explicitly attempt to meet the challenge of generally accepted standards of rigorous empirical experimentation in the social sciences. Except for its possible value as an informal exercise for heuristic purposes, Delphi should be replaced by demonstrably superior, scientifically rigorous questionnaire techniques and associated experimental procedures using human subjects."[5]

J. K. Carver, manager of futures research at the Monsanto Company, stated that "all of our research is done as part of our long-range corporate planning, the purpose being to give us some background against which to make today's decisions. So our emphasis is, first of all, on those matters that impinge on Monsanto and those things that are decisionable; that is, things that we can do something about."[6] He then describes the forecasting that aids this process: "Within this framework, we generally do three types of forecasting. One is good old reliable trend analysis. This requires a lot of data, but if you've got it and the trend is unmistakable, you had might as well pay attention to it. Expert opinion is used to bolster this, and it can be either one man's valued opinion or a group of experts'. We don't use Delphi a lot anymore because we found it to be rather time-consuming and that the rigid structure of Delphi left something to be desired. We use a sort of interview Delphi, presenting an expert with some kind of scenario or a set of facts or projections and ask him to comment. We try to keep this fairly structured. We get a lot of help in this from the Institute for the Future and from The Futures Group."[7] The third approach in the Monsanto futures research program is normative forecasting. "We ask, where is it that we want to be, say ten years out. If this differs from where the trend is taking us or where the experts say things are going, then what are we going to do to bridge the gap? You might call this scenario forecasting, but in our case we take the scenario to be something that is deliberately sought through our corporate planning process, an objective that we want to obtain, and then look for shortfalls in our effort or for pitfalls that we might run into." [8]

Several other qualitative techniques have been described in the forecasting literature. Cross-impact analysis is a methodology where the possible impact of every single event on every other event is systematically assessed to convert qualitative events into a quantitative forecast. Estimates are obtained for each of the possible events that can occur for their relative importance and probability of occurring. The Futures Group has done some interesting work in this area, including translating events such as diet programs, preventative heart disease programs, frequent medical checkups, and the like into effects on the sale of coronary vasodilators.

The Panel Consensus method is based on the assumption that several experts can arrive at a better forecast than one person. Shortcomings of this method, due to group dynamics, led to the development of the Delphi method.

The Historical Analogy method is a comparative analysis of the introduction and growth of similar new products. It bases the forecast on similarity patterns (for example, color television compared with black and white TV). Changes in consumer lifestyles and preferences make this approach less reliable than previously.

Market research also could be classified as a set of qualitative techniques, although quantitative methods are used to interpret the results. Once new products have been evaluated by market research techniques, or a rating-ranking approach, the comparative evaluations can be used to forecast future sales.

CAUSAL TECHNIQUES

Regression and correlation analysis is frequently used to determine whether relationships between two or more factors exist, that is, whether changes in the so-called independent variables will apparently lead to a change in the dependent variable. These are often called causal relationships, even though the correlations or concurrent variations may have occurred by chance, or the variables are in fact causally related to other factors. Variables included in regression analysis should accordingly be those among which there is some logical reason to believe that relationships exist. Regression analysis is an effective tool when applied correctly, being one of the techniques employed in the construction of econometric models. The PIMS (Profit Impact of Market Strategy) equations, derived primarily by regression analysis, provide insights on expected profit performance of different kinds of businesses under different competitive conditions and in a sense are a vehicle for forecasting business profitability. The March–April 1974 *Harvard Business Review* contained an article that described some interesting research findings.[9] Data from 57 corporations, with 620 diverse businesses, were used to analyze 37 factors and to establish relationships between planning factors and profit performance.

ECONOMETRIC MODELING

In econometric modeling it is often difficult to determine meaningful relationships between sales and economic factors. A few years ago a statistician at Corning Glass Works, in attempting to develop a forecasting model for gross sales of one of the product lines, concluded that the product line was not affected by the economic business cycle because he obtained poor correlations with the various economic factors. A later study revealed that the gross sales were buoyed by heavy promotion that was carried out during prior recessions. When the gross sales were adjusted for price promotions and pipeline inventories, the data showed that sales swings were similar to economic swings with respect to time and direction. The net sales were subsequently regressed with the economic swings, and that input, combined with a marketing input for price promotion and an estimated pipeline change in inventories, provided the final sales forecast. This forecasting approach has since been extended to a number of other Corning Glass Works established businesses. On the basis of experience to date (three to four years), there appears to be little question that the econometric approach yields better results. The key was the correct method of handling the economic, marketing, and other variables in the analyses and forecasts.

Since the forecasts are at least partially based on economic forecasts, one might ask: "How can the product line forecast accuracy improve when economic forecasts appear to be so bad?" During the past two years several economic scenarios were used, and by means of regular tracking it was possible to pinpoint what scenario or path the economy was most likely to follow. "Range forecasts" of the economy (that is, those in which ranges rather than single-point forecasts of economic variables are provided) were prepared and updated on a monthly basis throughout 1974 and 1975. The ranges were obtained by analyzing the forecasts of a number of economic forecasters, first grouping the forecasters according to the content of their forecasts and then establishing the ranges on the basis of the differences between groups.

For example, in tracking 20 reputable economic forecasters, we found that the forecasts tend to fall into three groups of 13, 5, and 2 forecasters. Since it appeared that similar methods and assumptions were used by forecasters within each group, it was decided that equal weights would be given to each group in computing the ranges. (Apparently, in general each group has one or two original thinkers, with others following their lead.) The group size is not necessarily an indication of accuracy. In fact, results of recent tracking of the forecasts of each group suggest that the smallest one is most accurate. However, unless one group demonstrates significantly greater accuracy over a long period of time, we feel the use of averages and ranges is more appropriate.

Just as in the case in a Delphi study, each group is providing some information that is of value and should be taken into account in preparing a forecast. This is particularly true for the 1976–1978 period, where varying boom or bust scenarios have been presented by economists. The economy for the next few years is highly uncertain and use of range forecasts will be the best approach to decision making.

However, while a range forecast is more meaningful, it also poses serious implementation problems. First, it requires the decision maker to analyze different options and then to make value judgments. He or she has to consider simultaneously the economic implications of alternative tactics or strategies and the likelihood that an environment exists that will make each strategy optimal. Nevertheless, we have found in the case of several consumer products that use of a single forecast leads to poor operating results and that consideration of risk is essential for optimizing long-term profits. A range forecast may reveal the potential risk of losing market share or an entire business, and such risks must be considered in planning for the future. Accordingly, the range approach will generally lead to contingency planning and awareness of the need to set up tracking systems.

Two very interesting papers relating to economic forecasting recently appeared in the September 1975 *Business Economics Journal*. In the first, Geoffrey H. Moore cites a quarterly survey of economic forecasts conducted by the American Statistical Association and the National Bureau of Economic Research,[10] in which it was found that, of the

50–60 forecasters participating in the survey, about one-half stated that the most important method they use is the "informal GNP model," 30 percent use econometric models as their prime method, while leading indicators are generally the second or third most important method. Moore also states that about two-thirds of those in the survey use leading indicators as well as models. (An informal GNP model is one in which the forecaster uses less rigorous methods than an econometric approach. For example, simple regression techniques or judgmental estimates, based on qualitative factors, would be included as informal GNP models.) He indicates that, as models have become more complex and comprehensive, their coverage of various indicators has increased. He discusses other advantages of using both indicators and models, stressing that many of the indicators give information on developments outside the boundaries of a particular model.

In the second article, Robert L. McLaughlin[11] describes the way he combines the use of several techniques in deriving and monitoring economic forecasts that are useful for various time periods. He tells how econometric models are primarily effective for medium-term rather than short-term forecasting, while indicators are more accurate for short-term forecasting. Essentially, the method involves the combination of what McLaughlin calls the Indicator Approach, the Econometric Approach, and the Judgmental Approach, which is the blending of causative models, various indexes and indicators, monitoring of recent trends, and consideration of qualitative information. McLaughlin recommends two new phases—the use of the federal government's economic policies as a leading indicator and the use of prices, the final effect of government policies—in addition to the three normal phases.

One of the major advantages of the econometric approach is that it allows a forecaster to test the implications of different assumptions. However, econometric models are by no means infallible, and it is sometimes necessary to set them aside temporarily and use more qualitative methods. This was done during the energy/oil crisis because econometric models did not properly reflect the impact of the oil embargo and subsequent increased costs. In another instance qualitative methods were substituted for an econometric model in forecasting demand for a product supplied by Corning to the automotive industry.

The changing dynamics of the automotive industry and deviations from historical trends were recently described in a September 4, 1975, weekly staff letter issued by David L. Babson and Company of Boston, Massachusetts. This letter notes that, during the past 15 years, automobile purchases have averaged 4.9 percent of disposable income, ranging from 4.0 percent during recessions to 5.5 percent in a boom year. Total automobile spending, including fuel and repairs, has consistently run between 10 and 11 percent. Spending on gas and oil, which used to average 3.2 percent of disposable income, has risen to 3.8 percent, because of the increase in oil prices. These changes lead some experts to believe that there has been a major change in automobile purchasing dynamics.

Another example of changing historical trends is the case of consumer nondurables. William T. Moran of Lever Brothers stated in a talk at a business outlook meeting given by The Conference Board on September 16, 1975, that, for the first time since World War II, in 1974 the real spending for consumer nondurables went down from the previous year (that is, there was a reduction in the volume of goods sold). Furthermore, there was considerable cross-product substitution within the amounts spent for nondurables.

MARKET MODELS

There are a variety of causal market forecasting models in addition to those based primarily on economic factors. Most of these utilize some specific knowledge about market dynamics, obtained through market research, by statistical analysis of market data, expert opinion, and so forth. In recent years a number of market research techniques have been developed that provide the relationships needed for accurate market forecasting models. Some of these are concerned with determining customer choices for varying product options and/or identifying the product features that contribute most to consumer decisions. In one of the more frequently used methods, customers being interviewed are asked to choose among product options and to indicate relative preferences.

Another approach that is being used increasingly is to ask potential customers to state preferences for different levels of product features, where they must indicate tradeoffs for paired comparisons of features as well as the different feature levels. This information, along with the proposed or existing feature levels of specific products, is used in models that compute the relative market values of the products. Various methods are then employed to extend relative product values to market-share estimates for forecasting purposes.

Several techniques are available for estimating features tradeoffs, with conjoint measurement and the Fishbein method being two of the more commonly used and publicized ones. Conjoint measurement is described in detail by Green and Wind in their article.[12] The Fishbein model and an alternative method are discussed in an article by Antola,[13] which contains references to several other articles describing the Fishbein method.

The Fishbein method is virtually identical to that utilized in SUMM (Single Unit Marketing Model), a technique developed by Eric Marder Associates, Inc., New York. Both SUMM and conjoint measurement have been used at Xerox to estimate customer acceptance of alternative new product designs.

SUMM and conjoint measurement differ primarily in the way the consumer is asked to assess tradeoffs. In SUMM the consumer is required to compare directly product features and levels of features on a ratio scale, whereas in conjoint measurement the consumer is asked for rank-order judgments/choices of features, and the ratio-scale values are then analytically derived. Both techniques then use models to aggregate the features to determine the relative values of products. In their article, Green and Wind describe how conjoint measurement results are used in marketing strategy simulations.

Thus far simulation models have been more effective for testing various marketing strategies than for market forecasting purposes, but some companies are developing simulation models that can be effectively used for market forecasting. A number of very large market simulation models have been described in the literature, with perhaps the largest being that developed by Amstutz and Claycamp for the prescription drug field.[14] These models attempt to incorporate factors that explain customer decision-making processes. In some instances the major portion of the model is a simulation of the customer acceptance (choice) of specific product or system offerings. A model of this type has been developed at Xerox.

Another type of simulation that has proved useful for planning purposes is the modeling of existing and proposed products to determine how they will perform in various customer environments and how that performance compares with competitive products. This permits the evaluation of alternative product designs and guides product development. These product simulation models may then be extended for use as marketing tools. This has recently been done for the Xerox 9200 Duplicating System.

In sum, causal models incorporate understanding of markets and the economy and make a more quantitative use of knowledge about specific relationships. Causal models are quite useful, but one must be careful to recognize their limitations. Forecasting is still an art and will probably remain so, but these tools can help the forecaster become a better artist.

TIME-SERIES ANALYSIS

Planning is concerned primarily with developing strategies that will achieve a desired future. Accordingly, planners frequently prefer to give relatively little attention to recent trends and patterns and therefore to avoid the use of trend projections, time-series-analysis techniques, and other such methods. These planners maintain that their objective is to create an environment that will enable them to deviate from historical trends and therefore that history has little value. However, there are several ways in which statistical projections are useful to planners, such as (1) projecting what will happen in the future if no radical changes are made within a particular business; (2) obtaining projections of the immediate future, so that longer-range forecasts are based on accurate short-range forecasts; and (3) measuring the potential impact of strategies versus a continuation of historical trends.

When historical data are used for short-term trend projections, analysts quite frequently use raw data and do not perform time-series analysis to identify seasonals, cycles, and current trends. This can result in serious errors concerning recent trends and the way sales are growing (or declining). For example, year-to-year comparisons may show a substantial increase in sales while the sales rate is presently declining. This would occur if there had been significant growth a few months to a year earlier.

Another potential error arises when a business has longer-term cycles, so that sales are in fact continuing on a long-term trend even though a cyclical pattern may make it appear that the trend has changed (for example, there appears to be a long-term cycle in the ophthalmic business). It is extremely difficult to observe these patterns by examining raw data, whereas various time-series-analysis techniques greatly improve the planner's ability to identify changes in sales trends, cycles, seasonals, and trends in seasonals.

Certain principles or assumptions underlie the use of statistical projection techniques: (1) the short-term future (three to six months out) has been determined by previous actions and new actions will not cause immediate deviations from historical trends; (2) there are generally statistical variations in historical data that will be repeated in at least the near-term future; and (3) short-term and long-term projections should both take into account the most recent rates and the way those rates are changing.

While most long-range planning is concerned with annual data or at best quarterly projections, we have found that there are advantages in working with monthly data or data representing relatively short time spans. This permits better identification of current trends and turning points and a basis for correlating trend and short-term changes with specific events such as marketing strategies, economic fluctuations, political or labor upsets (such as strikes), production constraints, and so forth.

Time-series-analysis techniques are particularly useful when the objective is to sort out the systematic fluctuations from random fluctuations. Depending on the particular technique, the seasonals, cycles, and trends are the systematic fluctuations, with most techniques combining trend and cycle. We have found it important to identify cyclical fluctuations, since it may appear that there is a downward trend, when in fact the long-term trend is upward and the short-term cycle is causing a reduction in the rate. The major objectives of the various techniques are to reduce the random fluctuations, that is, to maximize the amount of total variation in the data that can be attributed to systematic fluctuations. A related objective is to be able to identify turning points or recent deviations from historical patterns.

Two of the most commonly used time-series-analysis techniques are exponential smoothing and the Shiskin (Census Bureau X-11) techniques. The use of these, along with the Box-Jenkins method, has increased significantly as computer routines have become readily accessible from the computer manufacturers, software suppliers, and time-sharing operations. The calculations for most time-series-analysis methods, except for simple moving averages, are difficult to perform manually, but this presents no problem since computer programs are available at little or no cost for virtually all the technniques.

There are many variations of exponential smoothing (single, double, triple), with adaptive forecasting being a further extension. Some of these variations have deseasonalizing routines, while others do not, with a variety of approaches being used to derive seasonals, such as a moving average/ratio method or the application of a Fourier series. Exponential smoothing attempts to track recent changes in data, with the most recent data points being given greater weight than the less recent points. The weight to be assigned to the most recent point can be either judgmentally assigned or derived by an optimizing technique so that random fluctuations are minimized.

The major problem with exponential smoothing is the slowness in identifying recent trend changes, with the technique usually taking a minimum of three to four time periods to track new trends. Single exponential smoothing assumes that future data points will be equal to the most recent rate; double smoothing makes linear projections; and triple smoothing makes quadratic projections. In general, exponential smoothing should not be used for projecting more than 6–12 months into the future, with the accuracy decreasing significantly if there are frequent changes in trends. Exponential smoothing is used most effectively when there are many sets of time series to be analyzed, since it is a relatively inexpensive technique. When double or triple exponential smoothing is used, long-term projections can often indicate significant increases or decreases from current levels, but features setting upper limits on the projections are usually incorporated into the routines to avoid that problem.

A technique that we have found to be particularly effective is the Shiskin routine. While it is essentially a time-series-analysis technique (that is, it identifies historical patterns in data), it can be used to make short-term projections. Some of the more recent computer software packages have this feature. The Shiskin routine is especially effective in developing seasonals (it incorporates trends in seasonals) and in fitting curves to reflect recent trend changes. We have found that analyses based on studies of patterns of changes in the rates (or first differences) provide a good basis for making short-term projections up to one year into the future. By performing analyses for consecutive time periods and plotting the changes in the trend cycle (rates), we have been able to identify turning points as they occur, rather than two to three months after they have occurred. By turning points we mean points at which the first differences reach maximum or minimum rates, which are equivalent to inflection points on the trend cycle.

The Shiskin routine assigns weights to the data points according to the amount of fluctuation in the historical data (9, 13, 23 period moving averages are the options). This routine is useful not only in obtaining short-term projections to be incorporated into longer-range projections, but also in setting and cycling budgets and in doing short-term planning. It is essentially an iterative technique that systematically sorts out seasonals and trend-cycle fluctuations to obtain the "best" fit to the data (based on the curve-fitting algorithms in the computer routine).

Another form of time-series analysis is regression analysis, in which time is used as the independent variable. If there is seasonality in data, some method of deseasonalizing the data is generally combined with regression analysis. Projections can be either linear or curvilinear, depending on the particular option chosen. This technique is more commonly used for annual data rather than monthly or quarterly data. Regression analysis, as well as the previously mentioned techniques, utilizes some variation of the moving-average technique, with both exponential smoothing and the Shiskin routine using weights for the various points in the moving averages, while regression analysis uses equal weights for all points.

The most comprehensive time-series technique currently available, and one that is gaining in usage, is the Box-Jenkins method. This technique has many features that permit you to design your own model, specifying the length of the moving average, the weighting system, the curve-fitting mathematical form, the seasonality feature, and so forth. It requires a person well-trained in its application, and it is significantly more expensive to use than the techniques mentioned earlier. The costs of applying the various techniques are, in ascending order, moving averages, exponential smoothing, regression analysis, Shiskin, and Box-Jenkins, with the costs of regression analysis and exponential smoothing dependent on the options chosen.

With the exception of Box-Jenkins, time-series-analysis techniques do not usually sort out trends from cycles. We have found the identification of cycles to be important, and it is frequently of value to attempt to determine whether cycles exist and their lengths. Spectral density analysis is the most commonly used technique for identifying the existence and length of cycles.

Another type of cyclical analysis is that utilizing life-cycle patterns, where patterns for similar or analogous products are studied for their length and functional forms. Many consumer products are found to have similar life-cycle patterns, with the exact parameters of the curves depending on the product features and marketing strategies.

In summary, there are a variety of statistical projection techniques available to the planner. Most of these can be used to make short-term projections, and the short-term projections can be incorporated into longer-term forecasts, which are based on the techniques described in previous articles. The time-series and statistical projection techniques will also provide longer-term estimates of what will happen if nothing is done to change present trends.

REFERENCES

1. *Business Week*, "Corporate Planning: Piercing Future Fog in the Executive Suite," April 28, 1975, p. 46.

2. Ibid., p. 48.

3. "Future Shock Author Warns of Economic Woes," *Rochester Democrat & Chronicle*, May 5, 1975, p. 4E.

4. For example, North and Pyke, "Probes of the Technological Future," *Harvard Business Review*, May–June 1969.

5. *Technology Forecasts and Technology Surveys*, "Monsanto: Futures Research Aids Decision Making," March 1975, p. 3.

6. Ibid., pp. 1–2.

7. The writers have experienced a similar problem with Delphi, when applying it to business planning. This is described in the article by J. Chambers, S. Mullick, and D. Goodman, "Catalytic Agent for Effective Planning," *Harvard Business Review*, January–February 1971, pp. 110, 119.

8. *Technology Forecasts and Technology Surveys*, op. cit., p. 2.

9. Sidney Schoeffler, Robert D. Buzzell, and Donald F. Heany, "Impact of Strategic Planning on Profit Performance," *Harvard Business Review*, March–April 1974, pp. 137–143.

10. Geoffrey H. Moore, "Economic Indicators and Econometric Models," *Business Economics Journal*, September 1975, pp. 45–48.

11. Robert L. McLaughlin, "A New Five-Phase Economic Forecasting System," *Business Economics Journal*, September 1975, pp. 49–60.

12. Paul A. Green and Yoram Wind, "New Ways to Measure Consumer Judgments," *Harvard Business Review*, July–August 1975, pp. 107–117.

13. Ollie T. Antola, "The Vector Model of Preferences: An Alternative to the Fishbein Model," *Journal of Marketing Research*, February 1975, pp. 52–59.

14. Arnold E. Amstutz and H. J. Claycamp, "Simulation Techniques in the Analysis of Marketing Strategy," presented at the Symposium on Application of the Sciences and Marketing, Purdue University, 1966.

GEORGE E. HUMPHRIES

Technology Assessment— A New Imperative in Corporate Planning

THERE IS an evolutionary progression in corporate planning for new technology which goes: technology forecast, technology feasibility study, economic feasibility study, market feasibility study, technology assessment. A translation of this continuum reads: What is possible? Is it likely? Is it affordable? Will it sell? Will it hurt anything?

This contribution examines the end of this progression: technology assessment (TA) or consequence forecasting. It discusses why corporations should be both interested in and skeptical of TA and how the general concept of consequence forecasting should be adapted to corporate use.

In the continuum of corporate planning mentioned above, each successive element looks into the future with an increasing degree of specificity. Concomitantly, the difficulty of estimating future events also increases at each stage.

With an increase in difficulty comes an increase in cost and a decrease in the probable accuracy of the projections, estimates, forecasts, or predictions. This leads to the question: If pushing the range of corporate planning to the technology assessment phase is more difficult, more expensive, and less likely to be accurate, then why bother? The answers to this question are suggested below.

THE TRENDS

Corporate planners know how to discover past and present trends, and how to use extensions of them to estimate the future. Although it is probably impossible to detail the interactive network of elements which are changing, and in turn causing more changes, many believe that Western civilization may be approaching a watershed of attitude and mind sets. This means that a majority of the population of whole nation states may have a significantly different intellectual view of themselves and the world.

Although all the causes of this perceptual shift cannot be known, or the rate of change precisely set, some of the major causes are the rise in material affluence and the vast increase in quantity and content of communications media.

The affluence creates time to listen, think, and act. The communications increase provides data to think about. Together they provide a high level of awareness of what is going on and a realization that individuals can influence the decisions being made in their names by their governments.

Having the time to contemplate has also permitted more people to compare precepts and promises of the systems which affect their lives with the performance of those systems. The public is becoming less willing to accept the gap between promise and performance. People are beginning to question closely and intelligently the implicit cultural assumptions which they have previously accepted unquestioningly. Not all of those cultural assumptions bear close and intelligent scrutiny.

Not only are times changing, but they are changing at an accelerating rate. There are a number of indicators of the perceptual shift:

The change in attitude toward religion.

The change in attitude toward sex.

The change in attitude toward war as a necessary way of international "life."

The change in attitude toward the environment.

The change in attitude toward technology as an unalloyed "good," or as a costless, never-ending cornucopia of growth and wealth.

The changing attitude toward growth itself.

The changing attitude toward political responsibility.

The changing attitude toward sharing with all individuals the material wealth that collective enterprise has produced.

The changing attitude toward equality of the sexes, the "races," and the ethnic groups within our national borders.

The changing attitude toward sharing national affluence with less affluent nations.

The changing attitude toward the gap between the promises and the performance of the capitalistic system.

Some of these apparent shifts may not be secular trends. Instead, they may be cyclical oscillations which will ultimately reverse themselves. Certainly, each apparent change has produced a counterforce of reaction to that change. Yet taken together, and viewed over the past several decades, the changes appear to be more secular than cyclical. The conviction that the trends are evolutions to a different state becomes more certain when the permanence of their probable causes—affluence, leisure, communications, information, and actions—is taken into account.

Like the trends which seem to be demanding consequence forecasting, efforts to predict the impacts of projected change exist, and these efforts are not likely to stop in the face of a little criticism.

The National Environmental Protection Act and its creatures, the Council on Environmental Quality, the Environmental Protection Agency, and environmental impact statements, all, for better or worse, exist and are affecting our individual lives and our corporate practices.

The Congressional Office of Technology Assessment, in operation for more than four years, is beginning to have a direct impact on legislation, and indirect (but substantial) impacts on the behavior of the federal executive. Higher-order impacts on corporations are inevitable.

These manifestations of the will of the electorate, through action of the legislature, evidence not only the trend to view change as a mixed gamble, but the intention to do something about reducing the odds of that gamble.

The public's awareness and will is evidenced in other ways, too: in the consumer movement (and related legislation), in the continued activity of the environmental movement, and in the pressure to re-form and revitalize the regulatory agencies of the government.

ROLE OF THE PLANNER

What does all of this mean to corporate planners? Planners are expected to peer into the murky future and to offer suggestions to the intrepid captains of industry about the course most likely to lead to the achievement of corporate goals and that least likely to lose public acceptance.

If corporate planning is to fulfill this function in the sea of changes which society seems to be presenting to corporate navigators, then planners should take some soundings of these new waters. Since these new waters are different in social ways, those soundings should include forecasts of the social future.

Technology assessment offers a corporation the opportunity not only to improve management decisions and avoid the embarrassment of inadvertent antisocial acts, but also to avoid the losses in market, sales, and profits attendant on being "wrong" in the choice of a socially unacceptable product, process, plant, or action.

GOVERNMENT AND CORPORATE TECHNOLOGY ASSESSMENT

In the past, most technology assessments have been done for the government. Because this "impact estimation" is generally an input to decision and policy making, it differs as a function of the kind of decision and policy making it supports.

There are three major factors which distinguish corporate TA from government-sponsored TA. These can be summarized as cost constraints, technological constraints, and an evolutionary pace.

• A corporate TA must be worth what it costs. Better or perfect information has a value to the decision maker. To the extent that corporate planners can estimate the value of better information on consequences, a limit of resources is imposed on TA, and that limits the scope, scale, intensity, and extensiveness of the TA effort.

• Corporations are more likely to assess relatively smaller subjects than are governments. Whereas the government may want to assess fusion or fission as a source of electric power, industry may be concerned either with the differential between one fission method and another, or with the siting of a single plant.

A new product may require less effort to assess than offshore technology, geothermal energy, or similar gargantuan problems being assessed by the OTA and agencies of the federal executive.

• The most important difference between governmental and corporate TA is that government consequence estimation is usually made after the technology (product, process, project, or program) has been developed, while a company TA can be done concurrently with the development of the technology.

This is a vital and important distinction between corporate and government technology assessment. It is, in fact, the characteristic which allows corporate TA to be cost effective.

THE TECHNOLOGY ASSESSMENT PROCESS

Drafting proposals and blocking out study plans for assessments require increasingly detailed looks at the technology and its probable consequences.

Unlike the government, industry is usually involved with the development of new technology from the beginning, and with all of the studies of technology forecasting, technology feasibility, economic feasibility and market feasibility along the way. Therefore, it makes sense for corporations to assess consequences at each step in the development process. There are several reasons for this:

• One of the first tasks a conventional TA team faces is learning the technology. This usually means that the team must do this after the technology is fully developed and has a direction, momentum and established form of its own. Corporate TA has the opportunity of learning the technology as it evolves, and of aiding in the development of a better product from the beginning.

• A conventional, or one-look, assessment of yet-to-be implemented technologies is based on a long chain of questionable assumptions. As the future draws nearer, these assumptions become more clearly true or false, and the assessment more in need of revision. In any case, evolving assumptions and newly estimated consequences are sure to be different from those first made. Consequences once thought significant may disappear, but, more importantly, consequences invisible or vaguely seen at first may change in intensity and risk.

• Conventional, or government, TA is not usually involved with proprietary information. Hence it uses public information and publishes its findings. Corporate TA may well be concerned with an innovation which is designed to provide a competitive market advantage. For that reason, doing consequence estimation at each decision point in the innovation process, and doing it privately, may be a competitive necessity.

• Traditionally, TA's have been performed by large *ad hoc* aggregations of theretofore unassociated experts who then had to learn the technology, learn about TA, and learn to work with each other. Corporate TA, on the other hand, having only small consequence estimations to do early in the development process, can be done by a small group within the corporation. This permits the development of continuity of expertise alike in the corporation's technologies, in the skills of technology assessment, and in working together as an ongoing, closely knit team.

• In the corporate development process, decision milestones are set for the successive increments of funding in the continued development of the product. Each of these decision milestones should call for a consequence evaluation commensurate with the level of investment under consideration. The best time to discover a debilitating side effect is before the investment of large quantities of time, effort, and ego.

In the past, corporations have done some formal assessments in the *a posteriori* mode. After a product is well developed, and resources have been committed, some semi-independent element of the corporation, or a consultant, is asked to discover what the drawbacks of the new product, process, or service may be and how undesirable consequences might be avoided. The record is not clear on what has happened to products that were discovered by a TA to have undesirable consequences. Nor is the record clear on what happened to the reports citing the drawbacks, or what happened to the people who discovered and reported undesirable consequences of an otherwise profitable innovation. Executing the bearer of bad tidings has not ceased in Western culture; the means has merely become more subtle. In any case, it is undesirable to give corporate technology assessors the unenviable task of killing expensive corporate technological babies after they are fully developed. It is much better for the assessors to contribute to earlier and less expensive technological decision making during the development process.

THE ASSESSMENT TEAM

Technology assessment is the analysis not of a technology but of its consequences. While familiarity with the technology being assessed is useful in certain respects, it is not essential, and may even be a detriment to a good consequence evaluation. Many TA practitioners believe that TA experience is more important in consequence estimation than is experience in the technology involved.

Inasmuch as consequences can usefully be categorized as material (or physical), biological (or ecological), economic, and social (or cultural), it is much more important for team members to be qualified generally in each of these subject areas than for them to be deeply qualified in the esoterics of the generator of the consequences. A TA team never has the resources to qualify a chemist as a sociologist, but given a rudimentary idea of physical consequences, a sociologist can estimate social consequences.

But more than a collection of specialists, a TA team must be a group of generalists. Not only is there no time to teach economics to an engineer, there is not enough time to convince anyone that other disciplines are relevant and essential, or that the tools, language, and findings of all the relevant disciplines must be coordinated and blended into an integrated analysis. Persons qualified in two or more areas of study are very useful.

In addition to being proficient in a number of disciplines, TA team members must have a high degree of interpersonal facility and compatibility. Adherents of the physical and engineering sects frequently resist conceding that interpersonal processes are relevant to the conduct of scientific endeavors. Managers and social scientists know better. Problems of ego and communications can present insurmountable impediments to good interdisciplinary analysis.

As for the actual mechanics of generating and manipulating data, there are also some general rules to which experience has given credibility.

ECLECTICISM

There is no known universal tool, either in mechanics or in consequence estimation. The tool must fit the task, both in terms of the innovation being analyzed for consequences and the amount of resources allocated to do the job. A team of qualified generalists should know how to pick the tools which fit the situation.

QUALITY OF INPUTS

Consequence estimation involves four principal tasks:

Deciding what data are necessary.
Generating futures data.
Interrelating these data.
Interpreting or applying the resultant findings.

There are some practitioners who view a single one of these stages as the whole process, to the near exclusion of the others. For instance, the use of cross-impact and cross-support matrices is a good way of interrelating data. However, if the wrong elements go into the matrices, and if the futures data used in the matrices are worthless, the product is not just useless, it is dangerous.

Many futures data are generated by "navel analysis," that is, by contemplation of the belly button under the stress of expiring time and money. If the futures data are intuitively or subjectively generated by experts in the subject being considered, and if these experts base their conclusions on knowledge, experience, and thoughtful meditation, then the data have value. If, on the other hand, they are generated by enslaved graduate students or indentured junior researchers, the quality of the data is questionable. Those who hire TA consultants should insist on knowing the source of the data that are used, whatever type they may be.

CERTAINTY

A Chinese proverb states that "prophecy is a very difficult task, especially when it concerns the future." Just as technology forecasting, technology feasibility studies, economic feasibility studies, and market feasibility studies are subject to error, so is consequence estimation. It reduces risk, rather than eliminating it. And because it predicts reactions of people to a yet untried innovation, it is based on a chain of assumptions. Probably the accuracy diminishes as some exponential function of the number of assumptions in the chain. However, any thoughtful analysis, no matter how tenuous, is better than blind chance. Technology assessment has become much less tenuous than it appears to the uninitiated.

PATTERN FOR CORPORATE TA

The following ideas of corporate TA all support the conclusion that corporate TA should be done by an in-house group of consequence estimators:

1. Like other TA's, it is a repeatedly iterative process.
2. Unlike other TA's, it should be done concurrently with innovation, or the development of new technology.
3. Like other TA's, it is concerned primarily with consequences, and only secondarily with the technology.
4. Like other TA's, it is efficiently done only by generalists who work together well and who are familiar with TA and its inventory of tools.
5. It provides an imperfect, but highly useful and necessary, look into the future.

If the corporation is concerned with its long-term well-being, it is therefore necessary that a consequence estimation (or TA) capability be developed and perfected in the appropriate organizational location.

CONCLUSIONS

The public is demanding more and more that those who seek economic gain from innovations be held responsible for the general and social costs of those innovations.

The kind of consequence estimation activities that has evolved under the misleading name "technology assessment" affords corporations a means of protecting themselves against alienating their public by the inadvertent perpetration of socially undesirable costs.

Corporations can accomplish consequence evaluation of innovation most effectively and efficiently by integrating it into the innovation decision-making process.

The desirability and necessity of incorporating more formal and explicit consequence estimation into the corporate innovation process may be one of the most important planning issues of the 1980s.

E. Process Skills

**PAMELA SHEA CUMING AND
WILLIAM T. BECHARD**

Getting the Power to Plan

CORPORATE PLANNERS are charged with defining where the organization should be going and identifying how it might get there. To meet this challenge, the planner must be familiar with the diverse kinds of problems and opportunities confronting his organization, as well as with the resources available to solve the problems or respond to the opportunities. Unfortunately, being familiar with the problems, opportunities, and resources is not enough. If corporate planners are to go beyond recommending direction and approach, they must understand the nature of power and how to use it effectively. The objective of this article is to discuss the various types of power available to planners and how this power can be used to improve the effectiveness of planning skills.

POWER PROBLEMS AND ROLE TENSION

Corporate planners often complain that their role lacks power:

Boredom or frustration will sooner or later afflict the corporate planner. . . . One has described his discontent in rather specific terms. On most occasions, he says, he sees the dimensions of a problem or opportunity and alternative responses more fully and in sharper focus than the executives of the operating units. Yet, he can do nothing about having his view prevail, other than arguing for it. [1]

This corporate planner is referring to the frustration that results from insufficient power to act. When the responsibilities inherent in a role are not matched by power, the result is role tension:

Role tension exists when the power persons feel they need or can handle is not in line with the power inherent in the roles they represent. It exists when organization members are required to do something they feel they cannot do or do not believe is productive and worthwhile. It exists when members require certainty, predictability, and structure, and are placed in situations where expectations and procedure are ambiguous.[2]

Corporate planners are victims of multiple kinds of role tension. Many find themselves in relatively new organizational positions and are uncertain about what is expected. One study of the corporate planning function found that 63 out of 111 study participants were the first corporate planners in their organizations. An additional 34 had only one predecessor.[3]

Recency of position contributes as much to role conflict (being subject to contradictory expectations) as it does to role confusion. Line management often expects a variety of behavior patterns from the corporate planner. Oscillation between attempts to live up to the expectation that the planner be a decision-maker and the expectation that the planner be a teacher, counselor, or guide can lead to resentment and job ineffectiveness. Because operating managers frequently perceive planning as a threat to their own autonomy,[4] planners must be careful to guide and encourage rather than to direct and command, even though managers may interpret this effort to guide and counsel as a lack of decisiveness or pragmatism on the part of the planner.

Since many corporate planners report directly to the chief executive officer, the majority might be expected to adhere more closely to the expectations of the "boss" than to the expectations of others. For many, doing so may only lessen their chances of fulfilling their corporate obligations. Corporate planners cannot plan for management; they must rely on management's input and involvement if planned objectives are to be realistic and attainable. Because planners often lack the power to coerce line management to plan, they must cajole or catalyze the planning process. Those planners who resent the time and politicizing that may be involved in cajoling often experience the tension of insufficient role control—the ability or freedom to initiate action.

Role tension, experienced by planners as role confusion, role conflict, or the lack of role control, may account for the feeling of many planners that boredom and frustration are inevitable by-products of the corporate planning process. However, research and observation have indicated that these conditions are not inevitable, and some corporate planners have been able to empower themselves and, in the process, to minimize their role tensions. Role tension is alleviated as planners enter positions in which they can determine what others will and will not expect of them and in which they have the leverage to influence others in predictable ways.

Empowerment strategies used by staff personnel (among them corporate planners) can be broken down into two types: strategies to get formal power and strategies to get informal power. Because there are significant differences in the impact of the two strategies on organizational relationships, it is helpful to understand the key differences between formal and informal power.

FORMAL POWER

Formal power is not necessarily earned; it is automatically conferred upon anyone who holds a position. Kings have formal power over their subjects; captains have formal power over lieutenants; managers have formal power over subordinates; corporate planners typically have formal power only over subordinate members of their own staffs.

There are three kinds of formal power: coercive power, reward power, and legitimate power. *Coercive power* is the capacity to hurt or punish for noncompliance. *Reward power* exists when a person is in a position to give another something of value in exchange for compliance. *Legitimate power* encompasses the rights, privileges, and authority associated with hierarchical rank and status. Unlike reward and coercive power, legitimate power is dependent on the acceptance of and respect for the hierarchy. Parents have legitimate power over children only as long as children (and the larger society) respect the "right" of parents to control.

Because legitimate power is dependent on the willing acceptance of others, it is typically backed up by some measure of reward or coercive power. Children comply with parents not because of the inherent "rights" of parenthood, but because of the parents' ability to punish and to reward. The legitimate power of managers is backed up by the power to promote, demote, or fire.

INFORMAL POWER

Informal power resides not in the role, but in the person. Informal power must be earned; it cannot be conferred. Informal power encompasses expert power, referent power, and indirect power.

Expert power is the capacity to influence as a result of superior knowledge or skills. Expert power, however, can be carried to an extreme. The "expert" who causes others to say, "He may be the best in the field, but he doesn't understand my problems and needs" may have a diminished ability to influence.

Referent power is based on identification, felt similarity, and affection. If I like you and enjoy being identified with you, then you probably have the capacity to influence me. Planners who try to learn and use the jargon peculiar to operating divisions are attempting to build referent power. Planners who spend time socializing with line management often have a stronger referent power base than planners who are perceived as "loners."

Indirect power is visible when one person works through a second person to influence a third person. Indirect power can be a critical resource for those who must influence persons who are hierarchically removed or organizationally distant. Let's assume that the marketing director has referent power over a division head. If the corporate planner is in a position to influence the marketing director, he or she may be able to influence the division head by asking the marketing director to intervene. The danger is that the marketing director may distort the planner's original intent, particularly if the intermediary is using an inappropriate power strategy.

SELECTING AN EFFECTIVE POWER BASE

Referent and expert power are frequently more potent than the more formal kinds of power. Reward power is limited by the number of incentives available for use as "bait." Using reward power effectively requires precise knowledge of what is of value to the change target. Financial incentives may be less potent when they are used to influence wealthy employees. Corporate nursery schools may be of greater value than the corporate insurance plan to employees who are parents.

The limitations of coercive power are potentially even more severe. People who comply out of fear of punishment will be motivated primarily to frustrate the goals of the influencer when they can do so safely. Coercion frequently leads to mistrust and dislike. One broad-based study clearly indicated that a "worker who dislikes his supervisor tends to disagree with the instructions of the supervisor when he can do so privately without fear of punishment."[5]

Legitimate power also cannot be relied on. We are living in a decade characterized by demands for opportunities to earn privileges regardless of role. The women's movement has eroded many "male prerogatives." Equal Employment Opportunity Commission legislation has challenged the rights of union members to claim seniority privileges.

Unlike the formal power bases, referent and expert power can generate long-standing commitment to change, with behavioral modifications not dependent on continual rewards, surveillance, or maintenance of hierarchical rights and privileges. The potency of referent and expert power was illustrated in a study of successful and unsuccessful mayors in which it was found that mayors who relied on patronage (reward power) did not fare as well as mayors who relied on shared goals (a combination of referent and expert power). [6]

Planners and other staff personnel who lack formal power over their internal "clients" have reason to be encouraged by this kind of research and by studies which indicate that having formal power can be detrimental to the achievement of objectives. Frequently, managers who have no power to reward or punish build more productive work groups than their contemporaries who have a measure of formal power. The reason for this may be that the "powerless" managers have no choice but to try to build work relationships characterized by mutual trust and respect. Managers with formal power may be precluded from building such relationships because of the human tendency to resist being open with those in positions of higher authority.

SOLVING POWER PROBLEMS

Planners can resolve some of the power problems and role tensions they experience by using a different kind of power. The corporate planner who is incurring resentment might try to avoid use of coercive power and build up a referent power base. The planner who needs to get something done quickly might try a little coercion. It is possible to determine consciously which kind of power is most appropriate and then to follow the strategy associated with getting more of that kind of power.

1. *Reward power*—the candy-store strategy—works when it is possible to corner the market on available rewards, eliminating any options the change target might have. For the individual to get what he wants, he'll have to do as the planner says.
2. *Coercive power*—the arsenal strategy—is similar to the candy-store approach, except the attempt is to corner the market on available weapons. Getting into a position to control harm or injury insures compliance (and resentment).
3. *Legitimate power*—the crown prince strategy—is used when a person attempts to change his or her status relative to someone else's through promotion, demotion, or alteration of the role expectations associated with positions. Requesting a change in title is one manifestation of this strategy.
4. *Expert power*—the look-what-I've-done strategy—is used by people whose deeds or credentials are creditable. People who have long lists of letters after their names and who mention these letters whenever possible are using this strategy.

5. *Referent power*—the fraternity strategy—is being used when the planner gives others reasons to like, accept, trust, and identify with him or her. Being helpful or defining a shared goal may be manifestations of the fraternity strategy.
6. *Indirect power*—the network strategy—involves knowing many people who are influential in their own domains.

In the past planners have perceived a lack of support for their activities. The lack of formal power and the application of ineffective power strategies have been major limitations. Once planners overcome their power problems and alleviate their role tensions, they find themselves able to be more effective in their jobs.

REFERENCES

1. The Conference Board, Inc., *Planning and the Corporate Planning Director*, Report No. 627 (New York, 1974), p. 63.
2. Pamela Cuming, "Predicting the Human Reaction," *Planning Review*, Vol. 2, No. 5, p. 10.
3. The Conference Board, p. 1.
4. The Conference Board, p. 1.
5. Barry E. Collins and Bertram H. Raven, "Group Structure: Attractions, Coalitions, Communication and Power," in *The Handbook of Social Psychology*, Vol. 4, edited by Lindzer Gardner and Elliot Aronson (Reading, Mass.: Addison-Wesley, 1969), p. 176.
6. John Kotter and Paul Lawrence, "The Mayor, An Interim Research Report," February 1972, unpublished.

LYLE YORKS

Persuading Groups
to Buy Ideas

MOST EXECUTIVES find it necessary to make a number of persuasive presentations during their business careers. Planners must convince management committees to adopt new approaches or procedures; subordinates must convince their superiors that the organization should set out on a new course of action; home office managers must convince a group of field managers to pay more attention to service levels or a new product—the list of examples is endless. Such presentations are regular occurrences in all organizations.

Unfortunately, few managers are truly skilled in making presentations effectively. As a result, they often despair when the people to whom they are making a presentation remain unpersuaded and fail to adopt their recommendations. No matter how carefully or expertly a subject has been researched, unless a manager can convince others of the soundness of the conclusions drawn, the efforts will have been for nothing. The painful reality is that facts alone—or the basic validity of a proposal—will seldom carry the day. Rather, executing a persuasive presentation is a separate skill in itself.

WHAT IS A PERSUASIVE PRESENTATION?

There are many kinds of presentations. Three which most frequently occur in business are: informational, in which the objective is to explain the details about a program, proposal, or the like; problem solving, which is oriented toward getting the ideas and expertise of others in order to arrive at a course of action; and persuasive, in which the objective is to put across or sell a predetermined course of action. In many ways, the persuasive presentation is the most difficult because a positive response usually necessitates a commitment from the group in time, money, staff, or some similar resource.

One of the best ways to understand the essential character of a persuasive presentation is to consider what it is not. A persuasive presentation is not a lecture. A set of fundamental differences separates the two. In the persuasive presentation, unlike a lecture, the presenter is almost always more concerned about delivering the message than the listeners are about receiving it. Furthermore, the status roles of speakers vis-à-vis the group are usually reversed. Presenters, unlike lecturers, must subordinate themselves to the audience. After all, it is the presenter who needs approval from the group. Consequently, the presenter cannot demand the time and attention of the audience; at best, he or she can deserve it. Thus, the question which confronts the presenter is not "How much time do I need to do this subject justice?" but "How much time can my audience give me?"

The final result of these differences is that while a lecturer can often put the audience to some trouble to understand his or her ideas, a presenter must go out of his way to avoid putting the audience to trouble. He cannot talk about all the parts of a proposal which he finds interesting—only those of major importance to the listeners. He cannot demonstrate the range and depth of his expertise—only show how he can help the audience. A presenter cannot demand or expect the group to work to understand the intricacies of the presentation—he must make any intricacy as simple as possible.

An informational presentation differs from a persuasive one in equally important ways. The purpose of an informational presentation is to communicate descriptively or factually, with the emphasis on presenting a picture of things as they are. As such, the presenter can rely heavily on logical sequences (time, space, and deductive sequences, important elements) in structuring the basic message.

Persuasive presentations seek agreement from the group that an action is warranted. The emphasis is on eliciting belief or assent to ideas. Initially the group is more likely to be neutral or even opposed. Certainly they will be more critical than when listening to an informational presentation. Psychological sequences which are designed to deal with the logic of feeling, rather than ideas, become more important in this kind of presentation. The biggest mistake a presenter can make is structuring a persuasive presentation as though it were primarily an informational one. You may present the most important information, but if it is not packaged to be credible with the group, the presentation will fail.

While emphasizing the difficulties involved in preparing and giving a persuasive presentation, it should be noted that the presenter has a couple of advantages as well. The persuader has some freedom of choice regarding what to include or omit in the presentation. For the reasons discussed above, listeners generally expect the presenter to be selective in what is presented. This advantage carries with it the responsibility of not leading the group to erroneous or damaging conclusions through omission of important issues. Another advantage is that most persuasive presentations are preludes to further discussion. The objectives of the presentation are often limited to getting the audience to proceed to a more intensive involvement in the subject at hand. Thus, many persuasive presentations do not need to be comprehensive.

Many presentations do not succeed in persuading the audience because proper attention was not given to the preparation stage. Experience and research have shed considerable light on the kind of preparation which needs to go into a persuasive presentation. The discussion below highlights some of the most important preparatory elements. If followed, it can help a presenter avoid some of the more typical pitfalls.

Identify the objective of the presentation. Why are you giving the presentation? What specific action do you wish those listening to take? Many presentations fail to be persuasive because the content "wanders"—those listening find themselves asking "Why is he telling me this?" A precise objective might be "To convince the management committee to close down the plant in Albany by December 31st."

It is worth writing out the objective for reference during the preparation of the presentation. Such an objective is the most fundamental measuring stick to be used in deciding what should and should not be included in the presentation.

Identify the audience. The complementary question to "What am I trying to achieve?" is "With whom am I trying to achieve it?" The question the presenter must think through is "What is there about my proposal or product which is important to them?"

This is a more difficult question to answer than one might at first think. For example, having spent a considerable amount of time researching the feasibility of a new and technically complex product, it is easy for a presenter to spend much of the presentation talking about the technical subtleties of the product. Indeed, this may be what really excites him about the product. However, a group of manufacturing managers might be more excited about the fact that producing the product will not require much retooling in the plant. Or that assembly of the product readily lends itself to mass-production methods. Not to emphasize these factors, or worse, to bury them between technical data, is to invite a negative response.

In addition to the demands placed on the listeners by their jobs, a presenter should take into account their personal style preferences as well. As was discussed in earlier *Planning Review* articles,* people vary widely in their preferred personal styles. For example, psychologists have observed that some individuals are direct and to the point in their dealings with others. They are action-oriented and are at their best when responding to immediate problems. Such an individual tends to respond best to presentations which are brief, highlight the main points, and allow the person to ask his or her own questions about the content. These individuals tend to want presentations that are structured for a direct yes or no answer.

By way of contrast, another type of individual is analytically oriented. These individuals tend to be very precise and orderly in their dealings with others. As a result, they respond best to very structured presentations which invite them to follow the logical sequence in the argument. They tend to be uncomfortable with yes or no decisions, preferring instead to select from among a range of options.

A different personal style identified by psychologists involves people who like to make decisions based on the "feel" of a problem. These individuals tend to respond readily to their emotional reactions toward something. If other people are going to be affected by your proposals, these individuals like to think through the strategy of implementing the plan of action—what will the impact be on those involved? Research indicates that such individuals respond well to presentations which utilize anecdotes to demonstrate the points being made. They also respond well to presentations that begin with the familiar and proceed to the unfamiliar.

Yet another personal style is a conceptual, or intuitive, style. Individuals with a preference for this style tend to deal well with basic ideas and conceptual relationships. They especially like to examine trends and consider how a given course of action will have future benefits. An individual characterized by this style is uncomfortable with detail and too many nuances. He or she prefers to examine a proposal in a broad-brush manner and is most likely to respond to the general direction of a course of action.

Careful preparation in structuring a presentation so that it does not run counter to the style preferences of those in the group can help increase receptivity on the part of listeners. In many groups, more than one style will be represented. Therefore, the presentation must be balanced to include elements that might appeal to all the styles in the group.

---

*John D. Drake, "Communications—The Art of Getting Through to People," *Planning Review*, Part I, March 1975; Part II, May 1975; Part III, July 1975.

Lay out the crucial elements. Having identified both the objective and the audience, it is appropriate to decide what content will be included in the presentation.

The presenter should begin by listing all the points he wishes to make, both positive and negative. He should examine the list carefully to make sure each point is important to the stated objective, and trim from the list any points that are not. Then, he should go over the list a second time and identify which points are most likely to be important to the audience. These are the points which should be positioned for emphasis. Even at this stage, thought should be given to duration—how much time is required to adequately cover the points listed, relative to the amount of time available. It is most important to present those points which directly meet the needs of the objective and of the audience. In all probability, the list will need further trimming.

Having come this far, the presenter must now develop a logical sequence for the basic argument. The content must be laid out in a manner which makes sense to the listeners. Some possible sequences are: time sequences; important element sequences; problem–analysis–solution sequences; proposition–proof–conclusion sequences; and familiar–to–unfamiliar sequences.

Structure the presentation. The logical sequence needs to be structured into an actual presentation. Once again, the presenter needs to reassess time constraints. This time the question to be decided is "What points might best be left for any discussion?" Any content other than the basic "meat and potatoes" of the presenter's argument can often be most effectively utilized by holding it in reserve. This includes supplementary data and arguments. If necessary, the presenter can introduce this material during the discussion phase of the presentation.

Run through the presentation. Do it at least twice, if not more. Does it hang together? Once more, what about time? The presenter should always be conservative with regard to the amount of content included in the presentation. In the actual presentation, it is likely the content will "spread" as the group interacts with it. A presentation that is 15 minutes short seldom bothers anyone. But one that runs overtime may upset everybody.

A MODEL PRESENTATION

Assuming the presentation has been thoroughly prepared, the problem becomes one of delivery. Once again, experience and research have identified certain crucial elements that can either facilitate or hinder a presentation. The following model incorporates these elements into a strategy for making the presentation.

Overview. The presenter should begin by stating the purpose of the meeting and briefly outline how he intends to proceed. This lays the ground rules for the presentation and establishes the presenter as in control by providing an idea of what is to come. For example, the presenter might state: "The purpose of this presentation is to decide whether to make an immediate $150,000 investment in a new XYZ machine. After researching the matter thoroughly, we believe this would be a good decision. Today, we are going to share our reasoning with you for your consideration. I am going to present the major pros and cons associated with the investment and suggest a couple of possible alternative courses of action. Then I would like to open the presentation to your questions and comments."

Ask for any immediate inputs. A seldom-used, but often effective procedure is for the presenter to ask for any immediate comments from the group. This tactic accomplishes a couple of things. First, it tends to break the ice and put the group at ease; at the start they feel part of the presentation. Second, it often provides the presenter with data regarding the feelings or previous experiences anyone in the group may have on the subject. These comments may suggest to the presenter what points to emphasize or to discuss more fully. This is an easy step to implement. A comment to the effect of "Before I begin, does anyone have any questions he or she wants to be sure gets discussed?" is sufficient.

Actual presentation. This should be brief and geared to the needs of the group. Care should be taken to follow the predetermined presentation. If some aspect of the presentation has not been treated in sufficient depth, someone can be counted on to ask a question about it later. As long as the presenter has the supporting data ready, this is no problem. In fact, it is to the presenter's advantage as it gets the group involved in a discussion about the presentation.

Ask for reaction. If positive, go directly to the close. If it is negative, the presenter should explore the feelings in the group. He can ask open-ended questions, utilize restatement and reflection, and demonstrate interest in and understanding of the group's response. Above all, the presenter should avoid getting into an adversary relationship by bringing in more facts. More facts are likely to increase rather than decrease resistance from the group. At this point in the presentation, the presenter needs to know what the real concerns of the group members are. Chances are the group is not really sure at this point. Therefore, the presenter's best strategy is to encourage a discussion among the members of the group.

The presenter needs to be especially sensitive to any covert resistance that may be present. He should make an effort to draw everyone into the discussion. A comment such as "Frank, you look as though you have some real concerns about the proposal. What are your thoughts on this?" will often do the trick.

Next, the presenter needs to sharpen the differences in the group. Once the presenter believes he understands the positions of the various individuals in the group, this belief can be tested by summing up the situation. If the presenter is right, the group should agree with the summarization. This tactic enables the presenter to continue to direct the group and at the same time check to see if all the problems have surfaced. The presenter should not be overly eager to proceed to the next step. It is to his advantage to be sure the group has had sufficient time to think through his ideas and bring to light any concerns they might have regarding them.

Once the presenter feels he understands the concerns of the group, he can try to integrate the differences. At this point, the presenter is in a position to effectively provide additional input. He can offer information which specifically relates to the concerns of the group. This is the place where the presenter may wish to utilize some of the input omitted from his initial presentation. One way of doing this is to suggest alternatives to the group. Offering alternatives gives the group a measuring stick against which its members can compare the original proposals. In this process, the members of the group often accept the original proposals because they are now looking at them in a reasonably objective manner. The presenter should try to draw group members into offering alternatives. Such involvement on the part of the group can further help gain commitment from its members.

Close. The closing is an important part of the persuasion process. If the presenter has approached the presentation in the manner described above, he has made it possible for the group to make up its own mind through discussion of the presentation. Now, the presenter needs to get the group to act on this decision.

Sometimes this is a very straightforward process. If the group appears to be in agreement, the presenter can simply ask, "Well, what's the next step?" At other times it is necessary for the presenter to provide more structure to the closing.

When the key decision makers in the group are direct, action-oriented individuals, an effective close is to give a short summary of the key elements of the presentation and propose a next step. This makes it easy for them to respond in a direct, yes or no fashion. If the group contains individuals of a conceptual orientation, it is often useful to indicate how the next step is consistent with other activities being pursued by the organization. However, if the key decision makers are analytical thinkers, a somewhat different closing may prove more effective. A short summary that highlights the logical sequence of the presentation, followed by options for the group to choose from, is often a better closing for this type of individual.

Analytical individuals prefer to remain flexible and are most comfortable when they can see flexibility to meet unforeseen contingencies is part of any course of action. Emphasizing this factor during the closing will be an important plus to the presenter if these types of individuals are in the group.

There are no magic answers for preparing and presenting effective persuasive presentations. There are guidelines, however. Perhaps the most important is to choose a tack which encourages group participation, thus providing the audience with maximum opportunity to convince itself.

JOHN D. DRAKE

Communications—
The Art of
Getting Through to People

TRITE AS IT MAY SOUND, it is undeniable that the success of any corporate planner, and indeed any key executive, depends on his ability to communicate effectively. Whatever ideas or recommendations a planner may have, they are of little value if he cannot convey them to others.

Over the years, a variety of formats and methods have been suggested to help people communicate more effectively. These methods range from the Dale Carnegie "Hail, Fellow, Well Met" approach to Transactional Analysis to clinical counseling techniques. Each of these methods has its place in assisting in communications, but application of these methods is often difficult. In fact, frequently these techniques are helpful only after the fact, when the question, "What went wrong?" must be answered. Some are simply too clinical or too complex to be used effectively in day-to-day work-related communications.

In recent years the behavioral sciences have borrowed heavily from the work of Dr. Carl Jung, the famous Swiss psychologist. The present article deals primarily with a rather unique approach to communications that was derived from some of Jung's work. This approach is called "I Speak Your Language," hereafter referred to as I-SPEAK. As we shall demonstrate, it can easily be used by corporate planners in presenting their ideas and thoughts. In essence, it has to do with "getting through" to others. I-SPEAK is built around four fundamental premises:

1. Each of us has a recognized, habitual communication style. For example, we talk fast, or cautiously, or with a great deal of feeling and emotion.
2. It is possible to recognize and identify the communication style of others after a relatively short exposure to it.
3. We communicate most effectively with those individuals who have styles similar to our own, and we have significant difficulty com-

municating with those whose communication styles are different from ours.

4. We can readily adapt our style of communication in order to "speak the language" of those with whom we are conversing.

The advantage of the I-SPEAK approach is that it enables individuals to plan in advance the best way to make a statement or presentation to maximize the likelihood of its being heard receptively. Unless one adapts his communication style to that of his intended listener, the probability that he will be "tuned out" and not listened to is great. Most planners, for example, have experienced the frustration of attempting to convey to a busy executive a newly developed idea about some future course of action and finding it almost impossible to get the listener to focus on what is being presented. Another frustrating experience for a planner is to receive the "I've only got five minutes, what's on your mind?" response. In I-SPEAK terms, that question in the preceding sentence is symptomatic of a particular communication style, one frequently found among executives. The communication style of many planners, however, is quite different, and it is this difference that creates communication barriers.

The value of understanding I-SPEAK communication styles may become more evident as we learn a little about the type of individual that uses each style. Jung identified four different types: Intuitor, Thinker, Feeler, and Senser.

Intuitors. Intuitors are individuals who look forward to the future with a global perspective. They are good with concepts and often are able to relate diverse thoughts and ideas into meaningful wholes. Most Intuitors display good innovative ability and skill at looking at "the big picture." Most planners are Intuitors.

Thinkers. Thinkers are characterized by a desire to relate to their environment by thinking things through. As a result, Thinkers usually develop good analytical skills. Since facts and data are the tools with which one thinks, most Thinkers focus on being precise and systematic in their approach to problems. Many accountants are Thinkers. While the Intuitor's time orientation is the future, the Thinker typically focuses on the entire spectrum. Thinkers want to know about the factors that lead up to a particular situation (historical background), what is happening now, and what the outcome will be.

Feelers. Feelers prefer to deal with situations according to their "feeling" perceptions; that is, they frequently respond with "gut reactions." Feelers are highly sociable and use empathy and understanding in their solutions to problems. Most of them are perceptive of others' needs and are able to discern what lies beneath the surface. Their time orientation is essentially toward the past. Many sales persons are Feelers.

Sensers. The Senser's time orientation is immediate, the here and now. As a result, most Sensers respond to things they can touch, see, and feel—things of an immediate nature. They tend to be action oriented and are often valued for their ability to get things done. Sensers are often found in production and high-pressure job situations.

ANALYZE YOUR COMMUNICATION STYLE

Indicate below the order in which you feel each ending best describes you. In the space provided fill in the appropriate number (1, 2, 3, or 4), using 1 for the ending that best fits you, 2 for the next one that fits you, 3 for the next, and 4 for the ending that is least appropriate for you.

1. I am likely to impress others as
   a. practical and to the point.   a. _____
   b. emotional and somewhat stimulating.   b. _____
   c. astute and logical.   c. _____
   d. intellectually oriented and somewhat complex.   d. _____

2. When I work on a project, I
   a. want it to be stimulating and involve lively interaction with others.   a. _____
   b. concentrate to make sure it is systematically or logically developed.   b. _____
   c. want to be sure it has a tangible "pay-out" that will justify my spending time and energy on it.   c. _____
   d. am most concerned about whether it "breaks ground" or advances knowledge.   d. _____

3. When I think about a job problem, I usually
   a. think about concepts and relationships between events.   a. _____
   b. analyze what preceded it and what I plan next.   b. _____
   c. remain open and responsive to my feelings about the matter.   c. _____
   d. concentrate on reality, on things as they are right now.   d. _____

4. When confronted by others with a different point of view, I can usually make progress by
   a. getting at least one or two specific commitments on which we can build later.   a. _____

b. trying to place myself in the "others' shoes."   b. _____

c. keeping my composure and helping others to see things simply and logically.   c. _____

d. relying on my basic ability to conceptualize and pull ideas together.   d. _____

5. In communicating with others, I may

   a. express unintended boredom with talk that is too detailed.   a. _____

   b. convey impatience with those who express ideas that they have obviously not thought through carefully.   b. _____

   c. show little interest in thoughts and ideas that exhibit little or no originality.   c. _____

   d. tend to ignore those who talk about long-range implications and direct my attention to what needs to be done right now.   d. _____

To obtain an approximate indication of your primary communication style, enter below the number (1, 2, 3, or 4) you wrote next to each ending:

	Intuitor	Thinker	Feeler	Senser
Question 1	d. _____	c. _____	b. _____	a. _____
Question 2	d. _____	b. _____	a. _____	c. _____
Question 3	a. _____	b. _____	c. _____	d. _____
Question 4	d. _____	c. _____	b. _____	a. _____
Question 5	c. _____	b. _____	a. _____	d. _____
Totals	_____	_____	_____	_____

Now total each column. The column that has the smallest sum indicates your favored communication style; the column with the largest total is your least-used style.

ANALYZE SOMEONE ELSE'S STYLE

It is often possible to diagnose the communication style of another without actually meeting the person. Letters, proposals, memorandums, and telephone conversations all provide valuable information on which to base a preliminary diagnosis of style. The environment and surroundings in which the person works provide even more meaningful clues.

Here are a few environmental conditions that could help you determine an individual's style:

Condition of Desk

Examination of the condition of another's desk provides quick and easy clues to the worker's communication style.

Intuitor. Intuitors are usually involved in a variety of projects. They commonly have books piled on the desk, particularly those of the survey or theoretical variety. Reference works and scholarly reports may be in evidence, and are often in two piles, indicating that the individual is comparing two sets of data. The key here is a fairly large number of books.

Thinker. The Thinker's desk is likely to be neat and orderly, with only those things currently being worked with in sight. An electric calculator may be in evidence.

Feeler. In addition to business papers, personal memorabilia, such as photographs, meaningful paperweights, and pictures of the family, are often on the desk.

Senser. The Senser's desk is likely to be the most cluttered and disorderly, with piles of papers, correspondence, and projects in progress in no apparent arrangement. The general picture is one of chaos and disorganization.

Office Style

Once you have made a tentative diagnosis of style on the basis of an individual's desk, you could quickly look around the office and see additional confirming clues as to communication style. Let's consider the styles again.

Intuitor. If paintings are on the wall, they are often of an abstract nature. There undoubtedly will be a large number of books—almost always a bookcase. Again examination of the books shows them to be more of a theoretical or conceptual nature than practical. If any attention has been paid to surroundings, they are apt to be imaginative and somewhat avant-garde, or at least "different." Some Intuitors—particularly at the executive level—have offices resembling mini-think-tanks. A round conference table is typical.

Thinker. Here the office surroundings are apt to impress one as being neat, simple, sometimes sterile. Charts and graphs on the wall or on display are also clues. There will often be evidence of IBM computer printouts—a source of data that almost no Thinker can resist. Furnishings are apt to be tasteful and conventional.

Feeler. The Feeler's office, like his or her desk, often will be personalized. On the wall there are apt to be photographs of company outings, souvenirs, citations, and other personal documents. If there are books, they will probably be autobiographical and people-oriented. This office is likely to be the most warm and colorful of the offices of the various types.

Senser. Here again the office will be in the same state as the desk, that is, cluttered with half-finished projects and with piles of papers. It is common to find two or three briefcases. If there are paintings on the wall, they are apt to depict action or motion, to be aerial photographs of plants, or to be pictures of products. Many piles of papers in a somewhat disorganized office would be the most typical clue.

Clearly examination of an individual's office provides many clues to the person's style of communication. When you meet this person, additional information will be given by the mode and manner of dress.

Mode of Dress

As we will see, modes of dress of the different types have the same general characteristics as their desks and offices.

Intuitor. This type is often not fashion conscious, and may look more like an absent-minded professor than a business executive. These individuals care little about their clothing and the manner in which they present themselves. Those who are concerned with fashion may be quite stylish, although their clothes are likely to be somewhat out of the ordinary.

Thinker. This individual will strike one as being neatly dressed with careful attention paid to details such as color coordination and accessories. Most Thinkers will dress in a slightly conservative, understated manner. For men ties are often a significant clue: Thinkers tend to wear ties with geometric designs. A woman Thinker is likely to dress in solid or tweed suits, certainly nothing exotic.

Feeler. Of all the types, Feelers care most about how they and others appear. The Feeler tries to make an impression, and therefore frequently will wear casual and quite colorful clothing.

Senser. The Senser is often too busy to be neat. A male Senser typically would have his jacket off, his sleeves rolled up, and his tie loosened. A female Senser would probably be wearing something loose and casual, with few accessories, if any. Most Sensers incline toward simplicity in dress. If a person strikes you as being down-to-earth and action oriented, you are probably talking to a Senser.

A person's desk, office, and dress are only a few of the areas in which clues as to style of communication can be found. The other major diagnostic category, of course, is what an individual says.

Speech

Listed below are phrases that would typically be used by individuals of the four different types. Note that three examples are provided for each style.

Intuitor
a. "Your idea is only going to create more problems for us next year." (The important clue is "next year." Intuitors are future oriented.)
b. "How does your approach tie into our concept of . . . ?" (The clue phrase is "tie into our concept." Intuitors deal primarily with the world of concepts and ideas.)
c. "So what's so unique about it?" (The clue word here is "unique." Intuitors are interested in innovation and new ideas.)

Thinker
a. "What other options do you have?" (The clue word is "options." Thinkers like to think things through and weigh alternatives.)
b. "Let's go through your recommendation step by step." (The clue is "step by step." Thinkers like to work in an organized, systematic way.)
c. "You are going to have to be more precise about it before. . . ." (The clue word is "precise." Thinkers often use words like "exact" and "precise.")

Feeler
a. "Who else is using the program?" (The clue phrase is "who else." Feelers put considerable stock in the opinions of those whom they respect.)
b. "Most of the people in that department will not like the changes you are proposing." (The clue words are "most of the people in that department will not like." Feelers are very concerned about impact on others in the organization.)
c. "The way I feel about it is. . . ." (The clue word is "feel." Feelers will often use the word "feel" rather than "think.")

Senser
a. "I've only got five minutes, what's on your mind?" (The clue words are "only got five minutes." Sensers are always in a hurry.)
b. "You're nitpicking. Why don't you get it onstream and we'll worry about the exceptions later." (The clue words are "get it onstream." Sensers are impatient to get thoughts into action.)

    c. "Never mind all the details, how much is it going to save us?" (The clue words are "never mind all the details." Sensers have an abhorrence for minutiae—they like to get to the main point quickly.)

SPEAK TO THE OTHER PERSON'S STYLE

Knowing the fundamental characteristics of each style is basic to the diagnosis of an individual's style. The final step in this process is, of course, to be able to ascertain quickly the style of the person with whom you are communicating and to adapt your communication—whether written or verbal—to match that individual's style. This is referred to by the behavioral scientists as "opening in parallel," that is, trying to speak the language of the other individual so that he is responsive to and interested in what is being said.

Essentially, there are two ways in which one can modify presentations to match the style of the person being communicated with. These are:

1. Modify *how* one goes about presenting one's ideas—fast, slow, detailed, conceptual, emotional, and so forth.
2. Modify *what* words and phrases are used. Certain words have more meaning to some styles than others. As will be shown, it is possible to become discriminating in deciding which strengths of one's ideas or recommendations will have the most impact and meaning on persons of each style.

Intuitor. The Intuitor is a person whose time orientation is the future. His world is that of concepts and ideas. In communicating with an Intuitor, several suggestions can help you speak the Intuitor's language. These are:

1. *Allow ample time.* Intuitors frequently respond in terms of an intuitive thought pattern by linking one thought with the next. Often they seem to go off on tangents as their mind considers one thought after the other. Most Intuitors do not place a high premium on immediacy, and they enjoy the speculation of thinking a problem through by using their imagination in discussion.

2. *Be conceptual.* In your opening comments try to relate the specific topic at hand to a broader concept or idea. For example, if you have a specific suggestion for saving money, you might say, "I know, Mr. Intuitor, that you are very concerned with improving our return on investment. I have an idea that I think will contribute toward that concept."

3. *Stress uniqueness.* Try to mention something in your presentation about the uniqueness of your idea. Intuitors respond well to anything

new, out of the ordinary, or creative. Saying something like, "Here is something unique that has never been tried before," would strike a responsive chord with Intuitors.

4. *Emphasize future value.* Relate the impact that your idea or suggestion might have on the future. For example, "This idea will pay off even more next year."

5. *Do not stint on words.* When writing to an Intuitor, do not be afraid to use a lengthy narrative text. Intuitors read a lot and will not be dismayed by extended presentations. It might be well, however, to start your letter or proposal by indicating something about the *underlying* concepts or principles upon which your ideas, thoughts, or recommendations are built. In other words, start off with a global, broad treatment and work toward the more specific.

Thinker. The Thinker wants to think things through the same way you have and, therefore, needs background data to arrive at your conclusions by his own thinking. Be prepared to have plenty of facts to support your position. To determine how much data to present, ask yourself what a Thinker will need to reach the same conclusion you have reached.

1. *Be precise.* Avoid such phrases as "Generally speaking . . . ," or "It would appear that . . . ," or "Approximately . . . ," etc. Where it is not possible to be precise, state ranges ("ten to twenty-two percent") or probabilities ("forty percent of the time . . . will happen").

2. *Organize your presentations.* One possible format for organization would be chronological order. Tell what led up to the situation, what is evident at present, and what the outcome is likely to be. Another organizational scheme would be outline form. Break down your recommendations, ideas, or proposals into series of steps or phrases. It is very meaningful to a Thinker to hear, "This project has three parts: a, b, and c. Let's go through it step by step."

3. *Include alternatives.* A statement that rapidly turns off a Thinker is, "I've got it all worked out, and here is the answer." It is perfectly all right to recommend a course of action, but the Thinker likes to know you have considered other alternatives. You might say, "There are three approaches we can take. I recommend Approach A, but here are the pros and cons of Approaches B and C for you to review."

4. *Do not rush Thinkers.* Most of them want to think things through. When a Thinker says "I'd like to study this for a while," it is often not a stall, but a true need to study and think about the idea.

5. *Outline your proposal.* When writing to a Thinker, outline form is most appropriate, using sub-indentations of 1, 2, 3, and a, b, c.

Feeler. The Feeler likes to deal with others on a personal basis. Be informal. Conferences over lunch, over coffee, or in a friendly atmosphere are good.

1. *Allow for small talk.* Remember the Feeler determines his attitudes about you and your ideas through his emotions. Small talk allows the Feeler to evaluate the "vibes" between you. Do not begin the business part of your discussion until the Feeler gives you the clue to start. For example, Feelers will often make a comment such as "Well, what can I do for you today?"

2. *Explain how your proposal or idea can have a positive impact on others.* Show the relationship between your recommendations and its impact on people.

3. *Show how your idea has worked well in the past.* Whenever possible, show the traditional basis of what you are presenting.

4. *Indicate how others react.* The Feeler will respond favorably if people he knows and respects also think well of your suggestions and ideas.

5. *Use an informal writing style.* When writing to a Feeler, be informal, opening and closing with a personal comment. The best way is to write as if you were speaking face to face.

Senser. Be brief. The Senser responds quickly. He is always busy, and if you can start your conversation off with a comment such as "I only need five minutes of your time," you catch the Senser's attention.

1. *Indicate the results or conclusions first.* The Senser has neither time nor interest to wade through how you arrived at your position. Tell him first what the conclusions are and then he will tell you whether he is interested in hearing more.

2. *Do not offer many alternatives.* The Senser will want to know your "one best recommendation." It is all right to indicate that you have considered many options, but that your opinion is that alternative A is best.

3. *Stress the practicality of your ideas.* Indicate how your proposal will bring immediate tangible results.

4. *Use visual displays.* Remember, the Senser deals best with things he can touch, see, and feel. A graph often says as much as several pages. A replica or model of your idea or suggestion speaks volumes.

5. *Be brief.* When writing to a Senser, be succinct. One page is best. Proposals or letters of several pages most likely will end up in a pile of papers to be read; it may be a long time before the Senser gets to it. If your recommendation is complex and lengthy, attach an appendix. Limit

your cover sheet to one page and indicate the subject, the outcome, and your recommendation.

MODIFYING YOUR PRESENTATION OF WHAT YOU SAY

Certain phrases have more meaning for some styles than others. Some examples of phrases that would have significance for persons of the various styles are:

Intuitor
"We have a unique approach for you to consider."
"This idea is going to pay off even more in the years ahead."
"This idea ties in very well with the principle of. . . ."
Thinker
"I've got the entire plan spelled out here, step by step."
"There are several alternative ways to tackle your problem."
"Why don't you take our program and study it for a few days?"
Feeler
"Everyone is going to like the way it cuts down on overtime."
"Your friend, Bill Smith, over at XYZ Company, is also taking this approach."
"The plan we have here has traditionally worked for us. If you talk with those who have used it, you will find that it has been most effective."
Senser
"I only need five minutes of your time."
"We can start on it tomorrow!"
"I'm going to skip the details and just hit the highlights."

Planners can utilize the I-SPEAK concept by making a list of all the advantages of a plan or program. Then, opposite each benefit or feature, determine which of the four styles would be most receptive to that particular comment. By selecting the most appealing benefits for your presentations, you should be able to stimulate the interest of those whom you must influence.

In summary, I-SPEAK is a new and innovative tool to help command the attention of others. It provides planners with specific ways to effectively present their ideas, both personally and in writing.

JOHN D. DRAKE

Managing Conflict— The Art of Gaining Commitment

EVERYONE FACES problems in obtaining agreement or commitment from someone else every day of his life. In business this is particularly important for persons in sales and staff assignments in which the individual must influence without authority, that is, where commitment or agreement is needed, but the influencer cannot order or demand cooperation. Obviously, this is an issue that planners must deal with constantly—the problem of getting their ideas and recommendations accepted.

ADVERSARY MODEL

There are many ways by which an individual can influence others. Best known, and most frequently used, is the "hard sell" approach. At professional and managerial levels the hard sell is not blatant, but is usually manifested in sophisticated versions that come across as "pressure," "name dropping," and "persuasion" (threat). In essence, all these represent an adversary approach to gaining commitment. In effect, these approaches say, "I'm right; you're wrong." They lead to win/lose discussions. Almost all adversary models can be identified by what occurs after the other person (opponent) says "no" or disagrees. The classic response to the negative is for the influencer to say, "yes, but . . ." and then retort with more data or information to support his position.

The reason the adversary approach is rarely effective is that it leads to argument. There is an old saying that no one wins an argument. While this may be trite, it also happens to be true. Usually neither person objectively examines the other's point of view; each is caught up in the process of thinking about what else he is going to say to defend his own position. Thus, time goes on, dialogue takes place, but no real understanding or commitment occurs.

A NEW APPROACH: THE INFLUENCE OR COMMITMENT MODEL

Behavioral scientists today strongly advocate the use of communication models that minimize or eliminate the emotional elements (fear, anger, etc.) that typically arise from the adversary approach, so that the opponent will look at the influencer's idea or data in an objective, rational way. In such cases, the goal is to find the best answer—not a win/lose response; not a compromise, but a win/win solution—so that both parties leave the discussion with commitment because they are convinced that the best solution had been agreed upon. To help accomplish this kind of true commitment, the author has developed a commitment model (as opposed to an adversary model), which is described briefly below.

The influence or commitment model is based on the theoretical principle that for one individual to get another to change his mind or opinion, somehow the second person must internally—in his own words and his own terms—see that what is being presented is indeed a "good deal" for him. In this process the influencer becomes a catalyst to help the opponent convince himself. (Although in this model the two parties are not adversaries, for convenience we continue to use the term "opponent" for the individual being influenced.)

The model is related to the theories of management associated with MacGregor's Theory Y and other participative concepts. In order for this approach to be successful, the influencer must have the desire to obtain full acceptance and commitment from both parties. In achieving this end he must attempt to understand the attitudes, feelings, and opinions of his opponent. In so doing, however, he incurs the risk of being shown that he is wrong or that his original proposition has flaws.

In view of the above comments it should be clear that it takes a strong individual to operate in a participative manner, particularly in conflict. Once the door is open to the opinions and ideas of others, the influencer is often put on the defensive. The secret of success in influencing another lies in the influencer's ability to avoid becoming defensive when he is attacked or challenged. People who lack self-confidence will find this difficult. Those who are successful in using the influence model are usually characterized by maturity and a high level of self-assurance.

Application of the influence model begins once the opponent has said "no." Of course, people often say "no" other than by using the word. In fact, any response that is not positive must be dealt with as if it were negative, in the sense that the influencer must understand why the person is not positively going along with his ideas or suggestions.

Once someone indicates "no," an influencer has two options. He can either respond by providing additional data in an effort to overcome the objection. He can say, in effect, "yes, but. . . ." This response will lead to an argumentative or adversary posture. Or instead of coming back with the counterargument, he can ask a question or restate the opponent's position. The second approach is the start of the influence model.

STEP I. Explore the Differences. As soon as the influencer gets a negative response to the question, "What do you think of my idea?" he should avoid offering additional information and attempt to understand the other person's point of view. He can achieve this only be listening, by trying to draw out the other person so that the other person begins to discuss overtly his position.

STEP II. Sharpen the Differences. Once the opponent's point of view is understood, it is then possible for the influencer to point out the differences between the two positions and to test the extent to which he has understood the problems being expressed or felt by the opponent. An easy way for him to do this is to summarize his perception of the whole situation. He might say, for example, "Let's see now where we stand. As I understand it, you agree to A, B, C, and D, but we are still apart on E and F. Is that right?"

Once the differences are sharpened in this way, one of two things will happen. The opponent will say, "Yes, that's right," in which case the influencer can move on the Step III. Or the opponent will say, "No, that's not exactly right; there are some other problems here . . ." which is a signal to the influencer that he must go back to Step I and explore these differences further. When he again feels he understands his opponent's point of view, he can again test and sharpen the differences.

STEP III. Integrate the Differences. Once the two parties agree on what their differences are, the influencer can help bring about a resolution by creating a climate in which the opponent begins to weigh objectively the influencer's ideas or recommendations. The influencer does this by offering alternatives. He can say, for example, "If this isn't appropriate, suppose we do it this way. How would that be?"

In offering alternatives, the influencer need not compromise his position. He can even offer alternatives that are more favorable to his point of view. The main point is that the opponent should weigh objectively the original proposal as well as any alternatives. In this process the opponent often accepts the influencer's original position because he is now looking at it in a reasonably objective and nondefensive manner. If the original proposal has merits of its own, the opponent may convince himself that this is the most desirable course of action.

The influencer should recognize that he need not rely on himself to provide the alternatives; he can help the opponent to develop his own alternatives. He can say, for example, "How would you like us to approach this so that the proposal will be more acceptable to you?"

STEP IV. Obtaining Commitment or Agreement. Once the alternatives have been stated, the influencer's role becomes one of creating a situation in which the opponent can think through the various alternatives. The objective here is to help the opponent select that which he is convinced, in his own mind, is best for him. In a sense, we are creating a climate in which the opponent sells himself on an idea. Since he has convinced himself of what the best option is, the commitment that the influencer sought is usually obtained.

When this occurs, frequently the opponent begins to look at his viewpoint in a different perspective. Moreover, as new thoughts enter his perceptual framework, he almost always alters his position from a radical to a more central posture—usually one closer to the influencer's position—even though the influencer provides no data or input.

The influencer can best explore the other person's viewpoint by using open-ended questions, pauses, and by restating, in his own words, what he understands his opponent to be saying.

Part VII
PERSONALITIES

ROBERT J. ALLIO

The Galloping Cyberneticist

STAFFORD BEER has long been concerned with the rate of change which technological achievement represents, and comments: "It is to the rate rather than to the changes themselves that we have to adapt." He defines planning as the process of adjusting to a change in the environment. From his long inquiry into the task of organization and control in a fast-changing environment, he concludes that the line/staff distinction is now dysfunctional. Planners and other staff personnel are making many decisions because they have the information and the decision has to be made quickly. Dr. Beer argues that these people should be given the responsibility to match the power they in fact enjoy. That power derives from information, which should not be confused with the accumulation of data. Data becomes information only at the point where it effects changes in the individual or company receiving it.

Beer has long been a key figure in the fields of cybernetics, operations research, and management science. He has been a full-time senior manager in four British companies, one a large publishing house and another United Steel, where he founded and directed for 13 years what became the largest civil operations research group. He has acted as consultant to international organizations such as the UN and the OECD and to a number of governments, including those of the United States, Britain, France, and Chile, in the sciences of management and effective organization ("the science of effective organization" is his preferred definition of cybernetics).

Dr. Beer is Visiting Professor of Cybernetics at Manchester University, England, as well as Adjunct Professor of Statistics and Operations Research at the University of Pennsylvania. A conference speaker, broadcaster, and writer, he has published more than 150 papers and articles. Probably his best known books are *Cybernetics and Management* (1959), *Brain of the Firm* (1972), and *Platform for Change* (1975). In his spare time, Stafford Beer paints and writes poetry in his country home in Wales.

PLANNING REVIEW: In your writings and research over the past years you have been concerned with many important management issues. As a start, could you recapitulate the relationship between cybernetic theory and the planning process?

BEER: I always define cybernetics as the science of effective organization. This changes Norbert Wiener's original definition ["the study of control and communication in machines and living beings"], but I don't like his word "control" because it has the wrong connotation.

PR: You mean it sounds authoritarian?

BEER: Yes. Managers are supposed to organize effectively, and if there is a science of effective organization, managers should know about it. That's the first part of my answer: cybernetics ought to provide scientific insights into the total management structure and process. Planning is something that managers do within the structure. My key point about planning is that it requires active decisions; it is not a process of compiling reports, making forecasts, and so forth. This leads to the issue of how managers collect information to make those decisions, and how they can disseminate information to implement the decisions. I believe that cybernetics can improve the process of management enormously. What I would say to the managers is: "You are in the business of regulating a company and I am in the science of such regulation; we ought to get together."

PR: You stress information and communication as important elements of the management process. In my experience, organizations very often run aground not only because they fail to communicate internally and don't maintain the feedback loops, but also because the quality of what they communicate is poor. Isn't it becoming more and more difficult to get good information?

BEER: Yes, most people don't differentiate between communication and information; they confuse information with data. You can easily fill your files with data; with computers you can do it even more easily—and even more expensively. I maintain that data becomes information when it changes you, and information initiates an active decision when it changes you—and the company. When I refer to the scientific analysis of company structure, information is the commodity that I would use to describe the structure. The structure is not a series of boxes linked with lines on a piece of paper. Nor is it the way the corridors are laid out, in the architectural sense. The structure describes who relates to whom in terms of information. I regard the word "communication" more in a psychological sense: are you able to convey the information you've got? But if you haven't got the structure to turn the data into information, you can't even begin.

PR: In some of your earlier writings you identify one of the tasks of the planner or the manager as the design of structure for the organization. And yet a managerial axiom claims that structure should follow strategy. I'm confused by this apparent paradox: can you have structure before you have strategy?

BEER: I really don't like slogans, but I regard this as an iterative process. I would cheerfully agree to start with structure in the sense that one thing we know about the strategy from the outset is that you wish your organization to be a viable system. There is a basic skeletal structure without which, I contend, you don't have a viable system at all. Cybernetics makes an analysis of what constitutes a viable system, and this already determines something about the structure. Precisely how it is put together, and where the amplifiers and attenuators are in it, are determined by your strategy.

PR: You make the point that planning is a continuous process. I would suggest that for some organizations, a strategy can be selected that will remain constant over ten, twenty, thirty years. In other organizations, the environment is changing so rapidly that you need a new strategy every day. Taking those extremes, which are not so uncommon in the real world, one could argue that in the first case, planning is not needed and in the second case, planning is impractical. Yet it is precisely in that second case where the cybernetic notion applies.

BEER: I think you are in danger of reducing the concept to absurdity and then complaining that it is absurd. The environment is changing pretty fast, yes. You've only got to look at electronics to see the impact on any organization, whether it is in the electronics business or not. Companies continuously have the problem of adapting to change. What you need is machinery to keep the company in gear with that change—a different concept.

PR: By machinery, of course, you're talking about more than computers.

BEER: I'm still talking about the organization, the structure, but I mean the dynamic, information-gathering structure. Information is the key to it all, for the reason that command always lies where the information coheres. I saw this very clearly from my study of neurocybernetics and the brain. When I began to study organizations I found it was equally true. For an example of what I mean, suppose a company is going to buy a cyclotron or a computer or some very large technical equipment. The more expensive it is, the higher the committee level that has to approve it—and the less they know about it. So the decision is really going to be determined by two young men way off in a small office that nobody's heard of. They are going to concoct the story that will eventually get approved at the higher level, and the truth of the matter is that the command lies with them.

PR: No power without information.

BEER: Precisely—that is the whole secret and we'd better admit it. It is a total waste of time to have committee structures and approval patterns that don't recognize this reality.

PR: Do you mean that in most organizations, as we know them today, top management still make decisions that are ill-informed and arbitrary?

BEER: Well, that happens in bad organizations. In good organizations, project proposals go up and up until someone has enough authority associated with his signature to make a decision. But if he has any sense, he's taking the advice of his subordinates, isn't he?

PR: What then is the role of top management?

BEER: In the situation we have described, none. Decision-making is hinged on the false premise that as you become more senior and get more command of money, you get more knowledge about everything.

PR: You've often claimed that decision-making reaches its epitome in the "war room." In such a control center, all information on the operations of the firm would be collected in real time, processed, and presented to management for them to take decisions. I think this suggests to many people the dehumanization of the decision process.

BEER: Not at all. The whole idea of the control room, in the first place, is to provide the decision-takers with an environment that is human, not inhuman. We are so used to the boardroom with its polished table and its piles of papers that we think that's human—but it isn't. Nobody has access to information in such a boardroom. Chief executive officers are playing a ritual. I want to replace that ritual dance in the boardroom with an on-line control apparatus whereby people trying to take a decision can quickly command whatever information they want and can form real teams to solve their problems. Company management often boxes with each other and then defers the matter to the next meeting. I'm pointing to the humanization that results when we feed decision-takers the kind of information they can assimilate, not computer output which they can't; information in a form that makes sense to them. For instance, you rarely see photographs in a boardroom. Since most of the people taking the decisions have never seen, say, the plant they are talking about, why not show them a photograph of it? That's humanizing at the level of the decision-takers.

The control room I built for President Allende in Santiago, Chile, was tied directly to each of the major factories in the country. Real-time information on production and costs thus was available to management. But people are led by the fact that the control room looked like a set out of a science-fiction film to conclude that the decision-making process was dehumanizing. The intentions and the reality were both the opposite.

PR: The kind of information that is easy for a well-functioning corporation to access includes data on markets and product acceptance and costs. But nonquantitative data is an integral part of the decision-making process. The values and idiosyncrasies of the board may influence decisions far more than the discounted-cash-flow return on investment.

BEER: I agree.

PR: How do you make allowance for qualitative information in your decision-making process? How can you cope with the quirks of the board of directors?

BEER: Well, I feel that this gang of people is going to be like that anyway—that's the first part of the answer. To give them better rather than worse structure to work with can be bad, in the sense that it is absurd to pretend that by giving them a good structure you make them better people. Intuitive input to decisions is pretty damn important. As a matter of fact, when I talk about OR I always talk about narrowing the area of uncertainty. Anyone who says, "I'm going to do a linear program on this, and by God that's the answer," is out of his mind. Optimization routines ignore the possibility that if anything goes wrong with one of the million variables you may go too far. Any sensible manager wants some margin of safety, but we haven't yet got the mathematics to calculate these margins. That's where intuition comes in.

PR: Considerable advances have been made recently in the mathematics of discontinuous and divergent phenomena; that is, in analyzing situations where gradual changes in input lead to abrupt changes in performance. Can't these new developments in catastrophe theory be applied by planners?*

---

* E. C. Zeeman, "Catastrophe Theory," *Scientific American*, April 1976, p. 65.

BEER: As a matter of fact, that's what I'm working on now. For example, we need to help managers select strategies that yield payoffs without too much risk.

PR: What do you see as the next level in the evolution of planning? Some have forecast that planning, like management by objectives (MBO), management information systems (MIS), and PPBS, will fail to hold the interest of management.

BEER: The way I define planning, yes, but the way it's now becoming a slogan, no, because it will go the way of MBO and PPBS. As I define planning, with a small *p*, it is simply the process of adjusting to a change in environment; you can't stop doing that or you go bust. Now you can change the words, and planning as a staff function may go out. But if organizations don't adjust to their environment, they crash.

PR: With that settled, what then is the role of the planner in an organization?

BEER: I guess what you mean by that question is the guy who has "planner" on the door, the man who is helping the manager to make his decision. We must always focus on the manager, because he's the real decision-maker. The manager needs a team, and he'd better have a good team. I would like that team to be interdisciplinary; sometimes it will need behavioral scientists, sometimes accountants, sometimes planners, sometimes OR men, sometimes cyberneticists.

PR: The plant manager is usually preoccupied with day-to-day operations, and the pressure of the P & L statement gives him a very high discount factor for future-oriented actions. How can we get him to plan?

BEER: That's the big challenge for corporate management. Drastic environmental change is beating us. The manager always had to plan into the future, always had to commit the resources so that the future would be different. At a time when change is very slow, you can do that bit of your management job in your bath—and one bath a month would be sufficient. But keeping up with change these days can consume half your time.

Management education must encourage management to put an equal investment into the future as into the present. It is a fact of life that business is changing faster and that managers and organizations are not adapting. If you want the evidence, look at the crashing institutions all around us. The planner has to facilitate the ability of the manager to plan.

PR: Does this concept deny the planner his role as change agent? Are you saying that if the manager doesn't want to listen, the planner should go find someone else who will? Isn't that an abrogation of the planner's responsibility to the corporation?

BEER: I'm not suggesting he should abandon his company until he has had a damn good try. Yes, planners are agents of change and the manager needs prodding. Someone must say, "You are so busy managing, have you noticed that the building just fell down?" Planners become agents of change when they change their managers and their managing in accordance with the way the world is moving. The dilemma always is that the manager is looking for helpers who will reinforce preconceived opinions rather than changing them. But my main point is that the formalization of planning, as we know it, is manifestly dysfunctional.

PR: You're advising a practicing planner to break free of the ritual and into the on-line decision-making?

BEER: Right. The staff/line organization of most companies doesn't work. It may have made sense in the nineteenth century. A staff man could appraise situations, give you reports, and you had plenty of time to think about them. Decisions now have got to be taken so fast that the staff men are effectively taking them. When I now suggest that planners, to use their generic title, should be on-line, managers accuse me of seeking power for people like myself. Not so, exactly the opposite: these people already have the power; for God's sake, give them the responsibility.

PR: Let me ask you to return to the question of management and planner education. What's missing in the current curricula?

BEER: I think that the university curricula, in England especially, are very short on quantification. By that I mean sensible quantification, not mathematical masturbation; there's a very big difference. I think we're ignoring epistemology, the theory of knowledge, and this is a subject I want to see taught. Scientists often don't understand what they are doing because they haven't studied what we know and how we know it. We've got a lecturer in epistemology in the Manchester Business School, I'm happy to say.

PR: You haven't mentioned cybernetics?

BEER: Of course, I can't finish without including cybernetics. But the North American concept of cybernetics is not the view of the founding fathers—they were friends of mine and I think I can say that. It isn't engineering cybernetics we are talking about and it isn't about automation or robots or about bullying people. The rest of the trouble is getting the balance right. If you look at the great schools of management around the world, they are all lopsided: some of them are full to the gunwales with behavioral scientists and some are full of mathematicians. The team around the manager to help him must be interdisciplinary and, therefore, the planner should be interdisciplinary to equip himself to be a member of that team.

PR: Let me explore with you the issue of national planning. It seems to me that critics point to the difficulties of corporate planning to bolster their pessimism about successful national planning. Greater size, complexity, variety, and inflexibility are compounded at the national level. There is also the specter of loss of freedom. Yet in your work for Allende's administration in Chile you obviously felt that a national planning system was feasible.

BEER: Remember my definition of planning as the process of adjusting to the environment. In national planning, the formalization and ritualization have gone further than in the corporation, with even more bizarre results. What is normally paraded as a national plan is total nonsense and should be scrapped. Nonetheless, we do have to adjust to the world. Information even with computers is nine months out of date, so you probably lock onto the wrong half of the cycle. As a result, you take the decision to inflate just at the time when it's all over and you should be deflating. Then you pay armies of econometricians to try and discount this lag—which is impossible.

The clue to responding to change is to do it in real time. In my opinion, we now have the facility to regulate in real time. As for Chile, as you said, people's instinctive reaction to that is to say "My freedom's gone." This is pure hysteria. What I was trying to do in Chile was design a system that operated in real time. Detailed information about any one level could not get higher than one level above, and this was my prescription to avoid tyranny. Okay, that system could be abused, and you've got to take every conceivable step to stop abuse. I am utterly alert to the problem and doing everything I can about it. But while people are wasting their energies criticizing me for this, all sorts of other things are happening. Freedom is going out of the window all of the time, and nobody's taking any notice.

PR: You would argue then that the potential that national planning offers for improved efficiency, let's say of resource allocation, does not necessarily entail any abrogation of freedom.

BEER: Exactly.

PR: Are you willing to forecast that national planning will be operational somewhere soon—is that a real possibility?

BEER: No, I think national planning has been bureaucratized before it got started, before it's solved any problems. But sooner or later someone is going to have to try to develop a system that works.

ROBERT J. ALLIO

Interviewing Professor Mintzberg's "Right Brain"

PROBABLY EVERY PLANNER, while reading an article about managing, has felt a twinge of discomfort or gnaw of disbelief over the discrepancy between management as it is written about and management as it is practiced. According to the canons of business literary tradition, management's style and thought processes are presumed to be logical and orderly. Any MBA soon learns that top management does not behave as if it has read the right textbooks. Usually this discrepancy between real operation and literary tradition is dismissed with the Platonic argument that the real is always flawed when compared to the ideal.

But in 1976, Professor Henry Mintzberg of McGill caused a stir in the business community by observing that the textbook version of how managers operate is a fantasy. Managers may pay lip service to planning and tables of organization, pointed out Mintzberg, but they actually function quite well in near chaos. In a subsequent article, he identified managers as holistic, intuitive thinkers "who revel in ambiguity; in complex, mysterious systems with relatively little order." A record number of readers responded, most of them applauding Mintzberg's revelation.

Professor Mintzberg has synthesized data from some evocative physiological brain experiments with his perceptions of management thought processes. Physiologists now believe that each hemisphere of the brain has special abilities. In most people (right-handed ones) the right hemisphere controls conceptualization, intuition, synthesis, judgment. The left hemisphere employs logic, linear thinking, organizational abilities. According to Mintzberg, much of a manager's work involves such processes as following hunches in the midst of a chaotic problem-solving process, and this indicates that managers have exceptionally well-developed right brains. It is this "right-brainedness" that makes great corporate strategists capable of epoch-making leaps of conclusion. Planners and other staff aides, who Mintzberg says are left-brained, are best suited to taking their direction from these masters of strategy and tidying up the logic in the aftermath of the conclusion. It's a rather startling concept of the planner's role, so *Planning Review* asked Professor Mintzberg to discuss his theories and define his sense of the true function of the planner in more detail.

PLANNING REVIEW: Recent research suggests that the left hemisphere of the brain governs our logical, linear, and systematic thought processes while simultaneously the right hemisphere governs the holistic, relational, and intuitive thought processes. You've set forth the thesis that planners are "left-brained" and managers are "right-brained." That is, one hemisphere is more developed than the other.

MINTZBERG: I don't want to overemphasize that dichotomy. My guess is that people who are attracted to many of the staff positions—planning, operations research, management science, accounting, for example—tend to see the world in more structured and more linear ways than line managers.

PR: You would tend to categorize planners, accountants, and management scientists as professionals who think in a systematic mode. It's somewhat startling to think of managers as adept at a different mode of reasoning.

MINTZBERG: Yes, although I don't want to overemphasize the differentiation because I think managers mix the two. But it seems to me that a great many characteristics of management, and in the practice of managing, suggest it's a job for the right hemisphere. For example: the interruptions in the work, the lack of pattern in the work, the emphasis on verbal forms of communication. In all their tasks, managers have to know how to read a lot more than just the words. They assimilate gestures, feelings, moods. They like the interactive mode. They discourage written reports and management information systems. Everything about what managers do suggests that they employ what seems to be a very intuitive mode of thinking.

PR: So you are suggesting, Henry, that managers prefer soft data and planners prefer hard data.

MINTZBERG: Yes. And I am coming to think the reason this hasn't been more obvious is that management science's notion of measurement as a linear quantitative activity misses a lot of what goes on.

PR: Kelvin, the British mathematician and philosopher, insisted that only those things which can be measured are important. But you would take the position that the most important of a manager's inputs and outputs cannot be measured.

MINTZBERG: Yes, there are plenty of "inexpressibles" in management. This doesn't mean that they go unspoken because we can't articulate them. For instance, in a panel I was on, there was a women to whom I put the question: "What if I said you are attractive?" What am I expressing? Is "attractive" a kind of measurement or is it a Gestalt perception? In other words, am I saying to the woman "On a scale of one to seven, you are six because your nose is a certain shape or you've got big blue eyes"? Or am I reading a configuration of the variables associated with a face and admitting that there is no way to register it on any "Kelvin" scale? And I can go a step further. Sometimes "attractiveness" is definitely not based on facial appearance, but rather on the emission of a calm, relaxed kind of wave instead of an anxious one.

PR: As the song goes, they're emitting "good vibrations."

MINTZBERG: Yes, and that brings us back to where we started because "vibrations" is another Gestalt word like "attractive." We can even look into other people's eyes and see an emotion, like sadness. Somehow we know they have been through some hell recently. Another case: Ask a simple question like "What are you reading?" People respond with their eyebrows, contorting their eyes into frowns. There may be information coming straight from the eyes that we can read but not measure.

PR: Another communication mode.

MINTZBERG: Sure. ESP is a nice, convenient label for the fact that there is a sixth means of communication, and I think there is very little doubt that five means are insufficient to describe the way we communicate.

PR: Perhaps the sixth is the sum of the other five. Let's leave the subject of perception and review some of your current views on strategy, which you've defined as a mediating force between a dynamic environment and a stable operating system. Are planners sensitive to the dynamics of the strategy process?

MINTZBERG: We have traced strategies over time, asking how they change. You find some very surprising things. Some organizations have derived an excellent strategy and kept it for a hundred years. Does an organization need planning if it's not changing its strategy?

PR: But evidence is mounting that the business environment has become more unstable. Discontinuity is increasing; prediction is becoming more and more difficult. Don't businesses need contingency plans and "lifeboat" strategies?

MINTZBERG: Of course. But some situations defy planning, such as when John Foster Dulles went to the Geneva Conference in 1954. What strategic plan was he going to carry in his briefcase for that conference, since the day before they were to discuss the Vietnam issue Dienbienphu fell and then the French government pulled out and everything was topsy-turvy? How can you plan in such an incredibly dynamic situation? What you have to do, it seems to me, is be very flexible and very adaptive. The guy who is going to win is the one who can move fastest, which may mean very centralized decision-making with no planning whatsoever.

PR: My response would be that the initial strategy was not broad enough to accommodate possible changes in the environment. Many organizations find themselves in conflict now because their strategy was formulated last year and today things are different.

MINTZBERG: That's right. Bureaucracy says to the manager: "Give us a strategy. Any strategy. We need to buy machines, we need to hire workers, we need to take action; so give us a strategy without ifs or buts." So the manager formulates a clear strategy. They run with it. Six months later that strategy turns out worse than no strategy because the environment has changed 180 degrees and they are running in the wrong direction. So there are times when the manager should not produce a clear strategy because he can't be sure it's legitimate or because even if he could, it might be premature. The real dilemma is that the bureaucracy needs stability, the environment is changing, and management must mediate between the two.

Planning to me involves, as Drucker says, "making tomorrow's decisions today," but it may increase certain dangers since we don't know what tomorrow is going to look like.

PR: But can't planning increase your flexibility?

MINTZBERG: Planning decreases flexibility, because when you anticipate and put commitments on paper, you announce to your staff what you are going to do. If circumstances force you to repeatedly change your mind, then it becomes very difficult to keep telling everybody, "No, cancel yesterday's plans, we are doing something different today." If you've never issued a plan, you at least don't have this problem. I am not saying you shouldn't issue plans. Planning may have other advantages, but flexibility is not one of them.

PR: You don't seem to believe that the planning staff can make creative contributions to strategy formulation.

MINTZBERG: Probably not as a staff. My conception of a strategy is a plan based on a very complex interpretation of the relationship between the organization and its environment. This may require very sophisticated creative thinking by a single person. It could be that all the really effective strategies come from one very creative person in an organization who synthesizes huge quantities of information in a very adaptive way.

PR: And this creative integrated strategy is "right-brain" work. Hence your argument is that planning, done by left-brainers, tends to impede creativity.

MINTZBERG: Yes. That's not to say that a planner can't be creative. A creative guy who takes charge of a strategy-making process may be called a planner or a manager. Strategy formulation is a learning process that encourages creativity. But planning, as usually viewed in the organization, may interfere with creativity.

What exactly is planning? Can we draw a line between planning and not planning? We must either study planning as a formal technique, as planners do, or else study strategy formulation, encompassing all the decisional activities of managers. Every decision involves future thinking. So what is planning done by managers, exactly? Did they go through steps? Did they sit down at one meeting and say "Now we are assessing environment," and at the next meeting "Now we are assssessing our strengths and weaknesses," and three weeks later "Now we are putting those all together and generating alternative strategies," and come back a week later with "Now we are assessing alternative strategies"? I don't think managers ever do that, in that order. I think they do all those things but they are all mixed and welded together. Do you want to call that planning? It's what I call strategy formulation, in reality a very jumbled thing, not the way it's described in books. What's in the books, if done by anybody, is done by staff people in their own systematic order. What should planners be doing? I think they should have a variety of functions depending on the situation. An organization in a fairly stable situation may want formal planning. I think there is a place for that, but let's not try and superimpose it on creative strategy formulation. A planner's role may be to feed the relevant information to managers so they can make creative forecasts. But the planning should be almost on an ad hoc basis. Just keep pumping managers the data.

PR: How can planners understand the needs of the manager if the manager is "right-brained" and the planner "left-brained"?

MINTZBERG: I would not say the manager is only right-brained. The manager needs the potential of both hemispheres. The potential of his right or left hemisphere may have been ignored to some degree but both are still thinking. The planner should content himself with satisfying the manager's need for hard, quantitative information. Managers can't do without it. So the planner should make sure they get it in a form that can be used. And that suggests it shouldn't be integrated into some master plan. That integration is the manager's role. The planner's report should say "Look, this is where the economy seems to be headed," or "This is how our market seems to be changing," or "We seem to be running into trouble on these kinds of product lines." There are series of analytical inputs that are relevant.

PR: You would then argue that the planner should not be concerned with strategy formulation.

MINTZBERG: Yes, I guess you could say that. The manager should be in charge of strategy formulation because he has the whole set of data inputs which are crucial for strategy formulation. Planners don't. The other problem is that strategy formulation is not a periodic event that fits into the planning cycle.

PR: According to professional folklore, planning is continuous.

MINTZBERG: I don't know what that means to the operation of the company. Strategy may be formulated continuously. But does that mean planning is a continuous process? I am not sure. A company can be stable for a long period, in which case the strategy is fixed. Such planning could be called "operational planning"—relevant only because the strategy is fixed.

PR: There has been some research done to suggest that the latent capacity of the right side of the brain can be developed. Would you advocate that planners attempt it by trying sensitivity training?

MINTZBERG: The dilemma is that what may be beneficial for individuals may become a threat to the corporation. A few years ago, when the T group and encounter sessions were in full swing, I was asked by an interviewer from the Canadian Broadcasting Corporation whether such techniques should be used by corporations. My answer was, "It depends upon your point of view. The problem is that often managers go to encounter sessions and learn something so important to them that they quit the organization and go off and do something else they want to do." The interviewer started laughing because that was exactly what happened to him when he was the vice-president of a corporation. But I think in sum, society will benefit from mind development even if it causes organizations to become less concerned with efficiency and less obsessed with the economic values.

PR: Should organizations be hiring more "right-brained" people as planners? What about hiring more people whose life styles indicate their sensitivity to change—the kind of people who used to be called the avant garde?

MINTZBERG: It depends on what they can do with those people, but if they put them into traditional situations, they are not going to keep them very long. The organization would have to be open and flexible.

PR: Unfortunately, most corporations are prejudiced against change and changers. Changing the subject, your articles have cited the decline of PPBS and the MIS systems. Is planning going to suffer the same obsolescence?

MINTZBERG: It may emerge in a different form. I think there is a role for a staff person whose prime concern is the future of the organization.

PR: But he may not be a planner?

MINTZBERG: He may not make formal plans. He may be the future thinker in the sense that he keeps bugging management: "Where are we going? Look how the environment is changing. Think about this possibility." But management will synthesize; management will put intelligence together and make the decisions. But the planner should keep saying: "Think about it. Look at things differently. Did you look at this particular data? Here's an analysis that suggests things aren't what you think they are." I'm describing an ad hoc role, not an integrating role.

PR: Switching conversational direction, some recent writing on separate realities points out that there are different ways of viewing the world. Not just two ways—a large number.

MINTZBERG: Right. For instance, we've incorrectly described management as very analytic, very systematic. There's another reality— nonlinear, nonsystematic—which is much closer to what's going on out there. It's interesting how people lock in to certain views of the world. Later, these accepted theories have a way of coming true.

Canadians and Americans, for example, have different views of government. Canadians have nationalized activities like CBC and the National Film Board. Americans avoid nationalization because they think government can't be businesslike, and that turns out very often to be a self-fulfilling prophecy. If it's widely believed that government can't do anything right, then government can't recruit the best people and so mediocrities and politicians are hired instead. People lose respect for government, and ultimately government can't accomplish anything. It's obviously a vicious circle.

In many European countries, the opposite happens. The best students are attracted to government because they believe their governments are more powerful than their corporations. Having the pick of the talent, government is able to function more effectively. In certain European nations, they have too much faith in government intervention. Americans, it seems to me, worry too much about what government should not do.

PR: Can you offer a prescription for planners faced with some of the headaches you have diagnosed?

MINTZBERG: I guess my most important suggestion is not to work against management but with it. Not to think that managers are dumbbells because they are not operating the way planners think they should be. Planners need to develop much more sophistication about what's going on in a corporate society—about the way organizations function, the way managers work, the way decisions are made and strategies get formulated in organizations. They need to find a role that meshes with the subtle ways organizations have to function.

ROBERT M. RANDALL AND
ROBERT J. ALLIO

The Planner
Minding the Store

DONALD V. SEIBERT, Chairman of the Board of J. C. Penney, is a line executive who suffered through the experience of being nominated company planner without the benefit of academic training.

For this interview Mr. Seibert sat still for a two-hour lunch in one of his company's private dining rooms in the Manhattan headquarters. Speaking cautiously, with the restraint of a corporate spokesman who is well aware of the pitfalls that encircle the corporate state, Mr. Seibert outlined his view of Penney's present, its years ahead, and its place in the decades to come. Eventually, when talk turned to marketing strategy—parting the customer from his dollar in exchange for the quality merchandise for which Penney is famous—his voice became more fervent. A planner because he lives in an era in which planning is prudent capitalistic strategy, Mr. Seibert is obviously a retailer at heart.

Under his leadership Penney has achieved the following:

- Resumed earnings growth, partly by controlling expenses and increasing productivity.
- Increased both sales and net income.
- Survived a challenging economic period which saw the bankruptcy of one major retailer.
- Successfully maintained its image as a reliable merchandiser in a time when consumerism has held other firms up to the light and found tarnish.
- Held on through eight unprofitable years until the catalogue operation which he once commanded began to make a significant contribution to profit.

PLANNING REVIEW: In an interview with *The New York Times*, you joked that you were one of the few planners who ever got "kicked upstairs." You served as J. C. Penney's Director of Planning and Research during 1963 and then held a number of different positions

Table 1. Financial highlights (in millions except per share data).

	1975	1974
Sales	$7,678.6	$6,935.7
Percent increase from prior year	10.7	11.1
Net income	$ 189.6	$ 119.4
Percent increase (decrease)		
from prior year	58.8	(35.9)
Percent of sales	2.5	1.7
Percent of stockholders' equity	13.5	9.1
Net income per share	$ 3.16	$ 2.02
Dividends per share	$ 1.16	$ 1.16
Capital expenditures	$ 298.4	$ 262.5

SOURCE: J. C. Penney Company, Inc. 1975 Annual Report.

with the company before you became Director of Corporate Planning and Development in 1973. How would you characterize the transition from line to staff to the chief executive's office?

SEIBERT: The biggest adjustment was the first one, from an operating division to the corporate staff. The last move, from Director of Corporate Planning to my present function, was much easier. In fact, I've retained most of my planning responsibilities, and the units of the company that reported to me as Director of Planning report to me now.

PR: Did you ever have any academic training for planning?

SEIBERT: No. But over the past dozen years or so I have attended many seminars and conferences on planning. And I have learned a lot from the professionals that J. C. Penney hired to run our department. In 1963 I got the Director's job because I knew the company. We were then committed to establishing a formal planning function headed and staffed by professionals. We envisioned a two-way learning process between them and us. We taught them about J. C. Penney and merchandising, and they contributed their knowledge of sophisticated planning techniques. To this day I can't claim a nuts-and-bolts knowledge of, for example, a mathematical model. But I am aware of when models can be helpful and how to use them. And I have learned that if a model is going to be used on an optimal basis, it should be coupled with an operations research team. And I know that mathematical models shouldn't be all mathematics. (See Figure 1.)

PR: Did your management viewpoint change significantly on your promotion from Director of Corporate Planning and Development to Chief Executive Officer?

Figure 1. The J. C. Penney planning process.

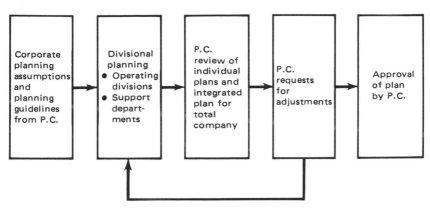

P.C.: Policy Committee, which is composed of management members
of the company's Board of Directors

SEIBERT: I now have a deeper appreciation of the human resources that make this company, and its plans, a success.

PR: Do you think planners neglect the human element in their equations?

SEIBERT: To take one example, it's the planner's function to project numbers of new stores, calculate the number of managers to staff them, and estimate the number of new trainees that will be needed. But when you get to be President you become aware of the chemistry that motivates these people and influences their behavioral patterns. From my point of view the human element affects the implementation of the plan.

PR: How much of your time is spent planning as opposed to running operations?

SEIBERT: That's always hard for me to sort out. In the broad sense, operating is something we're going to do tomorrow. Current organizational moves often affect a dozen years of operations, so it would be fair to call them planning, I suppose. If you also take into account the time I spend in Washington accumulating knowledge at meetings and hearings, perhaps a total of 50 percent of my time is spent planning.

PR: How is the planning team at J. C. Penney organized?

SEIBERT: The corporate development unit is responsible for publishing the plan. All the professional planners are in that group. Corporate development is divided into subgroups such as operations research, economic research, market research, international development, planning and research. Five of these entities—long-range strategic planning, planning and research, domestic development, international development, and organizational development—work as a team and continue to report to me, as they did when I was Director of Corporate Planning and Development. The five specialties together administer a corporate development plan which includes the company's long-range strategy (up to 1990) plus its ten-year and five-year plans. (See Figure 2.)

PR: Is there anybody with the word "planning" in his title on an operating level?

SEIBERT: No, but that doesn't mean we exclude operating people from the planning process. Quite the opposite. Penney's has a well-established planning approach that we characterize as a "bottom up, top down" process. This means that the operating people who are going to be involved in the results of the plan are required to be involved in its preparation. We try to get managers to think like planners. At the same time that we are producing direction, parameters, and guidelines for the plan from corporate headquarters, we ask store managers and regional managers to produce plans, from the

Figure 2. Corporate planning and development.

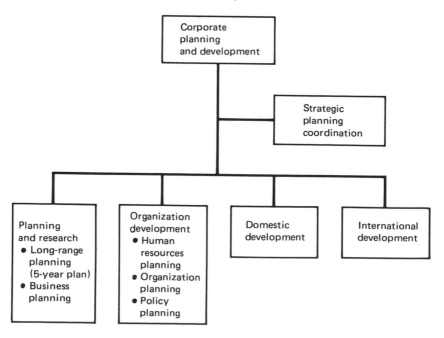

bottom up. Then together we negotiate our final product, the five-year plan.

PR: I suppose support units have their contribution to the plan.

SEIBERT: Right. And we have them duplicate the work of operations in a number of areas as a crosscheck for accuracy. For example, both the payroll department and store management prepare estimates of personnel costs. The duplication is needed because operations people are in touch with local conditions and trends, but the payroll department can take into account pending national legislation that could raise manpower costs.

PR: Do you also find this "bottom up, top down" approach a good communications tool?

SEIBERT: It can be a complex communication process. There are a lot of compromises and changes in any plan. After they have been made at the top, there's a danger that line people will think their input to the plan has been distorted or ignored. People in the divisions can decide that a plan just doesn't make sense after it has been written up by the professionals. Sometimes communications about the plan or changes in it made at the staff level can seem arbitrary. The trick is to get both sides to plan effectively without spending 90 percent of their time massaging numbers.

PR: At the "top," how are some of the guidelines set?

SEIBERT: Our international development group, for example, is engaged in studying markets broadly, from a retail standpoint. It collects information from operating divisions and then makes its suggestions to senior management about changing marketing strategy. This senior management is organized as a policy committee, our top-level long-range planning group.

PR: Are you a member of this group? And does resource allocation take place on this level?

SEIBERT: Yes to both questions.

PR: As Chief Executive Officer and a member of the policy committee, how would you describe the way you give leadership to the company? Do you have a vision of what Penney's should become and then ask your management to make you a plan that gets you there? Or do you ask them to analyze a probable future for the company?

SEIBERT: I have my own personal scenario of the future, one that has been influenced by exposure to the ideas of a lot of Penney people. Its concepts are deliberately couched in generalities. For example, I think Penney's wants to continue to be viewed as a growth company. That's an objective that doesn't have to be limited to statistical analysis. But we can examine the businesses that we are now in, consider their likely growth charts over the next 15 years, and determine whether we can continue to be a growth company by staying in our current markets.

PR: What are some of the other generalities in your scenario?

SEIBERT: A basic decision facing the company is whether we want to continue to be regarded as a value-oriented retailer, or whether we want to use the company's expertise in associated fields to diversify into new businesses. For example, because of our large real estate holdings and our experience financing shopping centers, we could consider moving into real estate development. Developing properties around our shopping centers could be the ideal way for us to achieve growth. Another opportunity for growth might be to become a manufacturer of certain products we now sell. We already have considerable expertise in the Penney organization because of the collaboration between our buyers and our laboratory engineers. A lot of such hypothesizing is just common sense, but at some point decisions have to be made. When alternatives represent differences of opinion within planning groups, they will be flushed up to the policy committee. If there is disagreement on the policy committee, then decisions are flushed up to me.

PR: What input do operating people, the "bottom up" people, make to such long-range plans?

SEIBERT: They are asked to prepare scenarios for their operating environments. We want them to consider the impact of change on the retail business and the ways that J. C. Penney should accommodate itself to those changes.

PR: And how do you relate this bird's-eye view to your five-year business plan?

SEIBERT: We can translate ten- and fifteen-year projections of the Penney character and operating objectives into five-year objectives of, for example, growth in a particular area or market, return on investment to be such and such. This gives our operating executives clear goals that they can relate to today's deals.

PR: Five years seems like a long lead time for planning a retail business.

SEIBERT: It actually takes more than five years to develop and supplement a business strategy for our kind of retailing. It may take three years, for example, to put together land deals, buy the real estate, and construct a full-line department store. By the time the store is built, we're committed to operating it for the next two years. The five-year time frame just doesn't give us the necessary flexibility for developing basic strategies. We do have supplemental sheets to our five-year plan which plot out several of our divisions' needs ten years ahead, for example, for catalogue distribution warehousing.

PR: Are you satisfied with your management's ability to react to contingencies not predicted by your five-year plan?

SEIBERT: No. I think we could have reacted better to the 1974 recession. We learned some important things.

PR: Would you agree that the modern business environment has so many potential discontinuities that it is fruitless to prepare contingency plans for each one, and that instead a company should try to keep its organization prepared to accommodate change?

SEIBERT: In general terms we try to think out ways of coping with possible futures in advance. We have considered what we would do if faced with a protracted period of high inflation and zero growth. If we don't change, how do we come out? If we don't like these numbers, then how do we change? I don't consider this contingency planning. But if we had an early warning signal that indicated that the economy was going to take such a course, then we'd start preparing a contingency plan. We do have contingency plans for dealing with the complex problems that can occur when plant capacity is exceeded, when additional distribution centers are needed, when storage capacity is inadequate. These can require delicate adjustments to the whole business. Should we decide to reduce the volume of our business by cutting the number of Penney's catalogues distributed in one season, then we must take into account the fact that such action will reduce the volume for the next season too. Fewer customers at Christmas means the start of a cumulative process that results in fewer customers in the spring and summer.

PR: Since your planners have no direct responsibility for operations, how do you evaluate their work? Have you found a way to tie their compensation to their skill at, say, long-range planning?

SEIBERT: We evaluate a planner both on the basis of the quality of work he produces and the extent to which he can influence operating people. I don't know a good way to reward a planner for long-range planning, nor has anyone proposed a good scheme for doing it.

PR: Taking a sidetrack for a moment, we'd like to get your views on the Humphrey-Javits proposal in Congress to institute some form of national planning machinery.

SEIBERT: I'm skeptical about the benefits of national planning as achieved by such legislation. I think it would lead to a controlled economy, or some variation, such as a regulated or semi-controlled one. There aren't any planned economies around the world that I prefer to our present system, even though I can find lots of faults in ours. I think a national planning function would simply begin to assemble and give power to officials who would sooner or later decide they were better able to make choices than the consumers.

PR: One of the main rationales for a national planning board is the deficiency in the current information system.

Seibert: That's a problem, but not a primary one. The energy crisis tracks back not to lack of information but to failure to act on information we had.

PR: Some forecasters have been troubled by instances of doctored or misleading information coming out of Washington. Have you found this a problem?

Seibert: Washington published a "profit" statistic recently that made it seem as if retailers were practically coining money. But you have to look underneath their percentages. Statistics have certainly become part of the system of politics. Economists are repeatedly bedeviled by the alteration of reasonable forecasts by political action.

PR: Does Penney's attempt political forecasting?

Seibert: Yes, on a short-range basis. We also work closely with legislative staff members to try to calculate the economic consequences of proposed legislation. Sometimes just a phrase dealing with record keeping or some other detail can add a $5 million "by-product" to the cost of a bill.

PR: What social legislation do you think will be unexpectedly costly over the next few decades?

Seibert: Increasing concern for the individual carries a substantial price tag. I would not suggest that this concern is inappropriate, but it nonetheless is costly to do the clerical work that guarantees an individual's rights—for example, his privacy.

PR: You are a former retailer, a planner, and now in a position to collect privileged information and have an overview of markets. What national changes do you foresee having an impact on Penney's business environment?

Seibert: The trend away from single dwelling units will affect our business, from carpets to lawnmowers. The increase in two-income families will change in-store traffic patterns; we'll need to expand sportswear departments for working women, perhaps. Technological innovations such as the maintenance-free battery will have fairly predictable effects. But we're blind about the future of the automobile itself fifteen years from now. If it might be replaced by mass transit, Penney's shouldn't be building free-standing automobile service stores in our shopping plazas. If energy costs merely limit automobile use somewhat, will the regional shopping centers that draw customers long distances continue to be viable?

Sometimes a dramatic change in demographics doesn't have the impact one would expect. While the birth rate is declining remarkably, for example, some specialists in the infant market say that business won't be affected very much because the first child in each family triggers all the major purchases—high chair, stroller, tricycle.

PR: You seem to have read a lot of projections of product lines. Do you enjoy keeping an eye on the store?

SEIBERT: I spend a lot of my time visiting stores, and when I get back from a trip I have a lot of input to the planning process.

ROBERT J. ALLIO

Planning at the Center

CANADA'S Department of Industry, Trade, and Commerce (DITC) is similar in many ways to the U.S. Department of Commerce. *Planning Review's* Editorial Director accosted Gordon Osbaldeston, the Department's urbane Deputy Minister, in Ottawa to ask some tough questions about how this key Department functions and the real place of planning in the federal government.

PLANNING REVIEW: Let's begin with a tendentious question: Is there any planning at the center of Canadian government?

OSBALDESTON: My answer is an unqualified yes, but when speaking about planning, one has in mind planning with respect to some objective. What is the objective of a government? That is about as philosophical a question as one can pose. And the closest that I've been able to come to an answer is that the objective of the government is to maximize the welfare of the nation.

PR: But no one would take the contrary position.

O: I don't think one can, which probably indicates the validity of the position.

PR: With such a general statement of objective, "validity" is difficult to measure.

O: Let's dissect that objective for a moment. What one person perceives to be an increase in his welfare, another may perceive to be a rip-off. The objective of government to some considerable extent lies in the eyes of the beholder. But you can't plan very easily with abstract objectives. Planning must begin by establishing some sort of indicators, for example, income, number of murders and the amount of crime, or investment in public roads. But even the use of indicators is difficult, because they are just components of the total welfare. Now to return to your question—"is there any central planning?" When you're working with about a hundred different goals, all of which are funneling up through the bureaucratic hierarchy, that's the only place one can see people planning. It's understandable why you ask, is there any central planning.

PR: Implicit in what we've been discussing is the notion that a certain degree of government intervention is required, which is to say that one cannot simply allow the free market system to operate.

O: You've moved into a very narrow component of my definition of total welfare, namely, the economic. Intervention is needed relative to national defense and some basic social services, no doubt about it. I believe that in the economic sector, government should do for the people what the people cannot do for themselves. That's as far as I would go.

PR: What they cannot do, or what they choose not to do.

O: My preference would be, what they cannot do, but the reality may be, will not do. But let me go a step further. Most of our economic systems are not perfect. I think governments compensate for an imperfect system. We don't have perfect competition; governments establish competition laws. So you're left not with deciding between intervention or nonintervention, but with the question of degree of intervention.

PR: And the trend has been for the federal government to assume responsibility for a larger and larger share of gross national product. Is that something that has been planned?

O: That share of the GNP going to government is running about 41%, having increased from 36% ten years ago. During the 40s, 50s, and 60s, there was a very real belief in unending growth and unending supply of government aid.

PR: A cornucopia?

O: Right, a cornucopia which could be allocated by government to do things which the people thought needed to be done. Bureaucrats, politicians, and the ordinary citizen shared in that view. An important point is that we transferred health care into the public sector during that period. It's a reallocation that probably no one would want to change. The second element of the growth of government spending is in the field of education. I think we're going to reallocate to the private sector some portion of that.

PR: It seems to me that social justice is one of the most significant issues which governments face in responding to their constituencies. Where social justice, in economic terms, entails redistribution of income, redistribution of income in turn requires what some consider to be an onerous tax burden, and also penalties on entrepreneurship. There's a basic conflict then between the objectives of growth and justice both of which, it could be argued, contribute ultimately to the welfare of the Canadian people.

O: The creation of wealth, in my view, is the role of the private sector not governments. Governments intervene to distribute wealth to correct what are perceived as imperfections. The real question is the degree of intervention and redistribution. My answer is that so long as there is sufficient wealth being created, and sufficient incentive present for that wealth to be created, then society is probably well served by the redistribution.

PR: Redistribution and the planning process you've mentioned imply a time horizon. Does the federal government have a time horizon longer than the three to five years common in business?

O: I think government's time horizon is much longer, contrary to the popular belief that there's only a four-year time horizon corresponding to the political cycle of election. Behind the electorate is a very large bureaucracy with the capacity to envision long-range scenarios. In the case of the corporation, management often acts as if it had a one-year horizon, because it must report annually to stockholders. Now, government doesn't have to make a profit every year. You might say that my masters have to show a profit every four-year period. The planning period for my Economic Branch is five to ten years.

PR: To repeat your point, you believe the electoral process does not significantly perturb the government planning process.

O: The planning process in government begins with the establishment of objectives by a politician. He puts these objectives to the bureaucracy and asks, how can I achieve them? The bureaucracy's job is to array the techniques for achieving those objectives. Over the past five years great strides have been made in the bureaucracy's ability to offer alternatives. Gibes that refer to bureaucrats as "mandarins" of government are really quite foolish since they don't make any decisions at all. They may extend their advice on the alternatives they array. As a bureaucrat I'd like to think I'm judged on two counts. First, my ability to identify and array alternatives. Secondly, my capacity to advocate the right alternative. But the politician is ultimately responsible for decisions. The politician can listen to me, and if he thinks I'm wise, perceptive, and judicious, he's likely to concur. Most planners should never engage in making recommendations. As Deputy Minister I have some obligation to do so. The professional planner below me has either very little obligation in that regard or none. He is not paid to make choices, and the day he starts, I say that's the day I'll fire him.

PR: But he is paid presumably to identify the strengths and weaknesses of various alternatives.

O: Absolutely.

PR: Are ministerial or political objectives ever made public, and how does the government assign priorities to different objectives?

O: Every four years the government goes to the electorate with their objectives. They present what they hope to achieve for the country, then they ask the electorate to vote. The complaint you may have as a professional planner is that those objectives are not very precise. Well, so be it. If the electorate feel that way, they will press the politician to be more precise. But I've got great sympathy for the politician in that process.

In the private sector, there's a very explicit bottom line, and therein lies an important difference between the corporation and the government. The bottom line in government is the greater welfare of all Canadians. When you demand more specific objectives, you're asking the politician to alienate many people. And that's a hell of a thing to ask of a person who has to win votes to keep his job.

PR: But doesn't the total of all the programs that are enacted by government constitute a de facto statement of objectives? The selection of those programs, then, in Industry, Trade, and Commerce or any other agency, in turn implies some priorities. Isn't this an ad hoc process?

O: By no means. When I was Secretary of the Treasury Board I lived through this process, and I can assure you that it's by no means ad hoc. It's very bureaucratized.

PR: Could you describe the process?

O: The government sets out certain general objectives. One year, for example, improving transportation and environment were objectives. The government's judgment was that certain components should be given attention, if necessary at the expense of other components. Bureaucracy is asked to propose alternatives, programs, the improvement of that sector. At this point government gets complicated, because many departments may have proposals. Flowing into the Treasury Board are sets of formal proposals. At the center, the decision becomes which of the 49 proposals to improve the transport sector are to be funded, given that one can only fund five. We set someone up with more information than anybody else, and indeed, he has to make the "infallible" choices of the five. Staff work has to be done, and then the Treasury Board and the Ministers have to make the final judgment as to whether the staff work is correct and the five proposals are the ones to be approved. Then come secondary problems: How do you split funds among the five, and how should priorities in different sectors be set?

PR: That's been exactly the stumbling block so far in applying the zero base budgeting process.

O: Yes. There's an enormous amount of work to be done in improving cost-benefit analysis within a sector. The field is enormously rich, incredibly complicated. The trade-offs exist in the minds of politicians who intuit a set of indices that nobody's ever been able to follow.

PR: Are you saying that the decision-making process at this level becomes one of political expediency?

O: Judgment.

PR: Or are you saying that there is an intuitive integrating process that results in good decisions?

O: You use the word "political expediency" in the pejorative sense.

PR: Yes.

O: Minor political expediencies occur. I've served under both Conservative and Liberal governments, and I think we've been blessed by politicians who make good political judgments. People rant at politicians when politicians have made tough judgments which in the long run will benefit the country. A very wise and long-lived politician said to me, and I agree with him heartily, that good programs are good politics.

PR: You would say then, just to recapitulate, that there is a decision-making process at the highest levels which, although it cannot be described in terms of conventional, rational procedures, is nonetheless very effective.

O: Exactly. And I want to stress this point. In a society or civilization the most difficult intellectual challenge is political judgment. People wish they didn't have to rely upon it. But people regard politics as some kind of tawdry profession that they wish did not have to be practiced. And that's a tragic misconception. The highest part of planning is carried on by the politician and with incredible skill when it's done well.

PR: That's a very interesting point of view. I don't disagree with you, but it's an unusual position.

PR: Let's spend a little time on the analysis of Canadian industrial planning. Cassandras claim industry is entering a period of rapid decline and imminent disaster. The absence of an industrial strategy, of course, has been cited as an important reason for the decline. Government has failed to come forward, it's alleged, with an industrial strategy.

O: Would you define what you mean by an industrial strategy?

PR: I was about to ask you that question.

O: Let me approach the matter another way. You and I agreed earlier that the role of government is minimum intervention, in large measure because of the importance of personal freedom. Once you say that, you start to circumscribe the question of industrial strategy. The Chinese have an industrial strategy, so do the Russians. In some degree, so do the French and the Cubans. So far as I know, the United States does not have an industrial strategy. The most successful industrial strategy is the one that doesn't exist, the United States strategy, of course.

PR: Let me suggest that the United States does have an industrial strategy, as does Canada. That strategy is the sum of the federal government's interaction with industry, both in terms of what it does and what it does not do.

O: If you can quantify that strategic program, I'll try and develop one for Canada. If you think of the context in which wealth is generated, and you think of the various industrial groups—ship building or footwear, for example—you can obviously have industrial policies for each group, and government policies for industry in general. These latter would include taxation or labor laws.

PR: Also monetary and fiscal policy.

O: Exactly. When I think of industrial strategies, I think of both types. Canada's industrial strategy, just like U.S. industrial strategy, is an aggregation of general and specific industrial policies.

PR: And then could we make a judgment as to whether the Canadian industrial strategy is effective, given the apparent deterioration of Canadian manufacturing industry in particular?

O: I can't answer that in the absolute. I look at rate of return on investment and I start to worry. I look at trade balance and I start to worry.

PR: Those are some of the indicators of the industrial "welfare."

O: Yes. They partly measure the quality of industrial strategy. But how to read them is a very complex question. In absolute terms, Canada's performance may be turning down, but not in relative terms. If you examine the OECD (Organization for Economic Cooperation and Development) countries, perhaps the only ones which are doing better than Canada are Japan and the United States. The rest aren't doing as well. But even if on relative grounds we're doing comparatively well, you have to ask whether we couldn't do better.

My own feelings, based on the premise that wealth is created in the private sector, is that trade group policy making generally is a form of government intervention. These trade group policies—shipbuilding subsidies, textile protection, and so on—tend to be a favorite of a great many of my friends in the private sector, whereas I favor them somewhat less. But when your ox is getting gored, I guess you'd like intervention. Now let's consider general industrial policies. These are generally aimed at a number of objectives simultaneously, and, indeed, may impact negatively on certain government goals. A simple example is minimum wage law. In terms of the redistribution of wealth we spoke about earlier, it's probably a valid instrument. But it has negative impact on the tourism industry. So you see, I cannot make the political decision that the pursuit of equity and social justice is more or less important than the creation of wealth. Industry, Trade, and Commerce cannot merely decide what will benefit industry, in terms of wealth creation. Composition of our total welfare must be considered. That's a difficult process. Society has to build a consensus.

PR: Do you think that's possible? Noncompetitiveness in certain industries is nurtured and sustained by trade policy and tariff policy. Can we get those industries competitive and off the back of the Canadian taxpayer and consumer by going to free trade? The political consequences of free trade, no doubt, would be very severe in the short term. Even if that policy were good for Canada in the long run, could you realistically expect that kind of political decision to be made?

O: Of course you could make that argument about the textile industry. An argument could be made, and I'm not saying I subscribe to it, that we obtain all the textiles abroad at a lower price. I don't believe that. But does one really want to put a proposition forward that 200,000 Canadians should be put out of work next week?

PR: You must put into play some transition program.

O: Exactly, and indeed we have such a program in place.

PR: What is Canada's economic model? Surely not Japan, the U.S., or Sweden, because I don't believe that those models fit. Yet, some would argue that Canadian industry's been trying to replicate the U.S. in the sense that we strive for a complete range of industrial capability.

Editorial Note: *At this stage in the dialog with the Deputy Minister, the private sector intervened by terminating power service to the ministry building in Ottawa. We were fortunately able to resume our discussion in a few minutes.*

PR: The appropriate Canadian model might entail building on comparative advantage.

O: The model we've always sought is the one which creates the greatest total welfare. But our own definition of welfare changes. The model has been changed to increase the emphasis on social justice. I would argue that it's changing again as we edge back to recognizing that we have to pay more attention to the creation of wealth.

PR: So you believe that industry and government in Canada will slowly evolve a program to optimize public welfare. Isn't the government alarmed by statistics that measure competitiveness, cost of labor, productivity, and so on?

O: Let me put out some signposts for you to read. Government published The Way Ahead, a position paper stating that more reliance would have to be put upon the private sector for the creation of wealth. It also stated that government intervention should decrease. Government reduced the benefits under unemployment insurance. It brought in an all-business budget in May of last year. It has not introduced increases in the social programs in over two years, and it's convened a First Ministers meeting for two and a half days on the state of the economy. I don't think business can point to any countervailing signals. These signposts indicate the government believes that the model has to be adjusted more in the direction of creation of wealth.

PR: Does that suggest also that the business community is going to have to play a more forcible role, vigorous role, take more initiative in correcting the problems or dealing with the issues?

O: If the rules are going to change, business had better speak up, and indicate the direction of changes that they think is necessary.

PR: Can we talk about the role of the planner in a government organization? You cited earlier the great importance of impartiality. What other aspects are there to the proper role of a planner?

O: Humility. Professionalism, heavily laced with humility. Where we are now in government planning—and I'm thinking of the evaluation techniques for either efficiency or effectiveness, not cost analysis—we are barely at the beginning of a very long trail.

PR: And where does the trail lead?

O: To capacity to quantify and capture the essence of public decision-making. I have nothing but admiration for those men who bring an intellect to this business that matches the task.

PR: What kind of skills or education or training should a planner in government bring to his task?

O: Traditionally planners' skills emanated from the economics profession. The problem is those skills don't take into account that which cannot be quantified.

PR: So you need men with a broad education?

O: They have to deal with the imprecision of human behavior, and somehow put that into the equation. I watch highly skilled professional planners converted through some magical process to recognize that the quantitative data are not reduced in quality by softening their numbers. That takes a man of considerable ability. After having spent eight years learning to add, he must learn to accept political arithmetic. That requires humility.

PR: One last question. How are we to judge the public planner?

O: The criteria of judging the planner in the private sector are different from the criteria in the public sector. The task is more difficult in the public sector, as we've discussed, because we're talking about the total welfare, not just a very specific bottom line number. Also the public planner supplies only a partial set of alternatives; decisions are made by the politician on the basis of other inputs as well. So, in a sense, one could say that the planner in the public sector should be neither blamed nor praised, because you'll never be able to understand what part his input had in the final decision.

PR: But he still has to be judged.

O: That's one of the difficulties in accountability in the public sector. Yes, you've got to judge, and that judgment must be made at the point of time on which he rendered his alternatives. Judgment on the result is not suitable, because the result is out of his control. That's one of the major problems in accountability in the public service in Canada.

ROBERT J. ALLIO AND
ROBERT M. RANDALL

Planner at the Helm

W. R. GOODWIN, President and Chief Executive Officer of Johns-Manville, is one of those rare chief executives who was promoted to top management after a stint as chief planner. Obviously, he is well acquainted with the methodology of planning, the various ways it can be utilized by a corporation, and its potentials.

The interview was informal and more a conversation than an interrogation. For this reason, specific and detailed questions about the Johns-Manville planning cycle and organizational structure were omitted. Instead, the time spent with Dr. Goodwin gave *Planning Review* an invaluable chance to learn about his attitude toward planning. Although the interviewers provided Dr. Goodwin with a list of questions in advance, these never became a central part of the discussion. Chief executives tend to answer questions they raise themselves.

PLANNING REVIEW: The Johns-Manville annual report indicates that you as chief executive officer are engineering a repositioning of the company. Have you formulated a planning "mechanism" for your intended changes?

GOODWIN: The word "mechanism" is too formal to be applied to our planning style. For planning to work, it has to be proceduralized, but, more importantly, it has to be thoroughly explained to the operating staff and accepted by them. Since I started studying Johns-Manville as a consultant in 1970, I've been working to get planning accepted as both a communications tool and a device for increasing the company's expectancy of a good return on investment.

PR: With only the limited muscle of a consultant, what was the scope of your original work?

GOODWIN: We first built up the planning system for one division. The first pass through the system was accomplished in nine months, and in a year and a half we had a real plan. The system required a thorough appraisal of the environment and the division's internal resources. We were conscious that the system we were devising could be used by the whole corporation. But what we wanted was to get results from our initial planning analysis that the division could use immediately.

PR: Do you think your early successes were crucial?

GOODWIN: Yes. Studies of customer attitude and an analysis of what the salesmen sold and who they sold it to gave the division answers it could sink its,teeth into. When we were able to prove that salesmen were being trained incorrectly, based on our analysis, the division became our boosters throughout the company.

PR: How would you characterize the style of planning you instituted versus the situation you found when you arrived?

GOODWIN: Formerly, the forecasting process was complex. The field people made their predictions; these numbers were sent on to a section in the corporate finance department called Profit Planning. This group would develop another forecast with different numbers. Then the corporate staff would revise the estimates, and the end result was three sets of forecasts, all different. We found that we got better results by depending more on the product manager, the general manager, and their people.

PR: You stressed the involvement of division staff and managers.

GOODWIN: Right. Plus the education of the general manager. The mandatory rule to follow is to have plans prepared by the group involved. A corporate planning staff can plan for the corporation qua corporation, but not for the elements of the corporation.

PR: What response did your planning effort provoke in the division?

GOODWIN: About halfway through the process everyone got provoked at all the paperwork. But the general manager's incentive to keep his people working on the plan was high because he was learning things about his division that he hadn't known before. We made the process complicated in order to get people in the habit of following all the procedures. Then we gradually simplified it, and now we have a workable planning system capable of supplying very detailed statistics. The plan puts out a four-year projection to facilitate capital planning. We use the projection as our stored expectancy; that way the divisions can't disregard their plans.

PR: But the divisions get a chance to revise their input?

GOODWIN: Certainly. This year we have modified plans about every quarter. I think this is good, since it suggests that divisions have learned that we use the plans and need the best available figures.

PR: Does Johns-Manville have an incentive system to tie division managers' compensation to adherence to the plan?

GOODWIN: Yes. But we may stop. Profit sharing is linked now to performance as compared with the goal set in the plan. We found that this practice tends to produce unrealistically low goals. Some companies have found that managers set their goals as low as possible in part, at least, to be sure they will meet their own quotas.

PR: Beyond studying a manager's record over a number of years, how do you monitor this tendency to make conservative predictions?

GOODWIN: We added a section to our plan which asks, "How does what you forecast for 1975 compare with what you forecast for that year in 1974?" We also have another kind of plan—due at six-month intervals—which asks the division managers to provide corporate headquarters with a picture of what could be done with the division if it had all the capital it wanted and no restrictions.

PR: In addition to this "positive" contingency planning, how does Johns-Manville plan for economic downturns? Your earnings suffered in 1975, like a lot of other companies.

GOODWIN: We have imposed a quarterly review. We also try to get the best economic information we can for our managers. To do this we have a small internal unit that specializes in economic analysis and issues regular reports on expected performance of economy.

PR: During a period of discontinuity, like the current one, what extra effort do you expect from your planners?

GOODWIN: We want them to focus closely on the everyday realities of our business. It's especially important to learn how Johns-Manville is doing vis-à-vis our competition—more so now than in good times. I expect the planner to re-examine the plan he's working from and decide, after conferring with division management, how to modify it.

PR: Are you planning to diversify your product line in order to make the company less susceptible to economic cycles?

GOODWIN: We have tried to become less dependent on cyclic business, like housing starts, by moving heavily into new kinds of insulation, a good energy-crisis business. Our home products group has diversified into remodeling and repair products, a more stable field. Johns-Manville has already become less susceptible to swings in the economy, and so have our competitors who followed the same strategy.

PR: Have you set any guidelines for how much of your future growth—these new businesses we're talking about—is going to result from internal development as opposed to acquisition?

GOODWIN: I don't know how to set such guidelines. I only know that a healthy company develops new business from within as well as without. If we don't develop new products internally, we shouldn't bother with having a $14 million research lab and pilot plant. We could just make do with a technical services department that solves process problems. As a matter of fact, prior to 1971, Johns-Manville didn't have a particularly good record in developing new businesses.

PR: Can planning improve the company's performance in this area?

GOODWIN: I appointed our head R&D man a vice president in charge of a development group which is split into three entities: internal development of new business, venture management, and process development. This last group is made up of about 70 engineers and applied scientists. They study every process in the company—new or old—but they follow a set of priorities set by division management.

PR: Is Johns-Manville now in a phase that emphasizes process improvement?

GOODWIN: Yes. We are saying that we plan to take existing capacity as of January 1, 1976, and to add 30–45 percent to that with only minor expenditures of capital.

PR: Wasn't Johns-Manville relying on process improvement to increase profits when you arrived at the company?

GOODWIN: That's right. Although profits weren't bad, the company was growing at a slower rate than the GNP. We planned a four-phase program. The first phase was to catalogue the company's assets and decide how we were going to recast the business. Second, we wanted to optimize our output without making major capital investments. Next comes phase three, which is to expand business created or emphasized in phases one and two. Phase four brings us back to a positive internal cash flow; we'll squeeze the most juice out of all the business developed in the first three phases.

PR: Does the business strategy benefit from the methodology of formal planning?

GOODWIN: Without planning it can become a dangerous "milking" process. For example, a manager who doesn't believe in planning, and who has had spectacularly successful years, can be lucky to move on before some situations catch up with him. He isn't able to foresee what will happen next year if, in order to be a hero, he spends all his resources this year to make an 11 percent return on investment.

PR: It's the CEO's job to make the entrepreneurs and the planners work together. Can you describe any situations in which they didn't cooperate?

GOODWIN: I can think of two types of "failure models." Company A, which shall be nameless, had the most powerful planning staff I've ever seen assembled: Operations research types, decision models, a corporate planning staff of about 40 people. Unfortunately, although they spoke at all the society meetings, within the company they seemed to speak only to themselves and to the chief executive. That was what was wrong with their approach.

PR: And type B?

GOODWIN: Type B does little or no planning. While these companies often do moderately well, in my opinion they usually could do much better.

PR: Company B sounds something like your description of Johns-Manville when you first were hired as a consultant. Did Johns-Manville have a plan in those days?

GOODWIN: The company had a profit-and-growth plan. But many people were just giving the plan lip service.

PR: And then there's the "malicious compliance" syndrome.

GOODWIN: Right! I'll have to remember to use that description in my speeches. Most of the staff at Johns-Manville is receptive to planning now. When I first started, there were plenty of skeptics. I ought to point out that Johns-Manville didn't even have a marketing department back then.

PR: A lot of older companies didn't become marketing oriented until quite recently. How did you overcome Johns-Manville's late start?

GOODWIN: Just last month we moved the corporate planning department into the marketing department. The director of planning is also responsible for economic analysis and market research. Having all these units together makes for a very nice alliance. Of course, each of our divisions must have a planning manager reporting directly to the division general manager.

PR: How has your view of your role in the corporation changed from when you first started to the present?

GOODWIN: Over the years it's become harder to stay objective. The pressures of the moment can assume an enormous amount of priority. Sometimes I think that's O.K. Planners can't foresee very much. Don't get me wrong. I'm not panning the planning process. Any time I detect anybody paying lip service to it, I shake things up. Planning is a very important tool for shaping the future, but it's not much good for predicting a future based on a string of sequential assumptions.

PR: You seem to place a lot of emphasis on communications between planners and line people. Is getting people to talk more important than the planning system itself?

Goodwin: All I can say is that our style of planning has placed Johns-Manville in a better posture by several standards of measurement. It has excited a lot of people who were pretty lethargic before it was instituted. It has served as a communications tool between people with very different jobs and training.

PR: Your approach seems somewhat influenced by your training in the behavioral sciences.

Goodwin: My philosophy is that planners are responsible for developing an idea grid. If a company has a common information base, then all information it develops fits somewhere. Companies that merely "operate" are just flying by the seat of their pants.

PR: Would you require your successor to take a major role in the planning process as part of his or her preparation?

Goodwin: Planning experience would be excellent preparation. I wouldn't make it a requirement, but I would make sure that any successor understood the planning process and believed in it. I'd consider a person's background. A production man, for example, would have to convince me of his firm understanding of the need to spend money for marketing planning. A financial expert needs to know planning so he can take into account the qualitative, rather than just the quantitative, aspects of the business.

PR: Speaking of finances, what are your corporate goals?

Goodwin: The corporate goal is not to fall below 11 percent return on assets, which we haven't achieved yet, and to reach 7 percent return on sales. If this interview is about over, there's one thing I'd like to say, since we're all planners here.

PR: Yes?

Goodwin: It sure has been nice to talk to a couple of fellow "giraffes" for a change.

Biographical Notes

MICHAEL G. ALLEN is vice-president for corporate strategy and systems at General Electric. Earlier he worked for McKinsey & Co., Marconi, and British Steel.

ROBERT J. ALLIO has recently joined the staff of Arthur D. Little, Inc., in Cambridge, Mass. Formerly he was president of Canstar Communications in Toronto and director of corporate planning and development for Babcock & Wilcox Company, N.Y. He is editorial director of *Planning Review*.

WILLIAM T. BECHARD is president and founder of Dialectics, Inc., Westport, Conn. Previously he was vice-president of Educational Systems and Designs, Inc.

JEANNE BINSTOCK is the director of Consumer and Management Trends, Inc., Boston and Ottawa, a consulting firm that specializes in lifestyle trends, social forecasting, and planning. Formerly she was professor of sociology at the University of Massachusetts. Dr. Binstock holds a Ph.D. from Brandeis University.

WALTER P. BLASS is director of corporate planning for New York Telephone. Previously he worked as an economist with AT&T and took a break to be Peace Corps country director for Afghanistan.

JOHN C. CHAMBERS is manager of management sciences of Xerox Corporation in Rochester, N.Y. He is a coauthor of *An Executive's Guide to Forecasting*.

WILLIAM F. CHRISTOPHER is director of marketing for Hooker Chemicals & Plastics Corporation in Stamford, Conn. Earlier he had a long career in marketing with General Electric. He has written two books, *Polycarbonates* (1962) and *The Achieving Enterprise* (1974), and numerous articles, and has done educational tapes and films.

JAMES R. COLLIER is senior vice-president of Marcona Corporation, a San Francisco-based mining, shipping, and resource development firm. Prior to joining Marcona, he was vice-president, corporate development, for Zenith Radio Corporation in Chicago.

PAMELA SHEA CUMING is a principal of Dialectics, Inc., Westport, Conn. Prior to joining Dialectics, she was at Educational Systems and Designs, Inc.

JOHN D. DRAKE is chairman of the executive committee of Drake-Beam & Associates, a consulting firm that specializes in behaviorial sciences. His book *Interviewing for Managers* is one of AMA's best sellers.

WAYNE DRAYER is manager of forecasting services, central management purchasing, at Babcock & Wilcox Company, Alliance, Ohio.

DARRYL J. ELLIS is manager of marketing, General Electric Medical Systems Division, Dental Operations, where he was formerly manager of strategy development. He has been director of planning and business development at Doric, Inc., and assistant director of planning at Estech, Inc., both subsidiaries of Esmark, Inc., in Chicago.

KENNETH R. FARRELL is Deputy Administrator, Economics, Statistics and Cooperative Service, U.S. Department of Agriculture. His long experience in agricultural economics has included teaching, government service, consulting, and numerous publications.

BRADLEY T. GALE is director of research for The Strategic Planning Institute and is a member of the economics faculty at the University of Massachusetts, Amherst. Dr. Gale has been with PIMS since it began at General Electric in 1972.

A. GEORGE GOLS is vice-president of Arthur D. Little, Inc., Cambridge, Mass., and is head of its management economics sections and Input–Output Forecasting Center. Dr. Gols recently created the Economic Advisory Service economic planning model in a joint venture with General Electric.

WILLIS D. HARMAN is director of the Center for the Study of Social Policy at SRI International. He specializes in analysis of major societal problems, social forecasting, and policy analysis.

DENNIS A. HAWVER is national program director for behavioral measurement and analysis consulting at RHR Institute, a division of Rohrer, Hibler & Replogle, Inc., New York City.

HAZEL HENDERSON is codirector of the Princeton Center for Alternative Futures. A writer, social critic, and economic adviser, she has written extensively and serves in many organizations including the National Science Foundation and Congress's Office of Technology Assessment Advisory Council.

HAROLD W. HENRY is professor of business administration at the University of Tennessee. He has worked at the Marshall Space Flight Center, Union Carbide Nuclear Division, and the University of Michigan Phoenix Laboratory in radiation physics. In addition to many articles, Dr. Henry has written two books on planning and pollution control.

GEORGE E. HUMPHRIES is president of Advanced Technology Management Associates, Inc., a consulting and research firm in Washington, D.C., and is vice-president of the International Society for Technology Assessment. Mr. Humphries writes and lectures on R&D management, technology assessment and forecasting, and social impact analysis.

FINN E. JERSTAD is managing director of Bayly, Martin & Fay AS Scandinavia in Oslo, a subsidiary of Sperry & Hutchinson Co., involved in offshore petroleum and marine insurance brokerage. Previously he established the corporate planning department for S&H. Earlier experience was in steel production, shipping, and publishing.

MICHAEL J. KAMI is president of Corporate Planning, Inc., Lighthouse Point, Florida. He was formerly vice-president of corporate planning for Xerox and corporate director of long-range planning for IBM. Dr. Kami's latest book is *Corporate Management in Crisis: Why the Mighty Fall.*

ABRAHAM KATZ is director of planning systems for IBM. Formerly he worked at the M.I.T. Digital Computer Laboratory, Marchant Research, R.C.A., and the Department of Commerce. He has consulted with the National Academy of Sciences and the Ford Foundation.

PARMANAND KUMAR is currently with Ralph M. Parsons Company. He was formerly with Jacobs Engineering after a long career of merger and acquisition consulting as vice-president of Parich International, Inc. Mr. Kumar has an MBA from the University of Southern California and degrees in engineering from universities in India.

FRED E. LEE is professor of organization planning and administration at SMU and is president of Fred E. Lee & Associates, a consulting firm. Previously he was with AMA, Glidden, Ford Motor, and Stromberg-Carlson.

MILTON LEONTIADES is associate professor of management at Rutgers University. He has held strategic planning positions with General Electric and I.U. International and was a consultant with Touche Ross. Earlier he did research for NYSE, the U.S. Treasury, and the N.A.M.

E. IRIS MARTIN is a research associate with GAMMA. She is a native of Scotland.

JAY S. MENDELL is visiting professor of business administration at Florida Atlantic University. Earlier he served as a futurist for Pratt & Whitney. He is editorial chairman of *Business Tomorrow* and is on the editorial board of *The Futurist.*

ARNOLD MITCHELL is senior social economist at the Center for the Study of Social Policy at SRI International. He specializes in studies of changing values, social trends, and long-range strategic planning.

GRAHAM T. T. MOLITOR is president of Public Policy Forecasting. Previously he was director of government relations for General Mills. He was on the White House Advisory Committee on Social Indicators and has had extensive corporate, government, and teaching experience.

JAMES G. MORRIS is associate professor of administrative science at Kent State University.

SATINDER K. MULLICK is manager of the economics and operations research department of Corning Glass Works. He is a coauthor of *An Executive's Guide to Forecasting*.

PETER P. PEKAR, JR., is director of business development for Quaker Oats. Formerly he was director of corporate economics and planning at Estech, Inc., in Chicago, and a consultant to NASA and the National Institutes of Health. Dr. Pekar holds a Ph.D. in business and economics from the Illinois Institute of Technology.

MALCOLM W. PENNINGTON is president of The Marketing & Planning Group, a consulting firm, and is senior editor of *Planning Review*.

JAMES E. POST is assistant professor at the School of Management of Boston University.

LEE E. PRESTON is professor of American enterprise at the School of Management, State University of New York at Buffalo.

ROBERT M. RANDALL is manager, research & product information, at Lederle Laboratories. Earlier he was writer/editor at Time Inc. He has been a newspaper journalist, medical writer, and editorial consultant to *Planning Review* since its inception.

MELVIN E. SALVESON is professor of business at Pepperdine University in Los Angeles and is chairman of Corporate Strategies International in Los Angeles. Previously he was group vice-president in charge of professional and scientific services at Control Data.

STEVE SEABURY is a systems analyst for GTE Data Services. He was previously with Babcock & Wilcox's operations research department, Alliance, Ohio.

PETER S. SINDELL is president of the consulting firm of Sindell Research Ltd., as well as senior research associate of GAMMA. He was a founding member of the Board of Directors of Manitou College, a native-run college in Quebec, and has worked extensively in the fields of northern development and Indian education.

SURENDRA S. SINGHVI is manager of corporate financial planning and analysis with Aramco Steel Corp. and adjunct professor of finance at Miami (Ohio) University. He received his doctorate from Columbia Business School and has published several books and articles.

J. GRAHAM SMITH is professor of management at McGill University and associate director of GAMMA. Dr. Smith has taught at several universities and has been a consultant to several government agencies and private corporations in Canada and abroad. He is economics editor of *Planning Review*.

ROBERT D. SMITH is professor of administrative science at Kent State University. Formerly he taught at the University of South Africa.

W. LYNN TANNER is associate professor of management at the University of Calgary and is on the editorial boards of *Business Tomorrow* and *Planning Review*. Earlier he worked with Pan Am and Boeing in the United States and Africa.

JOHN THACKRAY is a business journalist who writes for *The Institutional Investor, Financial Times,* and other American and British business publications.

KIMON VALASKAKIS is associate professor of economics at the University of Montreal and director of GAMMA. He has been a consultant to several Quebec and Canadian federal government departments and to various U.N. organizations. He has published extensively in the fields of futures, planning, and the economics of growth and development. He holds a law degree from the University of Paris and a Ph.D. in economics from Cornell University.

LYLE YORKS is vice-president of Drake-Beam & Associates, Inc., in New York City. He also teaches organization behavior at Eastern Connecticut State College and at the New School for Social Research in New York. His book *A Radical Approach to Job Enrichment* was published by AMACOM in 1977.

Bibliography

BOOKS AND SPECIAL REPORTS
Corporate Planning

Ackoff, Russell L.: *A Concept of Corporate Planning* (New York: Wiley, 1970).

Ansoff, H. Igor: *Corporate Strategy: An Analytical Approach to Business Policy for Growth and Expansion* (New York: McGraw-Hill, 1965).

Bennis, Warren G., Benne, Kenneth D., and Chin, Robert: *The Planning of Change* (New York: Holt, Rinehart and Winston, 1969).

Brown, James K., and O'Connor, Rochelle: *Planning and the Corporate Planning Director*, Report No. 627 (New York: The Conference Board, 1974).

Denning, Basil W.: *Corporate Planning: Selected Concepts* (New York: McGraw-Hill, 1971).

Egerton, Henry C., and Brown, James K.: *Planning and the Chief Executive* (New York: The Conference Board, 1972).

Ewing, David W.: *Long-Range Planning for Management* (New York: Harper & Row, 1972).

Hussey, D. E.: Introducing Corporate Planning (London: Pergamon, 1971).

Jain, Subhash, and Singhvi, Surendra: *Essentials of Corporate Planning* (New York: Planning Executives Institute, 1973).

Jantsch, Erich: *Perspectives of Planning* (Paris: OECD, 1969).

Kastens, Merritt L.: *Long-Range Planning for Your Business* (New York: AMACOM, 1976).

Liddell Hart, B. H.: *Strategy* (New York: Praeger Publications, 1967).

Mack, Ruth P.: *Planning on Uncertainty: Decision Making in Business and Government Administration* (New York: Wiley, 1971).

O'Connor, Rochelle: *Corporate Guides to Long-Range Planning*, Report No. 687 (New York: The Conference Board, 1976).

————: *Planning Under Uncertainty: Multiple Scenarios and Contingency Planning*, Report No. 741 (New York: The Conference Board, 1978).

Planning Series Part 4, Harvard Business Review, 1977.

Rosen, Stephen: *Long-Range Planning: A Presidential Perspective* (New York: The Presidents Association, 1973).

Rothschild, William E.: *Putting It All Together: A Guide to Strategic Thinking* (New York: AMACOM, 1976).

Schaffir, Walter B.: *Strategic Business Planning: Some Questions for the Chief Executive* (New York: The Presidents Association, 1976).

Smith, Theodore: *Dynamic Business Strategy: The Art of Planning* (New York: McGraw-Hill, 1977).

Steiner, George A.: *Top Management Planning* (New York: Macmillan, 1969).

————: *Pitfalls in Comprehensive Long-Range Planning* (Oxford, Ohio: The Planning Executives Institute, 1972).

————: *Strategic Managerial Planning* (Oxford, Ohio: The Planning Executives Institute, 1977).

Taylor, Bernard, and Hawkins, Kevin: *Handbook of Strategic Planning* (London: Longman Group Limited, 1972).

Forecasting

Bright, James R., and Shoeman, Milton E. F.: *A Guide to Practical Technological Forecasting* (Englewood Cliffs, N.J.: Prentice-Hall, 1973).

Butler, William F., Kavesh, Robert A., and Platt, Robert B.: *Methods and Techniques of Business Forecasting* (Englewood Cliffs, N.J.: Prentice-Hall, 1974).

Chambers, John C., Mullick, Satinder K., and Smith, Donald D.: *An Executive's Guide to Forecasting* (New York: Wiley, 1974).

Martino, Joseph P.: *Technological Forecasting for Decisionmaking* (New York: Elsevier–North-Holland, 1972).

JOURNALS

Futurist, World Future Society, Washington, D.C.

Long Range Planning, Pergamon Press, Oxford, England.

Managerial Planning, Planning Executives Institute, Oxford, Ohio.

Planning Review, Bell PubliCom, Inc., Dayton, Ohio.

Technological Forecasting and Social Change, Elsevier–North-Holland, New York.

Index